THE
HUMAN
RIGHTS
ENCYCLOPEDIA

THE
HUMAN
RIGHTS
ENCYCLOPEDIA

Volume Three

Foreword by Aung San Suu Kyi
Winner of the 1991 Nobel Peace Prize

Editors

JAMES R. LEWIS
University of Wisconsin at Stevens Point

CARL SKUTSCH
School of Visual Arts, New York, NY

 SHARPE REFERENCE
an imprint of M.E. Sharpe, Inc.

Contents

International Law

International law is the system of legal agreements, treaties, and traditions that is supposed to regulate the conduct of nations toward each other and toward their citizens. It is in the latter sense that international law has the most relevance for human rights.

INTERNATIONAL LAW AND HUMAN RIGHTS

The history of international law began with agreements between nations and groups of nations, and these agreements focused entirely on interstate relations (issues of war, trade, and fishing rights, for example). It was only in the nineteenth century that international law began to regulate the behavior of states toward individuals and thus create a body of internationally agreed upon human rights.

Before the expansion of international law into the human rights arena, human rights were defended by a long tradition of moral, religious, and philosophical guidelines that centered on a belief in the dignity and sanctity of human life. Such traditions, however high-minded, had no binding force and were often ignored. The first substantive international agreements on human rights issues were the Geneva Conventions, the first of which was signed in 1864. These international agreements regulated the conduct of wars, limiting, by common agreement, what countries could do to each other's citizens and soldiers in time of war. In 1949, the nations of the world agreed to a revamped set of Geneva Conventions that re-quired signatories to respect the human rights of enemy soldiers and civilians. More than 150 nations have signed the Geneva Conventions, and if few of them have obeyed them at all times, it seems clear that the agreements have helped to reduce some of the evils caused by war.

After 1945, the United Nations, in an attempt to make sure that the horrors of World War II would never be repeated, oversaw passage of a series of international agreements designed to make the defense of human rights a part of international law. The central document in these international agreements was the United Nations Universal Declaration of Human Rights. Passed in 1948, the Declaration outlines the rights that all governments are obliged to grant their citizens. Most of the world's nations have signed the United Nations Universal Declaration of Human Rights (although many of them do not scrupulously follow its articles). Supporting and expanding on the Universal Declaration of Human Rights are other documents, including the International Covenant on Economic, Social and Cultural Rights and the International Covenant of Civil and Political Rights, both of which were adopted by the United Nations in 1966.

There are also numerous other agreements that have been ratified by the United Nations, each of which covers some specific aspect of human rights and international law. Perhaps the most important of these is the Convention on the Prevention and Punishment of the Crime of Genocide, which was passed by the United Nations in

1948. This Convention requires all signatories to agree that "genocide, whether committed in time of peace or in time of war, is a crime under international law which they [the contracting parties] undertake to prevent and to punish." Other United Nations human rights declarations include the United Nations Declaration on the Elimination of All Forms of Racial Discrimination, signed in 1963, and the Declaration on the Elimination of Discrimination Against Women, signed in 1967.

INTERNATIONAL COURTS

One of the difficulties preventing the effective protection of human rights by international law is that there is no universally agreed upon supervisory body to regulate international law. The rights outlined in the United Nations–sponsored international treaties are noble ones, but the United Nations is often unable to enforce them.

One of the six principal organs of the United Nations is the International Court of Justice (ICJ)—also known as the World Court—but the ICJ hears only cases brought before it by states that have agreed to accept its jurisdiction. In 1947, the United Nations created the International Law Commission (ILC), but this body only has the authority to suggest changes in international law. It remains up to the United Nations General Assembly to act on the ILC's recommendations and pass treaties which lay out new codes of international law. Even then, these laws are not binding on a country until that country ratifies them. In essence, the whole process depends on the cooperation of the states involved. International law, as supervised by the ICJ and the ILC, is more like non-binding arbitration than a conventional court system. If, for the sake of international har-

mony, two disputing countries agree to be bound by the ICJ's opinions, a legal dispute can be resolved; if they do not, there is nothing the ICJ can do to stop them.

In 1993 and 1994, the United Nations created war crimes tribunals to prosecute the human rights violations that were then occurring in the states of the former Yugoslavia and in Rwanda. These tribunals prosecuted and convicted some of the criminals responsible for genocide in those countries, but were ad hoc courts, with no jurisdiction outside their assigned area of operations. To the extent that they were successful—and their success is debatable, as the most senior war criminals in both areas have managed to escape trial and incarceration—it was because they were backed by the military might of the industrialized countries, particularly the United States.

In order to prosecute future human rights crimes on a less ad hoc basis, the United Nations, in 1996, voted to create an International Criminal Court (ICC). The ICC was authorized to try crimes against humanity, including genocide, war crimes, slavery, mass rape, torture, and racism. Unlike the ICJ, the ICC was authorized to render legal opinions without the consent of all parties; in that sense, it functioned much more like a traditional law court. While the ICC was a step in the direction of a permanent world court, it was hampered by the reluctance of some nations, including the United States, to submit their sovereign power to an international body. Moreover, in practice, there is still the question of compliance. The ICC may convict a North Korean leader of crimes against humanity, but without its own police force, it cannot enforce its own ruling, and instead must rely on the military might of United Nations member states to ensure obedience to its legal decisions.

CONCLUSION

Paradoxically, international law remains both a vital and a weak defender of human rights. Internationally accepted codes of conduct, such as the United Nations Universal Declaration of Human Rights, provide a clear definition of the rights of all individuals, wherever they may live. But while these documents provide important moral and intellectual support for human rights defenders, they have only a limited effect against countries that choose to ignore their existence. Enforcement of international law requires the political, and sometimes military, cooperation of the nations of the world, and sometimes such cooperation is impossible to obtain. In cases like the attempted genocides in Bosnia and Kosovo, or the Iraqi invasion of Kuwait, it was possible to create an international coalition (in all three cases, supported by the United States, the world's biggest military power) to enforce international law. But when human rights violations are committed by powerful states—like Russia in Chechnya or China in Tibet—little can realistically be done. Yugoslavia's government can be pressured by American bombs into obeying international law, but no American president would try the same kind of pressure on nuclear powers like Russia or China. International law has done much to defend human rights, but its impact is necessarily limited by the realities of power politics.

Carl Skutsch

See also: Human Rights, Ethics, and Morality; Trials; United Nations; Universal Declaration of Human Rights.

Bibliography

Ball, Howard. *Prosecuting War Crimes and Genocide: The Twentieth-Century Experience.* Lawrence: University Press of Kansas, 1999.

Neier, Aryeh. *War Crimes: Brutality, Genocide, Terror, and the Struggle for Justice.* New York: Random House, 1998.

Shaw, Malcolm N. *International Law.* Cambridge: Cambridge University Press, 1997.

Martin Luther King, Jr.

Martin Luther King, Jr., was born on January 15, 1929, in Atlanta, Georgia. The son of an African-American Baptist preacher, he became a Baptist minister and rose to prominence as a civil rights advocate. King used Mohandas Gandhi's ideas of non-violence in his attempts to eliminate racial discrimination in the United States and thereby obtain for all African Americans their full human rights. He was assassinated on April 4, 1968.

BEGINNINGS

King obtained his education at Morehouse College, Crozer Theological Seminary, and Boston University, where he earned a Ph.D. During these years he studied philosophy, and first encountered Gandhi's ideas of non-violent resistance. In 1955, after leaving school, he went on to serve as the minister of a small Baptist church in Montgomery, Alabama. King's studies and background had long inclined him to the belief that the church should use its moral weight to support social change.

Montgomery, like the rest of the South, was a two-toned world; whites ruled, blacks obeyed. Blacks had no political power and were forced to humble themselves before whites or risk humiliation, violence, or even murder. In this racist world, King wished to use his pulpit to preach against the injustice of white oppression and black suffering.

King had his first opportunity to fight for black civil rights with the famous Montgomery bus boycott. On December 1, 1955, Rosa Parks and three other African Americans were asked to leave a row of seats to make room for one white man because blacks and whites were not allowed to sit in the same row, according to Alabama law. The other blacks agreed, but Parks refused and was arrested. King and other black leaders, hearing of the arrest, decided to organize a boycott in protest. Blacks in Montgomery were encouraged to avoid using the city's bus system until the city agreed to end segregation on public transportation. In a strong show of unity, most black residents refused to ride Montgomery's buses. This cost the bus company and Montgomery's white businesses a great deal of money. Whites responded with violence. Black boycotters were beaten up and King's house was bombed, but the boycott succeeded. It attracted outside attention, with the result that a federal court ruled segregation on buses to be illegal. King and his supporters were victorious in their non-violent protest.

CIVIL RIGHTS MOVEMENT

The Montgomery bus boycott marked King's entry into the civil rights struggle. After the successful boycott, King and other southern black ministers came together and created the Southern Christian Leadership Conference (SCLC). The SCLC became the driving force for civil rights in the 1950s. King traveled around the country, lecturing to crowds of whites and blacks, trying to bring about a change in American attitudes. He became the best-known civil rights leader in the country.

In 1960 he supported black student sit-ins at lunch counters in Atlanta eating es-

Children marching and singing during a celebration of Martin Luther King's birthday in Harlem, New York City.

tablishments. Many restaurants in the South were segregated or excluded blacks. To confront these policies, students would sit down in these restaurants and politely ask to be served. Although using non-violent methods, King and the students' actions invited violent reprisals from whites eager to stop blacks from gaining civil rights. Screaming verbal abuse, whites surrounded the students, pushed them, and shoved food into their hair and clothes. Trained by King and his associates to maintain discipline, the students did not fight back. During these demonstrations, King and some students were arrested, but the Georgia state government was forced to free him, and King and his cause attracted national attention.

King used his non-violent techniques in other places, organizing marches, more sit-ins, and holding larger and larger rallies. During a 1963 protest campaign in Birmingham, Alabama, the police attacked the demonstrators with fire hoses, clubs, and dogs. King and hundreds of other demonstrators were arrested. During his imprisonment in the Birmingham jail, King was criticized by some white clergy—they called his actions "unwise and untimely"—who thought that King, an outsider, should not have involved himself in Birmingham's problems. King responded with one of the most famous defenses of human rights in American history, his "Letter from Birmingham Jail." In the letter, he argued: "I am cognizant of the interrelatedness of all communities and states. I cannot sit idly by in Atlanta and not be concerned about what happens in Birmingham. Injustice anywhere is a threat to justice everywhere. We are caught in an inescapable network of mutuality, tied in a single garment of destiny. Whatever affects one directly affects all indirectly." King was arguing that the human rights of any person, no matter where he or she was, should be the concern of everyone else on the planet.

Later in 1963, King and others organized a civil rights march in Washington. A quarter of a million demonstrators gathered near the Lincoln Memorial to hear King speak. In this famous "I Have a Dream" speech, King told the audience: "I have a dream that one day on the red hills of Georgia the sons of former slaves and the sons of former slave owners will be able to sit down together at the table of brotherhood."

In 1964, King saw his efforts bear fruit. President Lyndon B. Johnson signed into law the Civil Rights Act of 1964, which outlawed most forms of discrimination. In that same year, King was awarded the Nobel Peace Price. In accepting the prize, King defended his non-violent techniques: "Nonviolence is the answer to the crucial political and moral questions of our time: the need for man to overcome oppression and violence without resorting to violence and oppression." King's defense of non-violence came at a time when many African Americans were becoming impatient with the slow progress of the civil rights movement. Some of them supported leaders like Malcolm X or the Black Panthers. Others turned to violence. From 1965 to 1968, cities across America faced riots led by poor blacks angry at continued white racism. As

King continued to preach non-violence, he was criticized and ridiculed by a younger generation of black leaders.

In the midst of these troubled times, King's preaching was silenced. On April 4, 1968, King was assassinated by James Earl Ray, a white, small-time criminal. Ray spent the rest of life in prison and died in 1998.

Martin Luther King, Jr., remains a towering figure in the history of the American civil rights movement and a symbol for human rights advocates the world over. During the religious conflicts in Northern Ireland, Catholic marchers sang the hymn that King made famous in his marches, "We Shall Overcome." King—like the man he admired so much, Mohandas Gandhi—was less admired and supported at his death than he had been in earlier years, but history has since seen his reputation steadily burnished. He is honored both for his efforts in bringing about the end of legalized racial segregation and for his unwavering commitment to non-violence.

Carl Skutsch

See also: Mohandas Gandhi; Racism.

Bibliography

Dyson, Michael Eric. *I May Not Get There with You: The True Martin Luther King, Jr.* New York: Free Press, 2000.

Garrow, David J. *Bearing the Cross: Martin Luther King, Jr. and the Southern Christian Leadership Conference.* New York: William Morrow, 1999.

Oates, Stephen B. *Let the Trumpet Sound: The Life of Martin Luther King, Jr.* New York: HarperCollins, 1994.

Kurds

The Kurds are a people living in the Middle East who have their own language, culture, traditions, and history, but no nation of their own. The area known as *Kurdistan* (which means "land of the Kurds") is divided among four southwest Asian countries: Turkey, Iran, Iraq, and Syria. While none of these countries particularly likes the other, they are all of one mind in opposing the creation of an independent Kurdistan. Such a country would, after all, take away parts of each of their own lands. If they allowed the Kurds to gain their independence, the Turks would lose much of the eastern part of their country, the Iranians the northwest of theirs, the Iraqis the north, and the Syrians the northeast. Therefore, the approximately 20 million Kurds who live in Kurdistan have no nation to call their own. In their efforts to suppress Kurdish nationalism, the four governments of the region have committed numerous human rights violations. And in suppressing the Kurds' efforts to achieve independence, these nations have denied the Kurds their human right to self-determination.

HISTORY

The Kurds have lived in the same general region for more than 3,000 years. With the Arab conquests of the seventh century they converted to Islam but retained their distinctive culture and language. Kurdish principalities have had some importance from time to time, and one Kurdish prince, named Salidan, was prominent in the twelfth century for opposing the invading Christian crusaders, but he ruled as a Muslim general, not as a Kurd.

Turkish armored cars pursuing fleeing Kurdish demonstrators, March 1992.

775

At one point in history, it seemed possible that Kurdish nationalist aspirations might come to be realized. The Turks had just lost World War I, and had been forced to sign the Treaty of Sevres (1920), which guaranteed the Kurds their own country. The Allied powers, prompted by the idealistic impulses of President Woodrow Wilson of the United States, were supporting the nationalist goals of many ethnic minorities who had previously had no country of their own, such as Czechs, Finns, and Hungarians. These groups demanded their own nations, as did the Kurds. The Turks, however, were unwilling to give up their Kurdish territories; they negotiated a new treaty (the Treaty of Lausanne, 1923) and used military force to bring the Kurds back under their control. Ever since, many Kurds have tried to regain what was lost in 1923.

REPRESSION

The Kurdish right to a country of their own would seem to be a human right as defined by the United Nations Universal Declaration of Human Rights (1948). Article 15 states that "everyone has the right to a nationality," while Article 21 states that "the will of the people shall be the basis of the authority of government." If the will of the Kurdish people is that they should have their own nation, would that not be a human right? Perhaps, but not in the eyes of the governments that rule over the Kurds.

In Turkey, where Kurds are most numerous, government repression has been severe. In the 1980s and 1990s the PKK (Kurdistan Workers Party) waged a guerrilla war against the Turkish government, and the government responded with unbridled force. The Turkish military used torture, bombing, and sometimes murder. (There

have been reports of Kurds being tossed from helicopters by Turkish officers.) Faced with continued Kurdish insurrection, the Turks responded by forcibly evacuating 3,000 Kurdish villages to take away the PKK's sources of support. This was a blatant violation of the human right to stay in one's chosen residence, and resulted in millions of Kurds being left destitute. Some 15,000 Kurdish civilians were killed. In the past, the Turks even denied the existence of the Kurds as a separate people, claiming that they were all actually "Mountain Turks." Kurds who speak out for independence, or merely write in Kurdish rather than Turkish, face police abuse and sometimes murder. The Turkish military's repeated violations of human rights during its campaign against the Kurds has been one of the main stumbling blocks in the way of Turkish admission into the European Union, which forbids the use of torture.

If Turkish repression of the Kurds has been severe, it pales beside that carried out by the Iraqi regime under Iraq's President Saddam Hussein. During the Iran-Iraq War (1980–1988), Kurds in northern Iraq attempted to gain their independence but were brutally suppressed by Hussein's army. The Iraqi soldiers used poison gas and conventional weapons to wipe out entire villages. This mass slaughter has been characterized as an attempt at genocide, and it is believed by some that as many as 180,000 men, women, and children were killed during the Anfal campaign of 1988. The use of poison gas during this campaign, which has been well documented, was a violation of the Geneva Conventions (1949).

The Kurds were subjected to Iraqi terrorism again in 1991. The Kurds had used the opportunity of the Persian Gulf War (1991) to rise up a second time against Hussein, and with the end of that war they faced renewed military attacks and forced relocations. Hundreds of thousands of Kurds fled Hussein's strafing planes, and it was only the intervention of American warplanes that prevented a wholesale slaughter of the Iraqi Kurds. The Americans, as part of their efforts to put pressure on Hussein, declared a "no-fly zone" above 36° north latitude. This prevented Iraqi air attacks, and allowed the Kurds to return and attempt to rebuild their homes and lives. The result has been that since 1992, the Kurds in northern Iraq have had de facto autonomy. But if the Americans ever lift their protective air shield, it seems quite possible that Hussein will renew his attempts to destroy the Kurdish people.

The Kurds remain a disenfranchised people. Subject to persecution in Turkey, Iraq, and—to a lesser extent—Syria and Iran, they have yet to achieve their full human rights. It is not clear that if allowed to, they would all vote for an independent Kurdistan (some Turkish Kurds, for example, have become prosperous in business, and might not be eager to leave the benefits of Turkish government), but it is clear that they are not likely to be given this chance in the near future. The right of self-determination makes it clear that this denial is a denial of their human rights.

Carl Skutsch

See also: Genocide; Universal Declaration of Human Rights; War; War Crimes.

Bibliography

Izady, Mehrdad R. *The Kurds: A Concise Handbook.* New York: Crane Russak, 1992.

McDowall, David. *A Modern History of the Kurds.* New York: I. B. Tauris, 1996.

Meisalis, Susan. *Kurdistan: In the Shadow of History.* New York: Random House, 1997.

Labor

The right to work is a basic human right and is protected in Article 23 of the United Nations Universal Declaration of Human Rights. This is a right which has rarely been properly defended in human history and whose importance is often ignored. It is enlightening to note that countries which respect labor rights almost always respect human rights, while those which persecute or abuse labor movements are also generally oppressive. A strong and well-protected labor movement is often a key factor in advancing human rights around the globe.

HISTORY

Karl Marx (1818–1883), the radical socialist intellectual and leader, believed that the central thread to history was the development and organization of labor. According to Marx, history can be explained largely by successive changes in the means of economic production and the way in which labor is organized. He believed that changes in the ownership of the means of production, manner of work, employment practices, and worker organizations determine all patterns of historical change.

The Industrial Revolution radically changed the scope of labor as well as the social and economic structures of society. From the mid-eighteenth century to the mid-nineteenth century, technological advances and the need to contract workers led to the development of the factory. The factory system employed large numbers of workers and used harnessed power and complex machinery. Large-scale production was characterized by a greater division of labor and specialized tasks, making products cheaper and more readily available. The workers came not only from workshops, but were recruited en masse from rural areas. The factory system gave birth to a new class of factory workers.

In the factory, mechanization automated the skills of workers. The factory also fostered a hierarchy of administrators and specialized professionals such as managers, engineers, specialized supervisors, bookkeepers, and others to help implement strict factory rules. The factory system reduced theft, established strict discipline and surveillance of workers, and made the capitalist owner indispensable for production. It also had the effect of turning the worker into a cog, much like those in the machinery that they worked on. The psychological effect of this can be significant. Workers who work in a factory often feel disconnected from their work, feeling that they are no more important than any machine on the factory floor. As a result, they often lose pride in their work. Marx called this the "alienation of the working class," and even non-Marxists recognize its debilitating effects.

ORGANIZED LABOR

In industrialized economies, conflicts arose between capitalists and laborers over the distribution of profits from production. The factory gave rich owners a powerful tool to control and exploit workers. A former age in which craft workers owned their own tools was replaced by a time in which workers were hired and fired at the whim of factory owners.

To combat poor wages and dangerous working conditions, the workers organized associations of workers in the form of trade unions to represent the interests of labor. The primary goal of a trade union is economic—for the workers to better their circumstances either immediately or in the near future—but it is also political since the members form a community that has a collective power. It can also be the focus of social and educational activity for its members. *Collective bargaining* is the term used to describe negotiations between labor and management. The goal is usually to obtain a labor contract that ensures certain benefits for the workers. The strike, a temporary work stoppage, is the most powerful mechanism workers use to put pressure on factory owners.

Early trade unions were very political in outlook. In 1864, Karl Marx founded the International Workingmen's Association, which promoted coalitions between trade unions and political movements. The Association was founded on socialist principles and held capitalism responsible for the social ills that industrialization created. In the late nineteenth century, labor parties were formed in Britain, Australia, New Zealand, and elsewhere. In several industrialized countries, organized labor in the form of national trade unions came to exert considerable power in government. In Western Europe, socialist labor parties gained strength in France, Germany, and Italy.

After World War II, labor and social movements, post-war economic depression, and, in Western Europe, a fear of workers' revolution, resulted in the establishment of the welfare state, which created social policies such as social security, unemployment insurance, pubic medical benefits, and income redistribution plans.

In Eastern Europe, union movements demonstrated the power of labor rights activists to be forces for improving human rights for everyone. Labor movements, starting with Poland's Solidarity union, were one of the factors that helped to bring the oppressive communist-bloc governments tumbling into oblivion in the late twentieth century. The importance of unions in obtaining freedom for Eastern Europe is demonstrated by the 1990 election of Lech Walesa as president of Poland in the country's first free elections after the fall of communism. Walesa first had been the leader of Solidarity.

THE UNITED STATES

In the United States, socialist labor coalitions did not mobilize mass numbers of workers politically as they did in Europe. Some militant groups, such as the Industrial Workers of the World in the early 1900s, gained influence for brief periods but seldom endured. Most American unions gravitated toward the conservative, craft-oriented American Federation of Labor (AFL), which was organized in 1886. In the 1930s, more radical labor leaders founded the Congress of Industrial Organizations (CIO), which organized millions of industrial workers. In 1955, the two unions merged to form the AFL-CIO, which remains today the largest umbrella union organization in the United States.

The leadership of the AFL-CIO focused on gaining better wages and working conditions for their members. As a result, union workers in core manufacturing sectors enjoyed high wages and benefits packages. These unions, however, were not as politically active or radical as their counterparts overseas. Often they cooperated with government attempts to root out alleged leftists in the labor movement. These government investigations were associated with the anti-communist witch-hunts of the 1940s and 1950s.

The power of labor unions lessened after the 1970s. Many new industries, such as computer manufacturing, resisted unionizing, while unions saw their jobs being transferred to cheaper workers in Third World countries. Currently only about 15 percent of the American workforce is unionized.

THE THIRD WORLD AND HUMAN RIGHTS THREATS

For the most part, the labor movement in the industrialized West was, and is, able to protect the rights of its workers. But safe conditions and relatively high wages are expensive for corporations. For this reason, many corporations have transferred their factories to Third World countries where human rights standards are lower, and, therefore, labor costs are cheaper.

This exploitation of Third World labor remains a critical issue for human rights advocates. Factories around the world often exploit workers, forcing them to work long hours for low wages. When workers try and form unions to fight for their rights, corporations are often able to get government support in breaking up these nascent labor movements. When police in Third World countries break up union strikes, it is an attack not only on labor rights, but on human rights as well.

In countries like the United States, factory workers resent the loss of jobs to low-

Sandinista strikers face police in Nicaragua, July 1990.

paid workers in countries overseas or across the border in Mexico. Many factory workers who have lost their reasonably well-paid union jobs are forced to find work in the growing, but lower-paying, service sector.

In this globalized economy, multinationals scour the globe for cheaper and cheaper labor, pitting countries and workers against each other to see who will offer the lowest wages and greatest tax breaks. Practices such as union busting, forced overtime, and penalties for slow production are instituted as laborers find themselves barely able to meet basic subsistence needs.

Present-day labor trends are largely the result of the growth of multinational corporations, globalization of the economy, and an increase in free-trade agreements. Since the 1970s, unions in the core industrialized countries have lost much of their gains as jobs have departed for the developing world. Labor in the developing world now faces similar challenges as did labor in industrialized nations in the nineteenth and twentieth centuries. Several factors suggest that twenty-first-century labor struggles in the developing world will be fought through global efforts, or at least with global solidarity. Transnational alliances between trade unions, non-governmental organizations, religious groups, and individual activists will advance the goals of the worker in the global economy. An increasing awareness of labor abuses, moral repugnance on the part of consumers, and media attention to labor conditions and organizing efforts will all lend not only attention to workers' efforts, but will also put pressure on multinational corporations responsible for poor labor conditions.

The issue of labor rights is sure to be one of the critical human rights issues of the twenty-first century.

Margaret Gray and Carl Skutsch

See also: Child Labor; Debt Bondage; Globalization and Multinational Corporations; Slavery; Trade Unions.

Bibliography

Rifkin, Jeremy. *The End of Work: The Decline of the Global Labor Force and the Dawn of the Post-Market Era.* New York: J. P. Tarcher, 1996.

Land Mines

Some argue that all weapons of war are inhumane, and that all are equally bad; however, most societies have consistently regarded some weapons as worse than others. Increasingly, many people are putting land mines into the category of weapons that should never be used. This is because once they are placed, they never go away; thus they attack soldier and civilian alike. For this reason, they are seen as an attack upon the human rights of innocents—including children—who should not be victims of war.

Land mines are small metal or plastic devices hidden in the ground, which explode when people or vehicles go over them or come in close proximity to them (land mines can also be detonated by remote control, but those are more expensive and less common). Primitive land mines have existed since the invention of gunpowder, but the modern land mine dates from World War II. During that war, all sides used land mines in large numbers to protect defensive positions. Land mines are relatively cheap, easy to deploy, and very effective in large numbers. After the war ended, land mines became standard equipment for most of the world's armies. Today's land mines are much more sophisticated than their predecessors. Many are designed to jump two feet in the air before exploding, thereby causing maximum damage to the abdomens of the triggering victim. Others are made mostly of plastic, thereby making detection almost impossible.

The problems with land mines are their ubiquity and their longevity. During a war, soldiers lay out minefields (areas filled with mines) wherever they station their troops.

By the end of a war, minefields usually will have been deployed throughout the entire combat area, and they do not go away. For years after a war has ended, the land mines remain in position, and innocent civilians run the risk of being killed by random explosions. This is what makes the use of land mines a human rights violation. As weapons of war they might be justified in their own right—wars have their own logic—but land mines kill long after the war is over. They are not aimed, like regular guns; they kill without conscience, without justification. Weapons of war target soldiers; land mines target everyone.

Land mines are particularly dangerous for children. Signs that warn off adults are ignored by children who either cannot read or who disregard the message. And when mines explode, children are more likely to be killed than adults.

In wars since 1945, land mines have been used in huge numbers and have left behind a terrible legacy of death and destruction. The United Nations estimates that Cambodia still has six million mines hidden in its fields and trails, that Angola has nine million, and that Afghanistan has ten million. Each year these land mines, left over from wars gone by, kill and maim more innocents. In Angola, it is estimated that 5,000 artificial limbs are needed each year. In Cambodia, there are an estimated 35,000 amputees who lost limbs because of land mines. Land mines are a serious problem in many other places including Bosnia, Chechnya, Iraq, and Somalia. The economics of land-mine use make them very hard to eliminate; land mines can cost

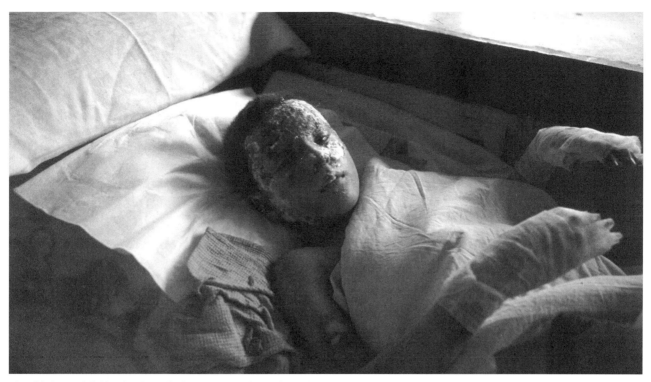

An Afghan child in the hospital. He was injured by a land mine while playing.

as little as $5 to deploy, but as much as $1,000 each to remove. (Most of the cost of removing land mines comes from the difficulty in finding them once they have been buried and hidden.) The cost factor is an obvious deterrent to removal.

The human effects of land mines are horrific. The web site landminesurvivors.org publicizes the stories of some of those who have survived land mine explosions. According to this organization, one of these survivors is "Marianne Holtz, an American nurse who has worked in Somalia, Southern Sudan, Rwanda, and Zaire. In 1995, Ms. Holtz worked in Goma, Zaire, as a Nurse Coordinator for the American Refugee Committee. She was driving in the countryside outside of Goma when her vehicle struck a land mine. She was severely injured by the explosion and rushed to a local hospital where doctors had to wire shut her fractured jaw, set her broken back and amputate both

of her legs below the knees. After further medical treatment, surgeries and rehabilitation, Ms. Holtz can now walk for short distances with her two prosthetic legs and a cane. She currently writes and speaks on the problem of land mines."

In 1992, several human rights groups banded together to form the International Campaign to Ban Landmines (ICBL; http://www.icbl.org/). The organizers of the ICBL saw land mines as a critical threat to human rights. In countries where land mines exist, the right to life, perhaps the most important human right, is under constant threat. The ICBL worked to publicize the dangers of land mines, particularly of the smaller, cheaper, and more prevalent antipersonnel mines, and to convince governments that they could and should do without them.

Under the leadership of the ICBL's chief coordinator, Jody Williams, the campaign against land mines attracted supporters from all over the world. Eventually more than a thousand organizations signed onto the campaign. Prominent celebrities, including Princess Diana of Great Britain, helped to draw attention to the issues involved. Their efforts paid off when, in 1997, more than one hundred nations met in Ottawa, Canada, to sign a ban on land mines. The Ottawa Convention—officially called the Convention on the Prohibition of the Use, Stockpiling, Production and Transfer of Anti-Personnel Mines and on Their Destruction—committed its signatories to destroy all the land mines in their armies' arsenals. The ICBL and Jody Williams were jointly awarded the 1997 Nobel Peace Prize for their efforts in fighting the use of land mines.

However, some of the world's biggest military powers, including Russia, China, and the United States, refused to sign the treaty, claiming that land mines are a necessary part of their defensive weaponry. The United States government, for example, claims that it needs land mines to defend the border of its ally South Korea from a possible North Korean invasion. There is some military validity to this claim, and certainly the United States is more careful in the deployment of its land mines than some other nations, but as long as these larger nations continue to build and deploy land mines, there is little pressure on other, smaller countries to cease using them.

Carl Skutsch

See also: Nobel Peace Prize; War.

Bibliography

Cameron, Maxwell A., Robert J. Lawson, and Brian W. Tomlin. *To Walk Without Fear: The Global Movement to Ban Landmines.* Oxford: Oxford University Press, 1999.

Winslow, Philip C. *Sowing the Dragon's Teeth: Land Mines and the Global Legacy of War.* Boston: Beacon, 1997.

Law and Justice

The law is intimately intertwined with human rights issues. The laws that a society enforces suggest which rights it considers important. But laws alone are not enough to protect people's human rights. There must also be a court system in place that effectively enforces those laws. In most countries, the law is enforced by the judiciary, which consists of the judges who sit in trial over the accused and pass judgment on the convicted.

There are two kinds of laws that protect human rights. The first are laws the prevent individuals from doing harm to one another. The second kind of law protects citizens from abusive behavior by the government. Both of these are important for the protection of human rights, but often the second kind is the more important.

Compared to their citizens, governments have vast powers. They control police, prosecutors, and the military. Governments are usually run by powerful figures who gained power in part because of their connections to wealth and influence. The law is often the only thing that stands between an individual and his or her government. For this reason, in countries where human rights are respected, the law gives the individual many protections against potential government excess.

In the United States, for example, the first ten amendments to the Constitution are known collectively as the Bill of Rights because they were designed to protect individuals against possible abuse by the government. The First Amendment protects rights such as free speech and freedom of assembly. The Fourth Amendment prevents police from searching a house without first obtaining a warrant from a judge. The Sixth Amendment guarantees a defendant a speedy trial.

Another important legal protection is the right of habeas corpus. This protection gives the judge the power to question whether a crime was actually committed and whether people in state custody are wrongfully imprisoned. If a judge doubts the state's honesty regarding a prisoner's disposition, the rule of habeas corpus allows the judge to demand that the prisoner be brought before him.

When such laws exist, human rights are only partially protected. But the laws must not only exist on paper; they must be enforced by a competent and effective judiciary.

To begin with, the judiciary must be independent. A judiciary that is easily influenced by politicians is more likely to defend the interests of the rich and powerful than the rights of the average citizen. An independent judiciary is required to stand up to the threats of powerful politicians or to ignore the demands of public popular pressure.

The judiciary must not only be independent from the political authorities, but must also maintain a healthy distance from prosecutors and police. A judge is supposed to be an impartial guardian of justice. When judges begin to see their role as one of facilitating the smooth functioning of criminal prosecutions, the judge ceases to be impartial. And the prisoner, in effect, loses his right to being presumed innocent. Furthermore, judges who are too closely tied

Trial of Marcus Vinicius Emmanuel. The Brazilian police officer confessed to being involved in the murder of eight Rio de Janeiro street children, April 1996.

to police and prosecutors are unlikely to be effective at punishing those police who commit crimes against society and against human rights.

The United Nations General Assembly endorsed the necessity of an independent judiciary with its 1985 passage of the Basic Principles on the Independence of the Judiciary. In its first four articles, this document makes clear the emphasis that the United Nations places on an independent judiciary:

1. The independence of the judiciary shall be guaranteed by the State and enshrined in the Constitution or the law of the country. It is the duty of all governmental and other institutions to respect and observe the independence of the judiciary.

2. The judiciary shall decide matters before them impartially, on the basis of facts and in accordance with the law, without any restrictions, improper influences, inducements, pressures, threats or interferences, direct or indirect, from any quarter or for any reason.

3. The judiciary shall have jurisdiction over all issues of a judicial nature and shall have exclusive authority to decide whether an issue submitted for its decision is within its competence as defined by law.

4. There shall not be any inappropriate or unwarranted interference with the judicial process, nor shall judicial decisions by the courts be subject to revision. This principle is without prej-

Mob justice in Sierra Leone. This man was suspected of looting, March 1998.

udice to judicial review or to mitigation or commutation by competent authorities of sentences imposed by the judiciary, in accordance with the law.

The judicial system should also be both efficient and relatively free of corruption. If the people feel they cannot rely on the courts to give them justice, they are likely to become disgusted with normal judicial procedures and try to take the law into their own hands. Corruption also allows the rich to subvert the normal workings of justice. In some countries, it is possible for business interests to buy a judge for a relatively small

sum of money. Compared to those in Western countries, judges in Asia, Africa, and South America are not well paid and so are often tempted to supplement their salaries by selling their integrity and independence.

Another requirement for justice to be served is legal aid for the poor. A legal system that truly protects human rights should provide free and competent legal aid to those who cannot afford their own lawyer. Without access to affordable legal services, the poor are likely to suffer abuses in the court system. When only the rich can afford lawyers, only the rich will have human rights.

Protestors denounce cuts to legal aid programs for the poor in Philadelphia, July 1995.

A diligent and vigilant judiciary is imperative to ensure that the state's obligations to promote and protect human rights are fulfilled. Beyond protecting local laws that guarantee human rights, the judiciary is also responsible for seeing that the country's executive respects international treaties that make human rights commitments.

In conclusion, for justice to be served, the law must protect human rights, the judiciary must be independent, and the state must provide sufficient legal assistance to all whom it prosecutes.

James R. Lewis and Carl Skutsch

See also: Habeas Corpus; International Law; Police and Law Enforcement; Victims' Rights.

Bibliography

Barnett, Randy E. *The Structure of Liberty: Justice and the Rule of Law.* New York: Oxford University Press, 2000.

Nelson Mandela

Nelson Rolihlahla Mandela was born July 18, 1918, at the Cape of Good Hope, in South Africa. He became a militant activist who fought for black rights against the white-controlled South African government. He spent twenty-eight years in prison, but eventually was freed and became the country's first black president, an office he retained until 1999.

FIGHT AGAINST APARTHEID

For most of Mandela's life, South Africa had been ruled under a system called *apartheid*. Apartheid—which means "apartness" in Afrikaans, the language of most white South Africans—required that whites, blacks, and other racial groups be separated as much as possible. In practice, apartheid meant that blacks, who made up the vast majority of the population, would be forced to be subservient, and whites, who made up less than 20 percent of the population, would have the best land, jobs, and lives.

Mandela came from a prominent Xhosa family (the Xhosa comprise one of South Africa's largest black ethnic groups) and was able to go to college and law school—a privilege most black South Africans could only dream of. Mandela, however, did not allow his privileged position to blind him to the injustice that characterized his country. He was determined to fight against it.

In 1943, Mandela joined the African National Congress (ANC), a black civil rights group dedicated to ending racial discrimination in South Africa. Although he sup-

Nelson Mandela on a visit to the United States shortly after his release from prison.

ported ANC goals, its approach was too moderate for Mandela and other young activists. In 1944, they formed the ANC Youth League, which had a more confrontational approach than the parent body. By 1947 Mandela and his allies were pushing the ANC to follow their more aggressive style. In 1960, responding to ANC-inspired anti-apartheid protests, South African police fired on hundreds of unarmed demonstrators at the township of Sharpeville. The resulting uproar of protest led the white-controlled government to ban the ANC. Mandela was transformed into a rebel. In 1962 he was charged with treason. At his trial he made a moving four-hour speech criticizing apartheid; the white court ignored his speech and ordered him imprisoned. He stayed in prison for the next twenty-eight years.

Mandela spent most of his prison time in Robben Island Prison, a dreary prison located off the coast of South Africa. In his memoirs, Mandela said: "Robben Island was without question the harshest, most iron-fisted outpost in the South African penal system. It was a hardship station not only for the prisoners but for the prison staff. Gone were the Coloured warders who had supplied cigarettes and sympathy. The warders were white and overwhelmingly Afrikaans-speaking, and they demanded a master-servant relationship. They ordered us to call them 'baas,' which we refused. The racial divide on Robben Island was absolute: there were no black warders, and no white prisoners. . . . Robben Island was like going to another country. Its isolation made it not simply another prison, but a world of its own, far removed from the one we had come from."

During his twenty-eight years of captivity, Mandela became one of the most famous prisoners in the world. The South African government tried to portray him as a communist revolutionary and troublemaker, but most of the world grew to see him as a dedicated man fighting for justice and imprisoned for political reasons. "Free Nelson Mandela" signs, posters, and bumper stickers became commonplace in many parts of the industrialized world. The prominence of Mandela as a prisoner helped to make many people aware of the evils of apartheid and prompted them to support economic sanctions against South Africa. After 1985, the white regime, recognizing Mandela's growing influence, tried to defuse his importance by repeatedly offering him a freedom in return

for a promise to cease his political activities. Mandela, not wishing to compromise his principles, refused these offers.

Facing growing opposition from both inside and outside the country, the South African government finally recognized that apartheid had to end, and that apartheid's most famous prisoner had to be released. President F. W. de Klerk released Mandela from prison on February 11, 1990. Mandela was chosen to be the leader of the ANC, and during the next few years he worked closely with de Klerk, his former enemy, to bring about a peaceful end to apartheid. The transition from apartheid to true democracy was marred by violence, much of it white on black, but Mandela consistently and continuously worked to calm tensions and avoid violent confrontations. In 1993, Mandela and de Klerk were jointly awarded the Nobel Peace Price. In 1994, Nelson Mandela was elected the first black president of South Africa.

As president, Mandela worked to heal the wounds caused by apartheid. Rather than seeking revenge, he organized the Truth and Reconciliation Commission, whose job it was to investigate the crimes that occurred under apartheid, but not to punish them. Mandela recognized that seeking justice for past crimes might have led to continued violence in South Africa; it also might have alienated many white South Africans, whose education and technical skills were required if the country were to prosper economically. In 1999 he ended his term as president and retired from political life.

Mandela's determination, even after years of imprisonment, and his magnanimity upon his release, marks him as unique among those who have fought for human rights. Many observers expected South

Africa to explode into violence as apartheid ended; it is probably Mandela's efforts, motivated by his respect for human life, that kept this from happening. For most of his life he was one of the oppressed; when he gained power, he refused to become an oppressor. He believed in human rights, not only for his people, but for all people.

Carl Skutsch

See also: Nobel Peace Prize; Political Prisoners; Racism.

Bibliography

Mandela, Nelson. *Long Walk to Freedom: The Autobiography of Nelson Mandela.* New York: Little, Brown, 1995.

Meredith, Martin. *Nelson Mandela: A Biography.* New York: St. Martin's, 1998.

Sampson, Anthony. *Mandela: The Authorized Biography.* New York: Knopf, 1999.

Marriage and Family

According to Article 16 of the United Nations Universal Declaration of Human Rights (1948): "The family is the natural and fundamental group unit of society and is entitled to protection by society and the State." As part of this basic human right, according to Article 16: "Men and women of full age, without any limitation due to race, nationality or religion, have the right to marry and to found a family. They are entitled to equal rights as to marriage, during marriage, and at its dissolution." In other words, having a family and entering into marriage are basic human rights.

A central article of the United Nations Universal Declaration of Human Rights states: "Marriage shall be entered into only with the free and full consent of the intending spouses." Marriage should be between two people who both want to be married to each other. This basic human right is often not protected. In many societies—India, Bangladesh—marriages are arranged by a bride and groom's families.

Women marching for more rights in marriage at the Fourth International Conference on Women, Beijing, China, 1995.

This is no violation of their human rights as long as they both freely consent to the marriage, but sometimes one party—almost always the woman—does not wish to be married and is forced to do so by family and societal pressures. While these sorts of forced marriages usually occur outside the industrialized West, they can occur anywhere. In the United States, for example, certain splinter sects of the Mormon church have been accused of forcing young girls into unwanted marriages.

Within marriages there can also be human rights violations. Women are almost always the victims of these human rights violations. In Pakistan, bride burnings have become a serious problem. Husbands, often helped by their families, will set fatal fires in order to rid themselves of an inconvenient or troublesome bride (usually after having received her dowry). Most violence within marriage is not this bad, but violence against wives remains commonplace worldwide. These attacks on women's human rights within marriage are fostered by the widely shared belief that wives should be subservient to their husbands. This belief denies women their basic human right to equality.

Not all people share in the universal human right to marriage and family. Gays and lesbians who wish to marry and form families are faced with many barriers. There are few countries that allow homosexuals to marry each other, and none use the word "marriage." Since 1989, gays in Denmark have been able to join in civil partnerships, with most of the rights and responsibilities of marriages. In France, gays and lesbians (and unmarried heterosexuals) can join in a *pacte civile de solidarité*, which grants rights similar to those of marriage. Other European countries have followed suit. In the United States, a strong religious tradition has made many hostile to the idea of gay marriage—in 1996, the federal government passed the Defense of Marriage Act, which said that only marriages between men and women would be recognized as legitimate. Going against this anti-gay marriage trend, the state of Vermont passed a law in 2000 that allowed gay couples to join in civil unions, which are marriages in everything but name. The law that legalized these unions (and that only confers state benefits, not federal benefits) declares: "The state has a strong interest in promoting stable and lasting families, including families based upon a same-sex couple." While this is a step forward for gay families, it is short of the full human right to marriage.

Divorce is another human right that is not easily accessible to all. In many cultures there is a strong bias against divorce, and strong social pressure by society to prevent people, particularly women, from trying to end their marriages. This social pressure is often supported by legal restrictions that make it difficult to obtain a divorce. In Morocco, for example, restrictive laws (and hostile judges) make it almost impossible for women to obtain divorces, even in cases where they have been physically abused by their husbands. As it is often the woman who suffers the most in unhappy marriages (women are almost always the victims, not the perpetrators of domestic violence), these restrictions on divorce are particularly restrictive of women's human rights. In many Muslim countries, "honor killings" are a common way of punishing women who seek divorce. These women are hunted down by their husbands or former husbands and assassinated. These killings are often supported by the women's own families and are tolerated by their governments.

In theory, marriage is a universally supported human right. In practice many marriages are less than ideal. Not all women have all the privileges of marriage as outlined by the United Nations.

Carl Skutsch

See also: Domestic Violence; Sexual Orientation and Homosexuality; Women's Rights.

Bibliography

Guggenheim, Martin. *The Rights of Families: The Authoritative ACLU Guide to the Rights of Family Members Today.* Carbondale: Southern Illinois University Press, 1996.

Mental Health and Psychiatry

Issues of human rights have always been intertwined with the history of psychiatry. In the history of many societies, the mentally ill were abused and treated without any respect for their rights or dignity. In some societies, such as medieval Europe, the mentally ill were thought to be possessed by demonic spirits. There were few attempts to cure them or ameliorate their suffering. In the early modern era, some countries funded "madhouses" for the mentally ill, but these were chambers of horrors, with screaming inmates chained to their beds, abused by ignorant and rapacious wardens. In the early nineteenth century, a new wave of doctors and reformers entered the profession and began to argue that the insane, as they were then called, needed to be treated with more humanity. By the twentieth century, treatment of the mentally ill had improved, but there remained, and remains, widespread human rights issues and abuses connected to mental health and psychiatry.

The right of the mentally ill to proper care is an internationally recognized human right. The United Nations International Covenant on Economic, Social and Cultural Rights (1966) states that everyone has the right to "the highest attainable standard of physical and mental health." The United Nations expanded on this statement with an additional document addressed directly to the plight of the

Patients in the psychiatric ward of Bugando Hospital, Tanzania.

mentally ill, the Principles for the Protection of Persons with Mental Illness and the Improvement of Mental Health Care (1991). The first two articles of this document state that "all persons have the right to the best available mental health care, which shall be part of the health and social care system," and "all persons with a mental illness, or who are being treated as such persons, shall be treated with humanity and respect for the inherent dignity of the human person."

INSTITUTIONS AND METHODS

Treatment for the mentally ill has progressed since the days when they were locked away in madhouses and insane asylums, but abuses still remain. The mentally ill are particularly vulnerable to mistreatment because they are often looked down upon by the rest of society, whose members prefer to forget that they exist. Often unable to voice their concerns and complaints, they are defenseless against the abuses of unscrupulous or uncaring nurses and doctors. But in spite of many abuses, modern mental health facilities, particularly in the industrialized countries, are far better than they once were. Part of the reason for this improvement is the increase in empathy for the plight of the mentally ill, the result of a corresponding increase in respect for the human rights of all people. However, perhaps the most significant change since the eighteenth century is the arrival of a new idea: that mental illness can be treated and either cured or lessened in severity.

In the late 1890s, doctors like Sigmund Freud greatly expanded the field of psychiatry and with it tried to cure those troubled by mental illness. Their successes were real, but limited. Some people could be cured, or helped, by Freud's talking cure;

others, particularly the severely troubled, showed little or no improvement. With the discovery of psychotropic drugs in the 1950s, the treatment of the mentally ill took a giant leap forward, as doctors found that certain chemicals could dramatically improve the behavior and mental state of their patients. Previous abusive treatments, such as electroshock (where a patient was subjected to a series of electric shocks, sometimes damaging their personality or memory) and lobotomies (an operation in which the nerve fibers of the frontal lobes of the brain are severed, often leaving the patient passive and dull, an empty shell of a human being), were abandoned in favor of the new drugs. Although drugs have greatly improved the lives of many mentally ill people—allowing some of them to re-enter the world as happy and productive members of society—they have also sometimes been used in abusive ways. Some institutions have used the drugs to sedate their patients in order to make them easier to handle, rather than out of concern for their well-being.

Places of treatment have also changed since the dark days of the eighteenth century. Insane asylums, themselves an improvement on the old madhouses, were replaced with modern mental hospitals, staffed by trained doctors and nurses. Increased budgets allowed these hospitals to provide various forms of therapy, including painting, theatrics, and other group activities. Nevertheless, abuses continue in hospitals around the world.

In the 1950s, governments in the United States and Great Britain began to release mental patients into the outside world in an effort to deinstitutionalize or mainstream them. The rate of mainstreaming was increased after the early 1970s, when mental hospitals, ignored by much of the

Women working in a Bulgarian mental hospital's workshop.

country, had reached a low point in their quality of care. This nadir was revealed in 1972, when a young reporter, Geraldo Rivera, smuggled a television camera into Willowbrook, a Staten Island institution for the mentally retarded, and revealed wards crowded with disabled children and feces-smeared walls. Since then there has been substantial, but uneven, improvement in the quality of care.

The main result of reports like Rivera's, however, was to accelerate the process of mainstreaming, because mental health advocates believed that the mentally ill might be best served by being released from mental hospitals and state institutions. The goal of mainstreaming may have been laudable, but the funds to support the patients in outpatient programs were not sufficient, and many mental patients ended up swelling the ranks of the urban homeless. This decision to leave hundreds of thousands of mental patients without sufficient care was and is a clear human rights violation, as defined by the UN resolutions on mental health.

For all its faults, mental health care in wealthy countries like the United States is reasonably good—certainly better than it was fifty years ago. In Third World countries, however, the situation of the mentally ill remains abysmal. Because these countries have too little money to help even the sane and healthy, the mentally ill are often ignored, aided only by the small amounts of money that trickle in from international charities. Abuses reminiscent of the old European madhouses continue in Africa and South America.

In Hidalgo, Mexico, a 1999 investigation by human rights advocates revealed a state mental hospital that epitomized the neglect with which mental patients are treated in much of the world. Inmates in the Hidalgo institution were locked in giant wards, with hundreds of men or women sharing a single dormitory-style room and only a few undertrained hospital personnel to supervise them. The hospital floors were covered with feces and urine, most patients went around shoeless and partially clothed, and some were entirely naked. Many of the patients were not even mentally ill, but rather mentally retarded, yet there were no provisions or plans for releasing them into the kinds of group homes for the mentally retarded that are common in the United States. And as bad as Mexico's mental health institutions can be, all around the globe there are many institutions that are worse.

One place, worldwide, where the mentally ill continue to face systematic abuse is in prison. Mentally ill prisoners can be the most troublesome, and for that reason prison authorities often treat them with excessive harshness. In many of the new super-maximum security ("super-max") prisons in the United States, mentally ill patients are locked in small, isolated cells for twenty-three hours a day. They may be kept in these cells for years, at great cost to their already unbalanced mental state. Human Rights Watch has called this treatment tantamount to torture, a clear violation of the United Nations Universal Declaration of Human Rights, which bans torture and other degrading punishments. Dr. Carl Fulwiler, a psychiatrist who investigated Indiana's placement of mentally ill prisoners in super-max facilities, said: "To force prisoners with serious psychiatric disorders to live in extreme social isolation and unremitting idleness in a claustrophobic environment is barbaric."

FORCED COMMITMENT

A human right violation connected to psychiatry is forced commitment. Governments, sometimes with the help of relatives, have the power to force people into mental institutions against their will. The United Nations Principles on Mental Illness state that "no treatment shall be given to a patient without his or her informed consent," but also allows such consent to be ignored if a person is judged incompetent to manage his or her own affairs. In some cases, this may be necessary—a mentally disturbed person may be a danger to himself and the community—but often forced commitments occur without sufficient evidence of any necessity. People forced into mental institutions may endure regimens of drugs and electroshock that can cause permanent psychological harm.

In some countries, these forced commitments have been a part of government policies of repression. In the Soviet Union, for example, the state forced political dissidents into psychiatric hospitals as punishment for their rebellious behavior. One self-serving rationale given by communist officials was that to be against the government was inherently to be mentally unbalanced, and therefore deserving of commitment in an institution. This use of psychiatry perverted the original intention of psychiatric hospitals and turned them into one more element of the human rights oppression that was built into the Soviet system.

Similar practices were carried out in other communist countries, making these human rights crimes endemic in the entire communist bloc. Ironically, some of those whose human rights were violated by forced commitment were being punished for their efforts to fight for human rights in their countries. In Yugoslavia, an army colonel named Radomir Veljkovic was accused of being insane because, according to the presiding court: "The accused says that laws are being broken on a large scale, that nepotism and bribe-taking have prevailed, that human rights are violated on a massive scale." Although these accusations were absolutely true, Veljkovic spent from 1971 to 1988 in a psychiatric hospital because the government claimed his accusations were the result of mental instability. Cases like that of Veljkovic were commonplace in all the communist states of Eastern Europe and Asia. With the collapse of the Soviet Union, systematic abuse of psychiatry has diminished, but human rights watchdog groups still accuse Russia and other nations of occasionally returning to their bad habit of forcing troublemakers into mental institutions.

DISCRIMINATION

There also remains a stigma attached to mental illness of all kinds. Many people with mental illnesses would be able to function in society if they received moderate support (often with the help of psychotropic drugs), but are unwilling to seek that help because of the shame they feel in confessing to mental illness. Illnesses such as depression and anxiety are treatable with therapy or drugs but, left untreated, can become worse, even leading a sufferer to commit suicide out of desperation.

The stigma attached to mental illnesses also leads to discrimination. Although the United Nations principles for the protection of persons with mental illness states that "there shall be no discrimination on the grounds of mental illness," such discrimination is common. Prejudice against those with mental illness—even curable illnesses like depression—remains strong.

CONCLUSION

The human rights situation of the mentally ill is far better than it has been in the past. In the Western world, trained psychiatrists, new drugs, and reasonably well-equipped mental hospitals provide sufferers with some chance of recovery. The problems that remain are mostly those of funding. There are still those in rich countries, however, who are unable to get the care they need; in poorer countries, the situation is much worse. The mentally ill still lack the human rights that United Nations resolutions have promised them.

Carl Skutsch

See also: Health Rights; Prisons.

Bibliography

Bluglass, Robert, and Martin Roth. *Psychiatry, Human Rights, and the Law.* Cambridge: Cambridge University Press, 1985.
Sayce, Liz. *From Psychiatric Patient to Citizen: Overcoming Discrimination and Social Exclusion.* New York: St. Martin's, 2000.

Migrant Workers

Migrant workers are laborers who move from place to place looking for work. Sometimes they move on a regular schedule, doing seasonal work. Migrant workers may also be long-term migrants to a particular country. These migrants hope to go home someday and see their work as a temporary way of supporting families in their home country. Migrant workers, thus, are often not residents of the country in which they work. For this reason, and many others, migrant workers are more subject to human rights abuses than many other kinds of workers.

According to the United Nations Universal Declaration of Human Rights (1948): "Everyone has the right to work, to free choice of employment, to just and favorable conditions of work and to protection against unemployment"; "Everyone has the right to a standard of living adequate for the health and well-being of himself and his family"; and "Everyone has the right to form and to join trade unions for the protection of his interests." These basic human rights apply to all people, not just migrant workers, but migrant workers, because of the peripatetic nature of their lives, are especially vulnerable to attacks on these rights.

Without settled roots in a community, migrant workers usually find it more difficult to achieve the respect and rights that are granted to permanent residents. Migrants are often seen as outsiders or troublemakers who are taking jobs away from locals—even though migrants tend to do the jobs that no one else wants.

Migrant workers are not a tiny part of the world's economy. In the United States, 3 to

Migrant farm workers in Honduras.

5 million farmer workers are migrants. Half of them were born in the United States; most of the rest are legal residents. American migrants pick cotton in Alabama, cherries in Montana, and oranges in California. Worldwide, the number of migrant workers may be as high as 100 million.

Abuse of migrant workers' human rights can be found around the world. In the 1960s in the United States, migrant workers on California's farms suffered under appalling working conditions. Their pay was low, their toilet facilities were ditches by the side of the road, their housing was unheated and overpriced, and child labor was commonplace. As a result of these terrible conditions, the average life expectancy of a migrant worker was forty-nine years. In 1962, with the creation of a National Farm Workers Association, led by Cesar Chavez, the condition of migrant workers slowly began to improve, although it still remains far behind that of settled workers.

Many nations export migrant workers, and the paychecks that they send home are vital to these countries' economies. Migrant workers from the Philippines, for example, go all over the world looking for work, and many of them end up working in near-slavery conditions. Filipino women hired as housekeepers and maids sometimes work sixty- to eighty-hour weeks, have their passports confiscated by their employers (making it difficult to leave their jobs), and are subjected to verbal and physical abuse. Trapped in a foreign country and unable to speak the language, migrant workers are easy targets for employers who wish to deny them their human rights.

In December 1990, to defend the specific rights of migrant workers, the UN General Assembly passed the International Convention on the Protection of the Rights of All Migrant Workers and Members of Their Families. This Convention reaffirms that migrant workers share all the rights of non-migrants, but goes farther in guaranteeing migrants the right to move freely between national borders in search of work. It also guarantees all migrant workers equal legal rights with nationals of the country in which they work; migrant workers cannot be singled out for special restrictions or penalties. Although the Convention has been adopted by the General Assembly, it has not been ratified by enough nations to be legally in effect as an element of international law; still, those countries that have signed it have committed, at least morally, to living up to its principles.

Carl Skutsch

See also: Labor.

Bibliography

Chang, Grace. *Disposable Domestics: Immigrant Women Workers in the Global Economy.* Cambridge, MA: South End Press, 2000.

Constable, Nicole. *Maid to Order in Hong Kong: Stories of Filipino Workers.* Ithaca, NY: Cornell University Press, 1997.

Rothenberg, Daniel. *With These Hands: The Hidden World of Migrant Farmworkers Today.* New York: Harcourt Brace, 1998.

Minority Rights

Throughout history the rights of minorities have been threatened by the power of the majority. This remains true today. All around the world, minorities struggle against attacks on their human rights. Some of these attacks are backed by government power, and others are merely the result of societal prejudice, but all must be dealt with if minorities are to share equally in the human rights accorded to all peoples.

To defend minority rights it is necessary to define *minority,* but the term has escaped a comprehensive and universally accepted definition. Does *minority* refer to speakers of a particular language, believers in a different religion, people who belong to an outnumbered ethnic group, or those whose sexual orientation is different from that of the majority? There are thus many definitions of *minority.* But although the question of defining a minority is difficult, it should not distract from the central issue of minority rights. For the purpose of discussing minorities and human rights, therefore, a minority can be defined as any group that is reasonably identifiable and cohesive and whose members face threats to their physical, material, psychological, or cultural well-being because of its membership in that identifiable group.

That minority rights are threatened is clear. From Jews to Kurds to gays, minorities are under attack. Some of these attacks threaten a minority's survival as an independent culture. Others affect their material prosperity, while still others threaten their very existence.

WHAT ARE MINORITY RIGHTS?

The United Nations proclaims its support for minority rights in a number of documents. The International Covenant on Civil and Political Rights (1966) declares, "in those States in which ethnic, religious, or linguistic minorities exist, persons belonging to such minorities shall not be denied the right, in community with the other members of their group, to enjoy their own culture, to profess and practise their own religion, or to use their own language." The Declaration on the Rights of Persons Belonging to National or Ethnic, Religious and Linguistic Minorites (1993) expands on the 1966 Covenant by detailing the specific rights adhering to minorities, starting with Article 1, which proclaims, "States shall protect the existence and the national or ethnic, cultural, religious, and linguistic identity of minorities within their respective territories and shall encourage conditions for the promotion of that identity."

The minority rights that should be protected fall into two categories: individual rights and group rights. Individual rights that need protecting for minorities are those rights that should be shared by all people, whether they belong to the majority or the minority, but are denied to a minority because of prejudice or government policy. Group rights are rights that are particular and peculiar to a specific minority culture.

Individual minority rights are the less controversial of the two types of minority rights. No reasonable person would deny that individual members of a minority should have the same access to rights as do members of the majority, including the rights to free speech, freedom of movement, and political freedoms. Yet minority individuals frequently are denied these rights.

The issue of group minority rights is more complex than that of individual minority rights. The United Nations' 1993 Covenant on Minorities defends the right of minority groups to maintain their cultural identity and calls upon governments to help them in this endeavor. Cultural rights might include the right to speak a language different from that of the majority, the right to practice different religious rituals, or the right to maintain distinctive styles of dress. As the Covenant puts it, "Persons belonging to national or ethnic, religious and linguistic minorities . . . have the right to enjoy their own culture, to profess and practice their own religion, and to use their own language, in private and in public, freely and without interference or any form of discrimination."

The question of group rights remains controversial for some. How far must governments go to protect minority language rights, for example? Must they ensure that some television and radio stations broadcast in the language of a minority, as some countries' governments do? And do cultural groups deserve special rights (as opposed to individuals in those groups)? In the United States, there is strong support for civil rights for all people, no matter what their racial or ethnic background, but there are also many Americans who think that all people should be required to use English in the work place or when dealing with government forms and offices. These Americans would grant individual immigrants all the rights that they themselves possess, but do not wish to allow for any protection for their culture. In a more extreme example,

the Turkish government claims to be willing to give all its Kurds (a minority ethnic group living in Turkey) the same rights as Turks, as long as they do not try and maintain their identity as Kurds. If the Kurds resist, as many do, the Turkish government uses the police and army in an attempt to force them to embrace Turkish language and culture.

ATTACKS ON MINORITIES

Minorities are under attack all over the world. These attacks can take many forms—physical violence, cultural assimilation, bias, and discrimination—but they all deny minorities their human rights.

At its worst, violence against minorities can result in genocide. In 1994, a racist Rwandan government led by extremist Hutus—the majority ethnic group in Rwanda—orchestrated a mass slaughter of approximately 800,000 Tutsis—who made up 15 percent of the population. Hutu government radio stations called upon the people to kill what they called *inyenzi* ("cockroaches"), and the people, led by pro-government militias, obliged. The mass killings took two months to complete and may have succeeded in eliminating at least half of Rwanda's Tutsi population. The killings only stopped with the successful invasion of a pro-Tutsi army based in Uganda. Other genocidal attacks on minorities have taken place in Iraq (where Saddam Hussein used poison gas against Iraqi Kurds), Indonesia (where government-backed Islamic militias slaughtered East Timorese Christians), and in Kosovo (where Serbian troops and militias attacked Kosovar Albanians).

In Europe, immigration from Arab and other Muslim countries has provoked an anti-immigrant and anti-minority reaction.

In some of these countries political parties have formed whose purpose is to attack the presence of these newcomers. In France, the National Front, led by Jean-Marie Le Pen, has called the Arabs outsiders—although many of them were born in the country—and ridiculed the "smells" that come from their neighborhoods. Police brutality against minorities is commonplace in French urban areas. (Le Pen's supporters have also attacked Jews, and the rise of his party has coincided with an increase in anti-Semitic incidents, including vandalism of Jewish cemeteries.) Germany is another country where racist attacks on minorities have become common. The attacks in Germany are backed by far-right-wing political parties with connections to "skinhead" and neo-Nazi groups. Not all people in France and Germany are hostile to the minorities in their midst, and the anti-minority violence has inspired the creation of groups supportive of minorities. These groups include both Muslim immigrants and people of European ancestry.

Anti-minority violence can also be the result of political struggles. In Northern Ireland, the Protestant majority has dominated the region's politics and economy for hundreds of years. In the 1960s, Catholic civil rights demonstrators began marching and protesting discrimination in jobs, housing, and education. Protestant gangs responded with violence and were countered by Catholic groups, most famously the Irish Republican Army (IRA). The violence lasted from the 1970s to the 1990s and was called "the Troubles" by those in Northern Ireland. A 1998 peace agreement gave the Catholic minority—who make up about 40 percent of the population—a share in the governance of the province, and may mark the end of anti-minority violence. (Anti-Catholic marches

continued in 2000, but were not given the same degree of support by the Protestant majority as they had in the past.) More than 3,000 people have died in Northern Ireland as a result of "the Troubles."

In other countries, attacks on minorities are less violent, but discrimination and prejudice remain problems. In the United States, all people, no matter what their ethnic or religious affiliations, share equal rights. Nevertheless, discrimination continues. African Americans have a lower average income per person than the general population and comprise a disproportionate share of the prison population. Until recently, there were clubs and resorts that excluded African Americans and Jews. Anti-minority violence, while not as common as in many places, continues. In 1982, an Asian American named Vincent Chin was beaten to death by two men who were angry at him because they blamed the Japanese for taking their jobs. Chin, however, was of Chinese descent. The men were convicted of manslaughter, but neither one served a day in jail. In 1998, a man named James Byrd, Jr., was dragged to his death on a Texas highway because he was black. In New Jersey, gangs of teenagers calling themselves "dot-busters" have harassed Indian immigrants (many Indian women wear painted marks on their foreheads as a religious sign).

A worldwide minority community that faces discrimination and attacks is that of homosexuals. Homosexual activity is illegal in many parts of the world, including most of Africa and the Middle East, as well as some states in the United States (although, in practice, the laws in the United States outlawing homosexual activity are seldom enforced). Even when gays and lesbians are not a legally persecuted minority, they face discrimination by homophobic people in public and in the work place. Violence against homosexuals is common throughout the world.

PROTECTION FOR MINORITIES

The protection offered to minorities—the protection called for by UN resolutions—varies greatly from country to country. Some countries go out of their way to offer protection for minorities and their cultures. In Scandinavia, the Sami, an indigenous people, have their rights guaranteed by law. The Sami language is supported by the government, and laws protect the Sami from violent attacks. Canada has similar, though less extensive, legal protections for the Inuit peoples of the northern territories.

In the United States, protection for minority rights is written into law. The original framers of the U.S. Constitution added the Bill of Rights, the first ten amendments to the Constitution, specifically to defend the rights of political minorities, and these rights apply to ethnic and racial minorities as well (although minorities have not always been protected by them in practice). The Constitution, combined with subsequent laws passed by Congress, makes it illegal to discriminate against people on the basis of their race, ethnicity, or religion. The United States has also enacted a variety of what are called "affirmative action" programs, which give job and educational opportunities to members of minority groups who might not otherwise have access to them or have historically been denied them. These affirmative action programs have been attacked in recent years; some critics call them a form of reverse discrimination, because majority groups are, in effect, being discriminated against. Affirmative action advocates respond by saying that affirmative

action programs merely counteract the racism that still bars advancement for minorities (as well as making up for past injustices that have left minorities at an economic disadvantage). Another form of minority protection is hate-crime law. These laws declare that crimes against certain groups—African Americans, Asian Americans, gays, and others—that are motivated by hatred deserve harsher penalties. Hate-crime laws are criticized by some because they penalize criminals not only for their actions but also for their thoughts, and thus are an indirect attack on the rights to free speech and free expression.

Although the United States has a body of laws protecting the rights of minorities, these laws are not universally respected or supported. Minority rights advocates argue that there need to be more laws, and they need to be more strictly enforced, before minorities can enjoy full human rights. Critics believe that the laws have gone too far and that what little prejudice exists in the United States is largely caused by programs like affirmative action.

Similarly, in Japan, there are strict laws designed prevent discrimination against the Burakumin, a cultural subcaste, but in practice these laws are ignored or subverted. Japanese companies do their best to avoid hiring Burakumin, and the average per capita income of the Burakumin is far lower than that of most Japanese.

While the idea of laws protecting minority rights is largely accepted by Scandinavia, hotly debated in the United States, and paid lip service to in Japan, in many other parts of the world it is rejected outright. In Guatemala, Myanmar (formerly Burma), Sudan, and Indonesia, for example, minorities have little or no legal protection against discrimination.

ASSIMILATION

Another threat to minorities is assimilation. This threat is more insidious because it does not take away the lives or property of individuals but, instead, subverts their culture. Members of minorities are encouraged to speak the language of the majority, dress like the majority, and forget their own cultural heritage. Assimilation can be forced, as in Turkey, where Kurds are made to speak and publish in Turkish, rather than Kurdish, or it can be the result of social and media pressures, as in Canada, where young Native Americans—surrounded by English television, radio, and movies—learn English rather than their ancestral tongues. In the United States, assimilation is often seen as a positive process. Immigrants coming from other countries are encouraged to forget their old ways and embrace the culture of America. While some accept this, others see it as an attack on their history and traditions.

Other countries have a similar tendency to assimilate minorities. Arab immigrants to France are encouraged to speak French, and pressure is put on Arab women to abandon their traditional veils. In the United Kingdom, citizens of South Asian background learn to love cricket, fish and chips, and the Queen, yet still face attacks by xenophobic fellow citizens. In Tibet, native Tibetans are increasingly outnumbered by Chinese immigrants and face political and economic pressure to forget Buddhism and their spiritual leader, the Dalai Lama, and instead embrace the culture and opportunities offered by China.

CONCLUSION

The United Nations has passed several resolutions defending the rights of minorities, but discrimination and persecution continue. Sometimes this persecution can be stopped by outside intervention, which is what saved the Albanians in Kosovo and the East Timorese in Indonesia; sometimes it is altered by a change in governments, as in Rwanda; and sometimes it simply continues. Even when individuals' lives are protected, their ability to maintain their culture is threatened: the pressures of the majority culture are often too much to withstand.

Carl Skutsch

See also: Anti-Semitism; Indigenous Peoples; Kurds; Nationality and Citizenship; Racism; Self-Determination; Sexual Orientation and Homosexuality.

Bibliography

Klinkner, Philip A. *The Unsteady March: The Rise and Decline of Racial Equality in America.* Chicago: University of Chicago Press, 1999.
Kymlicka, Will. *Multicultural Citizenship: A Liberal Theory of Minority Rights.* New York: Oxford University Press, 1995.
———. *The Rights of Minority Cultures.* New York: Oxford University Press, 1995.
Minority Rights Group International. *World Directory of Minorities.* London: Minority Rights Group International, 1997.

Nationality and Citizenship

Nationality refers to membership of a particular nation or state. It is a universal human right to belong to a nation. The United Nations Universal Declaration of Human Rights (1948) declares in Article 15 that "everyone has the right to a nationality" and "no one shall be arbitrarily deprived of his nationality nor denied the right to change his nationality." To be without a nationality is to be unattached to any one country, or to be stateless.

It is understandable that the United Nations declared nationality to be an essential human right, because, in practice, it is from nationality that many human rights flow. A person's rights are protected by the government of the country of which he or she is a citizen. Without that connection to a particular government, there is no organized guarantor of human rights. In an ideal world, all people would have human rights, no matter where they might live or what their citizenship might be; in truth, however, people's rights are protected by their own nation. If no nation is willing to acknowledge a person as a citizen, then there is nothing to protect their rights; they live in isolation, vulnerable to the whims of whatever force happens to rule their community.

Citizenship can be denied for many reasons. In recent years, for example, large numbers of Turkish and Kurdish workers

Slovak nationalists celebrating the birth of the Slovak Republic, December 31, 1992.

emigrated to Germany seeking jobs. For many years the German government, short on labor, encouraged these *Gastarbeiter* (guest workers). But much as it welcomed the Turks and Kurds as workers, it had no desire to grant them German citizenship. German citizenship is based on German ethnicity: if your ancestors were German, even if you no longer speak German, you can claim German nationality; if your ancestors were not German, you have no such claim. The result of this test is that Turks who were born in Germany, who speak German, and who have never seen Turkey are still considered foreigners; yet ethnic Germans born in the former Soviet Union, who speak only Russian, can (and do) emigrate to Germany and successfully claim German citizenship. These rules leave the Turks and Kurds in a no-win situation: the country where they live and work does not wish to offer them permanent protection (and many individual Germans are quite hostile to these "foreigners"), but the country where their parents or grandparents were born has no desire to have them come home. (Turkey has its own economic problems and is not eager for the *Gastarbeiter* to return.)

Germany is not alone in its stand on nationality. Many countries, including most European countries, make it difficult for foreigners to gain citizenship. Even France, which is more open-minded than most other European countries, does not automatically grant citizenship to children born within its borders of non-French parents but, instead, requires an application process before citizenship is granted. (This position is based on the reluctance of many French to see North African immigrants—of whom there are a great many in France—become citizens of their country.)

Many problems connected to nationality result from wars and the refugees those wars create. One of the most intractable of these problems is that of the Palestinian refugees who fled Israel after its creation in 1948. As a result of the bitter struggles between Jews and Arabs in the 1930s and 1940s, some 750,000 Palestinian Arabs fled their homes, fearful of the results of a Jewish victory. The new state of Israel, claiming that the Palestinians had abandoned their homes voluntarily, refused to allow the refugees to return or to grant them citizenship. Not wanting to accept the burden of this influx of foreigners (and also eager to keep the issue of Palestine alive), the Arab countries to which the Palestinians fled—Lebanon, Jordan, Egypt—also refused to grant them citizenship. As a result, the Palestinians lived in makeshift refugee camps, which turned into permanent refugee camps. Lacking citizenship in any country and lacking any internationally accepted nationality, they became stateless refugees.

Because they lack a government to protect them, the human rights situation of the Palestinian Arabs has been grim. Their camps are dirty and poorly supplied with sanitation and medical facilities, they are at the mercy of both their hosts and the occasional wars that have swept through the Middle East, and they dream of going back to a home that many of them—now the children and grandchildren of the original refugees—have never seen. There are currently approximately 4 million Palestinians living outside the lands controlled by Israel.

Other refugees made stateless by war or political turmoil include the Bosnian Muslims, chased out of their homes by Serbian militias; Tibetan followers of the Dalai Lama, living in exile in India; and Hutu refugees, living in camps in the Congo, afraid of the Tutsi-dominated regime in Rwanda.

Few countries have as open a policy on citizenship as the United States. While the United States does not accept all immigrants as citizens—and has been harshly criticized by human rights advocates for its treatment of refugees—it also has no ethnic hurdles that must be overcome before citizenship is granted. Anyone, no matter what their race, religion, or country of origin, can become a citizen by meeting the requirements of the Immigration and Naturalization Service and passing an examination on the history and political structure of the United States. Moreover, any child born in the United States, no matter what the status of his or her parents, automatically becomes a citizen, and thus acquires nationality.

For the human right of nationality to become a universal reality, the countries of the world would have to at least match the example of the United States. And, as the United States is far from perfect in its treatment of refugees, the world, including the United States, has a long way to go.

Carl Skutsch

See also: Minority Rights; Refugees; Self-Determination.

———————————

Bibliography

Kymlicka, Will. *Multicultural Citizenship: A Liberal Theory of Minority Rights.* New York: Oxford University Press, 1995.

Spinner, Jeff. *The Boundaries of Citizenship: Race, Ethnicity, and Nationality in the Liberal State.* Baltimore, MD: Johns Hopkins University Press, 1994.

Native Americans

The situation of the indigenous people of North America is intertwined with issues connected to human rights. The term "human rights" connotes something that is considered universal and applicable across time and cultures. Rights are often thought to apply solely to individuals, rather than to peoples. The relationship between Native American, or Indian, communities and the United States warns of the possible dangers and abuses of this ideal. Early European justifications for colonization rested on views of rights that were narrow and largely Eurocentric. The United States used the notion of individual rights to justify the genocide and assimilation of Native American peoples. Even today, the American conception of rights often clashes with Native American ideals. Of course, the United States is not alone in oppressing indigenous peoples, whose struggles for their human rights rage worldwide.

EUROPEAN JUSTIFICATIONS FOR COLONIZATION

From the start of the discovery of the so-called New World, European characterization of the indigenous peoples of the Americas as uncivilized savages was used to justify colonization and genocide. Human rights therefore applied to Europeans, or only those people who fit into a European framework of rights. Many Europeans proclaimed their duty to extend the Christian dominion and to save "heathens" and educate the "backward" Indians.

After the Protestant Reformation split Christianity, justifications that were more secularly grounded gained increasing prominence. A common argument was that the land of the Americas was empty and uninhabited. The indigenous people of the Americas were viewed as hunter-gatherer savages without civilized forms of government. Philosophers such as John Locke—who was an early proponent of the idea of human rights—argued that the "nomadic" natives of the Americas had not acquired a right to property or dominion because they had not settled, worked, and farmed the land in the Americas. Indians were left out of the European conceptions of rights because their cultures and governments did not operate in ways familiar to Europeans. The Indians thus were, in effect, not human and had no rights to be respected.

However, during the early periods of exploration, the British and French largely dealt with the tribes of North America as legitimate entities with which they had to make treaties and establish diplomatic relations. One of the complaints of American colonists in the American Revolution was that King George III of England had wrongly forbidden settlement west of the Appalachians in order to protect the Indians. Indian nations were often strong military powers and had to be treated with respect.

UNITED STATES AND THE INDIANS

In the context of U.S. constitutional law, the indigenous peoples of North America were considered "domestic dependent nations" within a nation. Chief Justice John Marshall (who presided over the Supreme Court in the 1830s) declared that the Indians and the United States existed in a "ward-guardian" relationship. The United States did not treat its wards well, and despite some Supreme Court rulings in their favor, the United States proceeded to take away Indian rights. The method of extinguishing Indian rights has varied in the United States, from mutually agreed upon treaties, to confiscation of land followed by later "compensation" (usually very paltry), to outright unilateral decisions made by the federal government.

The U.S. government has broken some part of every single treaty it has signed with Indians. Throughout history, Indian nations that refused to sign treaties often found themselves at war with the U.S. Army. The rush of American settlers westward created increasing demands on the Indians to cede more land to the United States. After the Civil War, the United States decided it was too expensive to keep making treaties that compensated Indians for their land, so it moved to take land and establish Indian reservations by congressional legislation. If any compensation was given, it was far below the value of that land and ignored that Indians in many cases had a special attachment to that land where their ancestors had lived. These actions were often justified by the idea that cheating the Indians was necessary to spread westward American democracy and rights.

The stated goal of American policy throughout the latter part of the nineteenth century, and supported by many self-proclaimed Indian rights advocates, was to assimilate and educate Indians as individuals into American culture and society. The 1887 General Allotment Act tried to break up the "tribal mass" of Indians on the reservations and force many Indians to become farmers on individual plots of land. The "surplus" Indian land was given to the military and

sold to settlers, with Indians usually being left with the most barren pieces of land. The breaking up of tribal lands helped to damage and weaken Indian culture.

As part of a program of assimilation (something that today would be considered "cultural genocide"), Indian children were forced to attend special boarding schools aimed at educating them in civilized Christian ways. Physically separated from their families for years, children were often brutally treated and forced to forget their tribe's culture, language, and heritage. Many Indian children grew up alienated from their tribe, but still never quite fitting into white society. Splits developed in native communities between traditionalists and those Christianized and educated in the boarding schools. The federal government often singled out the "educated" Indians for special favors and worked to destroy traditional forms of authority.

In the pursuit of this ideal of assimilation, rights that most Americans normally held were disregarded. The military and the powerful Bureau of Indian Affairs often ran the reservations, forcibly denying Indians the right to free speech and to practice Native religions.

The Indian Reorganization Act of 1934 changed the government's course somewhat by instituting some measure of self-governance back to the tribes. Government rhetoric spoke of allowing Indians to govern themselves, but the Bureau of Indian Affairs often insisted that tribes adopt constitutions that enacted "democratic" forms of government foreign to many Indian traditions. The federal government also still had control and veto power over many of the tribes' affairs.

In the 1950s, after the Supreme Court struck down the laws permitting "separate but equal" schools for different races, congressional policy headed in a new direction. The tribes were to be eliminated and their individual members absorbed into the larger culture. This was not the physical genocide of the nineteenth century, but it amounted to cultural genocide. The Indians as a tribal people were to be destroyed. This was the ultimate logical extension and conclusion of the U.S. policy of assimilation. By government fiat, several tribes ceased to exist legally as sovereign tribes, including (temporarily) the Menominee of Wisconsin.

The modern era of "self-determination" began when President Richard Nixon repudiated the goal of tribal elimination. The stated goal of the United States today is to encourage Indian tribes to govern themselves. While the United States unilaterally took away many Indian rights, the U.S.

courts held that the Indians' rights flowed not from American law, but from the Indian sovereignty that was still retained.

In the minds of many Americans, a tension exists between group rights and individual rights. The basis of group rights for Native Americans legally rests on the historical relationship between different political communities. Different arguments, such as protecting minority cultures, have been advanced for the continuing existence of Native American tribes. The United States had not given "special rights" to Native Americans. The rights Native Americans have are rights reserved by a sovereign group and are not rights granted by the United States.

Native Americans tribes also face a variety of other problems, as a result of both the legacy of genocide and of the continu-

Native Americans protest the testing of nuclear weapons near their lands.

ing attempts to limit their sovereignty. Poverty, unemployment, and crime are generally plentiful on reservations. Schooling, once a tool meant to assimilate Native Americans, is now so bureaucratized through the federal government as often to be ineffective. While some treaty rights, such as fishing rights, have been recognized to some extent, water rights and other rights are often not fully recognized. The issues are many and complex and do not always receive the full attention of Congress and the American public.

American notions of property often clash with Native Americans' desire to have access to sacred sites on private and government-owned land. Land once taken from Native Americans that is still sacred to them often cannot be accessed. The Supreme Court held in 1988 that government agencies managing public land can develop that land ("its land") without any concern for whether Native American sacred sites would be affected. Holy places must make way for new logging trails. The land that had been taken from Indians legally can be desecrated without any concern for the past at all.

Land claims still remain unresolved for many Native Americans; where they have been resolved, they have been "settled" by pennies on the dollar (or worse). An illustrative claim concerns the Black Hills of the Dakotas. In 1980, the Supreme Court ruled that the Black Hills were taken unfairly, in violation of the 1868 Fort Laramie treaty, and that the Sioux Indians were owed "just compensation," in the form of money. But the ruling did not allow the accounting of the billions of dollars of gold and minerals extracted from the Black Hills over the last century. Though the U.S. government has offered millions to the Sioux to settle the claims, the Sioux have consistently refused, claiming the land itself is sacred to them.

Senator Bill Bradley (D-NJ) introduced a bill several times in the 1980s that would have partially given the Black Hills back to the Sioux, but it did not pass. The Bureau of Indian Affairs has put the settlement money in a trust fund, considering the matter closed.

The criminal justice system also places many obstacles in the way of Native Americans. Federal, and especially state, courts are perceived by many Native Americans as racist (or at the very least, insensitive to cultural difference). Leonard Peltier, a leader of the militant American Indian Movement, has been held in jail for over two decades for being wrongly convicted of killing two FBI agents. Government officials have admitted that Peltier was not guilty of the killings and that it fabricated evidence. U.S. attorneys have said that Peltier would not be found guilty if he were retried today. Yet advocates for Peltier have been unable to get his conviction overturned or have him pardoned, making Peltier, in the eyes of many, a political prisoner.

OTHER NATIVES OF THE AMERICAS

To be fair, it should be said that the United States is not alone in its disregard for indigenous rights. Many countries refuse to recognize indigenous peoples or take their land claims seriously. Mexico faces the problem of dealing with the demands of indigenous peoples in Chiapas, for example. Brazil's development policies lead the government look the other way as settlers take land from its indigenous peoples, leading to further decimation of the rain forest.

While Canada has often been portrayed as more benevolent than the United States in its Indian policy, the truth is more complicated. Canada also signed many treaties, which were not all fully kept, with aboriginal peoples (or First Nations, as they are also called in Canada). Canada also instituted similar policies of assimilation, such as boarding schools. In 1969, the Canadian government announced its intention to eliminate any distinction between aboriginal people and "regular" Canadians. However, the government backed off this promise under a flurry of protest.

Today, Canada's constitution protects aboriginal treaty rights. Only in the last decade have Canadian courts begun to recognize that aboriginal rights do not come from Canada, but that aboriginal people retain some sovereignty derived from their ancient status as a people. In 1998, Canada allowed the admittance of a tribe's oral history as evidence in court, in recognition of the differences between cultures. Still, aboriginal rights in Canada are on the national agenda and under great discussion in a way that is almost inconceivable in the United States.

CONCLUSION

The fight for international recognition of indigenous rights has advanced, but it remains stymied. The right to self-determination has been an internationally recognized right, but its application has generally been limited to apply only to overseas colonies, not to indigenous peoples within a state. While there has been limited success, attempts to implement new human rights law in the United Nations, or to reinterpret old international law, have largely been blocked for political and economic reasons and because of the concerns and intents of powerful countries.

The fiction of a single unitary state containing equal rights for everyone has been an ideal fraught with problems. Early UN human rights documents gave minorities the right to assimilate into mainstream society, rather than to maintain their distinct identities. The ideal of human rights must not be cast in narrow individualist concerns. The world is divided into separate states, and current international law recognizes the rights of different political communities to exist within those states. Like other indigenious peoples, Native Americans have rights both as individuals and as groups, and those rights include keeping alive the tribal entities that are central to their culture and their sense of self.

Timothy Waligore

See also: Indigenous Peoples.

Bibliography

Deloria, Vine, Jr., and Clifford M. Lytle. *American Indians, American Justice.* Austin: University of Texas Press, 1997.

Jaimes, M. Annette, ed. *The State of Native America: Genocide, Colonization, and Resistance.* Boston: South End Press, 1992.

Pommersheim, Frank. *Braid of Feathers: American Indian Law and Contemporary Tribal Life.* Berkeley: University of California Press, 1995.

Nobel Peace Prize

The Nobel Peace Prize is one of five prizes created by the will of the Swedish inventor and capitalist Alfred Nobel (1833–1896). (The other Nobel Prizes are for physics, chemistry, physiology or medicine, and literature. A sixth prize, for economics, was added in 1969.) Originally the recipients of the Peace Prize were generally statesmen and officials who helped to bring about peace between nations, but in the last twenty years there has been a trend toward awarding prizes to activists who have worked to advance the cause of human rights.

Alfred Nobel's wording allowed such flexibility: "The whole of my remaining realizable estate shall be dealt with in the following way: the capital, invested in safe securities by my executors, shall constitute a fund, the interest on which shall be annually distributed in the form of prizes to those who, during the preceding year, shall have conferred the greatest benefit on mankind." It is ironic that Nobel himself did little to benefit mankind during his lifetime. He made his fortune developing new kinds of explosives, including dynamite and blasting gelatin, and later expanded his wealth by investing in the arms industry. He was called "the merchant of death" during his lifetime, and perhaps he founded the Nobel Prizes as a way of balancing his legacy.

The Nobel Peace Prize is awarded by the Norwegian Nobel Committee, which is made up of five individuals. Members serve a six-year term and are appointed by the Norwegian Parliament. The current members (for 2000–2002) are Gunnar Berge, Gunnar Johan Stålsett, Hanna Kristine Kvan-

Noble Peace Prize winner Nelson Mandela.

mo, Sissel Marie Rønbeck, and Inger-Marie Ytterhorn.

The following people and organizations are given the right to nominate Nobel Peace Prize candidates:

1. Present and past members of the Nobel Committee and the advisors at the Nobel Institute; 2. members of national assemblies and governments, and members of the Inter-Parliamentary Union; 3. members of the International Court of Arbitration and the International Court of Justice at The Hague; 4. members of the Commission of the Permanent International Peace Bureau;

5. members of the Institut de Droit International; 6. present university professors of law, political science, history, and philosophy; and 7. holders of the Nobel Peace Prize.

HUMAN RIGHTS ADVANCED

The emphasis in recent years has been to award Nobel Prizes for humanitarian reasons:

The 2000 Nobel Peace Prize winner was South Korean president Kim Dae Jung. Throughout his life he has worked toward reconciliation with North Korea, spoken out strongly for democracy and human rights, and denounced repression in Myanmar (formerly Burma) and East Timor.

The 1999 Nobel Prize recipient, Doctors Without Borders/Médecins Sans Frontières, is an organization of physicians dedicated to serving the sick and wounded in troubled areas of the world. They have been particularly active in war zones, which in recent years included Bosnia, Kosovo, Ethiopia, and Chechnya.

The 1997 prize was given to the International Campaign to Ban Landmines and Jody Williams, who helped to spark the grassroots movement to ban land mines. (Land mines cause thousands of deaths and dismemberments every year, even long after the end of the wars that led to their placement.)

The 1996 prize was given to José Ramos-Horta and Bishop Carlos Filipe Ximenes Belo. Both men spent many years opposing Indonesian oppression in East Timor. This prize angered the Indonesian government, which has denied human rights violations, but cheered human rights activists around the world who have called East Timor a human rights disaster.

The Nobel Peace Prize often has the affect of ruffling the feathers of governments accused of human rights violations. Indonesia is only one example of a government embarrassed by the world spotlight that the Nobel Peace Prize casts on it. The 1991 award of the prize to Myanmar activist Aung San Suu Kyi disturbed that country's repressive leadership, which had kept Aung San Suu Kyi under house arrest from 1989 to 1995. The Nobel Prize is probably one of the pressures that helped lead to her release (although she remains closely supervised by the government). Similarly, the 1989 award given to the Dalai Lama helped draw attention to the Chinese government's repressive behavior in Tibet.

Other prominent human rights activists awarded the Nobel Peace Prize include Rigoberta Menchú, Elie Wiesel, Bishop Desmond Tutu, Nelson Mandela, Lech Walesa, Adolfo Pérez, and Martin Luther King, Jr.

Carl Skutsch

See also: Aung San Suu Kyi; Mohandas Gandhi; Martin Luther King, Jr.; Land Mines; Nelson Mandela.

Bibliography

Abrams, Irwin. *The Words of Peace: Selections from the Speeches of the Nobel Prize Winners of the Twentieth Century.* New York: Newmarket Press, 2000.

Keene, Ann T. *Peacemakers: Winners of the Nobel Peace Prize.* Oxford: Oxford University Press, 1998.

Nuclear Weapons

Nuclear weapons are the ultimate weapons of mass destruction. At the moment they detonate, they kill by the intensity of the blast and the heat that they generate. They also produce radiation, which can travel through the atmosphere and cause illness or death within days or weeks after the weapon has been detonated. Even if not immediately lethal, radiation can also cause the later appearance of life-threatening medical conditions in a victim or genetic mutations in future generations. It can destroy the environment and make it uninhabitable. Nuclear weapons are indiscriminate in their devastating power, affecting combatant and civilian populations alike. There is a generally shared view that the suffering caused by their use cannot be justified by the accomplishment of any military objective. The use of nuclear weapons, no matter what the justification, is a gross violation of human rights.

From its inception, the United Nations has been vitally concerned with nuclear weapons and the threat to the right to life of all humanity posed by their possible use. The first resolution adopted by the General Assembly in 1946 set up the Atomic En-

In England, antiwar demonstrators protest the use of nuclear and other weapons of mass destruction, 1991.

ergy Commission and charged it with the task of developing possible plans for eliminating nuclear weapons. It also established various bodies, including the Disarmament Commission and the Committee on Disarmament, to work on an international level for nuclear disarmament.

Throughout the cold war and the nuclear arms race between the United States and the Soviet Union, the United Nations consistently advocated nuclear disarmament and the destruction of nuclear weapons stockpiles, citing its responsibility under the UN Charter to "maintain international peace and security" and "to promote and encourage respect for human rights and for fundamental freedoms."

The United Nations took many steps in the 1960s, 1970s, and 1980s to move the superpowers in the direction of disarmament. In 1961, a strongly worded General Assembly resolution stated that the use of nuclear weapons would violate the UN Charter, cause "indiscriminate suffering and destruction" and be "contrary to the rules of international law and to the laws of humanity." Any state employing such weapons would be "acting contrary to the laws of humanity and committing a crime against mankind." This resolution would be reissued several times over the next twenty years.

In 1966, the secretary-general released a report called "The Effects of Possible Use of Nuclear Weapons and on the Security and Economic Implications for States of the Acquisition and Further Development of these Weapons," which contained the findings of a group of experts on the ramifications of conducting a nuclear war. It concluded that the possible hazards for the world's population were too great to ever justify the weapons' use.

The United Nations also supported, and in several cases initiated, the numerous international treaties that were signed over the

years limiting the uses of nuclear weapons and technology. The major treaties include:

1. The Nuclear Test Ban Treaty (1963), which prohibited testing nuclear weapons in space, above ground, or underwater.
2. The Outer Space Treaty (1966), which banned putting nuclear weapons into space.
3. The Nonproliferation Treaty (1968), in which countries with nuclear weapons agreed not to assist countries without nuclear weapons in acquiring nuclear weapons or technology.
4. The Seabed Treaty (1972), which banned placing nuclear weapons on or under the seabed or ocean floor.

There have also been a number of treaties signed by the two major nuclear powers, the United States and the Soviet Union (now Russia). These include:

1. The Strategic Arms Limitation Treaties I (1972) and II (1979). The first treaty limited antiballistic missile launch sites and imposed a five-year freeze on the testing and deployment of certain types of nuclear weapons; the second treaty limited the numbers of offensive nuclear weapons each country could maintain.
2. The Intermediate-Range Nuclear Forces Treaty (1987). It eliminated medium- and short-range missiles.
3. The Strategic Arms Reduction Treaty I (1991). This was the first treaty in which the superpowers agreed to begin to reduce their nuclear weapons stockpiles.
4. The Strategic Arms Reduction Treaty II (1993). This calls for reduction of long-range missiles and the elimination of certain other types of nuclear weapons.

While supporting all of these treaties, the UN General Assembly had also, in 1981, reiterated its own stance on nuclear weapons with the "Declaration on the Prevention of Nuclear Catastrophe," which unequivocally stated that "nuclear weapons are capable of destroying civilization on earth" and therefore "states or statesmen that resort first to the use of nuclear weapons will be committing the gravest crime against humanity."

The years since the breakup of the Soviet Union and the end of the cold war have generally seen positive movement toward the non-proliferation of nuclear weapons. In spite of the fact that many more nations now possess nuclear weapons and technology, the number of states that have signed the Nonproliferation Treaty is well over 150 and growing. Nuclear weapon–free zones have been established in Antarctica, the South Pacific, the Caribbean, and South America; and the United Nations periodically calls for the establishment of such zones in the Middle East and southern Asia as well.

James R. Lewis

See also: Conventional Weapons.

Bibliography

Evan, William M., and Stephen Hilgartner, ed. *The Arms Race and Nuclear War.* Englewood Cliffs, NJ: Prentice-Hall, 1987.

Forsberg, Randall, et al. *Nonproliferation Primer: Preventing the Spread of Nuclear, Chemical, and Biological Weapons.* Cambridge, MA: MIT Press, 1995.

United Nations Department for Disarmament Affairs. *Nuclear Weapons: A Comprehensive Study.* New York: United Nations, 1991.

Palestine and the Palestinian Authority

Palestine is not an internationally recognized national entity, but the Palestinian Authority (PA) governs certain areas in the territories controlled by Israel (the Occupied Territories), and there are hopes, among Palestinians, that these areas will eventually be granted full independence. The areas under Palestinian Authority governance include parts of the West Bank, which lies between Israel and Jordan, and the Gaza Strip, which lies between Israel and Egypt.

There has been no accurate census of the Palestinian Occupied Territories by Israel. The majority of the population are Sunni Muslims. There is a minority Christian population divided between Catholic, Orthodox, and Protestant denominations, based in and near the neighboring cities of Ramallah, Jerusalem, and Bethlehem.

ISRAEL AND THE OCCUPATION

The human rights situation in the Occupied Territories is closely linked to the Palestinian-Israeli conflict. The series of battles from 1947 to 1949 between the Arabs and Jewish settlers led to the separation of UN-mandated Palestine into what became Israel, on the one hand, and Jordanian- and Egyptian-controlled Arab territories, on the other. As a result of this war, around 750,000 Palestinian left their homes as refugees, many migrating to neighboring countries, to the West Bank, and to the Gaza Strip. Ever since this war, Arabs and Israelis have been in dispute about these Palestinian refugees—should they be allowed to return to their homes (something that most Palestinians favor and most Israelis oppose), the borders of Israel, the status of Jerusalem, and other security matters.

These issues of dispute have led to a protracted series of conflicts and an intermittent state of war between Israel and Arab countries. In the June 1967 Arab-Israeli war, Israel occupied the remaining areas of Palestine, including the West Bank, East Jerusalem, and the Gaza Strip. This placed many Palestinians under direct Israeli authority and has led to conflicts ever since. The wars and Israeli control of the Occupied Territories have also involved many human rights violations.

In 1993, the Palestine Liberation Organization (PLO) and Israel embarked on a peace process that was designed to end the conflict between the Palestinians and Israelis. Israel and the PLO agreed to a five-year interim period during which the issues in dispute would be resolved. Subsequent agreements have called for the withdrawal of Israeli forces from parts of the Occupied Territories and the transfer of powers to an interim Palestinian Authority, established by the PLO and headed by its chairman, Yasser Arafat.

By 2000, the Palestinian Authority had military control over small sections of the Occupied Territories and civil control over a larger area. The remaining areas of the Occupied Territories are in Israeli hands. Except for the increasingly expanding Jerusalem municipality, these areas of the Occupied Territories are administered by an Israeli military administration.

Across most of the Occupied Territories, Israel retains overall control for security under the agreements and can demand that the Palestinians ensure Israeli security in areas controlled by the Palestinian Authority. This includes the power to demand that suspects be handed over on request and without a formal extradition process and the right to chase Palestinians into the Occupied Territories, even those parts administered by the PA.

Whether Israel will allow Palestinians complete control over all the Occupied Territories is a critical and hotly debated question. Many Israelis wish to have peace with their Arab neighbors and so are eager to give them the independence they desire. Other Israelis fear that, once free, the Palestinians will use the West Bank and the Gaza Strip as staging areas for attacks on Israel, which some Palestinian Arabs wish to retake entirely. And still others believe that the Occupied Territories rightfully belong to Israel as outlined in the

Bible. The debate inside Israel is matched by debates and animosities among Palestinians. Extremists on both sides are willing to use violence and terror to achieve their ends.

Israeli operatives have been known to undertake intelligence and other security operations in Palestinian Authority areas and the Israeli Parliament has declared that Israeli courts have jurisdiction to try Palestinians for actions in their own territories that may harm Israeli security. These actions clearly demonstrate that the PA is not a sovereign government.

The limitations on the Palestinian Authority's power mean that the Palestinians do not have their own independent state. They are forced to acknowledge Israeli authority. Although this causes great resentment among many Palestinians—and has been called a general human rights violation by international observers—Palestini-

Hamas fighters wearing masks lead a demonstration in the Gaza Strip. Hamas is an extremist Palestinian political group, 1993.

ans have more self-government today than they have ever had in the past.

In areas under its own security controls, Israel continues to pursue practices that sometimes violate human rights. Arrest, harassment, detention, interrogation, and imprisonment all occur with some degree of human rights violation. Although the numbers of Palestinians killed and injured has been substantially reduced, perhaps due to the removal of Israeli military from population centers, incidents are reported each year. Israel also pursues policies, particularly in and around Jerusalem, that the UN monitoring committees have found result in the violation of Palestinians' economic, social, and cultural rights. Israel argues that human rights treaties to which it is signatory do not afford protection to those living in the Occupied Territories.

In October 2000, renewed violence between angry Palestinian crowds demanding political rights and Israeli security forces led to the death of more than 140 Arabs (and at least eight Jews). The death toll from this new violence continued through the end of 2000. The new violence has placed the ongoing peace negotiations on hold and in jeopardy.

THE PALESTINIAN AUTHORITY

In 1996, the Palestinians elected their first government, consisting of an elected assembly, the Palestinian Legislative Council, made up of 88 members, and a chairman, Yasser Arafat. Arafat then appointed a cabinet, the majority of whose members are drawn from the legislature. There is also an appointed judiciary. Although a Basic Law was passed by the Palestinian Legislative Council, Arafat has been unwilling to sign it. Consequently, there is no formal constitution for the Palestinian Authority, though constitutional protection is to be found in numerous instruments of Palestinian law.

As the Palestinian Authority is not the government of a state, it does not have the capacity to sign international treaties. Nonetheless, at a meeting with Amnesty International in July 1994, the head of the Palestinian Authority confirmed the intention to respect all human rights treaties. Despite this confirmation, the PA does not protect many human rights in the areas under its control.

Democracy is not respected by the Palestinian Authority. The laws passed by the Legislative Council are seldom signed by the chairman, while over 100 executive decrees are enforced without approval or vote by the Legislative Council. Legislative Council members have been beaten, arrested, and imprisoned by PA security services, despite the legal immunity granted by their office. The Council has also been unable to constrain the executive, including cases where there are confirmed reports of ministerial corruption and misadministration.

Political cases are decided arbitrarily, and defendants have been denied the right to a fair trial. Political cases may be decided by any senior member of the executive, which may include governors of districts, mayors, and other local functionaries. In these instances, evidence, witnesses, and opposing parties may be interfered with in advance of trial. Even where trials take place, unsatisfactory judgments may not be enforced by executive agencies.

The Palestinian Authority has created parallel systems to the legislature and courts. Communal systems, political parties, executive authorities, and the security establishment all provide alternatives to the legislature and judiciary. These systems tend to be more cognizant of political considerations and less concerned with formal considerations of equality in law, justice, or fairness. Critics argue that these systems are dominated by nepotism, corruption, and bribery.

The Palestinian Authority has also established the State Security Court, which is a military tribunal that will try and convict without ensuring a defendant's rights or due process. The perfunctory nature of the trial process has led many human rights groups to question the independence and impartiality of the court. There is no appeal from the State Security Court, and it operates outside the civilian court system. Three people have been executed following cursory trials and convictions in the State Security Court.

Critics and independent forces—such as the media, civil society, and political parties—are frequently intimidated, threatened, and harassed by executive authorities, whenever they criticize the Palestinian Authority. Numerous editors, journalists, and human rights activists have been arrested and detained for this reason. Usually these arrests are without warrant and detentions are without recourse to a tribunal and without the rights of access to a lawyer, family, or judicial authority.

Freedom of the press exists but is under pressure. Newspapers and radio stations have been closed down or distribution obstructed, usually temporarily. Political opponents and critics are regularly arrested. Groups with extremist beliefs, such as Hamas, Islamic Jihad, and the Popular Front for the Liberation of Palestine, have been subject to numerous arrest campaigns, sometimes at the insistence of Israel following bomb attacks. In many cases of arrest and detention, security forces have used excessive force, and interrogation has involved ill treatment. More than 350 people were arrested in 1999 for political reasons, some of whom were political extremists arrested in response to pressure from the Israeli government. Torture is alleged to have occurred after some of these arrests. Serious injuries have been inflicted on detainees, some of which have led to fatalities.

Competing and confused government structures are a feature throughout the Palestinian Authority. Critics have argued that the lack of regulation and supervision has encouraged abuses of power and human rights violations. In addition to civil and political human rights violations, social and economic inequalities also present problems. The economy remains underdeveloped, and many resources remain under Israeli control. The Palestinians have little command over their borders and lack money and materials for production. Most of the gross domestic product is generated by the large migratory workforce traveling daily to Israel, and the treasury relies heavily on international aid.

Rhys Johnson

See also: Cairo Declaration on Human Rights in Islam; Self-Determination; Terrorism.

Bibliography

Amnesty International. *Amnesty International Report 2000.* New York: Amnesty International Publications, 2000.

Human Rights Watch. *World Report 2000.* New York: Human Rights Watch, 2000.

Peace

It can be argued that peace is the primary subject of international law and the main objective of organized international cooperation. When the United Nations (UN) was founded at the end of World War II, it was visualized as an international organization whose most important function was to keep the peace and to prevent another war. Article I of the UN Charter enumerates the organization's purposes. The first purpose listed is "to maintain international peace and security, and to that end: to take effective collective measures for the prevention and removal of threats to the peace, and for the suppression of acts of aggression or other breaches of the peace." Peace was, and is, considered a necessary condition for the full development and enjoyment of human rights by the world's population.

There is a strong tendency to think that if nations divest themselves of their arsenals of weapons, especially their weapons of mass destruction, then there will be peace. But, although the UN and other organizations continue to work toward disarmament, there is a growing awareness in the international community that the concept of peace encompasses much more than the laying down of weapons and that disarmament is only one of the steps that must be taken to achieve peace.

Today, in peace studies, much stronger emphasis is placed on the complete interdependency of peace and human rights, with peace increasingly being defined as a human right itself, one part of the "third generation" of human rights. The first generation consists of civil and political rights; the second of economic, social, and cultural rights; and the third, of rights like the right to peace and the right to development. These third-generation rights are collectively referred to as "solidarity rights," because they define the rights of individuals in relation to their membership in a collective society.

By examining some of the relevant documents, it is possible to trace the UN's shift toward this conception of peace as a human right. The Declaration on the Essentials of Peace, adopted by the UN General Assembly in 1949, in the early years of the cold war, emphasizes that for an enduring peace, nations must "refrain from threatening or using force . . . and from any threats or acts, direct or indirect, aimed at impairing the freedom, independence or integrity of any State," and they must "cooperate to attain the effective international regulation of conventional armaments . . . and the prohibition of atomic weapons." Peace was seen primarily as the absence and opposite of war. In 1968, however, an international conference on human rights was held in Teheran, Iran, and its Proclamation of Teheran demonstrated that the concept of peace was beginning to evolve into something more. It called for "recognizing that peace is the universal aspiration of mankind and that peace and justice are indispensable to the full realization of human rights and fundamental freedoms."

These concepts of the complete interrelationship of human rights and peace and of the necessity for a climate of peace in which human rights can flourish are stated in the UN Declaration on the Preparation of Societies for Life in Peace, adopted by the General Assembly in 1978. The Declaration affirmed that states should, in the interest of establishing and maintaining a durable climate of peace, observe several basic principles. Those principles included recognizing that "every nation and every human being . . . has the inherent right to life in peace. Respect for that right, as well as for the other human rights, is in the common interest of all mankind and an indispensable condition of advancement of all nations" and that "every State, acting in the spirit of friendship and good neighborly relations, has the duty to promote all-around, mutually advantageous and equitable political, economic, social and cultural cooperation with other States, . . . with a view to securing their common existence and cooperation in peace."

Finally, in 1984, the UN General Assembly issued the "Declaration on the Right of Peoples to Peace," an unequivocal statement asserting the view that peace is a basic human right and a necessity for the full and unfettered enjoyment of all other human rights. It affirmed that "the main-tenance of a peaceful life for peoples is the sacred duty of each State" and that "the preservation of the right of the peoples to peace and the promotion of its implementation constitute a fundamental obligation of each State." It called on states and other international organizations "to do their utmost to assist in implementing the right of peoples to peace."

Today, the UN continues to espouse this view of peace as a basic human right. Sadly, the world remains wracked by war.

James R. Lewis

See also: War; War Crimes.

Bibliography

Claude, Richard Pierre, and Burns H. Weston. *Human Rights in the World Community.* Philadelphia: University of Pennsylvania Press, 1992.

Forsythe, David P. *Human Rights and Peace: International and National Dimensions.* Lincoln: University of Nebraska Press, 1993.

Police and Law Enforcement

Police are at the center of human rights. They face in two directions, with two possible attitudes toward the protection of human rights. First, the police can be the main defenders of people's human rights. In free societies, the police are the first people citizens turn to for protection against crime, domestic abuse, and racist attacks. In repressive societies, however, the police play the opposite role. They become the people's main oppressors and the primary tool of authoritarian governments bent on denying their citizens full human rights. And even in free societies, the amount of power given to the police can sometimes lead to abuses of that power and to violations of human rights.

It is unfortunate that the police are more often viewed as attackers of human rights rather than its defenders, but the latter role is vital. All people have the right to live in a safe and secure environment, to be protected from assault, rape, or robbery, and to have equal access to justice. A well-trained and well-led police force is essential for protecting these human rights. Without police, we would live in a world of anarchy and mayhem, where no rights would be possible.

According to international human rights watchdogs, the police forces of Western and Northern Europe, Canada, and the United States have the best human rights records

Guatemalan police face peasants protesting excessive taxes.

(Even so, of course, these police forces are not perfect, as is outlined later.) The police in these nations are professionally trained, reasonably well paid (many police officers are able to retire after twenty years of work), and watched over by well-regulated court systems.

Beyond the benefit of serving their own citizens, police can also be used to train other police to work more effectively. In 1994, the dictatorial government of Haiti was overthrown by American troops and replaced with a democracy. Haiti's old police force had been responsible for numerous human rights abuses and was viewed by most Haitians as more of a threat than a protector. To solve this problem, the United States spent almost $100 million to train a brand-new police force, unmarred by any of the crimes of the past. Taking part in their training were police from the United States. This new force, numbering 6,000, has been one of the few modest successes in a Haiti, which continues to struggle with human rights problems. Similar police training efforts have been carried through in Cambodia and East Timor.

POLICE ABUSE OF HUMAN RIGHTS

While many police forces work hard to protect human rights, all too often they are responsible for many of the human rights abuses in their countries.

Even in countries with well-trained and professional police forces, human rights abuses occur. In Western Europe—whose police, as has been said, have a generally good human rights record—there has been a recent rise in police brutality toward ethnic minorities. These human rights crimes are particularly common in Germany, Austria, Switzerland, and Belgium. Observers speculate that the large influx of Slavic war

refugees (from Kosovo and Bosnia) and Turkish immigrants to these countries has helped to raise ethnic tensions, and the police may simply be part of an unpleasant xenophobic trend in European politics. For example, in 1999 a Sudanese refugee being deported from Germany was gagged during a plane flight; he died as a result. Such deportations are themselves human rights violations, and similar events have happened all across Europe.

The police in the United States are also usually well trained and professional in their behavior, but there are many individual exceptions. As in Germany, many of these incidents involve black victims and white police officers. Again, as in Europe, racism may be at the root of many of these police abuse cases. Moreover, human rights groups have accused some American urban police departments of covering up the human rights abuses that occur, rather than trying to prosecute the guilty officers and thereby contributing to a pattern of abuse. In the 1990s, there were a number of police brutality cases that received national attention. In 1991, the Los Angeles police stopped a speeding African-American motorist named Rodney King and, in the process of subduing him, beat him repeatedly; much of the beating was captured on videotape and replayed for shocked American television viewers. After the incident, one of the officers was recorded on his car radio as saying, "I haven't beaten anyone this bad in a long time." Anger over the incident—and at the continued police brutality toward African Americans that it seemed to represent—resulted in a large riot in Los Angeles in April 1992. In a horrific 1997 incident, Abner Louima, a Haitian immigrant in New York City, was taken to a police station and tortured; the police at first tried to hide what had happened, but some of the officers involved were eventually convicted for their crimes.

Police abuse in the United States, as horrible as it is when it occurs, is generally agreed to be the exception rather than the rule. Even organizations such as Amnesty International—which has strongly criticized American police departments—agree that most police in the United States act professionally and show respect for human rights. Elsewhere this is less true. Many countries have police forces that ignore human rights as a matter of policy. Some of these departments are able to do so, in part, because they receive widespread support from both the government and the general population, which both see a strong and determined police force as more important than the defense of human rights.

In Turkey, for example, police brutality, including torture, is standard practice. Some officials have expressed fear of what might happen if the Turkish police were forced to abandon these traditional methods. A minister of the Turkish government said, "People are happy with the performance of the police. The police are capable of extracting confessions from the culprits. What's the use of creating a lot of fuss as long as public opinion endorses what the police do?"

If police respect for human rights in Turkey is weak, in much of the rest of the world the situation is far worse. The Turkish government has been at least making efforts to improve the behavior of its police forces (motivated by its desire to join the human rights–conscious European Union). The police in countries like China, Cuba, and Syria consistently violate the 1948 United Nations Universal Declaration of Human Rights' codes on torture and the proper treatment of prisoners. (For example, some Tibetan monks report Chinese police using electric prods to punish them for their loyalty to the Dalai Lama.) These countries lack any independent judiciary, and the primary function of the police is to serve the oppressive will of the state.

In some parts of the world where human rights violations had been common, this kind of police brutality is becoming a thing of the past. Chile, for example, where during the Augusto Pinochet regime the police used to arrest people and then have them "disappear," has begun to built a modern and responsible police force. Other Latin American countries have moved in the same direction, and South and Central America have much better police forces than they did in the 1980s and early 1990s. Brazil remains an exception. There, the police have been accused of murdering without trial people they think might be criminals. In 1993, in a particularly infamous example of police human rights abuses, a group of off-duty Brazilian police opened fire on a group of street children, killing eight of them; the police did this because they found the children, who were often petty thieves, to be a nuisance. This was not an isolated event. Human rights activists accuse Brazilian police of being involved in at least 500 murders a year during the late 1990s. Almost all of those suspected of being murdered by the Brazilian police were poor—many of them criminals or homeless—and so wealthier Brazilians have tended to ignore the problem.

In the Third World, police brutality is sometimes caused by political commands from the government, but more often it is the result of poor training and corruption. Local police officers in some parts of Africa are paid very little and have almost no incentive to treat those they arrest with any respect for human rights. Innocent and guilty alike are crammed in small jails under conditions that are the equivalent of intentional torture. In some Rwandan jails, it has been alleged that the crowding is so severe that the prisoners cannot even sit down. Police in these countries often resort to extortion and even robbery of citizens to supplement their meager paychecks.

CONCLUSION

If the job of the police is to protect human rights, it is clear that, worldwide, they are failing. In Western Europe and North America the police are largely, with occasionally glaring lapses, respectful of human rights. In the rest of the world, the police are often the source of most human rights abuses.

Juvenal, an ancient Roman author, once wrote, "*Quis custodiet ipsos custodes?*" (Who shall guard the guardians?). The question is especially applicable to modern police forces. If they are the main defenses of the public, they can also be one of the most serious threats to human rights. With a monopoly of force in its hands, and with few legal restrictions, an unprofessional, unrestrained police force can become a threat to the society it was supposed to defend.

Carl Skutsch

See also: Crime; Domestic Violence; Prisons; Victims' Rights.

Bibliography

Human Rights Watch. *Shielded from Justice: Police Brutality and Accountability in the United States.* New York: Human Rights Watch, 1998.

Parenti, Christian. *Lockdown America: Police and Prisons in the Age of Crisis.* New York: Verso Books, 1999.

Political Prisoners

Political prisoners are prisoners denied their freedom not because they have committed what are normally considered crimes—murder, robbery, assault—but because they are considered politically dangerous or troublesome. They usually are citizens of totalitarian or dictatorial governments who have tried to exercise their human rights to free speech, freedom of religion, or freedom of assembly. They are quintessential human rights victims, because they are almost always in prison because of their attempt to defend human rights. Many victims of human rights abuses are civilian casualties in the war against human rights abuse; political prisoners are usually the war's frontline soldiers.

BACKGROUND

The category of political prisoners has a long history. It begins with the modern era, when a nascent belief in human rights prevented governments from killing their opponents outright; instead, trumped-up charges such as treason would be slapped on the victim, and they would be whisked away to a dark fortress prison, never to be seen again. Alexander Dumas' mid-nineteenth century novel *The Man in the Iron Mask* is a story about such a prisoner locked away in the French Bastille. Although fictional, it is based on the true stories of many political adversaries who were locked away by the kings of France in the seventeenth and eighteenth centuries. In the nineteenth century it was the tsars of Russia who filled the vast expanses of Siberia with revolutionary activists (including many famous writers, such

as Fyodor Dostoyevsky). Then, in the twentieth century, when those same revolutionaries (or their heirs) had turned Russia into the communist Soviet Union, it was the Communist Party leaders Joseph Stalin, Nikita Khrushchev, and Leonid Brezhnev who locked dissidents away in the Soviet gulag (prison camp system).

It was in the Soviet Union and the other Eastern bloc countries that the modern image of political prisoners was formed. The Soviet Union under Stalin created a vast camp system to contain those who opposed them, or those they simply deemed enemies regardless of truth. The most famous description of this camp system is Aleksandr Solzhenitsyn's *The Gulag Archipelago* (1973–1975). Solzhenitsyn showed how the gulag functioned, how the prisoners were treated, and how their human rights were denied.

Solzhenitsyn was the most famous political prisoner in the gulag, but the gulag was not the only system with political prisoners. In authoritarian countries, like Augusto Pinochet's Chile and Francisco Franco's Spain, anyone who tried to exercise his or her human right to free speech was likely to become a prisoner of the state. Even democracies had their political prisoners: Israel locked up Palestinians who were deemed a threat, and South Africa's apartheid-era regime imprisoned thousands of African National Congress members (the most prominent of these prisoners was Nelson Mandela, who later became South Africa's first black president).

With the ending of the cold war in the early 1990s, the political prisoners in the communist world gained their freedom. Elsewhere, the arrival of democracy—in Chile, Taiwan, Argentina, and other countries—led to an end of the government policies that had created political prisoners. But not all the political prisoners have been freed. Around the world, there are still governments that deny their citizens their rights and that will imprison those who oppose them.

A SELECTION OF MODERN PRISONERS

In recent years, perhaps the world's most famous political prisoner has been Aung San Suu Kyi, a Myanmar (formerly Burma) pro-democracy activist who was imprisoned by Myanmar's dictators because of her popularity with the people. For six years—from 1989 to 1995—she remained under house arrest, at first with no visitors allowed (which led to rumors that she had been killed by the government), and later with limited visitation privileges. She was awarded the Nobel Peace Prize in 1991 and became a symbol around the world because of her determined resistance to human rights abuses.

Although the government released her in 1995, Myanmar did not relax its repressive policies, and the government still holds many political prisoners. These people may be less famous than Aung San Suu Kyi, but their imprisonment is just as politically motivated and just as much a violation of human rights standards. For example, in July 1999, the Myanmar authorities arrested Ma Khin Khin Leh, a schoolteacher, whose only crime was being married to a pro-democracy student activist. Ma Khin Khin Leh was sentenced to life imprisonment for "disrupting security" and "contact with illegal organizations." She, like many others in Myanmar, remained a political prisoner as of mid-2000.

China, like Myanmar, is home to many of the world's political prisoners. Even though the Chinese government succeeded in crushing the 1989 Tiananmen Square protests, Chinese political dissidents have continued to organize political protests and pro-democracy activities. In response, the Chinese government has continued its policy of imprisoning its people because of their political opinions and words, denying them their basic human rights of self-determination and free speech. It was only in 1998 that Wei Jingsheng, perhaps the longest-serving political prisoner of the Tiananmen demonstrations, was released and deported to the United States, and many others remain in prison who are more recent victims of China's anti–human rights policies. Among those currently imprisoned are veteran dissidents Xu Wenli in Beijing, Qin Yongmin in Hubei Province, and Wang Youcai in Zhejiang; each is serving a long prison term because of membership in the China Democracy Party (CDP). They are a mere few among dozens of CDP political prisoners. Other Chinese political movements have faced similar repression and have had their members imprisoned for their pro-democracy and pro-reform beliefs.

In Tibet, many monks and nuns who support the exiled Dalai Lama have been imprisoned because of that support. The most prominent of these prisoners is the Panchen Lama. The Dalai Lama had declared a young boy, Gendun Choekyi Nyima, to be the reincarnation of, and therefore the next, Panchen Lama, who is the second most important figure in Tibetan Buddhism. China's government refused to recognize the Dalai Lama's choice and instead recognized another boy, Gyaltsen Norbu, as the Panchen Lama, putting Gendun Choekyi Nyima under arrest. No one has seen the original Panchen Lama or members of his family since 1995. He is assumed to be a prisoner somewhere, a victim of China's repressive policies toward Tibet. The common use of torture in Chinese prisons makes the Tibetan political prisoners' situation a particularly ugly violation of human rights. Even after release from prison, some Tibetans' health is so badly damaged that they soon die. A monk, Ngawang Jinpa, died two months after serving his full four-year term, and Gandan Norbu, another monk, died almost three years after severe prison beatings damaged his kidneys. Both men were in their early twenties.

Some political prisoners are jailed not for what they have done, but as convenient scapegoats for crimes or actions a government wishes to punish, but for which they cannot find the actual culprits. In Peru, between 1992 and 1995, the government of President Alberto Fujimori carried out a large-scale anti-terrorism campaign as part of its war against the Maoist Shining Path guerrillas. Accused guerrillas were tried and convicted by secret tribunals. The procedures used to convict them were slipshod, with no juries and no cross-examinations. Trials sometimes lasted as little as twenty minutes. Many of those arrested were tortured in order to gain confessions (and many people confessed to whatever the authorities wanted, just to avoid torture). All these methods were blatant violations of the United Nations declarations on the human right to a fair trial. Although the trials did prosecute some real Shining Path members, they also tried hundreds of innocent people. These people languished in Peruvian prisons for as long as eight years before being freed, and hundreds of innocent people may still be in prison. They were not political prisoners in the usual sense of the word because they were not being punished for their political views, but

they were prisoners of politics, innocent victims of a justice system unhampered by scruples or accountability. Although most of the "innocents," as the Peruvians call them, have been freed, their lives, bodies, and minds remain badly scarred by years of cruel treatment.

POLITICAL PRISONERS IN THE UNITED STATES

Mumia Abu-Jamal is perhaps the best-known alleged political prisoner in the American prison system. Mumia was a radio journalist well known for supporting radical black causes. In 1981, he was involved in a shooting incident in which a Philadelphia police officer was killed. Mumia claimed that he was merely intervening in a beating of his brother by police and that he was not responsible for the shooting (other men were alleged to have fled the scene of the shooting), but the police put the blame for the officer's death on Mumia. After a relatively quick trial—which critics say was characterized by falsification of evidence and lying police witnesses—Mumia was sentenced to death. His defenders claim that he is a political prisoner, railroaded because of his radical beliefs. His opponents, and the widow of the dead police officer, call him a cold-blooded murderer. Mumia's cause has attracted national attention and many prominent supporters.

Another alleged political prisoner in the United States is Leonard Peltier. In 1975, during a shootout on the Pine Ridge Indian Reservation, two Federal Bureau of Investigation (FBI) agents and one Native-American activist were killed. Peltier fled to Canada, but was later extradited, convicted of murder, and sentenced to life in prison. Peltier's defenders claim that Peltier did not kill anyone, and in any case the shooting took place at a time of high tension between federal agents and members of the American Indian Movement (AIM). Dozens of Native Americans had been killed as a result of a conflict between AIM and more conservative tribal leaders (who were supported by the FBI). In this environment, according to supporters, Peltier and the other AIM activists reacted understandably to the appearance of an unmarked car with two armed men inside. In a separate trial, two other AIM members involved in the shooting were found innocent by reason of self-defense. Amnesty International has designated Peltier a political prisoner and called for his release, and he has acquired a long list of celebrity supporters, including Robert Redford.

CONCLUSION

Political prisoners, or prisoners of conscience, as Amnesty International calls them, are living symbols of human rights abuse. They are in prison because they would not cooperate with the state, because they demanded basic human rights, or because they were politically troublesome when free. Political prisoners are sometimes freed, such as Wei Jingsheng in 1998, but there are always more put into prison to replace those who have left. Political prisoners act as a kind of reverse canary in the mine shaft of human rights: just as canaries were carried by coal miners to warn them when oxygen was getting low, as long as political prisoners remain behind bars the world knows that human rights are not yet shared by all.

Carl Skutsch

See also: Aung San Suu Kyi; Nelson Mandela; Prisons; Trials.

Bibliography

Ginzburg, Eugenia. *Journey into the Whirlwind.* New York: Harcourt Brace, 1975.

Kohn, Stephen M., and Howard Zinn. *American Political Prisoners.* New York: Praeger, 1994.

Solzhenitsyn, Aleksandr. *The Gulag Archipelago.* Westport, CT: Westview, 1997.

Wei Jingsheng. *The Courage to Stand Alone: Letters from Prison and Other Writings.* New York: Penguin, 1998.

Poverty

Woman stands in a breadline in the United States, 1989.

In 1948, the Universal Declaration of Human Rights called for "the advent of a world in which human beings shall enjoy . . . freedom from fear and want." It was affirmed as self-evident that extreme poverty is incompatible with human rights. By including in the Declaration economic, social, and cultural rights, those who drafted this agreement were arguing that human rights involve more than simply protecting individuals from abusive treatment, but also involve guaranteeing them decent health care, education, shelter, and food.

Not all people agreed, or still agree, with this point of view. Some people believe that government only has the responsibility to protect its citizens' political rights; their physical well-being is a private matter and has nothing to do with human rights. Not surprisingly, it is usually those who have no worries about finding food and shelter—those who are middle class and wealthier—who are most likely to emphasize political rights over economic rights. For the poor, the right to have enough food to eat has a lot more meaning than either the right to vote or the right to speak freely.

Those who deny that poverty is a human right tend to deny the necessity of providing assistance to the poor. Subsidized housing, welfare payments, government sponsored health care, all these are viewed by some conservatives as props for people who are unwilling to work. These attitudes have been responsible in cuts in social pro-

grams from the United States to the United Kingdom.

In 1989, the United Nations Commission on Human Rights affirmed explicitly for the first time that extreme poverty was a violation of all human rights. After years of opposition by conservatives, a report was commissioned, and in 1996 Leandro Despouy presented to the Commission his Final Report on Human Rights and Extreme Poverty.

This report marked a definite shift in the Commission's attitude. Mary Robinson, the new High Commissioner for Human Rights, worked with non-governmental organizations dedicated to helping the very poor. She opened the 2000 session of the Human

Labor rally in Philadelphia calls for more jobs and an end to welfare cutbacks, 1997.

Rights Commission in Geneva with these powerful words: "The first session in a new century is a good time to reflect and take stock. It is a good time to recognize that the central role human rights now plays in international and national life is no accident. . . . What I urge is that we recapture the spirit when the Commission first began under the Chairmanship of Eleanor Roosevelt with the commitment of prestigious representatives from every region of the world. If they were sitting here with us now, what human rights issues might they want to raise? I believe they would be shocked by the inequalities of our world, where a thousand million people lack access to clean water and where thousands of children die each day from preventable diseases. Eradicating extreme poverty is the greatest human rights challenge we face, and this Commission has the responsibility to develop the human rights framework within which it must be achieved."

How then is extreme poverty a violation of human rights? Despouy report begins by noting references to extreme poverty in international reports, as well as recommendations by the World Summit on Social Development held in Copenhagen in 1995. It gathers general statistical data on health, revenues, and housing—including the fact that one billion people live on less than one dollar a day.

The report goes on to show how extreme poverty is an actual denial of twelve specific rights: (1) the right to a decent standard of living; (2) the right to housing; (3) the right to education; (4) the right to work; (5) the right to health; (6) the right to protection of the family; (7) the right to privacy; (8) the right to recognition as a person before the law and the right to be registered; (9) the right to life and the right to physical in-

Impoverished man sewing in a Bangladesh slum, 1992.

tegrity; (10) the right to justice; (11) the right to take part in political affairs; and (12) the right to participate in social and cultural life.

To survive, the poor often must do things that deny their basic humanity, such as rooting through garbage to find food; begging for money from strangers; and engaging in prostitution to earn money.

Extreme poverty denies people's basic humanity. Without sufficient food, shelter, and health care, all other human rights are irrelevant. Poverty, therefore, is the one of the most pervasive and insidious obstacles to realizing human rights.

Haitian child roots through a garbage dump. Searching for "valuables" in garbage is a full-time job for some poor, 1994.

The difference between those living in poverty and others is that they rarely have the means to effectively speak for themselves or to protect their rights. Extreme poverty has isolated them from others, so that people who do have a voice in society tend not to identify with them. With no one able or willing to fight for their human rights, they often end up having very few.

Bruno Tardieu

See also: Housing Rights and Homelessness; Hunger.

Bibliography

Rosenfeld, Jona, and Bruno Tardieu. *Artisans of Democracy: How Families in Extreme Poverty, Ordinary Citizens and Social Institutions Become Allies to Overcome Social Exclusion.* Lanham, MD: University Press of America, 2000.

Wronka, Joseph. *Human Rights and Social Policy in the 21st Century.* Lanham, MD: University Press of America, 1998.

Prisons

In Fyodor Dostoyevsky's novel *The House of the Dead* (1862), he wrote, "The degree of civilization in a society can be judged by entering its prisons." Dostoyevsky finished the novel after spending years in imperial Russian prisons, so he was familiar with prisons from the inside. Most people will never see the inside of a prison. This may explain why prisons remain shameful evidence of the world's often disappointing degree of civilization and its support, or lack of support, for human rights.

Article 5 of the United Nations Universal Declaration of Human Rights states, "No one shall be subjected to torture or to cruel, inhuman or degrading treatment or punishment." In 1955, the United Nations expanded on Article 5 by issuing the United Nations Standard Minimum Rules for the Treatment of Prisoners. These rules set the minimum standards that the world's nations should meet in their treatment of prisoners. These rules make it clear that even prisoners have human rights. But these rights are violated on a regular basis in almost every nation on the planet. Prisoners are raped, beaten, jammed into overcrowded cells, and locked up without enough air, food, or exercise. Prison authorities are eager to keep the general population unaware of the abuses that go on inside their prisons. For this reason, prisoners are often prevented from communicating with the outside world. When they do succeed in getting their message out, they often are met with apathy. Many people do not care what goes on in prisons; they simply wish that criminals be put away. Once criminals are imprisoned, there is the belief that nothing that happens to them matters.

PRISON OVERCROWDING

Prison overcrowding is a constant problem throughout the world. In many countries, some of the prison overcrowding is caused by the large number of prisoners who are being held while awaiting their court dates, but have not been convicted of any crime; they are being detained because they are suspected of having committed a crime. In Bangladesh, Chad, Guatemala, India, Peru, and Venezuela, for example, unsentenced prisoners make up the majority of the prison population. Some of these prisoners can spend years behind bars before finally being brought before a judge. Then, in many cases, they are found innocent of the crime with which they had been charged.

The number of people imprisoned in the United States is enormous. Approximately 2 million Americans are behind bars, the highest number in the world. (In 1990, this number was 1 million; in other words, America doubled its prison population in only ten years.) Russia, the next runner-up, has more than 1 million prisoners. In the United States, much prison overcrowding is the result of mandatory sentencing laws. People convicted of possessing or selling relatively small amounts of cocaine or marijuana can end up spending many years behind bars. Once in prison

Prisoners crowded together in Rwanda's Kigali Prison.

they tend to be barbarized by their surroundings; once freed from prison, they tend to quickly return, knowing no skills other than those they learned from other criminals while incarcerated.

In poorer parts of the world, prison conditions are so harsh that prisoners die at a rate far outstripping what is normal for the general population. Some of these deaths are caused by prisoner-on-prisoner violence, but most result from overcrowding, bad food, poor medical care, and the prevalence of disease (worsened by malnutrition and the lack of medical care). Tuberculosis (TB) is particularly prevalent in prisons.

Cramped conditions and poor health care help spread this deadly disease. Russian prisons are especially hard hit by TB; an estimated one in one hundred Russian prisoners is infected with the disease. Approximately 20 percent of those infected have the multidrug resistant (MDR) strain. The breeding of MDR strains of TB in prisons has the potential to be a health catastrophe for the entire world.

PRISON CHARACTERISTICS

Prisons in many parts of the world are understaffed. Without enough guards to watch the prisoners, the prison authorities tend to let the prisoners create their own social pecking order. The result is a world of brutality and violence. Occasionally the tensions engendered by this unchecked viciousness explode into riots and prison uprisings. An April 1998 riot in a Colombia prison left fifteen inmates dead; a May 1998 riot in a Brazilian prison killed twenty-two. In Venezuela, there are so few guards in the prison system that prisoners are able to smuggle in guns and grenades. These weapons are then used to intimidate or kill those prisoners who do not cooperate with inmate leaders. The prisoners form gangs, and those prisoners who do not join the gangs suffer constant abuse. In the United States gangs are usually organized along racial or ethic lines: white, black, or Hispanic. White gang members sport Aryan Nation tattoos and spout racist slurs. Racism is commonplace in these prisons.

In some countries' prisons, conditions are so bad that prison authorities severely restrict the access of any outside visitors, particularly journalists or human rights representatives. To deal with their manpower shortages, many prisons resort to barbaric methods of controlling prisoners. Pakistani prisoners are hobbled by heavy weights, which make walking a painful ordeal. Prison authorities wish to hide their methods of controlling prisoners, particularly their use of torture. Torture is commonplace in many of the world's prisons, including those in Egypt, China, and Brazil. In Turkey, years of allegations of torture by human rights groups—allegations that had always been denied by the Turkish government—were finally confirmed when a Turkish parliamentary committee in charge of investigating prison abuse issued a long re-

port on the use of torture in Turkish prisons. In addition to extensive inmate testimony, their report included photos of torture devices and maps showing where special torture cells were located in different prisons and police stations across the country.

The quality of the world's prisons varies from ultramodern to antique and decaying. Both types have human rights problems. The older prisons often lack modern plumbing facilities, central heat, or safe structural framework. In prisons without decent toilets, prisoners are sometimes forced to defecate into a shared bucket. The ultramodern prisons, sometimes called super-maximum (or super-max) prisons have a different set of problems. First developed in the United States, they were designed to keep troublesome inmates isolated from one another. Each inmate is locked away in his own antiseptic cell, unable to see his fellow prisoners or even a glimpse of the outside world. Prisoners in these facilities spend twenty-three hours a day in their cells, with limited access to recreation or education. Rather than suffer degradation, they are left to molder slowly in their own solitude.

CONCLUSION

The United Nations says that even prisoners deserve to have their human rights protected. Our sense of humanity should tell us the same thing. But the evidence is that this is not yet happening. Human rights remains the province of the free; the incarcerated live in world where human rights are few and where torture and suffering are more common than justice.

Carl Skutsch

See also: Crime; Domestic Violence; Police and Law Enforcement; Political Prisoners; Torture; Victims' Rights.

Bibliography

Burton-Rose, Daniel, Dan Pens, and Paul Wright. *The Celling of America: An Inside Look at the U.S. Prison Industry.* Monroe, ME: Common Courage Press, 1998.

Morris, Norval, and David J. Rothman. *The Oxford History of the Prison: The Practice of Punishment in Western Society.* Oxford: Oxford University Press, 1997.

Parenti, Christian. *Lockdown America: Police and Prisons in the Age of Crisis.* New York: Verso Books, 1999.

Privacy

Of all human rights, privacy is among the most difficult to define. Definitions of privacy vary widely according to context and environment. Privacy rights are frequently seen as a way of drawing the line at how far society and government can intrude into the affairs of an individual. How exactly to define this line is difficult.

In the 1890s, future U.S. Supreme Court justice Louis Brandeis articulated a concept of privacy that it was the individual's "right to be left alone." Brandeis argued that privacy was the most cherished of freedoms in a democracy, and he was concerned that it should be reflected in the Constitution.

Years later, in his authoritative work *Privacy and Freedom* (1967), Alan F. Westin defined privacy as the desire of people to choose freely under what circumstances and to what extent they will expose themselves, their attitudes, and their behavior to others. More recently, in 1994, the Preamble to the Australian Privacy Charter stated: "A free and democratic society requires respect for the autonomy of individuals, and limits on the power of both state and private organizations to intrude on that autonomy. . . . Privacy is a key value which underpins human dignity and other key values such as freedom of association and freedom of speech. . . . Privacy is a basic human right and the reasonable expectation of every person."

The lack of a single definition should not imply that the issue lacks importance. As one writer observed: "In one sense, all human rights are aspects of the right to privacy." Privacy rights can be divided into four key areas: information privacy, bodily privacy, communicative privacy, and territorial privacy. Information privacy involves the establishment of rules governing the collection and handling of personal data such as credit information and medical records. Bodily privacy is concerned with protection of one's physical person—one's body—against invasive procedures such as drug testing and cavity searches. Communications privacy covers the security and privacy of mail, telephones, e-mail, and other forms of communication. Territorial privacy concerns the setting of limits on intrusion into the home, workplace, and other geographic or physical locations.

The concept of privacy can be traced as far back as 1361, when the Justices of the Peace Act in England provided for the arrest of "peeping toms" and eavesdroppers—those who invade or intrude upon other people's space. In the centuries that followed, various countries developed specific protections for privacy. In the United States privacy protection is reflected in numerous Supreme Court decisions. The modern privacy benchmark at an international level can be found in the 1948 United Nations Universal Declaration of Human Rights (UDHR), which protected territorial and communications privacy. Article 12 states: "No one should be subjected to arbitrary interference with his privacy, family, home or correspondence, nor to attack of his honor or reputation." Everyone, the Declaration proclaims, has the right to be protected by law against such interferences or attacks.

Numerous international human rights covenants give specific recognition to privacy as a right. The International Covenant on Civil and Political Rights reinforced the UDHR, while the European Declaration of Human Rights expanded the concept of "private life."

Concern with the right of privacy increased in the 1960s and 1970s with the advent of information technology (IT). Newly created computer systems and databases enabled governments and private organizations to accumulate vast amounts of information on people without their knowledge or permission. The surveillance potential of powerful IT systems prompted demands for specific rules governing the collection and handling of personal information.

The genesis of modern legislation in this area can be traced to national privacy and data-protection laws passed by Sweden (1973), the United States (1974), West Germany (1977), and France (1978). Two crucial international instruments evolved from these laws. Both the Council of Europe's Convention on the Protection of Individuals with Regard to the Automatic Processing of Personal Data and the Organization for Economic Cooperation and Development's Guidelines Governing the Protection of Privacy and Transborder Data Flows of Personal Data articulate specific rules covering the handling of electronic data.

The expression of data protection in various declarations and laws varies only by degree. All require that personal information be obtained fairly and lawfully; used only for the original specified purpose; adequate, relevant, and not excessive to purpose; accurate and up-to-date, and be destroyed after its purpose is completed.

While the protection of privacy is enforced primarily at a national level, two recent initiatives have had the effect of laying the foundations for a global privacy standard. In 1994, the European Parliament passed two Europe-wide directives that will provide citizens with a wider range of protections over abuses of their data. The Data Protection Directive sets a benchmark for national laws throughout the European Union (EU). Each EU state must pass complementary legislation. The Telecommunications Directive establishes specific protections covering telephones, digital television, mobile networks, and other telecommunications systems.

Several principles of data protection are strengthened under the Directives. These principles include the right to know where the data originated, the right to have inaccurate data rectified, a right of recourse in the event of unlawful processing, and the right to withhold permission to use data in some circumstances. As an example of this last principle, individuals will have the right to opt out free of charge from being sent direct marketing material, without having to provide any specific reason.

The Data Protection Directive contains strengthened protections over the use of sensitive personal data in such categories as health and finances. In the future, the commercial and government use of such information will require the individual's "explicit and unambiguous" consent. The Directive also imposes an obligation on member states to ensure that the personal information relating to European citizens is covered by law when it is exported to and processed in countries outside Europe. This requirement has resulted in growing pressure outside Europe for the passage of privacy laws. Those countries that refuse to adopt meaningful privacy laws may find themselves unable to conduct certain types of information exchanges with Europe.

The Telecommunications Directive imposes widescale obligations on carriers and service providers to ensure the privacy of users' communications. The new rules will cover areas that until now have fallen between the cracks of data-protection laws. Access to billing data will be severely restricted, as will marketing activity. Caller-identification technology must incorporate an option for the blocking of number transmission.

Some countries, such as the United States, have avoided general data-protection rules in favor of specific laws governing each privacy issue; for example, laws have been passed preventing the dissemination of video rental records and financial records.

With the recent development of commercially available encryption-based technologies, privacy protection has also moved into the hands of individual users. Any user of the Internet can employ a range of programs and systems that will ensure varying degrees of privacy and security of communications.

It is clear that the power, capacity, and speed of information technology are accelerating rapidly. The extent of privacy invasion—or certainly the potential to invade privacy—is increasing proportionately. Despite efforts to pass laws protecting privacy, government agencies and private businesses still retain huge databases charting the behavior and habits of much of the population. This greatly concerns privacy advocates.

Privacy issues are often of more concern in rich, technologically advanced countries that have the infrastructure to support camera, telephone, and Internet surveillance. But it is often the citizens of Third World nations that face the greatest invasions of privacy. Basic techniques, such as opening mail or paying neighbors to act as spies, are less sophisticated than electron-

ic invasions of privacy but can be equally invasive. Governments of developing nations can also rely on industrialized countries to supply them with technologies of surveillance, such as digital wiretapping equipment, deciphering equipment, scanners, bugs, tracking equipment, and computer intercept systems. The transfer of surveillance technology from richer to poorer nations is now a lucrative sideline for the arms industry. In its 1995 report "Big Brother Incorporated," the watchdog organization Privacy International highlighted the extent of this trade. This view was supported by a 1997 report, "Assessing the Technologies of Political Control," commissioned by the European Parliament's Civil Liberties Committee and undertaken by the European Commission's Science and Technology Options Assessment office.

The international trade in surveillance technology—sometimes known as the repression trade—involves the manufacture and export of technologies of political control. These technologies involve sophisticated, computer-based technology that vastly increases the power of government officials. When the government knows everything its people are doing, it is much easier to control them and deny them their human rights.

The Privacy International report listed the companies that export such technology to developing countries with a poor human rights record. The attempt of the reports by the European Parliament and Privacy International to raise awareness of the dangers to human rights involved in the transfer of such technology has been augmented by recent studies by Amnesty International, Human Rights Watch, and Oxfam. All these reports make it clear that the threat to privacy in the Third World is also a threat to human rights.

The surveillance trade is almost indistinguishable from the arms trade. More than 70 percent of companies that manufacture and export surveillance technology also export arms, chemical weapons, or military hardware. Surveillance is a crucial element for the maintenance of any nondemocratic infrastructure and is an important activity in the pursuit of intelligence and political control. Many countries in transition to democracy also rely heavily on surveillance to satisfy the demands of the police and military.

Much of this technology is used to track the activities of dissidents, human rights activists, journalists, student leaders, minorities, trade union leaders, and political opponents. Large-scale identification systems are also useful for monitoring larger sectors of the population. As Privacy International observed: "In the absence of meaningful legal or constitutional protections, such technology is inimical to democratic reform." Such matters demonstrate that, as technology grows ever more sophisticated, the issue, scope, and definition of privacy will keep evolving in the twenty-first century.

Simon Davies

See also: Right to Life; Women's Rights.

BIBLIOGRAPHY

Australian Privacy Charter Group. *The Australian Privacy Charter.* Sydney: University of New South Wales, 1994.

Banisar, David, and Simon Davies. *Privacy and Human Rights 1999: An International Survey of Privacy Laws & Developments.* London: Electronic Privacy Information Center, 1999.

Davies, Simon. *Big Brother: Britain's Web of Surveillance and The New Technological Order.* London: Pan, 1996.

Flaherty, David. *Protecting Privacy In Surveillance Societies.* Charlotte: University of North Carolina Press, 1989.

Westin, Alan F. *Privacy and Freedom.* New York: Atheneum, 1967.

Property Rights

The right to property is not only a human right, it is also one of foundation stones of the tradition of all human rights. John Locke (1632–1704), the British philosopher, argued that all governments exist solely because of the right to property. As Locke put it, "The great and chief end, therefore, of men's uniting into commonwealths, and putting themselves under government, is the preservation of their property." If a government protected property rights, it was a good government; if it did not, it should be overthrown. (Locke's ideas were used by Thomas Jefferson in drafting the United States Declaration of Independence.)

The United Nations brought Lockean ideas into the twentieth century with the Universal Declaration of Human Rights (1948). Article 17 of that document declares: "Everyone has the right to own property alone as well as in association with others," and "no one shall be arbitrarily deprived of his property."

Property, according to Locke and others, is the result of labor; if you work on a farm or work as an artisan, what you produce is yours because you made it. If you are paid a salary, it is your work that gives you a right to that salary, or property. The basis of property rights, it can be argued, stems from the most basic of all human rights: the right to life. If a person spends a year earning enough money to buy a house, and then that house is taken away from him, one could argue that a year of his or her life has been stolen.

Department store being looted in Capetown, South Africa, April 1993.

The question of property rights becomes philosophically more complex when large numbers of workers are involved. When a factory worker labors in a factory, it is the factory owner who usually gets the largest share of the factory's profits, even though the factory would have produced nothing without its workers. Property rights defenders argue that owners deserve the profits because without their property—the factory—no profits could have been made. This view has not been universally embraced. Pierre-Joseph Proudhon (1809–1865), the French founder of anarchism, declared, "Property is theft!" (*"La propriété c'est le vol!"*), because the labor of the factory worker was stolen and converted into profits by the factory owner. The socialist and communist followers of Karl Marx felt similarly and declared that all private property should be abolished. It was the ideas of Marx that fueled the Russian Revolution of 1917 and the Chinese communist victory in 1949. Both these states outlawed most forms of private property. However, not only did property rights disappear but so did other human rights, such as the right to free speech, freedom of assembly, and freedom of religion. For those theorists who argue that full human rights are based on the existence of property rights, the oppression that existed in the Soviet Union goes some way toward making their case. Most (but not all) modern political theorists agree that Marx and Proudhon misunderstood the importance of the right to private property.

Property rights have also been intertwined with the advance of human rights for women. Throughout history, most human societies have denied women full equality, and one of the rights most often denied them has been the right to property. The right to own property and control the wages they earned was one of the main issues behind the feminist movement in the nineteenth century. At that time, a woman might inherit property, but whatever she technically owned would be under the legal control of a male guardian: her father, if she was unmarried; her husband, if she was married. Without the ability to control their property, women could not manage their financial affairs without the help of men. Legally, women were little more than property themselves, dependent on the opinions and actions of the men around them. It is for this reason that early women's rights advocates made the acquisition of property rights one of their first goals.

Not all societies have shared the Western tradition of private property and property rights—many societies tended to reduce the power of private property in favor of the state or ruler—but it is the Western idea of property as a human right that seems to have been most effective at supporting all human rights. When people have a sacred right to the products of their own labor, they are free from some of the more egregious attacks on human rights to which governments are prone. This is not to say that property rights do not have some negative human rights implications—the vast disparity between rich and poor in some countries can be a human rights problem in and of itself—but most people are better off defending the right to property if they wish to keep all other treasured human rights.

Carl Skutsch

See also: Human Rights, Ethics, and Morality; Poverty.

Bibliography

Waldron, Jeremy. *The Right to Private Property.* Oxford: Clarendon, 1988.

Prostitution (Forced)

Forced prostitution is a practice in which girls and boys, usually between the ages of ten and twenty, are tricked, kidnapped, or otherwise lured from their homes by "brokers" representing a brothel or prostitution network and brought to urban areas to serve as prostitutes, receiving little or no wages for their work.

A recent development is the growth of forced prostitution in Eastern Europe. With the economies of Eastern Europe suffering from the economic repercussions of communism's fall, many women are desperate for jobs. Unscrupulous pimps, who are usually part of organized crime rings, trick girls and young women from the countryside—those from Ukraine are particularly targeted—into going to neighboring countries to get good jobs. They are told they will be prostitutes only after they cross the border and have their passports confiscated.

Eastern Europe, however, is not the area of most serious concern. While forced prostitution takes place in countries throughout the world, it is most widely practiced in Asia, especially in Thailand.

PROSTITUTION IN THAILAND

Japan and Southeast Asia have a flourishing sex tourism industry, which is fed by prostitutes who are often imported from Thailand. While forced prostitutes do not often service foreign tourists, who make up much of Asia's sex tourism industry (prostitutes serving this "high end" of the market tend to be voluntary), sex tourism has created a business climate that is conducive to sexual slavery. The economic boom that Thailand has experienced in recent years has created opportunities for many Thais to earn higher wages; this, combined with a climate in which sex tourism is the norm, creates a higher demand for cheap sex. Enslaved women and girls satisfy this demand in brothels frequented primarily by working-class Thai men.

In Thailand itself, this demand for prostitutes is supplied by girls, and some boys, from the economically depressed northern mountainous region of Thailand, and from the neighboring countries of Myanmar (Burma) and Laos. Burmese and Laotian prostitutes are more likely to have been directly enslaved. Because the borders between Myanmar, Laos, and Thailand are chaotic and unpoliced, female emigrants from Myanmar and Laos who are deported are often dropped in the jungle at the border. Pimps and other recruiters follow the trucks transporting the deportees and then offer the women work in Thailand. Without other alternatives, these women often agree to go with the pimps, only to find that the "work" is prostitution. Once in the pimps' control, the women are forced to remain in the brothels, suffering beatings and rapes if they try to leave. Other Burmese and Laotian women, traveling into Thailand unaccompanied, are kidnapped at bus and train stations by pimps who drug them, bring them back to a brothel, and force them to work as prostitutes.

Thai prostitutes from the northern mountains are less likely to have been directly kidnapped or coerced into prostitution.

While brokers do sometimes trick parents by offering well-paid work as dishwashers or servants in the city, more often they are open about the type of work they are offering. Several factors combine to create a situation in northern Thailand in which selling a daughter, even into prostitution, while not preferred, is an acceptable choice. In this economically depressed farming region, the sale of a daughter has long been an accepted way of alleviating the effects of a poor harvest or other financial disasters. As the demand for prostitutes in southern Thailand grows, daughters are increasingly sold to brokers for brothels. Because so many northern Thai girls are sold by their parents to become prostitutes in the south, young northern girls are aware of prostitution and realize that they themselves could become prostitutes one day. Prostitution's ubiquity has served, however, to soften its image and to remove the stigma once attached to it. In a survey taken of northern Thai girls, most reported that they believed prostitution to be "wearing Western clothes in a glamorous restaurant."

Once the girls are sold into prostitution, pimps use a system of debt bondage to keep enslaved. After these girls are sold, usually for about 50,000 baht ($2,000), they are taken south by brokers and sold to brothels for about 100,000 baht. In addition to these sums, the girls must pay rent of approximately 30,000 baht per month for their rooms in the brothel, as well as fees for food, medicine, and fines if a customer is displeased. The total of all of these sums is considered to be a debt which the girls must pay before they can send money home or leave the brothel. Because this "debt" is so large in comparison to the fees the girls earn as prostitutes, most are never able to pay the debt, or even meet monthly food and rent payments. The pimps running the brothels also frequently falsify accounts so that even those prostitutes who have paid off their debt are kept at the brothel in debt bondage.

AIDS AND PROSTITUTION

The AIDS epidemic in Thailand, as well as the belief in many Asian countries that sex with a virgin increases virility, has created a market for younger prostitutes, sometimes as young as age ten. For men concerned about HIV infection and sex tourists attempting to restore their virility, then, virgins carry a special value. Because many newly recruited prostitutes are ten to twelve years old, many men are willing to pay more to have sex with these girls. This situation provides pimps with a way both to break down the resistance of new arrivals to their new life as prostitutes and to reap a larger profit.

New girls are beaten, raped, and then forced to service a chain of clients from night until morning. This continues until the girl stops objecting or attempting to escape. Pimps benefit because many clients are willing to pay large sums for the privilege of performing the initial rape, while the girl, because she is so young, can be falsely presented as a virgin to subsequent clients, who will also pay higher fees to have sex with a girl they think is "clean."

Very few of these young prostitutes are ever able to pay their debt and benefit from their own sexual slavery. While pimps occasionally declare some prostitutes' debts paid and allow them to send money home as a way of calming rebellious behavior, these girls, whose families benefit financially from their daughters' prostitution, are unable to return home because their parents prefer that they remain prostitutes and continue to send money home.

Without this option, and with no other way of earning money, these women have nowhere else to go, so they often remain at the brothels. Most eventually become infected with HIV or other sexually transmitted diseases and, once this happens, are thrown out to manage for themselves on the streets. The plentiful and cheap supply of new girls provides little motivation to provide any kind of medical care to prostitutes when they fall ill or become too old to work.

GOVERNMENT INVOLVEMENT

This system of prostitution is ubiquitous in Thai society, partly because of tacit government support. A full set of laws against forced prostitution is unenforced, while police and other local officials receive regular bribes from brothels and are regular patrons themselves. In 1992, Thai Prime Minister Chuan Leekpai commented that if "the problem [of forced prostitution] cannot be solved, I will not order the authorities to tackle it." Also, because brothels are not individually owned but are part of the business interests of prominent members of Thai communities, prosecution of those profiting from forced prostitution becomes difficult. These "billionaire slaveholders" suffer no stigma on account of their brothel ownership.

Thai women, including those in southern Thailand, are also brought into other countries to work as prostitutes. Often lured by promises of well-paid work as cooks or domestics, or else by glamorous stories of life as a foreign prostitute, these women and girls, like northern Thai, Burmese, and Laotian women in their own country, are brutalized and enslaved by debt bondage (the girls are held responsible for airfare, false passport fees, and other costs) once they arrive. In Switzerland, Thai girls are brought into the country on "artist" visas and so must work as exotic dancers in addition to being prostitutes, while in Germany, Thai girls work as waitresses and are sold to men by bartenders or bouncers. In other countries, such as Japan and the United States, Thai girls are simply placed in brothels.

Despite frequent stories in the Thai and Western press exposing child prostitution and sexual slavery, the Thai government has done little to solve the problem. In 1992, the government set up an anti-prostitution task force consisting of six men. In 1994, this force arrested 64 brothel owners and 472 prostitutes and rescued 35 child sex slaves. With an estimated 1 million sex workers in Thailand, of whom an estimated 35,000 are child sex slaves, their efforts affected only a small percentage of the total.

Campaigns by non-governmental organizations, such as the End Child Prostitution in Asian Tourism group, have brought some changes, such as the 1997 revision of the laws on prostitution. The new laws impose a maximum 60,000 baht fine and three-year prison sentence for anyone having sex with prostitutes under age eighteen, and a maximum 400,000 baht fine and twenty-year prison sentence for anyone having sex with a prostitute under age fifteen. Human Rights Watch also did an investigation of child sex slavery in Thailand in 1993 and published a report outlining seventeen steps for the government to take in ending forced prostitution. A Thai organization, the Center for the Protection of Children's Rights, rescues children from brothels and provides medical and psychological care, while the Foundation for Women and the Global Alliance Against Traffic in Women, as well as the Task Force to End Child Sexploitation, all raise awareness in Europe and North America and urge the Thai government to enforce laws against prostitution.

Despite these efforts, forced prostitution remains a serious problem in Thailand and other Southeast Asian countries and is a growing problem in parts of Eastern Europe.

Autumn Smith and James R. Lewis

See also: Child Pornography; Women's Rights.

Bibliography

Bales, Kevin. *Disposable People*. Berkeley: University of California Press, 1999.

Public Relations, Propaganda and Human Rights

Propaganda is the strategic, tactical, and hidden manipulation of public opinion, information, and policy to serve the objectives of vested political and economic interests, typically conducted by public relations (PR) professionals with backgrounds and expertise in communications, politics, and marketing. Although the goal of public relations is often benign—to help a company or individual improve its image—the goal of propaganda is not. Propaganda is destructive to democracy because it attempts to manipulate society invisibly for the benefit of an elite, often to hide or cover up crimes and misdeeds by the governments or businesses funding the propaganda campaign. Propaganda can subvert human rights by hiding the truth about human rights crimes and abuses.

The modern PR industry has its roots in World War I and the campaigns by the participating governments to gain public support for the war. In the United States, Edward L. Bernays, Ivy Lee, and others who are considered the founders of PR worked on the war propaganda campaign and afterward counseled tobacco companies and other emerging multinational businesses and political leaders.

Australian academic Alex Carey wrote: "The twentieth century has been characterized by three developments of great political importance: the growth of democracy, the growth of corporate power, and the growth of corporate propaganda as a means of protecting corporate power against democracy." Carey noted that today propaganda is in the form of advertising, especially public relations. Public relations is closely related to advertising, and most big PR firms are owned by advertising companies. But while advertising is usually obvious, PR is purposely invisible as it attempts to put its carefully honed messages in the mouths of people likely to be trusted and believed—such as journalists and experts—by the audience being propagandized.

Today the propaganda industry is immense and global. While exact figures are impossible to collect because of its hidden nature, governments and corporations spend an estimated tens of billions of dollars annually on PR campaigns and activities, both for in-house practitioners and for the hiring of outside consultants and firms. In 1999, the six largest international PR firms were, in descending order, Burson-Marsteller, Hill and Knowlton, Porter Novelli International, Shandwick International, Fleishman-Hillard, and Edelman. Their combined net income exceeded $1 billion. All of them but Shandwick, a British company, are headquartered in the United States; however, their presence is worldwide.

Burson-Marsteller, for instance, calls itself "a global perception management communications consulting company" whose purpose is "to manage perceptions which motivate behaviors that create business results." Burson-Marsteller employs 2,000 professionals in seventy-five offices to "manage issues by influencing—in the right combination—public attitudes, public perceptions, public behavior and public policies." Like most of its competitors, "B-M," as it is called, refuses to divulge a complete list of its hundreds of corporate and government clients, but they have included such powerful interests as Philip Morris, McDonald's, Monsanto, Coca-Cola, Eli Lilly, Ford Motor Company, General Electric, the UNITA guerrillas in Angola, the World Bank, and the governments of El Salvador, Saudi Arabia, Indonesia, South Korea, and Mexico.

While most people associate propaganda with brutal totalitarian regimes, Alex Carey points out that "propaganda plays an important role . . . in technologically advanced democratic societies where the maintenance of the existing power and privileges are vulnerable to popular opinion." Totalitarian governments that might utilize terrorism, torture, and murder to repress citizens at home often also employ PR firms to influence and manage the attitudes of citizens and officials in other countries in an attempt to hide or rationalize their brutal ways and human rights violations.

During the military dictatorship that "disappeared" and murdered thousands of Argentines, the country hired Burson-Marsteller to improve its image internationally. The government of Colombia, deeply enmeshed with cocaine cartels, hired the Sawyer/Miller firm to persuade the American people and U.S. Congress it was a struggling democracy fighting for freedom and justice. The royal family of Kuwait spent over $10 million hiring the Hill and Knowlton firm in 1990 to set up a front group called Citizens for a Free Kuwait, which even staged phony congressional testimony about a non-existent incident of baby-killing to lobby for a U.S. war against Iraq.

A recent tactic of PR firms are so-called astroturf organizations. These are groups that appear to be genuine grassroots democratic movements but are actually created, subsidized, and run by political or economic interests. For instance, on behalf of Philip Morris, and with tens of millions of dollars from the tobacco giant, the Burson-Marsteller firm established the National Smokers Alliance, a 3-million-member lobby for "smokers rights." With funding from the American Legion organization, Burson-Marsteller runs the Citizens Flag Alliance, which promotes amending the U.S. Constitution to outlaw flag burning.

As the news media become more and more concentrated among a handful of giant media corporations, independent and investigative journalism is in steep decline. On any given day, much of the news and information seen, heard, or read is actually PR, placed or spun by public relations campaigns. Sometimes it is a verbatim reprint of a news release or the airing of an audio or video news release that radio and TV news directors broadcast as if it were their own reporting, but is actually fake news provided by a PR firm on behalf of a client. Journalists usually fail to inform citizens about PR campaigns because so much of the news is dependent upon PR and because the same powerful advertisers that bankroll the media through advertising also use PR firms to manipulate news and information. The use of PR is rising, and more and more news and information in the twenty-first century will likely be spun and manipulated by hidden persuaders, making propaganda a growing threat to democracy.

John C. Stauber

See also: Freedom of the Press.

Bibliography

Carey, Alex. *Taking the Risk Out of Democracy: Propaganda in the U.S. and Australia.* Sydney: University of New South Wales Press, 1995.

Stauber, John, and Sheldon Rampton. *Toxic Sludge Is Good for You: Lies, Damn Lies and the Public Relations Industry.* Monroe, ME: Common Courage Press, 1995.

Tye, Larry. *The Father of Spin: Edward L. Bernays and the Birth of Public Relations.* New York: Crown, 1998.

Racism

The United Nations Universal Declaration of Human Rights (1948), lays out its opposition to racism in its first two articles:

Article 1. "All human beings are born free and equal in dignity and rights. They are endowed with reason and conscience and should act toward one another in a spirit of brotherhood."

Article 2. "Everyone is entitled to all the rights and freedoms set forth in this Declaration, without distinction of any kind, such as race, color, sex, language, religion, political or other opinion, national or social origin, property, birth or other status."

Despite these words, racism exists and remains one of the main barriers dividing people and preventing everyone from enjoying the same human rights. Racism is the theory that people can be put into categories based on their physical appearance—skin color, hair, texture, shape of the face—and that those physical categories also serve to define those people's intelligence, attitudes, and behavioral traits. The end result of this process of categorization is that races are ranked in a ladder of worth, with people belonging to some races declaring themselves to be superior to people belonging to other races.

BACKGROUND

There is nothing natural or scientific about the division of human beings into racial categories. The "traditional" division of the human species into three races ("Caucasian," "Mongoloid," "Negro") is inherently arbitrary. By tracking the physiognomy of peoples, a vast array of types and looks can be charted. Not all Europeans look the same, however, nor do Asians, nor do Africans. The Chinese look similar to the Burmese, who look similar to the Nepalese, who look similar to the Indians, who look similar to the Iranians, who look similar to the Greeks, who look similar to the Italians, who look similar to the French. So why do the Chinese and French not belong to the same race? The reason is that race is a cultural construct. People invented the idea, and many believe it to be real. But although racism may be a figment of people's imaginations, it has very real consequences.

In the ancient world, racism as it is understood today did not exist. People had prejudices, but they were based on culture, not skin color. The Romans looked down on the Gauls because they felt they had a superior culture, not race. (When the Romans took slaves, for example, they were of all different skin tones and physical types.) Modern racism was born with the rise of African slavery in the Americas and the simultaneous spread of European empires. Europeans justified their enslavement of Africans by arguing that the Africans were inherently inferior, that they naturally were racially beneath the Europeans. When Europeans went on to conquer much of the world during the seventeenth, eighteenth, and nineteenth centuries, they justified their conquests using the same racial ideas: they believed they were entitled to conquer non-Europeans because they considered themselves racially superior.

Modern racial categories were developed by Johann Blumenbach, a German naturalist, who, in the 1700s, put forward a theory that divided all human beings into five races: Mongoloid, Ethiopian, Caucasian, American, and Malayan. Blumenbach had no scientific basis for his categories; they were based entirely upon appearance. His ideas were expanded upon by the nineteenth-century French writer Joseph de Gobineau, who argued that the white race was superior to all other races (something Blumenbach had never said). The ideas of Gobineau and his successors were used to justify much of the racism that existed in the late nineteenth and early twentieth centuries, including, most infamously, the racism of Adolf Hitler and the Nazi Party.

With the decline of European empires and the rise of civil rights movements around the world, racism—at least officially sanctioned racism—has been on the retreat. The American civil rights movement of the 1950s and 1960s led to the dismantling of the racist structures that had existed in the United States. Apartheid, South Africa's system of racial separation, was abolished in the early 1990s.

RACISM TODAY

Despite the pronouncements of the United Nations and the victories of civil rights movements, racism still persists around the world, limiting the human rights of its victims.

Racism means more than simply not liking someone because of his perceived race. Racism leads to racial discrimination, which directly affects the lives of its victims. Racial discrimination results in people not being hired, not being allowed to live where they please, not being treated with respect in public or in their place of employment, and having to send their children to substandard schools. Racial discrimination can be subtle—a white real-estate agent might

"forget" to tell a black couple about an available house in a white neighborhood—or it can be overt and ugly—white police officers stop cars driven by blacks because they assume that blacks commit most crimes—but it always detracts from the human rights of those targeted.

In the United States, racism takes many forms. In one North Carolina slaughterhouse, for example, jobs are divided by race. Although nothing is said officially, whites dominate supervisory positions, blacks hold many of the slaughtering jobs, and Hispanic immigrants have the low-paying work of cutting up the carcasses.

Racism can have tragic consequences. In 1998, a black man, James Byrd, Jr., was dragged down a Texas highway and killed by a truck driven by a white man looking for someone black to hurt. Racist hate groups, such as the Ku Klux Klan, have also targeted blacks, harassing, assaulting, and sometimes killing them.

Prison statistics suggest racism, too: African Americans make up only 13 percent of the population, but more than 45 percent of prisoners are black. African Americans are far more likely than whites to be put on death row.

In Brazil, Eduardo Brito, the secretary of justice for the city of São Paulo, was pulled over by police, who assumed that a black man in an expensive car must have stolen it. Brazil, a country with as complex a racial mix as the United States, has often claimed to have avoided America's racial problems. But although Brazil lacks the sharply defined color barriers of the United States, it is quite clear that lighter-skinned people have better chances of success than those with darker complexions. Television, movies, and politics are all dominated by those with lighter complexions. Brazilians

Two member of the Ku Klux Klan—an American, racist hate group—dressed in hoods and robes.

with African roots, who make up half of the population, do not have the same opportunities that whites have.

Not all racism in the world is white on black or black on white. Anti-Semitism, or hostility toward Jews, persists and is widespread (anti-Semitic books have even been published in Japan, a country with no native Jewish population). The Internet is filled with web sites claiming that Jews control the world's money and that they are trying to take over the world, the same ideas that Hitler used to maintain his control in Germany. The Roma are another people persecuted by Hitler who still face racial discrimination today. The Roma have suffered from racist prejudice in the Czech Republic, Hungary, Romania, and many other European countries. Roma have been murdered and their houses burned by racists who see them as outsiders.

In Japan, the Ainu and Burakumin, along with Korean immigrants, face constant discrimination; some Japanese corporations are known to have bought lists of Burakumin so as to avoid hiring them (in one of the oddities of racism, Burakumin look no different from other Japanese). Koreans and Ainu face similar discrimination in employment and social situations.

In France, North African immigrants also face discrimination based on race. There is even a political party, the National Front, whose goal is to expel North Africans from France. In Germany, immigrant Turks can be born in the country, speak perfect German, and yet never be treated as fully German. Turkish homes and businesses in Germany have been firebombed by racist groups, many of which honor Adolf Hitler as a hero. In Indonesia, ethnic Chinese are viewed with suspicion by many ethnic Indonesians and have been subjected to racist attacks. Most of these Indonesian Chinese have lived in the country for many generations.

One of the key organizations in the fight against racism is the United Nations Educational, Scientific, and Cultural Organization (UNESCO). UNESCO has undertaken massive efforts to eliminate racism through education and international treaties. It is joined by many other private non-governmental organizations. Despite their efforts, racism continues to flourish. Until it is expunged, people will not all share the same human right to be treated with equality and dignity.

Carl Skutsch

See also: Apartheid; Genocide; Martin Luther King, Jr.; Universal Declaration of Human Rights; War; War Crimes.

Bibliography

Bulmer, Martin. *Racism.* Oxford: Oxford University Press, 2000.

Cose, Ellis. *Color-Blind: Seeing Beyond Race in a Race-Obsessed World.* New York: HarperCollins, 1997.

Hacker, Andrew. *Two Nations: Black and White, Separate, Hostile, Unequal.* New York: Ballantine, 1995.

Kleg, Milton. *Hate Prejudice and Racism.* Albany: State University of New York Press, 1993.

Marx, Anthony W. *Making Race and Nation: A Comparison of South Africa, the United States, and Brazil.* Cambridge: Cambridge University Press, 1998.

Refugees

A refugee, narrowly defined in international law, is a person with a well-founded fear of persecution on account of race, religion, nationality, membership in a particular social group, or political opinion, who is outside the country of his or her nationality and is unable or unwilling to return. The term is often popularly understood in far broader terms, however, encompassing persons fleeing war, civil strife, famine, and environmental disasters.

REFUGEES ACCORDING TO INTERNATIONAL LAW

The drafters of the 1951 United Nations (UN) Convention Relating to the Status of Refugees, the primary instrument of international law concerning refugees, not only limited the modern definition of refugee to persons fearing a relatively narrow range of human rights abuses, but also restricted its scope to migrants in Europe who fled as a result of events occurring before 1951. In 1967, a protocol dropped the Convention's geographic and temporal limitations. As of 1999, the Convention or protocol had been signed by 134 countries.

Although the protocol universalized the applicability of the Convention, it did not expand the refugee definition. In the developing world, the Convention's and protocol's definitions were often seen as inadequately encompassing the many reasons people fled their homelands to seek protection elsewhere. A wider definition was adopted by the Organization of African Unity (OAU) in 1969, extending its definition of a refugee to include persons compelled to leave their place of habitual residence because of external aggression, occupation, foreign domination, or events seriously disturbing public order. Similarly, representatives of Central American states in 1984 issued the Cartagena Declaration, which includes as refugees persons fleeing generalized violence, international conflicts, and serious disturbances of public peace.

Although the office of the United Nations High Commissioner for Refugees (UNHCR) was created in 1950 to assist and protect refugees remaining in Europe at the close of World War II, through the years, the High Commissioner has also helped groups that did not necessarily fall strictly within the refugee definition in the Convention and protocol. For example, the UNHCR assists about 265,000 displaced persons in Cyprus who are not technically refugees because they are still within their nominal home country. In Africa, the UNHCR offers assistance and protection to refugees meeting the OAU definition.

Falling outside the mandate of the UNHCR, and overlooked by Cartagena and the OAU as well, are internally displaced persons, people who flee their home district for the same reasons as refugees, but who do not cross an international border. By not actually leaving their countries of origin, internally displaced persons are frequently more vulnerable than the refugees outside their homelands who are the beneficiaries of international protection and assistance. In 1999, the U.S. Committee for Refugees estimated that worldwide there are 17 million internally displaced persons, along with 13.6 million refugees and asylum seekers.

Refugee camp of those displaced during the 1989 U.S. invasion of Panama, September 1990.

HELPING REFUGEES

In all cases, the UNHCR promotes three durable, long-range solutions for refugees. Its first preference is voluntary repatriation, a solution that assumes that the original causes of refugee flight have been ameliorated sufficiently to permit the safe return of the refugees. If this is not possible, the UNHCR attempts to integrate the refugees locally, in what are known as countries of first asylum, states that usually border the refugees' country of origin, and to which they flee in the first instance. The UNHCR tries to support local host populations to encourage them to be receptive to the refugees in their midst, often linking refugees with kinship groups or other populations with whom they have linguistic or other cultural ties.

The UNHCR's third durable solution is third-country resettlement. Considered to be the most expensive solution and one that can help the fewest refugees, it nevertheless is promoted for especially vulnerable individuals and groups who are not able or allowed to remain safely in countries of first asylum and for whom countries outside the region might have a special humanitarian concern. For example, in the mid-1970s, more than a million Southeast Asian refugees were settled outside the region, mostly in the United States, following the defeat of U.S.-backed regimes in Vietnam, Laos, and Cambodia.

Most of the world's refugees still await durable solutions for their plight. Most have been granted, at best, provisional or temporary asylum in neighboring countries, and are not able to regularize their status or integrate into the host country. Instead, millions live in squalid refugee camps, where rights to move and work are often highly restricted, and where educational and recreational opportunities are often non-existent or severely lacking. At times, refugees are subject to attack, either by local security forces or by cross-border incursions from their country of origin. At times, host governments forcibly return them to places of persecution.

ASYLUM AND NON-*REFOULEMENT*

The return of people by force to places where they were persecuted violates the most fundamental principle in international refugee law: the concept of non-*refoulement,* or the prohibition of the forced return of a refugee. This principle is enshrined in Article 33 of the Convention Relating to the Status of Refugees, which says that no state "shall expel or return (*refouler*) a refugee in any manner whatsoever to the frontiers of territories where his life or freedom would be threatened on account of his race, religion, nationality, membership of a particular social group, or political opinion."

Long before any international system was created to assist refugees or to prescribe their protection from forced return in international law, refugees fled persecution and sought protection outside the reach of the power they were fleeing. Refugees, broadly understood, can be found in the earliest literature, as wanderers in exile, seeking asylum.

The theme of exile recurs throughout religious writings. In the Bible, for example, human history begins with the expulsion of Adam and Eve from the Garden of Eden. The Israelites escaped from slavery in Egypt

Refugees fleeing into Bangladesh from Myanmar, 1992.

and wandered through the desert in search of a new home. The Christian birth narrative in the Gospel According to Matthew (2:13–18) says that an angel came to Joseph telling him to take the child and his mother and flee to Egypt in order to save the baby from Herod, who subsequently killed all the male children in Bethlehem who were two years old or younger. The theme of escape from persecution is also central to Islam. One of Islam's central events, the Hegira—from the word for exile, "Hijrah"—marks the flight of the prophet Mohammed from persecution in Mecca to Medina in the year 622. The theme of exile is also found in Eastern religious traditions. In the Hindu epic poem the Ramayana, on the eve of his ascendancy to the throne, the hero, the god Rama, is banished to the forest to live in exile for fourteen years.

Most of these religious traditions also promote the idea of asylum, that is, of providing refuge to persons seeking protection outside their homelands. The ancient Israelites were admonished, "Do not mistreat or oppress a foreigner; remember that you were foreigners in Egypt" (Exodus 22:21). In biblical times, penalties for manslaughter were severe and exacting, so a person who killed another by mistake would still face "eye for an eye" vengeance. However, if a person accused of manslaughter could escape to certain designated "cities of refuge," local residents would protect those accused of involuntary killing from retribution. In the New Testament, Jesus identifies himself as the stranger—"I was a stranger, and ye took me in"—so that his followers would consider that feeding and clothing any stranger was akin to comforting Christ himself (Matt. 25:35–45). The Christian church developed a practice of offering asylum to persons who sought its sanctuary. The principle of church asylum

was affirmed by the Council of Sardis in 347 and confirmed by the law codes of both Theodosius in the fourth century and Justinian in the sixth century. In 1140, Pope Gratian codified ecclesiastical law on asylum, excluding perpetrators of certain crimes from the church's protection. Until 1983, the Code of Canon Law of the Roman Catholic Church included the canon (number 1179) that "a church enjoys the right of asylum, so that guilty persons who take refuge in it must not be taken from it, except in the case of necessity, without the consent of the ordinary, or at least of the rector of the church."

The principle of asylum has a valued place in Islam as well. According to the Koran (14:35–37), the most sacred site in Islam, the Kaaba and the Haram that surrounds it, was established by Abraham in Mecca with the words "Lord, make this place a land of safe asylum." Traditionally, anyone who took refuge in the Haram was protected from harm. In fact, much of Islam's high regard for the principle of asylum derives from pre-Islamic Arabic traditions of hospitality that required the desert Bedouin tribes to shelter strangers in distress. According to custom, Bedouins were obligated to provide asylum (*igra*) for three days to the unarmed stranger. Under Islam, this protection was even extended to idolaters seeking refuge in time of war. The Koran (9:6) says, "If an idolater seeks asylum with you, give him protection so that he may hear the Word of Allah, and then convey him to safety."

Although the logic of refugee status dictates some form of asylum, a place where the refugee can exist outside the home country where he or she has lost the protection of his or her government, in fact, international law is decidedly weak on this right to asylum. Although the non-binding

Universal Declaration of Human Rights states, "Everyone has the right to seek and to enjoy in other countries asylum from persecution," the meaning of "to enjoy" is rather vague. Governments grant asylum; individuals "enjoy" it. The refugee's right to enjoy asylum is therefore limited by the willingness of the government to proffer it. So, although states are prohibited under international law from returning refugees to persecution, they are not required to take them in. A UN conference convened in 1977 failed to draft a Convention on Territorial Asylum that would require states to provide asylum to refugees. Instead, it came up with a declaration that states "shall endeavor" to grant asylum on their territory to eligible persons.

HISTORY OF ASYLUM

The idea of asylum can be found in the earliest Anglo-Saxon legal code, that of King Ethelbert in 597, which sets penalties for violating a church's offer of sanctuary. In 887, Alfred the Great's legal code expressly provides that any man who flees to a monastery shall be protected for three days, during which time he may come to terms with those seeking him out. As the power of the crown grew in England under the Tudors and Stuarts, and that of the church waned, the power of the church to grant sanctuary eroded. By 1540, the Parliament under King Henry VIII abolished church sanctuary for a wide range of crimes, but also designated eight cities where fugitives could find refuge. Under James I, the British Parliament abolished sanctuary entirely in 1603–1604. Following the religious upheaval and English civil war of the seventeenth century, the British Parliament in 1708 allowed foreign Protestant refugees seeking refuge in England to become citizens.

Refugee movements mark key milestones of American history. The Pilgrims, who started settlements in New England in the seventeenth century soon after James I abolished sanctuary, were refugees fleeing religious persecution in England. Many waves of subsequent immigrants to this country were, in fact, refugees fleeing various forms of persecution.

Within the United States, a refugee movement of sorts occurred in the face of the Fugitive Slave Act of 1850, which prohibited transporting or harboring escaped slaves, when the abolitionists "conducted" the Underground Railroad, smuggling escaped slaves north to freedom. Among twentieth-century refugees who have made significant contributions to American life are Albert Einstein, Henry Kissinger, and Rudolf Nureyev.

The most recent refugees to the United States include Vietnamese, Laotians, and Cambodians who fled after the American withdrawal and the communist takeover of their countries. Hundreds of thousands of refugees have also fled Cuba by boat and raft since a revolution in 1959 brought Fidel Castro to power. By some estimates, one-tenth of Cuba's population have become refugees, starting new lives mostly in the United States, primarily in the Miami , Florida area. American generosity has been selective, however. Throughout the 1980s, as civil war and repression wracked El Salvador and Guatemala, whose governments were backed by the United States, more than 97 percent of Salvadorans and Guatemalans applying for asylum in the United States were denied. During that same time, 75 percent of applicants from the Soviet Union were approved, and approval rates for asylum seekers from other communist countries were generally high. Presidents Ronald Reagan, George Bush, and Bill Clinton all pursued a policy of interdicting Haitian asylum seekers and automatically sending them back to Haiti without first making a determination as to whether they might qualify as refugees. As such, it is likely that genuine refugees among them were returned to persecution.

Refugees have also played a prominent role in continental European history. One of the most common reasons for forced migration in Europe has been religious and ethnic intolerance. The history of the Jews in Europe is that of a religious minority that never achieved firm protection from sovereign powers and frequently was forced to flee official or officially condoned persecution, including their expulsion from Spain in 1492, their flight from pogroms in Russia in the late nineteenth and early twentieth centuries, and their exile from Germany, Austria, and the Sudetenland in the 1930s.

Protestants in Europe were also forced to flee at key points in their history. On October 18, 1685, King Louis XIV of France revoked the Edict of Nantes, marking the end of tolerance of the French Protestants, known as Huguenots. Within days, Friedrich Wilhelm, the Great Elector of Brandenburg, issued the Edict of Potsdam, offering asylum to the French Huguenots. The English word *refugee*, in fact, has its origin in the French *refugie*.

Although religious persecution caused most mass movements of refugees during the Middle Ages and through the Reformation, political ideology characterized most European refugee flows from the French Revolution in the late eighteenth century through the end of the Cold War. Article 120 of the French Constitution of 1793 marks a new political consciousness about political exile by providing asylum to foreigners exiled "for the cause of liberty."

As state power grew in the nineteenth century, European governments concluded extradition treaties with one another. However, these same governments saw the rationale for exempting political offenders from extradition. Implicit in these treaties was the recognition that refugees ought to be protected from forced repatriation. In 1832, France made that recognition explicit in the Law Concerning Foreign Refugees Residing in France, which defined foreign refugees as persons residing in France without their own government's protection.

The lack of protection from one's own government is a key element in the concept of refuge. A refugee has been denied the rights associated with citizenship, fearing persecution at the hands of his or her own government. Denied rights due them as citizens, refugees become a uniquely human rights concern, as they are forced to seek protection from outside their homeland.

The Balkan Wars of 1912–1913 touched off mass refugee movements in southeastern Europe that continued throughout World War I; in the aftermath of the war, the Russian Revolution created another 1.5 million refugees, placing enormous strains on European stability. In 1921, in response to the Russian exodus, the League of Nations appointed the Norwegian explorer Fritjof Nansen as the first High Commissioner for Refugees. Aware of the lack of protection that accompanies lack of documents, Nansen produced documents for Russian refugees, known as Nansen Passports, which afforded the refugees recognition and protection.

In short order, new refugee movements outside Russia, particularly of Armenians fleeing severe persecution in Turkey, placed similar demands on the High Commissioner to issue more Nansen Passports. His office also assisted hundreds of thousands of

Greek and Turkish refugees who were displaced in the early 1920s. With Nansen's death in 1930, the Office of the High Commissioner lapsed.

The rise of Nazism in Germany in 1933 produced a new wave of refugees, but the international community was ill prepared to assist and protect those who might otherwise have escaped the atrocities to come. The League of Nations provided minimal financial support to the newly constituted Nansen Office, and a Convention Relating to the Status of Refugees drafted by that office in 1933 was ratified by only eight countries.

THE UNITED NATIONS AND REFUGEES

World War II displaced an estimated 30 million people, and a United Nations Relief and Rehabilitation Administration in 1943 and the International Refugee Organization (IRO) in 1947 were created to assist "displaced persons" and refugees. In 1946, the UN General Assembly declared that no displaced person or refugee who had shown satisfactory reason for not being returned to his or her country of origin should be forcibly returned.

The Soviet Union opposed the creation of the IRO, seeing it as promoting flight of refugees from the newly communist states of Eastern Europe. Throughout the Cold War, the Soviet bloc remained aloof from the international system, including the UNHCR, created to protect and assist refugees. Until the end of the Cold War, none of the Soviet bloc countries ratified the 1951 Convention Relating to the Status of Refugees.

Modern refugee movements have by no means been limited to Europe. More than a million Palestinian Arabs fled or were evicted after the partition of Palestine in 1948. A specialized United Nations agency, the UN Relief and Works Agency for Palestine Refugees in the Near East (UNRWA), was created on their behalf in 1950. In 1967, as a result of the Six Day War, hundreds of thousands of Palestinians were displaced, many for a second time. By 1999, UNRWA had registered 3.5 million Palestinians as refugees in the West Bank, Gaza Strip, Jordan, Lebanon, and Syria.

UNRWA operates with a different mandate, and employs a different refugee definition, than does the UNHCR, which is responsible for protecting and assisting other refugee groups. UN General Assembly resolutions define Palestinian refugees as persons who resided in Palestine two years prior to the outbreak of hostilities in 1948 and who lost their homes and livelihoods as a result of that war. Unlike the UNHCR's three durable solutions, the UNRWA mandate recognizes only repatriation or compensation as permanent solutions for the Palestinian refugee problem.

OTHER REFUGEE TROUBLE SPOTS

The partition of the Indian subcontinent in 1947 was accompanied by brutal communal fighting, which, in turn, forced millions to flee. Most of the refugees fled from the Punjab, Indian Delhi, and the Pakistani North West Frontier Province, where communal violence was heaviest. Masses of traumatized Hindus and Sikhs fled to India, while Muslims, in turn, fell victim to vicious persecution by Hindus and others in India, prompting a mass exodus into Pakistan. The two sides formally agreed to a population transfer after the majority had already fled in the midst of violent attacks. A 1951 census in West Pakistan put the number of Muslim refugees from India at 5.8 million;

Refugees from ethnic conflict in Bangladesh, April 1992.

an Indian census in 1949 counted 4.4 million Hindu and Sikh refugees who had arrived from West Pakistan. Perhaps as many as a million did not survive the ordeal.

Three decades later, Pakistan and India would again endure mass influxes of refugees. In 1971, 10 million refugees fled from East Pakistan (now Bangladesh) to India, after tensions between West and East Pakistan erupted into violence. The mass influx of refugees was a major cause of India's declaration of war on Pakistan in December 1971 and the subsequent declaration of independence by Bangladesh, following which the refugees were repatriated. Between 1979 and 1983, about 3 million Afghan refugees fled into Pakistan, while nearly 2 million others fled into Iran. Most

of the refugees endured a life of exile for more than two decades. Even after the end of the cold war, the withdrawal of Soviet troops from Afghanistan, and the defeat of the Soviet-installed government, the bulk of the refugees did not go home. Ethnicity-based civil war replaced the proxy battle of the superpowers, and ongoing insecurity thwarted reconstruction as well as refugee repatriation.

Conflicts surrounding the African independence movements of the mid-1960s and the consolidation of newly independent states contributed to refugee flows throughout much of the continent. In the Horn of Africa and southern Africa, in particular, ethnic conflicts, repression, and war, exacerbated by droughts and famines, continued to produce massive flows of refugees in the 1970s, 1980s, and 1990s. Refugees would crisscross borders, for example Ethiopian refugees fleeing to Sudan even as Sudanese refugees fled to Ethiopia. Others, in places like South Africa or Somalia, became internally displaced.

Although the end of the cold war and reforms in South Africa resulted in reduced tensions and significant voluntary repatriation of Namibian, Mozambican, South African, Ethiopian, and Eritrean refugees, the long-awaited repatriations to Sudan, Rwanda, and Angola failed to materialize, as civil strife based on ethnic and political divisions continued unabated and created new refugee flows out of Liberia and Somalia. By 2000, two-thirds of the world's uprooted—combining internally displaced and refugees—were in Africa and the Middle East.

Nationality- and ethnicity-based persecution has become an increasingly common cause of refugee flight in the post–cold war era. In 1992–1995, ethnic and religious persecution in the former Yugoslavia forced more than three million refugees from their homes in Bosnia and Croatia. In 1998–1999, the conflict in Kosovo displaced additional hundreds of thousands both inside and outside Kosovo. After the rapid return of the overwhelming majority of ethnic Albanian Kosovars in the summer of 1999, more than 200,000 ethnic Serbs and Roma were forced to flee, mostly to Serbia proper and Montenegro.

Kosovar refugees, fleeing from Serbian death squads, move into Macedonia, April 1999.

To an unprecedented degree, the conflicts in the former Yugoslavia stretched the mandate and resources of the UNHCR and the international regimen of refugee protection and assistance. The UN secretary-general charged the UNHCR with the task of providing humanitarian assistance to besieged communities still within Bosnia and Kosovo. Traditionally, the UNHCR has remained outside a country's borders protecting and assisting refugees, who, after all, are defined as being outside their country of origin. But in the post–cold war era, first in northern Iraq with Kurdish refugees displaced in the aftermath of the Persian Gulf War, and then in Bosnia and Kosovo, the UNHCR crossed the line of state sovereignty to intervene on behalf of vulnerable groups before they actually became refugees.

Some see this development as a historic advance and challenge to the presumption of refugee protection from the earliest times: that a refugee is to be protected only after he or she has gone into exile. This view sees the starting point of protection as the persecution or threat of persecution that causes a person to flee. Stopping the persecution, according to this view, would prevent the refugee problem from occurring at all.

Others see the international community as unable or unwilling to redress the massive human rights abuses and violence that cause major refugee flows and argue that outside governments find it more expedient simply to prevent would-be refugees from entering their countries, while using humanitarian intervention as an excuse for denying asylum.

In the early 1990s, this debate focused on would-be refugees still living within Haiti, Bosnia, China, Somalia, and Iraq, among others. The ability of the world community to assist and protect such vulnerable populations, while still in their home countries pending resolutions of the situations that threatened them, as well as its effectiveness in alleviating the causes of their misery, would determine the meaning of the term *refugee* and the relevance of the need for asylum in the twenty-first century.

Bill Frelick

See also: Asylum; Exile and Deportation.

Bibliography

United Nations High Commissioner for Refugees. *The State of the World's Refugees 2000: 50 Years of Humanitarian Action.* New York: Oxford University Press, 2000.

Reproductive Rights

While reproductive rights have gained their greatest recognition during the past two decades, they are firmly rooted in some of the most basic human rights principles. As noted in the Programme of Action of the 1994 International Conference on Population and Development (Cairo Programme of Action), "Reproductive rights embrace certain human rights that are already recognized in national laws, international laws and international human rights documents and other consensus documents." Broadly speaking, the concept of reproductive rights encompasses two principles: the right to reproductive health care and the right to reproductive self-determination. Measures may be taken to ensure these two rights overlap and are interdependent. Their international legal foundations, however, are distinct, and their broad implications bear separate examination.

THE RIGHT TO REPRODUCTIVE HEALTH CARE

The right to reproductive health care is rooted in the provisions of international human rights instruments protecting life and health. The right to life is protected in provisions of most of the principal human rights instruments, including Article 3 of the United Nations Universal Declaration of Human Rights (Universal Declaration) and Article 6 of the International Covenant on Civil and Political Rights (Civil and Political Rights Covenant). While traditionally read to protect individuals only from arbitrary execution by the state, the right to life has been interpreted by the Human

Rights Committee, the body that monitors compliance with the Civil and Political Rights Covenant, to require governments to adopt "positive measures" aimed at preserving life. In particular, the Committee recommends that states take steps to "reduce infant mortality and to increase life expectancy." Implementation of both of these recommendations requires an investment in health care, including reproductive health care.

The right to health is recognized in Article 12 of the International Covenant on Economic, Social, and Cultural Rights (Economic, Social, and Cultural Rights Covenant), which requires states to "recognize the right of everyone to the enjoyment of the highest attainable standard of physical and mental health." The World Health Organization (WHO) has defined health as "a state of complete physical, mental and social well-being, not merely the absence of disease or infirmity." According to the Cairo Programme of Action, "reproductive health" is total well-being "in all matters relating to the reproductive system and to its functions and processes." While the right to health does not guarantee perfect health for all people, it does encompass a government duty to ensure health care. Article 12(2)(d) of the Economic, Social and Cultural Rights Covenant requires states to create "conditions which would ensure to all medical service and medical attention in the event of sickness."

The international community's earliest explicit acknowledgment of the right to reproductive health care appears in provisions relating to maternal and child health. Article 25(2) of the Universal Declaration provides that "[m]otherhood and childhood are entitled to special care and assistance." Similarly, Article 10(2) of the Economic, Social and Cultural Rights Covenant declares: "Special protection should be accorded to mothers during a reasonable period before and after childbirth." Article 12(2)(a) requires states to provide for "the reduction of the stillbirth rate and of infant mortality." All of these provisions suggest a government duty to provide pre- and post-natal care, as well as medical assistance during childbirth.

A broader obligation to provide the full range of reproductive health services has support in principles of non-discrimination. Article 3 of the Civil and Political Rights Covenant and Article 3 of the Economic, Social and Cultural Rights Covenant obligate governments to ensure the equal enjoyment of the rights protected in these instruments. To ensure equal enjoyment of the rights to life and health, states must take into account the particular health needs of both women and men. This point is recognized in the Convention on the Elimination of All Forms of Discrimination Against Women (Women's Convention). Article 12(1) of that Convention requires states to ensure "on a basis of equality of men and women, access to health care services, including those related to family planning."

Reproductive health is a fundamental aspect of women's well-being. Without regular access to safe, high-quality services, women become vulnerable to a host of health complications, which may include death or injury during childbirth, unwanted pregnancy, and sexually transmitted diseases (STDs). The right to reproductive health care thus gives rise to a governmental duty both to ensure the availability of reproductive health services and to remove legal barriers to reproductive health care.

States must take affirmative measures to ensure that reproductive health care is available and accessible to all women. The Committee on the Elimination of Discrimination Against Women (CEDAW), the body that monitors compliance with the Women's Convention, has addressed government obligations pertaining to reproductive health care. In its recommendation on Women and Health, it declares: "States should implement a comprehensive national strategy to promote women's health throughout their lifespan. This will . . . ensure universal access for all women to a full range of high-quality and affordable health care, including sexual and reproductive health services."

Comprehensive reproductive health care should include measures to promote safe motherhood, care for those infected with HIV/AIDS and other STDs, abortion, infertility treatments, and a full range of quality contraception (including emergency contraception). An implicit element of the right to health care is the right to information necessary to protect one's own health. Article 10(h) of the Women's Convention recognizes the importance of information in fulfilling the right to health, stating that governments shall ensure "[a]ccess to specific educational information to help to ensure the health and well-being of families, including information and advice on family planning." Women and adolescent girls should be given the information they need to protect themselves from such threats to their health as unwanted pregnancy, STDs, and harmful traditional practices such as female genital mutilation.

Governments are also bound to remove legal barriers to reproductive health care. CEDAW, in its General Recommendation on Health, has stated that "barriers to women's access to appropriate health care include laws that criminalize medical procedures only needed by women and that punish women who undergo those procedures." In many countries, women's access to abortion is severely restricted by criminal legislation. Many reproductive care advocates argue that abortion is a medical procedure. Because an unwanted pregnancy subjects a woman to undesired risks to her physical and mental health, an abortion may be her preferred medical option. Furthermore, when a pregnancy puts a woman's life or health in immediate danger, an abortion may be necessary to ensure her safety. Restrictive abortion laws thus, in this view, impede access to health care. Other legal barriers to reproductive health include laws that restrict advertising of contraception, laws that require a hus-

band's consent to obtain contraception, and laws that criminalize voluntary sterilization procedures.

REPRODUCTIVE SELF-DETERMINATION

A fundamental aspect of reproductive self-determination is the right to plan one's family. This right has been declared by the international community in documents adopted at international conferences and in the Women's Convention. The right to determine "freely and responsibly" the number and spacing of one's children and to have the information and education necessary to do so was first articulated in 1968, at the International Conference on Human Rights in Teheran. It was reaf-

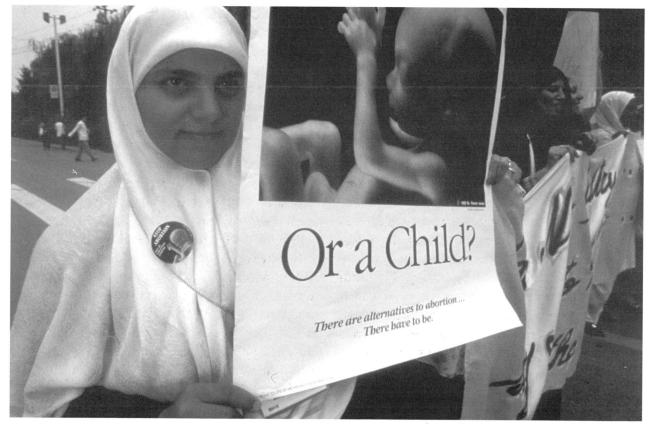

Muslim women protest against abortion at the 1995 United Nations Fourth World Conference on Women in Beijing, China.

firmed in 1974, at the World Population Conference in Bucharest; in 1984, at the International Conference on Population in Mexico City; in 1994, at the International Conference on Population and Development in Cairo; and, most recently, in 1995, at the Fourth World Conference on Women in Beijing. (However, at all these conferences, some women, often from conservative Muslim countries, opposed the mainstream's demands for more reproductive rights.) The right was given legal force in Article 16(e) of the Women's Convention, which provides that states shall ensure men and women "[t]he same rights to decide freely and responsibly on the number and spacing of their children and to have access to the information, education and means to enable them to exercise these rights." States are thus obligated to ensure that men and women have access to a full range of contraceptive choices and reproductive health services and that they have information about family planning and sexual and reproductive health.

The principle of reproductive self-determination also encompasses the right to freedom from interference in reproductive decision making. This right relates to broader notions of bodily autonomy, often referred to as the right to physical integrity. The principle of physical integrity has roots in the right to respect for human dignity, the right to liberty and security of the person, and the right to privacy. Physical integrity is explicitly protected in Article 4 of the African Charter of Human and People's Rights and Article 5(1) of the American Convention on Human Rights (American Convention). It protects women from unwanted invasion of or intrusion into their bodies and other non-consensual restrictions on women's physical autonomy.

Abortion is a critical part of the right to reproductive self-determination. Denying a woman the option of avoiding pregnancy or childbirth, for example, interferes with her right to decide on a matter having tremendous implications for her body and personal liberty. Nationally and internationally, the right to privacy has been invoked to support the principle that women are entitled to make decisions about their bodies, free of interference. Privacy and family life are protected by Article 12 of the Universal Declaration of Human Rights, Article 17 of the Civil and Political Rights Covenant, Article 11 of the American Convention, and Article 8(1) of the European Convention on Human Rights (European Connection). The European Commission on Human Rights has held that laws that restrict a woman's choice to terminate a pregnancy, for example, touch on the right to privacy protected in Article 8(1) of the European Convention.

Of course, a few human rights advocates believe that the right to reproductive self-determination, which allows an abortion is not sufficiently strong to override the fetus' right to life. Negotiating a path between these two rights remains a controversial issue in many countries.

Reproductive self-determination implies freedom, not just from intrusive laws and policies, but from all forms of violence and coercion that affect a woman's sexual or reproductive life. One such coercive practice, forced marriage, has long been recognized by the international community as a violation of human rights. Article 16(2) of the Universal Declaration provides that "[m]arriage shall be entered into only with the free and full consent of the intending spouses." This requirement is echoed in Article 10(1) of the Economic, Social and Cultural Rights Covenant and Article 23(3) of the Civil and

Political Rights Covenant. A broader notion of self-determination has been recognized in more recent years. The Cairo Programme of Action notes that women are entitled to "make decisions concerning reproduction free of discrimination, coercion and violence."

Violence against women is often directed specifically at a woman's sexual or reproductive capacity. Rape and other forms of sexual violence, female circumcision/female genital mutilation, and forced or coercive sterilization are examples of the types of violence that infringe upon reproductive self-determination.

CONCLUSION

It has been widely recognized that reproductive rights are critical for the attainment of women's equal status in the world. Full enjoyment of reproductive rights depends, in turn, on profound social, economic, and political change. In the short term, governments can promote reproductive rights by realizing legislative and policy change, building a culture of human rights through enhancement of legal literacy and access to legal recourse, developing indicators for monitoring enjoyment of rights, and ensuring the political commitment to allocating resources toward these efforts.

Anika Rahman and Laura Katzive

See also: Abortion; Right to Life.

Bibliography

Hartmann, Betsy. *Reproductive Rights and Wrongs: The Global Politics of Population Control.* Boston: South End Press, 1995

Right to Life

In the context of the contemporary discussion of human rights, the right to life refers to the right not to be arbitrarily deprived of life. In this context, one should note that most discussions of the right to life are not primarily concerned with the anti-abortion movement, which has adopted the "right to life movement" as a self-designation. The issue of capital punishment is also involved with the right to life, but is only one of many associated issues. Other issues discussed under the category of the right to life are deaths that occur during routine police actions and during actions taken by authorities to suppress riots, as well as the duty of the state to prevent acts of murder by private citizens and others.

The right to life is obviously a precondition for enjoying the exercise of other human rights. Article 3 of the Universal Declaration of Human Rights states: "Everyone has the right to life, liberty, and security of person." Article 6 of the International Covenant on Civil and Political Rights deals with the right to life in greater detail:

1. Every human being has the inherent right to life. This right shall be protected by law. No one shall be arbitrarily deprived of his life.
2. In countries which have not abolished the death penalty, sentence of death may be imposed only for the most serious crimes in accordance with the law in force at the time of the commission of the crime and not contrary to the provisions of the present Covenant and to the Convention on the Prevention and Punishment of the Crime of Genocide. This penalty can only be carried out pursuant to a final judgment rendered by a competent court.
3. When deprivation of life constitutes the crime of genocide, it is understood that nothing in this article shall authorize any State Party to the present Covenant to derogate in any way from any obligation assumed under the provisions of the Convention on the Prevention and Punishment of the Crime of Genocide.
4. Anyone sentenced to death shall have the right to seek pardon or commutation of the sentence. Amnesty, pardon or commutation of the sentence of death may be granted in all cases.
5. Sentence of death shall not be imposed for crimes committed by persons below eighteen years of age and shall not be carried out on pregnant women.
6. Nothing in this article shall be invoked to delay or to prevent the abolition of capital punishment by any State Party to the present Covenant.

Finally, Article 1 of the Second Optional Protocol to the International Covenant on Civil and Political Rights adopts the position that eliminating capital punishment will enhance human dignity and develop human rights:

1. No one within the jurisdiction of a State Party to the present Optional Protocol shall be executed.
2. Each state shall take all necessary measures to abolish the death penalty within its jurisdiction.

This position reflects the changing sensitivity to capital punishment, which has emerged as a major issue in recent decades.

At first glance, it may appear paradoxical that many anti-abortion activists support the death penalty while opponents of capital punishment often adhere to a pro-choice position. These superficially contradictory views can, however, be supported by, in the former case, making a sharp contrast between the innocence of the unborn and the guilt of candidates for capital punishment; and, in the latter case, by drawing a sharp distinction between the personhood of individuals on death row and the non-personhood of the unborn.

The debate over the personhood of the fetus is reflected in the contrast between Article 6 of the International Covenant on Civil and Political Rights, and Article 4 of the American Convention on Human Rights (adopted in San José, Costa Rica, on November 11, 1969). The American Convention asserts that the right to life begins "from the moment of conception." Efforts to include similar wording into the International Covenant on Civil and Political Rights were defeated, although, by stipulating that pregnant women should not be executed, Article 6(5) cited above seems to impute personhood to the human fetus. Minus this sort of stipulation, the implication is that an unborn fetus is a non-person without rights, which can therefore be aborted without violating the right to life principle.

James R. Lewis

See also: Abortion; Capital Punishment.

Bibliography

Campbell, Tom, David Goldberg, Sheila McLean, and Tom Mullen, eds. *Human Rights: From Rhetoric to Reality.* New York: Basil Blackwell, 1986.

Dinstein, Yoram. "The Right to Life, Physical Integrity, and Liberty." In Louis Henkin, ed., *The International Bill of Rights: The Covenant on Civil and Political Rights.* New York: Columbia University Press, 1981.

Roma ("Gypsies")

The Roma—commonly but incorrectly known in English as "Gypsies"—number between 7 million and 8 million in Europe and are that continent's largest and most oppressed minority. Of north Indian origin, they reached Europe in the late Middle Ages and maintain their own language and customs. They have been persecuted throughout Europe for centuries and were, along with Jews, targeted for extermination by Nazi Germany. About 500,000 to 600,000 were killed during the Holocaust.

Repression and discrimination continued after World War II. Many Eastern bloc countries launched forced assimilation policies that tended to negate Romani identity. After the cold war ended, long-submerged bigotry emerged, which led to violent attacks and expulsions—often with police approval or participation—of the Roma from Eastern Europe. The Roma suffer from discrimination in education, employment, health care, and other public services across Europe.

The ongoing discrimination against the Roma encompasses a multitude of human rights crimes. The United Nations Universal Declaration of Human Rights forbids discrimination on any grounds, including that of racial or ethnic background. Nevertheless, throughout much of Europe, the Roma are denied their right to national self-determination, participation in the government, security of person, and freedom of movement and residence. In its first article, the Universal Declaration of Human Rights states: "All human beings are born free and equal in dignity and rights. They are endowed with reason and conscience and should act toward one another in a spirit of brotherhood."

Yet all too often the Romani people are treated with little dignity or respect for their rights. In recent years, human rights advocates—sometimes prodded by Romani civil rights groups—have begun to insist that the struggle to gain full human rights for the Roma is one of Europe's most important human rights arenas.

Romani civil rights movements and organizations have been assembled in several countries, notably Germany, Spain, and Italy. The European Roma Rights Center, based in Budapest, monitors the human rights status of the Roma. Other organizations whose purview is not limited to the Roma, such as the Princeton, New Jersey–based Project on Ethnic Relations, include the Roma struggle as part of their work to prevent ethnic conflicts in Europe.

HISTORY

Although the word *Gypsies* derives from the notion that the Roma's ancestors came from Egypt, Western scholars have recognized, since the late eighteenth century, that the group's origins lie in northern India. Their Indo-Aryan language is rooted in old Indic, the scholarly form of which was Sanskrit. According to Professor Ian Hancock, the group's name in that language—Rom—derives from the Sanskrit word rama, meaning "man" or "husband."

The Roma have been the victims of prejudice and repression in Europe since their arrival there. According to anthropologist Gabrielle Tyrnauer, they were "regarded . . . with a mixture of envy, fear, nostalgia, and contempt." The names they have been given in European languages reflect their history as outsiders to the established Christian political and social culture. "Gypsy," the Spanish *gitano,* implies a supposed Egyptian origin. Other names, like Zigeuner in German or tsigane in French, are derived from the name of a Manichean sect to which the Roma were widely—and wrongly—believed to belong.

Over the centuries, groups of the Roma split off, and, in isolation, the subgroups developed separate cultural patterns and acquired separate names. Sinti, for example, is the name for Germanized Roma, whose ancestors settled in German territory as early as the fifteenth century.

European countries imposed a variety of punishments on the Roma, including death, torture, and expulsion. One historian has counted 148 such laws in German territory alone from the fifteenth through the eighteenth centuries. The Roma were expelled from the Holy Roman Empire in 1500 and from England by a series of laws in the sixteenth century. Saxony expelled them in 1579, and a law authorized in 1648 condemned them to death. In 1710, Frederick I of Prussia condemned all adult male Roma to forced labor, women to be whipped and branded, and children to be taken from their parents. In the same year, Emperor Joseph I of Austria-Hungary ordered Romani men to be hanged. In Bohemia, boys and women had their left ears cut off; in Moravia the right ones were cut off. "Gypsy hunts" were common sport in many countries.

Enlightenment scholarship did little to eradicate this persecution. Heinrich Grellmann, the eighteenth-century German ethnographer who confirmed the Roma's Indian origin, contended that the 700,000 to 800,000 Roma who then populated Germany prompted "serious consideration . . . [since] . . . most of these people [were]

idlers, cheats, and thieves." Cesare Lombroso, a leading Italian criminologist of the late nineteenth century, believed that certain anthropological traits were associated with particular "criminal types," and he characterized the Roma as "the living example of a whole race of criminals."

In 1899, Bavaria created the Gypsy Affairs Office, later called the Central Office for Fighting the Gypsy Menace. A census taken by the agency in 1905 described the Roma as "a pest against which society must unflaggingly defend itself." In 1926, the Bavarian Law for Combatting the Gypsies, Vagabonds, and Idlers provided that Roma with criminal records could be expelled from municipalities and states, and forced to travel on prescribed routes and live in prescribed areas. It also gave the police power to seize and send for two years to an Arbeitsanstalt, or labor institution, any Romani person over sixteen whose police records did not prove "steady employment." In 1928, the Roma were made subject to permanent police surveillance, and, the next year, the Munich center allied with Interpol in Vienna to register and detain Roma.

A book published in 1920 by a psychiatrist-judge developed the idea of *lebensunwertes Leben*—"lives unworthy of life"—and advocated the killing of those who were *Ballastexistenzen*—"dead weight"—upon humanity, including the Roma. A treatise of 1928 by the influential anthropologist Hans Günther asserted that it was the Gypsies who "introduced foreign blood into Europe."

NAZI PERSECUTION

The Third Reich established by Adolf Hitler in Germany in the 1930s inherited the deep, long-standing structure of anti-Roma laws and customs and carried it to new heights. As Gabrielle Tyrnauer has noted, the

Roma's "experience with the Third Reich was . . . a new kind of persecution. . . . It was total, ideological, and aimed at the extermination of their entire ethnic group—in short, genocide, as it came subsequently to be called." Indeed, "among all those who suffered under the Nazi Terror only Jews and Gypsies were marked for total extermination."

In one of Nazi Germany's earliest actions in July 1933, the Roma were categorized as having "innate feeblemindedness," under the *Gesetz zur Verhutung erbkranken Nachwuchs* (Law for the Prevention of Genetically Unsound Offspring). This categorization permitted their forced sterilization. The Roma accounted for some 94 percent of all forced sterilizations in Nazi Germany. The first mass arrest of the Roma occurred in January 1934. Classifications labeled the Roma as "racially inferior asocials and criminals of Asiatic ancestry."

Although the Roma were not mentioned by name in the Nuremberg Laws of September 15, 1935, authoritative commentaries included them as distinctive racial minorities of "alien blood." In 1936 the government created a principal institution to deal with the Roma, the *Rassenhygienische und Bevolkerungsbiologische Forschungsstelle* (Racial Hygiene and Criminal Biology and Research Unit) of the Ministry of Health. Robert Ritter, a psychiatrist who had tried to prove the Roma's distinctive racial qualities by studying their genealogy and genetics, was named head. The agency used biological and anthropological theories to classify the Roma and concluded that they were inherently diseased. These studies formed the basis of Nazi official Heinrich Himmler's *Runderlass*, or circular decree, of December 8, 1938, on Combatting the Gypsy Menace, which advocated "the reso-

lution of the Gypsy question based on its essentially racial nature."

As early as 1935, the Nazis had established an internment camp for the Roma in Cologne. More camps were set up in Düsseldorf in 1936, and in Frankfurt in 1937. The largest camp, Berlin-Marzahn, was created to rid Berlin of the Roma for the 1936 Olympics. Across Germany in 1938, many Roma were arrested, often those already in internment camps. Many were deported to Sachsenhausen, Buchenwald, Dachau, Mauthausen, and other concentration camps. After Germany took over Austria in 1938, camps for the Roma were set up there as well. Roma property, including gold, was confiscated.

World War II broke out in 1939. Three years later Nazi propaganda minister Joseph Goebbels asserted that "Jews and Gypsies should be exterminated unconditionally." In December 1942, Heinrich Himmler, the Nazi leader in charge of the concentration camps, issued the *Auschwitz-Erlass,* which ordered the deportation of all "mixed-blood Gypsies, Rom-Gypsies, and Gypsies of 'Balkan blood origin'" to Auschwitz-Birkenau.

Thousands of Roma were also sent to other death camps, such as Belsec, Sobibor, and Treblinka. Thousands more were simply shot. On the evening of July 31, 1942—*Zigeunernacht,* or "Gypsy Night"—all but 1,500 of the Roma at Auschwitz were killed by poison gas. Thus, the Roma joined the Jews in being victims, albeit on smaller scale, of the human rights crime of genocide. The Roma suffered other atrocities as well. At Auschwitz, Dr. Josef Mengele conducted medical experiments on them. These included the killing of Romani twins to study comparative eye coloration and the study of fetal development by artificially inseminating Romani women and then forcibly performing abortions at various stages.

On the Eastern front, the Roma, like Jews, were killed under explicit orders by firing squads. In November 1942, it was reported that all Roma in Serbia had been killed. In Croatia, the fate of the Roma was left to the pro-Nazi Ustasa regime, which is believed to have killed all but 1 percent of the prewar Roma population. Estimates of Romani deaths during World War II have ranged from 219,000 to more than 1 million.

POSTWAR CLIMATE AND TREATMENT

The age-old hostility toward the Roma continued throughout Europe after World War II. East Germany, considering itself a new, socialist state with no connection to its Nazi past, disclaimed any responsibility for Nazi horrors inflicted on the Roma. The West German government transferred to its agencies the "Gypsy" files that had been collected during the Third Reich.

Anti-Roma regulation continued in force. The Cologne municipal authorities, for example, expressly accepted the validity of Himmler's 1938 *Runderlass* on Combatting the Gypsy Menace. Cologne regulations also maintained Nazi restrictions on issuing licenses for Roma with itinerant trades, such as musicians, craft workers, and traveling vendors, and mandated the registration and surveillance of all local Roma employment.

Persecution of the Roma was especially strong in Eastern Europe after World War II ended. In 1958, Czechoslovakia adopted a measure aimed at the Roma that forbade "nomadism." This law led to the government slaughter of Romani horses that had formerly pulled their caravans. Bulgaria and Poland also passed laws designed to prevent the free movement of the Roma.

In Western Europe, increasing civil rights activism led the Roma to organize national Roma assemblies for the purpose of fighting for Romani civil rights. This civil rights movement inspired the First World Romani Congress, held in London in 1971 and attended by Romani representatives from fourteen countries. This landmark event marked the coming of age of a Romani human rights struggle that continues to the present day. Although there have been other World Romani Congresses, the fight for Romani human rights has largely been fought country by country, as the Roma in different European states can often be faced with substantially different barriers to achieving full human rights.

NATIONAL CONDITIONS

Today, living conditions for the Roma and their human rights situation vary from one country to another. Below is a breakdown of countries with a significant Romani population.

Romania: Romania is home to the single largest Romani community. Estimates range from 1.35 to 2 million, or more than 9 percent of the population. Former dictator Nicolae Ceausescu, who ruled Romania from 1965 to his execution in 1989, followed a policy of "homogenization" of Romanian society by integration of minorities. This assimilation program led to the suppression of Romani language, history, and culture. Attempts were made to settle the Roma who lacked fixed addresses. Some old Romani quarters were destroyed and traditional occupations prohibited.

Since the 1989 revolution that overthrew the Ceausescu regime, the Roma have gained political and cultural rights, but hatred and violence toward the Roma—which had been suppressed under that regime—have become overt and severe. Mob attacks on people and property became so common in the mid-1990s that the Ministry of the Interior developed a Mob Violence Prevention Program. Even after that plan was enacted, however, local police forces have themselves been accused by Romani and human rights organizations of conducting unjustified and violent raids against Romani communities, sometimes under the rubrics of "illegal domicile" or "fighting crime."

Bulgaria: In Bulgaria, where the Romani population is estimated at 6 to 7 percent, discrimination and violence toward the Roma have remained a serious problem since the fall of the Communist government in 1989–1990. There have been reports of organized police beatings and the arbitrary arrests and jailings of the Roma, as well as of attacks by skinheads. It has been difficult for the Roma to apply for social benefits and to claim land to which they were entitled under the law disbanding socialist farming cooperatives. In 1998, the government announced that it would develop a long-term program to integrate ethnic and religious minorities, including the Roma.

Spain: Spain has the largest Roma community in Western Europe, with estimates ranging from 650,000 and 1 million, or roughly 2 percent of the population. They have historically been marginalized and still suffer social and economic discrimination. According to some Romani sources, 75 to 80 percent of the Spanish Roma have "informal sector" employment in farm work and peddling. A Madrid ordinance against peddling was invalidated by a court but is reportedly still enforced in some places, and other municipalities have enacted similar bans. Truancy, dropout, and illiteracy rates are high. Housing conditions are often poor; Roma were estimated in 1990 to constitute 95 percent of the squatter population. There have been some efforts to relocate squatters, but the housing to which they were transferred has been substandard. Non-governmental organizations like Gypsy Presence advocate for improved conditions, as does the Office of the People's Defender.

Hungary: The situation is much the same in Hungary, where, at about 350,000, or 5 percent of the population, the Roma are the largest minority group. Here, too, Romani leaders and organizations assert that both discrimination and police and judicial harassment have worsened since the fall of communism in 1989. Romani unemployment is estimated at 70 percent, and the Roma are discriminated against in education, housing, and other public functions. The Roma have been evicted by local authorities in the name of eliminating substandard housing. The law prohibits discrimination, but it often goes unenforced.

In 1994, in the first elections for minority self-government, 477 Romani governing bodies were chosen, a number that increased to 770 in 1998. These governments have, however, been criticized for underfunding and for allowing the local governments to disclaim responsibility for the welfare of their poorest citizens. Publications and broadcasting are available in the Romani language.

In 1998, the prime minister accused Romani communities of embracing criminal elements. The mayor of Patka gathered one thousand signatures in support of barring out the Roma from another town, and the mayor of Isaszeg ordered an eighteen-member Romani family to leave. An agreement with the European Union the same year required Hungary to "ensure justice and protection for the Roma."

Slovakia: Roma are the second largest minority, after Hungarians. Estimated to number between 300,000 and 520,000, Roma make up to 10 percent of the population, one of the highest proportions in the world. Racist attacks by skinheads and others have been common. The police have often denied the existence of these crimes and have sometimes brought charges against the Romani victims. The use of the Romani language in colloquial speech is widespread, but its official recognition is ambiguous. The right to use languages other than Slovak in official communications was effectively discouraged by a 1995 law.

The Roma have also been subjected to geographic exclusions. Local residence permits are mandatory, and local authorities have applied the requirement in a discriminatory fashion to block the Roma from moving into cities and to expel them from existing locations, thus separating them from the larger society.

Russia: Reports on the human rights status of the Roma in Russia, where they number an estimated 375,000, or 0.3 percent of the population, are sparse. There is widespread discrimination against them in the Caucasus and Central Asian regions. The Roma have been attacked by skinheads and targeted by police for harassment, arrest, illegal penalties, and deportation from cities.

Czech Republic: The Roma, estimated at 200,000 to 275,000, are the second largest

In Prague, demonstrators march in defense of Roma rights. A nearby rally of racist skinheads is marching against the Roma, May 1992.

minority after Slovaks. Discrimination and sporadic violence against the Roma are a principal human rights problem in the country. Popular prejudice is deeply ingrained, and the Roma suffer from poverty, unemployment, illiteracy, and disease. Many cases have been identified of the failure of police to act on reports of attacks on and threats against the Roma. Some politicians and organizations openly promote hatred against the Roma.

A citizenship law enacted in 1993 at the time of the split with Slovakia effectively deprived many Roma, who had been citizens of Czechoslovakia, of Czech citizenship. Under a 1969 law, most Roma had been designated as Slovaks, and after 1994 they had to undergo naturalization to become Czech citizens. Roma without Czech citizenship are unable to vote or receive health and other social benefits.

In 1998, the 1958 law aimed at the Roma prohibiting nomadic lifestyles was repealed. Except for an advisory council on nationalities, which has three Romani members, there are few Roma in government positions. The state funds some broadcasting and print media for the Roma.

Greece: The estimated 150,000 to 300,000 Roma in Greece, once largely migratory, have been gradually settling into suburban slums. Plagued by poverty and illiteracy, they suffer widespread discrimination in fields like employment and housing. The Roma have also been targets of police brutality. There have been some reports that the Roma have been refused employment registration on the ground, or pretext, that they failed to meet residency requirements.

Italy: The Roma number approximately 60,000 to 80,000 citizens and 45,000 to 60,000 immigrants, mostly from the former Yugoslavia. Without valid identity documents, the immigrant Roma often have difficulty obtaining legal residency or employment and in some cases have turned to begging and petty theft. Those who are citizens with established places of residence have achieved relatively equal treatment in the economic sphere. About 130 nonprofit organizations represent Romani people, although the groups are not well funded. There have been reports of police mistreatment of Roma.

Albania: The Roma, who number from 100,000 to 120,000, reached what is now Albania in about 1400, around the same time the area was conquered by the Ottoman Empire. Most adopted the Islamic faith. Their treatment was relatively benign through the establishment of an independent Albania in 1912 and the Italian occupation during World War II. The Enver Hoxha regime, which ruled Albania from 1944 to 1985, sought to submerge all separate ethnic and cultural identities, including that of the Roma. Since the end of the cold war and especially since the near-collapse of civil society in 1997 in the wake of economic scandals—during which false rumors flourished that "the Roma are rich"—conditions for the Roma worsened.

Human rights violations are widespread and affect far more than the Roma. The Roma are, however, the most neglected minority group and are subject to discrimination and economic disadvantage. They have not generally been singled out for violent attacks by the police or others.

Ukraine: The Roma are concentrated in Transcarpathia, a sliver of territory in the southwestern corner of the country that borders Slovakia, Hungary, and Romania. They have lived in this region since the fifteenth century. The Soviet Union, which ruled Ukraine for much of the twentieth century, forcibly resettled the Roma, forbidding "vagrancy" and "parasitism" on penalty of hard labor in prison camp.

With their traditional nomadic lifestyle outlawed, the Roma in independent Ukraine have turned to what has been called the "neo-nomadism of the outcast." In that marginalized position, they have been targeted for violence by both the police and private individuals.

Poland: The national government does not practice overt discrimination against the Romani population, estimated at 40,000 to 45,000, but some local governments discriminate in the provision of services. Some schools place Romani children in separate classes, asserting that they are behind others in socioeconomic status and literacy. As in other central European countries, Roma have been attacked by skinheads, but relatively sporadically, and police authorities pursue criminal actions.

Croatia: The Romani population, estimated at 35,000, faces discrimination and lack of official response to complaints. Reports of exclusion from public education are common. The government finds the source of the problems in linguistic and cultural differences that obstruct the integration of the Roma into society.

Germany: An estimated 110,000 to 130,000 Romani live in Germany. About 60,000 of these have German citizenship, including the Sinti who settled in German territory beginning around 1400. After World War II,

a Romani civil rights movement slowly began to form in West Germany. In the early 1980s, Romani activists, with the support of the *Gesellschaft für bedrohte Volker* (Society for Endangered Peoples), formed the *Zentralrat Deutscher Sinti und Roma* (Central Council of German Sinti and Roma), which later received political recognition and financial support from the West German government. Other grass-roots organizations were also formed, such as the Rom and Sinti Union in Hamburg, later called the Roma National Congress. The newer organizations, independent of the government and less strictly German in outlook, supported civil rights for immigrant and stateless Roma within Germany.

In 1995, five years after the reunification of Germany, the government officially recognized Sinti and Roma as a national minority. Two years later, the government committed itself to protecting and fostering the languages and cultures of traditional minority groups, including the Roma and Sinti. Despite these efforts, there has been considerable resistance to the idea that the Romani language should be protected and cultivated by the state. Romani leaders assert that public statements by officials and the media perpetuate prejudice against the Roma.

United States: Roma have been in the United States since at least the early nineteenth century. They live throughout the country and are concentrated in large cities. No reliable count of the Romani population exists. Some estimates range up to 1 million, which would place the United States second to Romania in the number of Roma.

Misunderstanding and hostility have followed the Roma in their North American migrations. They continue to meet discrimination in many sectors, including housing, employment, and criminal justice. The idea of the Roma as rootless is pervasive and has led to results ranging from restrictive zoning to denials of probation.

Many communities have sought to exclude the Roma by enacting laws against "fortune telling," as the ritual of drabarimos—a method of healing to help people achieve a more spiritual way of life—is known to many Roma. A leading police publication advised passage of such laws to "deter Gypsies from inhabiting your community." In 1985, the California Supreme Court invalidated such a ban, and similar decisions have followed elsewhere.

Barry A. Fisher

See also: Racism.

Bibliography

Crowe, David, and John Kolsti, eds. *The Gypsies of Eastern Europe.* Armonk, NY: M.E. Sharpe, Inc., 1991.

Kenrick, Donald, and Grattan Puxon. *The Destiny of Europe's Gypsies.* London: Heinemann-Chatto-Sussex, 1972.

Tebbutt, Susan, ed. *Sinti and Roma: Gypsies in German-Speaking Society and Literature.* New York and Oxford: Berghahn Books, 1998.

U.S. Department of State. *Hungary Country Report on Human Rights Practices for 1998.* Washington, DC: Bureau of Democracy, Human Rights and Labor, 1999.

———. *Romania Country Report on Human Rights Practices for 1998.* Washington, DC: Bureau of Democracy, Human Rights and Labor, 1999.

———. *Slovakia Country Report on Human Rights Practices for 1998.* Washington, DC: Bureau of Democracy, Human Rights and Labor, 1999.

Science and Technology

The development of new sciences and technologies can have a major and often detrimental impact on human rights. While some developments, such as the Internet, may aid the cause of human rights by making more information available to a wider public, many technological advancements pose grave threats to civil liberties. Sophisticated listening and tracking stations around the world, spy satellites that can take pictures accurate almost to the inch with startling clarity, and increased computing power to maintain Internet firewalls and monitor staggering amounts of electronic communications all have the potential to undermine the cause of human rights and endanger basic freedoms.

ELECTRONIC SURVEILLANCE

The United Nations Universal Declaration of Human Rights (1948) states, "No one shall be subjected to arbitrary interference with his privacy, family, home or correspondence, nor to attacks upon his honour and reputation. Everyone has the right to the protection of the law against such interference or attacks" (Article 12). Yet in every country, technology is making it easier to interfere with the right to privacy. There is mounting evidence to suggest that the National Security Agency (NSA) of the United States, in conjunction with intelligence agencies in Canada, England, Australia, and New Zealand, operates a massive computerized information gathering system known as Echelon, which analyzes all electronic communications in every country. Communications via telephone, fax, emails, and radio, captured by a massive array of listening stations and communication satellites, are searched for voice patterns and "keywords." All communications that the system deems suspect are then flagged for further analysis by intelligence personnel within the agencies.

While rumors of the Echelon system have raised hackles in Europe, within the United States Echelon has allegedly been used to arbitrarily monitor both private citizens and "suspect" organizations such as Amnesty International, Greenpeace, and even congressional representatives. These activities violate both the United Nations Declaration of Human Rights and the First, Fourth, and Fifth Amendments of the U.S. Bill of Rights. Congressional oversight of the activities of the NSA, especially in the past two decades, has been sparse. Scattered evidence of Echelon's intrusive activities, along with continual secrecy about the very purpose of the NSA, and constant reports of new surveillance satellites worry private citizens and human rights activists alike.

THE INTERNET

The Internet has been lauded as a new, technologically advanced highway of free speech. Because of its relatively open nature, the Internet presents a particular problem to authoritarian countries such as China, which is trying to make the transition from a centrally planned to a market-based economy, while simultaneously suppressing all forms of dissent within its borders. Traditionally, print and broadcast media are easy targets for suppression—by threatening broadcasters and journalists, Chinese authorities impose a high degree of self-censorship on the national press. Internet content is more difficult to censor and control. In an attempt to do so, the Chinese government increased its monitoring of the Internet in 1999 with some degree of success. Banned web sites in China include foreign news services such as CNN and the BBC, and web sites belonging to persecuted religious factions such as the Falun Gong, a Buddhist offshoot that has been outlawed by the Chinese authorities.

Although information transmitted over the Internet is difficult to censor, it is just as susceptible to surveillance as phone calls or faxes, if not more so. All government agencies with access to telecommunications switchboards can intercept data as they are sent and received. Internet service providers (ISPs) can open and read the emails of their users and allow the authorities to do so. In China and Tunisia, ISPs are compelled to grant server access to their respective governments. These activities on the part of even the most liberal governments present a massive and outright attack of every individual's basic right to privacy, which neither human rights organizations nor representative governments can afford to ignore.

GENETICS

As genetics advances as a science, its possible uses and misuses also become a human rights issue. In 2000, scientists at both the multinational Human Genome Project and a private firm announced decryption of the entire human genome. These new genetic revelations are extremely significant from both a scientific and a human rights standpoint.

Genetics has positive implications for world health. Diseases that cannot be cured today, such as cancer and AIDS, can perhaps be eradicated through the use of genetic manipulation. This same manipulation, however, can be used in ways that violate human rights. As with all new technology, control of genetics will reside within the countries which have developed it—the developed world. If genetics becomes a privatized industry, it is doubtful whether people in areas such as sub-Saharan Africa and central and south Asia, desperately in need of what genetics might produce, will be its beneficiaries. And if they do benefit from such advances, it will likely be long after the rest of the world. People in these areas might even become victims of genetic engineering.

CONCLUSION

Human rights and technology may not be mutually exclusive. Perhaps it is possible to chart a course that minimizes human rights violations and encourages free expression while allowing for technological growth. But the relationship between the interests of science and technology and the interests of human rights remains ambiguous. Vigilance against tyranny must maintain parity with the outermost technological developments if we are to uphold and expand the rights that have been guaranteed to all people.

Eric Busch

See also: Bioethics.

Bibliography

Ball, Desmond, and Jeffrey Richelson. *The Ties That Bind: Intelligence Cooperation Between the UKUSA Countries.* Boston: Allen and Unwin, 1985.

Whitaker, Reg. *The End of Privacy: How Total Surveillance Is Becoming a Reality.* New York: New Press, 1999.

Self-Determination

The right to self-determination is the right of a people to determine their own national status. Those denied the right of self-determination are usually ethnic or national minorities, living within a larger country, that would like either to be independent or to have some degree of autonomy. (Although during the decades after World War II, the main seekers of self-determination were the peoples living in colonies under European control, by 1970, most of these colonies were independent states, and the issue of colonial self-determination had virtually disappeared.) The primary motivation behind the desire for self-determination is usually nationalism.

The United Nations has declared the right to self-determination to be a basic human right. In the United Nations International Covenant on Civil and Political Rights (1976), Article 1 states: "All peoples have the right of self-determination. By virtue of that right they freely determine their political status and freely pursue their economic, social and cultural development." Article 27 adds, "In those States in which ethnic, religious or linguistic minorities exist, persons belonging to such minorities shall not be denied the right, in community with the other members of their group, to enjoy their own culture, to profess and practice their own religion, or to use their own language."

Despite these pronouncements, self-determination is a right more often denied than protected. The reason is clear. When ethnic or national minorities demand the right to self-determination, it suggests that they might wish to break away from the country in which they are currently citizens and create a new country with new borders. This would necessarily make the old, parent country smaller and weaker, and so it is something that most governments tend to resist. In those countries where there is more than one ethnic minority, perhaps even a majority of minorities, allowing each group its right to self-determination might lead to the complete destruction of the state. This is exactly what happened to the old Ottoman and Austrian Empires after World War I, and it also happened to the Soviet Union, causing its collapse in 1991.

Modern movements for self-determination vary widely, as do the reactions to them. In some cases what is desired is outright independence. The reaction to such demands is most often one of severe repression. At other times, an ethnic minority may merely wish for some form of political autonomy—meaning control over some parts of its members' civil and political lives, but usually not extending to such national elements as independent armies or foreign embassies. Sometimes, as in the cases of the Tibetans and the Kurds (discussed elsewhere in this volume), there is no consensus on what the eventual goal of self-determination may be. Some Tibetans, for instance, want outright independence; others are quite willing to settle for limited autonomy under the control of the Chinese government. This ambivalence has done little to aid the cause of those seeking self-determination. Both China and Turkey (the country where most Kurds live) have reacted with equally harsh repression to both those seeking independence and those seeking autonomy.

Sometimes the desire for self-determination breaks out into open warfare. The Chechens, a people living in the Caucasus under Russian control, have long considered themselves an independent people. When the Soviet Union collapsed, they declared their independence. Russia, however, refused to acknowledge their right to self-determination. For two years, from 1994 to 1996, Russian tanks and troops attempted to force Chechnya to give up its dream of independence. After much brutal fighting, which devastated most of Chechnya, the Russian troops left. Chechnya's victory was brief. In 1999, Russian troops returned to finish their conquest. Their repeated bombardments left the Chechen capital of Grozny a complete ruin, with almost no buildings left standing. The fighting continued beyond 2000, with Russia in control of Chechnya's cities and Chechen guerrillas raiding the countryside. Russia's decision to deny Chechens their right to self-determination has left a human rights disaster in Chechnya. Beyond the estimated 150,000 deaths, the Chechen war has turned hundreds of thousands of Chechens into refugees. There are some who suggest that Russian generals wish to destroy Chechnya and its inhabitants to avoid giving it up. If so, this would be genocide, a crime against humanity.

Other movements for self-determination have resulted in more sporadic violence. In the Basque sections of Spain, fighters for ETA (*Euzkadi Ta Azkatasuna*, Basque for "Basque Homeland and Liberty") have carried out a terrorist campaign of assassinations, their targets being Spanish officials and Basques who cooperate with the Spanish. Perhaps as a result of their activities, the Basques have achieved some political autonomy while still remaining under Spanish control. This seems to have satisfied most Basques' desire for self-determination. ETA, which desires full independence, continues to carry out assassinations, but has lost the support of all but the most extreme Basque nationalists.

A more peaceful resolution to the question of self-determination has taken place in Canada. There, the province of Quebec, which has a French-speaking majority, has been able to gain political and economic rights while staying within the Canadian state, which has an English-speaking majority. While there was some violence by French nationalists—particularly during the 1960s—for the most part the process of giving Quebec near-autonomy has been peaceful and has not been strongly resisted by the Canadian government. Today, most French Canadians seem satisfied with the degree of self-determination that they have achieved.

Unfortunately, the peaceful granting of the human right of self-determination to the French in Canada is exceptional. In most of the world, demands for self-determination result in violence and repression, as in Chechnya and Spain. There are dozens of simmering civil wars that result from thwarted desires for self-determination: the Tamil rebellion in Sri Lanka, the Christians in southern Sudan, the Turks in Cyprus, the Palestinians in Israel, among many others. Self-determination remains a right largely confined to powerful majorities and denied to struggling minorities.

Carl Skutsch

See also: Dalai Lama; Indigenous Peoples; Kurds; Minority Rights; Nationality and Citizenship.

Bibliography

Clarke, Desmond M., and Charles Jones. *The Rights of Nations: Nations and Nationalism in a Changing World.* New York: St. Martin's, 1999.

Gall, Carlotta, and Thomas de Waal. *Chechnya: Calamity in the Caucasus.* New York: New York University Press, 1998.

Halperin, Morton H., and David J. Scheffer. *Self-determination in the New World Order.* Washington, DC: Carnegie Endowment for International Peace, 1992.

Kurlansky, Mark. *The Basque History of the World.* New York: Walker, 1999.

Sexual Orientation and Homosexuality

A gay activist, speaking in defense of gay rights, recently wrote that gay rights are human rights "because families are defined by love, not gender. Because hatred is not a family value. Because equal rights are not special rights." These passionate words are not yet universally accepted. The issue of homosexuality and sexual orientation is one of the more controversial for human rights advocates at the beginning of the twenty-first century. Although many writers, religious leaders, and large numbers of the general public believe that sexual orientation and homosexuality should be protected human rights, there is a long tradition of hostility to homosexuality, one that continues to this day and has led to attacks on those with differing sexual orientations.

BACKGROUND

The history of homosexuality is long, as old as that of humanity. Famous homosexual leaders in history include Alexander the Great, Richard the Lionheart, and Frederick the Great; famous homosexual artists and thinkers include Socrates, Leonardo da Vinci, Walt Whitman, Oscar Wilde, Gertrude Stein, Truman Capote, and Andy Warhol. Although homosexuality has been universal in human society, through most of history it has been condemned. Both Judaism and Christianity, for example, have traditionally considered homosexuality a sin, pointing to proscriptions in the Old Testament for justification. There have been societies in which homosexuality was open-ly accepted—that of ancient Greece, for example—but these have been exceptions. Many societies saw homosexuality as a crime against nature and maintained laws condemning homosexuals to imprisonment or even death.

Despite prohibitions against homosexuality, however, many societies have also tolerated homosexuals, particularly those of high social status or political importance. There was often a large difference between the legal and actual risks of homosexuality. In many societies, homosexuality was simply not discussed; its existence was an accepted secret without a label. In the nineteenth century, close friendships between same-sex couples existed and were accepted because many people did not realize they might have a sexual element—and often, of course, they did not. In the late nineteenth and early twentieth centuries, the newborn science of psychiatry defined homosexuality as a mental disorder (a position that the American Psychological Association repudiated in 1974, but is still held by many) and helped bring it into the public spotlight. (It was then that the word "homosexual" began to be used to discuss people who preferred same-sex relationships.) With the rise of awareness of homosexuality came an increase in persecution. Famous trials like that of the playwright Oscar Wilde in 1895 for indecent acts inaugurated a new period of legal and social repression in the West. People exposed as homosexuals could be prosecuted, lose their jobs, and see their lives ruined.

The 1960s saw a backlash by homosexuals angry at violations of their privacy and rights. On June 27, 1969, patrons at the Stonewall Bar in New York City fought back against an attempt by police to arrest them for indecent behavior. The event came to be known as the Stonewall Riots and marks a key date in the gay rights movement. After the Stonewall Riots, homosexuals in the United States, and soon elsewhere as well, fought for their rights, including the right to be called something other than homosexual. Feeling that the word had too much negative history, they opted instead for *gay*, when applied to men, and *lesbian*, when applied to women. As acceptance of gays and lesbians grew, other terms were added to the lexicon of sexual orientation, including *bisexual* (those who pursue sexual relations with members of both sexes) and *transgender* (meaning those who have crossed away from their gender as defined at birth). In recent years, there has been a trend among many activists to use the word *queer* as a catchall for gay, lesbian, bisexual, and transgendered people—a trend that has not been embraced by mainstream gay and lesbian organizations.

SEXUAL ORIENTATION AND INTERNATIONAL ORGANIZATIONS

Gays and lesbians face many threats to their safety, and their human rights are often endangered. They have been murdered by death squads in Brazil, fear the death penalty in many Islamic countries (Iran, Saudi Arabia), and face discrimination in most nations of the world. Only South Africa has a national constitution that explicitly forbids discrimination on the basis of sexual orientation (although many local, state, and city governments, particularly in the United States, have passed legislation protecting gays and lesbians from discrimination).

Robert Filippini and gay activist Yaroslav Mogutin attempted—unsuccessfully—to be married in Moscow, April 1994.

In international law, the rights of gays and lesbians are unprotected. The United Nations does not have an official policy on sexual orientation. Gays and lesbians have no special mention in the Universal Declaration of Human Rights (1948) or any other UN human rights document. There has been some sign of change in the attitude of the United Nations: in 1998, United Nations High Commissioner for Human Rights Mary Robinson (formerly president of Ireland), met with the International Lesbian and Gay Association and discussed the issue of making homosexual rights a part of human rights. Nothing was concluded, but both sides called the meeting successful.

Outside the framework of the United Nations, other multinational institutions have offered some protection to lesbians and gays. Gay and lesbian rights have always been strongest in Europe and North America, with their strong traditions of pluralistic civil societies. Organizations promoting gay and lesbian rights in Asia, the Middle East, Africa, and Latin America have faced the difficulty of overcoming cultures that have historically placed a heavy emphasis on traditional family and sex roles.

In Europe, the European Court of Human Rights has been at the forefront of granting gays and lesbians full human rights. The court, created in 1959, is an outgrowth of the European Convention on Human Rights, ratified in 1950, which itself was an attempt to give institutional substance to the United Nations Universal Declaration of Human Rights. Even though neither the Universal Declaration nor European Convention explicitly defends the rights of homosexuals, the European Court has repeatedly ruled in favor of granting homosexuals the same rights as heterosexuals in many areas. Like many courts around the world, the European Court has based its position on the strong defense of privacy contained in the European Convention on Human Rights, the argument being that interfering in activities of gays and lesbians requires interfering in their right to privacy, a universally accepted human right.

The European Parliament has joined in this stance by passing laws defending the rights of lesbians and gays to live free of persecution. The most important of these was a February 1994 resolution calling on all European countries to grant homosexuals greater legal protection. Article 10 of this resolution called "upon the Member States, together with the national lesbian and homosexual organizations, to take measures and initiate campaigns to combat all forms of social discrimination against homosexuals." All of this falls short of defining human rights as including homosexual rights, but puts Europe ahead of the rest of the world in its defense of the rights of lesbians and gays.

SEXUAL ORIENTATION AND HUMAN RIGHTS WITHIN NATIONS

Discrimination against gays and lesbians varies greatly from country to country. Toleration and acceptance are greatest in Western Europe and North America, and weakest in Asia and South America. There are exceptions to these generalizations: South Africa, under the guidance of Nelson Mandela, ratified a 1996 constitution that outlawed discrimination on the basis of sexual orientation (although in practice much discrimination continues), while Australia has been at the forefront of demanding equal rights for gays and lesbians. In 1996, the Australian minister for foreign affairs, Alexander Downer, said: "I am strongly committed to individuals having the freedom to conduct their lives as they wish so long as that freedom does not impinge upon the freedom of others. I will carry out this commitment as foreign minister by ensuring that in its diplomatic representations abroad and in multilateral fora, Australia continues to oppose the persecution against individuals on the basis of religion, ethnic grouping, or sexual preference."

Nevertheless, despite good examples, much of the world views homosexuality as wrong and does not consider the free choice of sexual partners to be a human right. More than eighty-five countries have laws that declare sexual activity between persons of the same sex illegal. Not all of these laws are enforced—some were passed long ago and simply remain on the books—but they all serve to deny gays and lesbians their basic human rights. And, in some countries, homosexuals are prosecuted. In Romania, for example, gays and lesbians have been put in jail merely for propositioning someone of the same sex. Discrimination goes even further in some nations. President Robert Mugabe of Zimbabwe has made attacks on homosexuals part of his state's official policies. Blaming them for many of Zimbabwe's problems, Mugabe has said that homosexuals have no human rights.

In the United States, the situation is complex. The country is home to one of the world's strongest and most active movements advocating full rights for homosexuals, and gays and lesbians have made much progress. Police no longer arrest people for homosexual activity; many entertainers, and even some politicians, are openly gay; and Americans watch television and movies with positively portrayed openly gay characters. But prejudice against gays and lesbians remains widespread. From locker-room jokes to pronouncements by well-known entertainment or political figures on the nature of homosexuality, gays and lesbians face a constant barrage of attacks on their human rights. Popular radio talk-show host Laura Schlessinger is not alone when she calls homosexuality "deviant" and a "biological error." Similarly, journalist and presidential candidate Patrick Buchanan once announced that he would never hire a homosexual to serve in his cabinet because being gay is "a disorder." These people are part of a strong movement in the United States that wishes to limit or reduce the social acceptance and legal and human rights successes of homosexuals.

Legally, gays have won only limited victories. In 1986, the U.S. Supreme Court ruled that homosexual acts are not protected by the Constitution, thereby allowing some states to maintain laws that criminalized homosexual behavior. And in 1993, in a much-criticized compromise with President Bill Clinton, the U.S. military kept its anti-gay stance by endorsing a policy of "don't ask/don't tell," which supposedly protected gays in the military from being questioned as to their sexual orientation, but allowed the military to discharge them if they publicly admitted to it. The strange result has been an increase in gay soldiers being forcibly discharged from the army and other branches of the U.S. military.

Opponents of the rights of gays and lesbians attack laws giving them rights by saying that "homosexual rights are special rights" (which is also the name of an anti-gay video put out by the Reverend Louis Sheldon's conservative Traditional Values Coalition). Gays and lesbians counter by saying that all they want is human rights, not special rights, but the "special rights" slogan has helped anti–gay rights groups gain ground. While gay and lesbian organizations see the right to marry each other or to adopt children as basic human rights, their opponents disagree. Among other actions, these opponents have managed to get more than thirty states to pass bans on same-sex marriages. (Ironically, one of the accusations hurled at gays has been that they are sexually promiscuous, yet when they wish to be monogamous and marry, conservatives oppose them.)

The high level of prejudice against gays has consequences that go beyond legal discrimination. Individuals, believing that homosexuals are bad or sick, feel authorized to take out their own hatred and aggression on gays that they meet or know. Human rights activists say that this kind of prejudice leads to killings like that of Matthew Shepard, a young Wyoming college student, who, in 1998, was tortured and murdered because he was gay. In a similar 1999 case, Billy Jack Gaither, a thrity-nine-year-old Alabama gay man, had his throat slit, was beaten badly, and then was burned by two men, one of whom, Steven Mullins, said in defense of his acts, "[Gaither] didn't need to live any longer."

Although gays and lesbians have made strides toward full human rights, they still do not have many basic rights enjoyed by heterosexuals. They are not guaranteed the right to marry each other. They are not guaranteed the right to raise children together. They are not guaranteed the right to freedom from discrimination in their place of employment. And as some brutal crimes have shown, they sometimes lack the most basic right of all: the right to life.

Carl Skutsch

See also: AIDS/HIV and Human Rights; Marriage and Family; Privacy.

Bibliography

Duyvendak, Jan Willem. *The Global Emergence of Gay and Lesbian Politics: National Imprints of a Worldwide Movement.* Philadelphia: Temple University Press, 1998.

Miller, Diane Helene. *Freedom to Differ: The Shaping of the Gay and Lesbian Struggle for Civil Rights.* New York: New York University Press, 1998.

Richards, David A. *Identity and the Case for Gay Rights: Race, Gender, Religion as Analogies.* Chicago: University of Chicago Press, 1999.

Wintemute, Robert. *Sexual Orientation and Human Rights: The United States Constitution, the European Convention and the Canadian Charter.* Oxford: Oxford University Press, 1997.

Sikhs

Khalistan is the Sikh name for the Sikh homeland, a region that India calls Punjab. A group of Sikhs declared Khalistan's independence on October 7, 1987. At that time the Council of Khalistan was designated to lead the Sikh struggle for freedom. India refused to acknowledge the Sikh attempt to declare independence.

The population of the Punjab is about two thirds Sikh. The country remains under Indian occupation. There are about 22 million Sikhs worldwide. Fifteen million Sikhs live in Punjab, and there are another three million living elsewhere in India. There are about 500,000 Sikhs living in the United States, and another half a million live in Canada. The United Kingdom about 800,000 Sikhs, the highest concentration outside India.

The Sikh religion is monotheistic. It is not a part of Hinduism, Islam, or any other religion. It was founded by Guru Nanak Dev Ji (1469–1539) in Punjab, in the late fifteenth century. Guru Nanak Dev Ji preached a simple message of devotion to the one God, the creator of the universe. He exhorted his followers to develop inner strength, spiritual awareness, and harmony between the individual self and the universal self. The Sikh religion does not believe in the caste system that is integral to Hinduism. In 1699, the last of the ten Sikh Gurus, Guru Gobind Singh Ji, instituted the Order of the Khalsa Panth. He instituted the "five Ks," the symbols of Sikhism: Kesh (unshorn hair, symbolizing a saintly and natural appearance); Kanga (a special comb for cleanliness of the hair); Kara (a steel bracelet signifying discipline and gentility); Kachh (a special type of undershorts, a sign of chastity); and Kirpan (a sword, an emblem of commitment to justice, truth, freedom, and human dignity). He proclaimed that his mission was to uphold human virtues and destroy the forces of evil and tyranny.

Punjab, or Khalistan, was not historically a part of India. Banda Singh Bahadar established Sikh rule in Punjab in 1710. Sikh rule lasted until the British conquest of 1849. Since the British annexation of the subcontinent in 1849, the Sikh nation has been struggling to regain its sovereignty. Sikhs actively participated in India's independence movement against British imperialism.

When India won its independence in 1947, three nations were to receive sovereign power. The Hindus received India, the Muslims received Pakistan, but the Sikhs were not granted sovereign status and instead were incorporated into India.

Sikhs are seeking self-determination in accordance with Articles 1 and 55 of the United Nations Charter. In violation of these international rights, Indian executive law declares it illegal for Sikhs or any minority group to advocate peacefully for the independence of their homeland. Since 1984, Sikhs who have peacefully advocated an independent Sikh state of Khalistan have risked imprisonment, torture, and even death for themselves and for their families.

The Indian government maintains that Sikhs have never supported an independent Khalistan. Yet it stations 500,000 troops in Punjab, or Khalistan, to suppress the supposedly unpopular freedom movement. India refuses to hold a plebiscite (or vote) to decide the future of the region in a free and fair decree by the people.

At the Sikh nation's 300th anniversary celebration in Washington, D.C., in April 1999, General Narinder Singh and Justice Ajit Singh Bains, Sikh leaders from the region, said that there is no rule of law in Punjab. In July 1997, Narinder Singr, a spokesperson for the Golden Temple in Amritsar, had told an interviewer from the U.S. radio station National Public Radio, "The Indian government, all the time they boast that they are democratic, they are secular, but they have nothing to do with a democracy, they have nothing to do with a secularism. They kill Sikhs just to please the majority."

According to officials of the Punjab State Magistracy, the Indian government murdered more than 200,000 Sikhs from 1984 through 1992. A coalition of human rights groups and journalists reported that the regime killed over 50,000 more Sikhs in 1994 alone. These murders were part of an Indian government campaign to silence the voices of Sikh widows, orphans, and elders who had seen their loved ones lynched, burned alive, tortured in police custody, killed in police encounters, and terrorized by Indian police death-squads.

Amnesty International, Human Rights Watch, and other human rights organizations have documented the genocide against the Sikhs and other minorities by the Indian government. In June 1999, Amnesty International reported that thousands of Sikhs and others remain in illegal detention in India. Many of them have been held since 1984 under the repressive Terrorist and Disruptive Activities Prevention Act, even though it expired in May 1995. This law permitted persons to be held for up to two years without charge, trial, or access to legal counsel.

According to human rights groups, over 50,000 Sikhs have "disappeared." The U.S. State Department's 1999 Country Report on Human Rights Practices condemned India for "serious human rights abuses," including extrajudicial and other political killings; excessive use of force by security forces; torture; rape; and death of suspects in police custody. The 1994 U.S. State Department's Country Report on Human Rights Practices in India stated that between 1991 and 1993, the regime had paid more than 41,000 cash bounties to police officers for killing Sikhs.

The United Nations Working Group on Enforced and Involuntary Disappearances echoed these findings in its January 1998 report, "Question of the Human Rights of All Persons Subjected to Any Form of Detention or Imprisonment; Question of Enforced In-

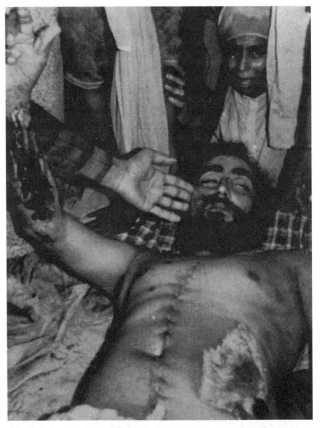

Young Sikh allegedly tortured to death by Indian police.

voluntary Disappearances." The report stated that "all provinces have adopted the practice of not filing arrest reports or registering detentions. Since there are no records, the police are reportedly able to deny holding a detainee." It further noted that "new cases of disappearances continue to be reported to it, and that very few cases on the Working Group's files have been clarified."

The report further stated that "although there has recently been a decrease [from previous years] in incidents of police excesses in the Punjab, including disappearances, human rights workers and activists are said to be subjected to threats and abuses by members of the security forces, including disappearances." *The Hitavada,* an Indian newspaper, reported that the police murdered a three-and-a-half-year-old Sikh boy, who the police then claimed was a "terrorist" killed in an "encounter."

India has not allowed Amnesty International or other independent human rights monitoring organizations into Punjab since 1987. Because of this, news of atrocities against Sikhs emerges very slowly, sometimes months after they occur. However, through internal sources, human rights organizations have been able to document many of the Indian government's violations of human rights in the region.

James R. Lewis

See also: Self-Determination.

Bibliography

Grewal, J. S. *The Sikhs of the Punjab (New Cambridge History of India).* Cambridge: Cambridge University Press, 1998.

Slavery

In the twenty-first century, slavery exists on an unprecedented scale. In fact, in the year 2000, over 27 million people live as slaves. Differing little from their predecessors in bondage, they serve as carpet weavers, sugarcane cutters, camel jockeys, sex slaves, and even as chattel. Chattel slavery is widely practiced in Mauritania and Sudan, and, although it is the most destructive form of slavery, other forms of forced servitude persist around the world.

Under international law the practice of slavery in all its forms is prohibited as specified under the 1948 Universal Declaration of Human Rights. Article 4 states, "No one shall be held in slavery or servitude; slavery and the slave trade shall be prohibited in all their forms." This instrument of law is applicable to all members of the United Nations. The practice of slavery also contravenes International Labor Organization Convention No. 29, which provides for the abolition of forced labor. Article 2 (1) defines forced or compulsory labor as all work "which is extracted from any person under the menace of any penalty and for which the said person has not offered himself voluntarily." Despite these human rights declarations, slavery still goes on.

SLAVERY IN MAURITANIA

Perhaps the most shocking cases of contemporary slavery occur in Mauritania and Sudan. In contrast to Sudan, in Mauritania slavery has existed for over 700 years. Though successive governments outlawed slavery three times, as many as one million slaves still suffer in Mauritania. These slaves come from the lowest of the country's three social classes. The ancestors of these black slaves were the sole inhabitants of Mauritania until the year 1300, when white Arab-Berbers swept into the northwest African nation and seized control, enslaving the local blacks. Though most of the conquered people converted to Islam, the religion of their captors, the racial distinctions have made slavery a continued reality for the descendents of Mauritania's black population.

The Mauritanian slave system is deeply embedded in the cultural and political heritage of that nation. Arabs of every social class possess slaves to perform the routine, manual tasks required to support the household. These slaves have been told from birth that slavery is their ordained position. Many truly believe that serving their masters is their religious duty. A slave's infractions, no matter how minor, are severely punished. For trivial misdeeds, the slave might be beaten with a wet cord while naked, denied food and drink, or bound and exposed to the desert sun. More severe tortures, however, await the slave who greatly displeases his master. Such punishments might include burning coals applied to the inner thighs and genitals or the "insect treatment," which involves stuffing the miscreant slave's ears full of insects and sealing them with stones and a headscarf. The slave's hands and feet are tied, and the individual is left to suffer for several days. Often, he is reduced to insanity.

SLAVERY IN SUDAN

In 1987 non-governmental organizations reported slavery's reemergence in Sudan. Since 1992 international organizations, including the United Nations and the International Labor Organization, have issued reports on this human rights violation in Sudan. The United Nations Commission on Human Rights Resolution 1997 (59) stated that it was "deeply concerned about continued reports of slavery, servitude, the slave trade and forced labor, the sale and trafficking of children and their abduction and forced internment, often at undisclosed locations . . . ideological indoctrination or cruel, inhuman, and degrading punishments, especially but not exclusively affecting displaced families and women and children belonging to racial, ethnic, and religious minorities" from southern Sudan, the Nuba Mountains, and the Ingassema Hills areas.

The 1996 UN Special Rapporteur on Sudan, Dr. Gaspar Biro, said, "The total passivity of the government after having received information for years regarding this situation can only be interpreted as tacit political approval and support of the institution of slavery."

In 1996, the National Islamic Front–backed government of Lieutenant-General Omar Hassan al-Bashir, which had seized power from the democratically elected government in a military coup in 1989, responded to international pressure on the issue of slavery by establishing investigative committees, while simultaneously denying that it existed in the country. Today the government remains deliberately blind to the problem of slavery in Sudan.

Although there are no precise figures on the number of people enslaved in Sudan,

it is estimated to be many thousands, and continuing reports confirm that slavery persists, primarily as a result of Sudan's ongoing civil war.

Slavery is not new in Sudan. Until the early twentieth century the country was an active participant in the slave trade. For centuries Turko-Egyptian traders as well as Sudanese from the north raided villages in the south, particularly those in the southwestern region of Bahr al-Ghazal, one of the main centers for slave raiding. Slavers would catch people and beat them. They would then tie them together and walk or ship them to their destinations to be sold as domestic workers, farm laborers, soldiers, or concubines in the north or abroad to Egypt, Libya, and other surrounding countries.

Influenced by the European drive to abolish slavery, Egypt, which ruled Sudan in the nineteenth century, closed the slave markets in the Sudanese city of Khartoum in 1860 and developed a military fashioned on the European model, which was not dependent on slaves for soldiers. The move to end slavery advanced in August 1877 with the adoption of the Anglo-Egyptian Slave Trade Convention, which pledged to prohibit the sale and purchase of slaves in Sudan by 1880. By the time Sudan became independent in 1956, slavery had effectively died out.

Slavery was reborn during the civil war, which began in 1983. Rebels in the south, consisting mainly of black Christians, animists, and Muslims, took up arms against the largely Arab Muslim north, which controlled the government. Fighting was brutal, and the government-assisted militias launched fierce campaigns against the Dinka, southern Sudan's largest ethnic group, in Bahr al-Ghazal Province. War and widespread famine killed a staggering 1.5 million people, and many villagers, displaced and defenseless, became victims of a new kind of slave trader. Soldiers, officers, and militiamen loyal to the northern government conducted a massive slave trade involving black Africans of southern Sudan. The majority of those enslaved in the late twentieth and early twenty-first centuries are Dinka. As in the nineteenth century, most slaves come from the northeastern part of Bahr al-Ghazal Province, although some also come from other wartorn areas.

Women and children captured in raids have been forced to walk to southern Darfur and southern Kordofan to be used as farm laborers and domestic workers or to be sold. Unlike the wealthy slave holders of the nineteenth century, the contemporary equivalent is a small farmer owning a few dozen acres of land or a small herd of cattle or camels. Since the National Islamic Front seized power in 1989, most of the captors are government-armed militias. Members of the Popular Defense Force, a government paramilitary unit created in 1990, along with some regular army officers, are known to be involved in slave raids.

Because slaves are rarely freed with the help of police or the courts, the Dinka have developed a "retrieval committee" to free women and children. Through fundraising among the southern community in Sudan and accumulating evidence of slave catching to bring to the attention of the state government of Darfur, the committee has had several successes, including the release of 103 children who had been captured in December 1989.

In the mid-1990s, several foreign organizations started to pay "ransoms" or "re-demptions" for the release of slaves. This involved paying agents to visit areas in which captives are held and secure their release, and then accompany them back to Dinka-controlled areas. This practice has been internationally criticized by a number of organizations, including Anti-Slavery International, as possibly helping to perpetuate the cycle of slavery, rather than ending it.

When the United Nations Commission on Human Rights agreed in April 1999 to abandon its criticism of "slavery" and refer instead to "abductions" and "forced labor," the Sudanese government responded by establishing the Committee for the Eradication of Abduction of Women and Children. Its mandate is to investigate reports of abductions of women and children, the causes of such abductions, and to release the women and children affected. By early 2000, it had secured some releases, but had done nothing to punish slave-holders. Thousands of Dinka still remain enslaved.

TROKOSI SLAVERY

A trokosi is a virgin girl who is dedicated (married) to a priest as a penance for a crime committed by a member of her family. The girl then spends the rest of her life as a trokosi. When she dies, the family must dedicate another virgin to the priest to continue paying for the crime, which, in some cases, was committed generations earlier. Girls are also given to the priest to please the gods, as ill fortune and sickness may have afflicted the family. The system of trokosi dates back hundreds of years. It continues today in Ghana, Togo, Nigeria, and Benin, although it is most prevalent among the Ewe people of Ghana. In 1998 the locally based non-governmental organization International Needs Ghana estimated that 4,000 women were enslaved in shrines in the Volta and Greater Accra Regions of Ghana alone.

Some girls are given to the priest when they are age ten or younger. Once they are trokosi, they must farm, cook, and clean for the priest, receiving no money for their labor and depriving them of their right to an education. Their only source of income is their family, although in many cases these families are too poor to provide support.

Once the girls reach puberty, they are forced to sleep with the priest, often becoming pregnant when they are twelve or fourteen years old. The girls end up looking after their children themselves. Even though they labor for the priest, they do not receive money from him. By the time the women have reached middle age, the priest either keeps them in the shrine or allows them to leave. However, even if they leave, they are unable to remarry because they are trokosi and remain married to the priest.

The system of trokosi is illegal both internationally and in Ghana. It violates all the United Nations conventions, which apply to human rights, the right to education, children's rights, women's rights, labor rights, and marriage rights. Even though Ghana has ratified all these treaties, the practice continues, and many Ghanaian officials do little to enforce the law against the practice. Ghana is also a signatory to the African Charter on Human and Peoples' Rights, which specifies that "particular traditional practices, which are injurious to the health and well-being of a person, are abolished."

The trokosi system is not as prevalent as it was several years ago, and growing pressure has led to the release of the girls from the shrines. To gain the release of these girls and women, International Needs Ghana is paying compensation to the priests for their loss of earnings. Abolition remains difficult, however, as this system is deeply rooted in traditional belief, involving both priests who enslave girls and the families that dedicate their daughters to the shrines. As one ex-trokosi said: "I was not old, just about ten years old, when I was sent to a shrine. I asked my parents why I should leave them to stay at a different place. They gave the reason that it was understood that they have offended the fetish at our place and unless I am sent there the whole family would die and my going there would close the gate of death."

CHILD SLAVERY IN ASIA

In India, Pakistan, and Nepal, slavery primarily takes the form of bonded child labor. Though these children work in similar conditions to other child laborers, they are neither paid wages nor allowed to leave. They are, therefore, slaves. These child slaves serve in their masters' factories, usually as carpet weavers. Some children are ostensibly paid a small salary, but they rarely see it. The children report poor treatment and inadequate food. They suffer from a variety of lung diseases triggered by dust from the carpets, and their eyesight steadily declines from performing tedious tasks in dark rooms. Furthermore, the sharp instruments used in carpet weaving often mutilate the children's hands. Many of the children's masters acquired them through an underground slave trade. Slavers kidnap village children, taking them to sell on the black market in the larger cities.

Other children serve as debt-bondage slaves. Because their families are unable to pay outstanding debts, creditors take the children as payment. These child slave laborers work for years to pay their family's debts; often, no records are kept, and their debt is never cancelled. They remain in bondage for many years. One of the best known of these child slaves was Iqbal Masih, a Pakistani carpet weaver who traveled throughout the West to tell his story. Masih was assassinated upon his return to Pakistan.

In other parts of Asia, children serve as concubines and sex slaves, kept by the owners of brothels to grant sexual favors to Western and Japanese men. These men make sex trips to certain Asian countries—particularly Thailand—to obtain pedophilic sex without significant fear of recrimination. Several hundred thousand children, some as young as eight years old, are enslaved in this way. The brothel owners control them, retain their wages, and give them only the bare essentials of survival. Like the bonded child laborers, many of those sex slaves were attained through the underground, the black market, or through debt bondage. Slave owners purchased others, however, from destitute parents, relatives, or even friends. Some children were sold or exchanged for modern conveniences, such as a television, videocassette recorder, or automobile. Other children were promised good jobs with fair wages by employment agencies.

Recently, child sex slavery in Thailand acquired an international dimension. With the worldwide growth of AIDS and other sexually transmitted diseases, Asian prostitution was in decline. To combat this trend, brothel owners started to acquire younger children to serve as prostitutes. Because these smaller children are less likely to be infected with diseases like AIDS, they are considered "safer" for the sex pa-

trons. In order to obtain more inexperienced and younger children, Thai brothels owners now kidnap and purchase younger children from the surrounding nations of Myanmar (Burma), China, and Cambodia. Though some of the children held as sex slaves have been freed, rehabilitation has been extremely difficult. Experts say that sexual exploitation has proved even more traumatizing to children than war.

Many of today's slaves live in Africa or Asia and a large number are children, yet slavery is not exclusively limited by geography or age. It extends into the Western Hemisphere and includes people of every age and gender. In the Dominican Republic, sugar plantation workers and even police arrest Haitian men and take them to shantytowns to cut sugarcane for Dominican landowners. The masters confiscate their men's belongings and give them machetes to cut sugarcane. In order to be given even small meals of dried fish and rice, the Haitians must work in the cane fields. Though these slaves are ostensibly paid a small sum—$2.00 per ton—many of them never see this money. Escape attempts are punishable by death, forcing most Haitians to remain on the plantation throughout the sugar harvest season.

CHILD TRAFFICKING IN WEST AND CENTRAL AFRICA

According to a conference organized in 2000 by the United Nations Children's Fund (UNICEF) and the International Labor Organization on child trafficking in West and Central Africa, this region is active in the selling of children for forced labor and other purposes. The rise in the regional trade in human beings since the early 1990s is largely due to poverty, the easing of trade and labor restrictions between countries, and rapid population growth.

Child trafficking refers to the transport of a child from one place to another, whether within or across national borders, where the trafficker experiences economic or any other form of gain resulting from this movement. This process can be described as a transaction regardless of whether money was exchanged at the time the child was handed over. In 1998 UNICEF identified several types of trafficking in West and Central Africa. These include the abduction of children for sale by traffickers at a later date, trafficking for embezzlement, whereby the trafficker places the children in employment and benefits from receipt of their wages, and "bonded placement." In the case of bonded placement the amount spent in transporting the children to their place of work, as well as that spent on maintenance is deducted from their pay, meaning that the children receive no money for their labor.

Children as young as eight years old from Benin, Burkina Faso, Ghana, Mali, Nigeria, and Togo are trafficked to Congo, Côte d'Ivoire, Equatorial Guinea, and Gabon. According to UNICEF's 1998 report on the trafficking of child domestic workers, the number of children intercepted at the Benin border rose from 117 in 1995 to 802 in 1997.

Once in the "receiver" country these children are forced to work in various fields: on agricultural plantations, in fishing, as market traders, and as domestic servants, beggars, and prostitutes. The majority of those bought and sold along these routes are young girls. Girls are preferred because they are considered less likely than boys to rebel and more suitable for domestic work. In many cases, they are also expected to move away from the family home soon after puberty.

Traffickers or brokers usually approach poor families in which parents are struggling to feed, clothe, and educate their children. The prospect of having their children learn a trade, as promised by some brokers, induces parents to give the brokers their children in return for money. In some cases, however, children are themselves tricked or abducted by the brokers. In some cases those trafficked have achieved the income or training they were promised, but this is rare and only serves to blind parents to the risks involved.

The journeys involved can be dangerous, and there have been reports of children dying along the route, particularly when traveling by sea. One child in Gabon told of running out of food and water and being forced to drink seawater.

Those who survive these brutal voyages are subjected to harsh living and working conditions at their destination. Basic food, health, sanitation, and clothing needs are not met, and sometimes the children are not paid for their labor. In addition they are vulnerable to physical, psychological, and sexual abuse.

The effect of trafficking on children is devastating. Apart from these deprivations, they are in danger of being cut off from their roots and losing contact with both their families and their culture. They are denied the fundamental rights of education and recreation crucial to their social and psychological development. Many never return home and are trafficked more than once. Even when they do manage to return to their villages, they face difficulties in adjusting.

Despite its growth there are international conventions prohibiting child trafficking that have been ratified by most of the countries where it is found. These include the United Nations Convention on the Rights of the Child; the International Labor Organization's Convention No. 29; the United Nations Supplementary Convention on the Abolition of Slavery, the Slave Trade, and of Institutions and Practices Similar to Slavery; and the Organization of African Unity's African Charter on the Rights and Welfare of the Child.

Anti-Slavery International, Holland Webb, Carron Sommerset

See also: Child Labor; Child Pornography; Debt Bondage; Mauritania; Prostitution (Forced).

Bibliography

Adihou, Alain Francois. *The Trafficking of Children Between Benin and Gabon.* London: Anti-Slavey International, 1999.

Bales, Kevin. *Disposable People: New Slavery in the Global Economy.* Berkeley: University of California Press, 1999.

Verney, Peter. *Slavery in Sudan.* London: Anti-Slavery International, 1997.

State of Emergency

The framers of the United Nations human rights documents recognized that, during a state of emergency, authorities might need to limit certain human rights until the emergency is over. This partial suspension is usually referred to as a *derogation*, a term that refers to a treaty violation (the International Covenant on Civil and Political Rights [ICCPR] and the International Covenant on Economic, Social and Cultural Rights—both core human rights agreements—are technically treaties). Article 4(1) of the ICCPR specifies the scope of a possible derogation of human rights during such an emergency. This provision also notes that certain rights cannot be derogated and specifies that nations that officially declare a state of emergency must duly inform other nations participating in the ICCPR through the secretary-general of the United Nations.

Despite the cautious manner in which the ICCPR set limits to states of emergency, there was still concern about the way in which a government's declaration of a public emergency might be used as a pretext for abridging human rights. All too often, a state of emergency becomes permanent and even institutionalized, particularly in the case of political opponents of the ruling party who are locked up without due process. In 1969, the European Commission of Human Rights set forth more explicit criteria for determining whether a given crisis might merit the declaration of a state of emergency:

1. It [the emergency] must be actual or imminent.
2. Its effects must involve the whole nation.
3. The continuance of the organized life of the community must be threatened.

The crisis or danger must be exceptional, in that the normal measures or restrictions permitted by the Convention for the maintenance of public safety, health, and order are plainly inadequate.

The only problematic item here is the second one, which seems to imply that the whole nation must be engulfed in crisis before an emergency can be declared. Subsequent discussion has clarified that this was not the intention behind the "whole nation" criterion and that a crisis meriting the declaration of a state of emergency can exist in only one part of a country.

James R. Lewis

See also: Derogation.

Bibliography

Buergenthal, Thomas. "To Respect and to Ensure: State Obligations and Permissible Derogations." In Louis Henkin, ed., *The International Bill of Rights: The Covenant on Civil and Political Rights.* New York: Columbia University Press, 1981.

Terrorism

On the face of it, it might appear that terrorism—the indiscriminate use of violence to achieve political ends—almost by definition involves human rights violations. This is especially clear in cases of state terrorism, in which governments employ terrorism against their own citizens.

The definition of terrorist, however, is often in dispute. German forces occupying conquered territories during World War II referred to partisan guerrillas as "terrorists." The allies saw these guerrillas—quite rightly—as freedom fighters. Not all cases of mislabeling are so clear. Terrorist or freedom fighter, the lines are not always so easy to draw as they were in World War II. How different is the situation of World War II partisans from contemporary groups like Palestinian guerrillas (also labeled terrorists) struggling against Israeli occupation forces? This is not, of course, to equate these two struggles but, rather, to make the point that terrorism admits to a certain ambiguity—an ambiguity succinctly captured in the expression "One man's terrorist is another man's freedom fighter."

Such ambiguity derives, at least partially, from a conflict between different sets of rights. This conflict, in turn, finds expression in different United Nations (UN) documents. On the one hand, the core documents of the International Bill of Rights stress the right of individuals to enjoy freedom from fear—the very hallmark of terrorism—and various UN bodies have issued formal resolutions condemning terrorism, such as the UN Commission on Human Rights in Resolution 1994/46; the Sub-Commission on Prevention of Discrimination and Protection of Minorities in Resolution 1994/18; and the General Assembly, in Resolutions 48/122 and 49/185. On the other hand, the United Nations has also strongly supported the right of peoples to self-determination (e.g., the Declaration on the Granting of Independence to Colonial Countries and Peoples, adopted by the General Assembly in 1960), a right that appears to legitimate at least certain kinds of armed insurrections, particularly by clearly defined ethnic groups within a larger nation-state.

Such insurgencies, however, almost inevitably involve terrorist acts. Because so many of the countries that joined the UN in the decades immediately following World War II had only recently thrown off the colonial yoke, there was little support for anti-terrorist resolutions that could be interpreted as condemning nationalist movements. This was still the situation in 1972, following the Munich Olympics massacre, when Secretary-General Kurt Waldheim asked the United Nations to respond to terrorism. Because the representatives of so many member states tended to view "terrorism" as a colonialist label for anti-colonialist struggles, the most the UN General Assembly was able to agree upon was the 1973 Convention on the Prevention and Punishment of Crimes Against Internationally Protected Persons, Including Diplomatic Agents. It is no coincidence that it was a different body, representing nations with a longer history of political independence, namely the Council of Europe, that was able to ratify a Convention on the Suppression of Terrorism in 1977.

The support for revolutionary struggles diminished, however, as the emergent nations became established and began to experience their own internal insurgencies. As a consequence, international opinion shifted so that by the final decade of the twentieth century, the UN began issuing strong condemnations of terrorism—condemnations such as those contained in the resolutions mentioned earlier. However, this new consensus merely obscures, rather than resolves, the tensions between competing sets of human rights.

One suggestion for addressing terrorism is to use actions that would be regarded as war crimes in an international armed conflict as criteria for distinguishing terrorism from legitimate insurgencies. In other words, groups that confined their attacks to military targets would be freedom fighters, while groups that attacked civilians would be terrorists. This criterion, however, ignores the fact that the very nature of an insurgency consists in the fact that most insurgents simply do not have the equipment, training, or manpower to face a conventional military force. This criterion also ignores the fact that in modern warfare, civilian populations are routinely targeted—such as in the massive bombing campaigns associated with World War II and the Vietnam War—as a way of demoralizing the enemy. How different is this reasoning from the rationale behind a terrorist attack? To apply the terrorist label to small, contemporary insurgencies but not to the bombings of Dresden and suburban Tokyo during World War II, and to the bombing of North Vietnamese villages during the Vietnam War, can seem to some to be hypocritical and self-serving.

Hence, the effort to apply war crimes criteria to this issue ultimately breaks down, and it is likely that any other attempt to formulate objectivist criteria would be frustrated as well. Perhaps the paradox of terrorism is merely part of the paradox of war in general. Terrorism may be a human rights violation to the same extent that all wars are human rights violations.

James R. Lewis

See also: War; War Crimes.

Bibliography

Crenshaw, Martha, and John Pimlott, eds. *Encyclopedia of World Terrorism.* Armonk, NY: Sharpe Reference, 1997.

Ratner, Steven R. and Jason S. Abrams. *Accountability for Human Rights Atrocities in International Law: Beyond the Nuremberg Legacy.* New York: Oxford University Press, 1997.

Torture

According to the United Nations Convention Against Torture (1984), torture is "any act by which severe pain or suffering, whether physical or mental, is intentionally inflicted on a person for such purposes as obtaining from her or a third person information or a confession, punishing him for an act he or a third person has committed or is suspected of having committed, or intimidating or coercing him or a third person, or for any reason based on discrimination of any kind, when such pain or suffering is inflicted by or at the instigation of or with the consent or acquiescence of a public official or other person acting in an official capacity." In other words, torture is the deliberate use of pain by a government employee for officially sanctioned purposes.

Although the Convention Against Torture defines torture and called upon all nations to prevent torture, the United Nations Universal Declaration of Human Rights had already outlawed it in 1948. Article 5 of that Declaration states: "No one shall be subjected to torture or to cruel, inhuman or degrading treatment or punishment." Unfortunately, the United Nations Declaration had proved to be ineffective at preventing torture, as has the more recently passed Convention Against Torture. This central human right, the right to be safe from torture, remains ignored, and every year, people around the world continue to be tortured. Some are tortured in countries with authoritarian governments, which have little respect for human rights. More shockingly, torture also goes on in advanced democracies, sometimes sanctioned by the government, sometimes allowed through inaction. And torture seems likely to continue unabated.

BACKGROUND

Torture is as old as government. The ancient Romans and Greeks both used torture. According to early Roman law, only slaves could be tortured, but eventually free people were also subject to torture. In early modern Europe, torture was commonly used to gain confessions in criminal cases. During the Enlightenment, inspired by the humanitarian ideas of the eighteenth century, Europeans began to outlaw the use of torture. By 1800, torture was almost unheard of in Europe. But in the twentieth century it made a terrible comeback—first under the totalitarian governments of Adolf Hitler and Joseph Stalin—and later spreading to the rest of the world.

Torture was not limited to dictatorships. In the mid-twentieth century, democratic France used torture in attempts to crush the Algerian and Vietnamese independence movements. (It appears that it is easier to torture those who are different from the mainstream of a society, particularly those of another race or ethnicity; blinded by racism, the torturers may not see the victims as completely human.) Likewise, democratic Great Britain used torture in its campaigns to stop Catholic resistance in Northern Ireland.

The twentieth century saw changes in the techniques of torture. While in the past the emphasis had been on inflicting raw pain, modern torturers developed more subtle methods. Sleep deprivation became one of

Man tortured by the Haitian Army, left lying in the street as an example to others, October 1988.

the favored torture methods. Police and military torturers discovered that by working in rotation they could keep a prisoner awake for days. People who have been awake for that long tend to lose connection with reality and become delusional. They may then confess the desired information. This method was called "the conveyer belt" by Stalinist torturers, and it has the advantage of causing great suffering without leaving any marks on the victim's body. Still, although the use of the conveyer belt and other psychological tools increased, old-fashioned pain infliction continued to be used by torturers around the world.

RECENT TORTURE

One of the problems with torture is defining it. Some examples of torture are clear:

physical pain directly and deliberately inflicted usually qualifies as torture. But what of conditions that are horrible but do not involve the direct infliction of pain? Jamming dozens of men into a cell designed to fit only a few may not fit a dictionary definition of torture, but it surely subjects them to "inhuman or degrading treatment," to quote the Universal Declaration of Human Rights.

Sleep deprivation is not the only innovation in the field of torture. Modern torturers also use humiliation. They shower their victims with constant verbal abuse, scream in their faces, and then refuse to let them use the toilet. Soiled with their own urine and feces, the humiliated victims feel their self-esteem disappear and become willing to do anything or confess to anything their torturers desire. Also common in modern torture is the use of a bag tied around the victim's head. This serves the double purpose of having the prisoner feel increasingly alone and isolated—which can help break down resistance—as well as shielding the identity of the torturers, which they hope will prevent any legal repercussions in countries where torture is supposed to be illegal.

Another form of torture common in the twentieth century has been rape. Soldiers or militiamen rape their prisoners, usually women, as a means of humiliating them and destroying their self-esteem. The purpose of rape is rarely to gain information; it is more often part of some general campaign of intimidation, such as ethnic cleansing. During the Bosnian conflict (1992–1995), there were repeated reports of large-scale rapes carried out, usually on Bosnian Muslim women, by Serbian militiamen.

Torture does not exist only in war zones or under repressive dictatorships. In the 1980s, police departments around the United States were accused of using torture. In New Orleans, suspects had their heads covered with plastic bags and were then hit with telephone books. In New York, police used stun guns, which cause agonizing pain and burn marks, in their attempts to gain confessions from suspects.

If torture occurs in the United States occasionally, it remains commonplace elsewhere. Turkey has been constantly criticized by the international community for its use of torture in its war against Kurdish insurgents. Amnesty International claims that torture in Turkey is "routine and systematic."

Israel is another democratic country that has been accused of tolerating torture. In a well-publicized 1988 incident, a group of Israeli soldiers were ordered to arrest some Palestinian civilians, residents of a village called Hawara, and break their arms and legs. No reason was given, except the need to intimidate other Palestinians and perhaps thereby encourage them to behave better. The soldiers obeyed their orders. At a subsequent court-martial, one of the soldiers described their actions as follows: "We covered their mouths in order not to arouse provocation. We wanted to break limbs as quickly as possible and as quietly as possible. . . . The officer gave orders. . . . There were four soldiers for every prisoner. . . . After a few seconds of beating most of them stopped screaming. After a half minute of beating they were no longer conscious. We took the scarves out of their mouths, broke the handcuffs, and left the field." The Palestinians, limbs broken, were left to lie unconscious in the open field. Only one Israeli officer was court-martialed for the Hawara beatings, but he was given no prison sentence.

According to Amnesty International, more than two thirds of the world's nations use torture or something approaching torture in their treatment of prisoners. Nations that are highlighted for their particularly egregious use of torture include China, Colombia, Turkey, and Russia. In China, electroshock is used, particularly on Tibetans who resist China's control of Tibet. Tibetan monks have electric prods applied to their ears, teeth, and genitalia, causing excruciating pain. Electroshock devices are favored by torturers because, if used properly, they tend to leave few if any marks.

Amnesty International has also alleged that the use in the United States of electroshock devices and pepper spray to punish prisoners is tantamount to torture. The group draws a line here between the use of such devices to subdue someone who is unrestrained and a possible threat and the use of these devices on prisoners who are handcuffed or tied onto a chair and is therefore no threat to anyone. In the latter case, the only reason for the pain is punishment, and therefore it qualifies as torture.

TORTURE JUSTIFIED

Governments always find reasons to justify torture. In the 1970s, British government officials denied that suspected Irish guerrillas had been tortured, but admitted that they had been subjected to "rough" treatment. The officials justified this not-quite-torture by saying it was necessary to fight the evil of terrorism. Many people, fearful of Irish Republican Army bombs, were willing to accept this argument. Better that someone else be tortured, their thinking went, than that I risk being bombed, even though I should know that sometimes the wrong person, an innocent person, is caught and tortured. The same blinkered attitudes supported the French policy of torture in Algeria in the 1950s and the American use of torture in Vietnam in the 1960s.

During the cold war, many Americans accepted that extreme methods, including torture, might be necessary to fight the threat of communism. In 1946, the American military established the School of the Americas in Georgia, the purpose of which was to train Latin American soldiers in counter-insurgency methods so they could better oppose leftist guerrillas in their own countries. One of the techniques taught by the school's American instructors was torture. The school became infamous in the 1970s and 1980s for training soldiers from Central and South American countries to use all possible means to suppress their opponents. The Defense Department eliminated torture from the curriculum in 1991 and, in 2000, renamed the school the Defense Institute for Hemispheric Security Cooperation.

THE TORTURER

Individuals justify their role as torturers in differing ways. Usually they are not responsible for giving the orders to torture and so can pass the blame to those in authority above them. On the other hand, those in authority can feel less guilty because they themselves are not actually carrying out the torture. A lengthy chain of command makes torture much easier for all the participants.

Torturers are usually portrayed as evil fiends, but most are ordinary people who see themselves as merely doing their jobs. Their victims were guilty, or might be guilty, and it was their job to discover the truth, or punish, or do whatever else they were told.

The idea that only evil men can commit torture was dispelled by the 1960s experiments of Stanley Milgram, a Yale psychologist. Milgram approached ordinary men on the street and asked them to apply electric shocks to other men if they failed to answer certain questions correctly. Most of the men complied, even when their victims were screaming in pain. (The pain was simulated; there were no real shocks given, but the men applying the shocks in the experiment did not know this.) The subjects were not guards, soldiers, or law enforcement personnel; rather, they were ordinary men who had received no special orientation that might have made them insensitive to the treatment of prisoners. Milgram later experimented on women, with equally disturbing results. Milgram's experiments suggested that many people are capable of inflicting torture.

CONCLUSION

Torture is an extreme violation of a person's human rights, perhaps the most extreme violation short of murder. Instinctively most people recognize the inherent inhumanity of torture. It is a universally accepted violation of human rights, and yet it continues, causing incalculable damage to countless victims. The victims suffer during the process; and then they and their families spend years trying to recover from the psychological scars. Until torture is outlawed in practice as well as in theory, this suffering will continue.

Carl Skutsch

See also: Apartheid; Genocide; Kurds; Martin Luther King, Jr.; Universal Declaration of Human Rights; War; War Crimes.

Bibliography

Conroy, John. *Unspeakable Acts, Ordinary People: The Dynamics of Torture.* New York: Knopf, 2000.

Innes, Brian. *The History of Torture.* New York: St. Martin's, 1998.

Weschler, Lawrence. *A Miracle, a Universe: Settling Accounts with Torturers.* Chicago: University of Chicago Press, 1998.

Totalitarian Ideologies

Governments that follow totalitarian ideologies seek complete control over the lives of all individuals living in a society. The word *totalitarism* was coined in the twentieth century to describe systems such as fascist Italy, Nazi Germany, and the Soviet Union. Totalitarian states are usually distinguished from mere authoritarian states by the degree of control they seek to gain.

Authoritarian states—traditional dictatorships—merely wish to maintain a monopoly of political authority; what their citizens do in their private lives is unimportant to traditional dictators. Totalitarian states wish to control ever aspect of their citizens' lives. There is no "private" in a totalitarian society. Motivated by an ideology which they deem more important than anything else—whether it is Adolf Hitler's belief in the destiny of the master race, or Joseph Stalin's belief in the inevitable spread of communism—they are willing to sacrifice everything, particularly the rights and lives of their citizens, to achieve their goals.

HISTORY

Benito Mussolini was the first of the twentieth-century totalitarian leaders. In the gloom following World War I, he organized an Italian political party he called the *Fasci di Combattimento* ("group of fighters"). It was dedicated to bringing pride back to the Italian people after the humiliations of the war. Mussolini emphasized the importance of loyalty to the nation, strength, and unity. He ridiculed democracy as being weak and ineffectual, while he attacked communism (which was on the rise in the 1920s) as

being a threat to national unity. Backed by crowds of violent supporters, Mussolini came to power in Italy in 1922.

The transformations he made of Italian society were largely unplanned. He had prepared no blueprints in advance for his future fascist state. Nevertheless, Mussolini's dictatorship would become the model for the other totalitarian systems. He outlawed all other political parties, declaring the Fascist Party to be the only legal party. All organizations, public or private, were forced to put themselves under state control or supervision. As Mussolini put it, "All within the state, none outside the state, none against the state." Under this system, the individual existed to serve the state.

This central philosophical attitude of fascism—which it shares with all totalitarian ideologies—is directly opposed to the traditions of personal liberty that grew out of the European Enlightenment. Seventeenth- and eighteenth-century writers, such as John Locke, Voltaire, and Thomas Jefferson, emphasized the rights of the individual. In their eyes, the purpose of the state was to serve the needs of the individual. Fascism and other totalitarian ideologies argue the opposite. And because the state is more important than any person under its control, concepts such as private life and individual rights are discarded.

Although Mussolini was the first modern totalitarian leader, he was surpassed in ruthlessness by two other twentieth-century totalitarian dictators: Adolf Hitler and Joseph Stalin. Hitler's Nazi Party, which came to power in 1933, was similar to Mussolini's Fascist Party, in that it emphasized nationalism and duty of the individual to serve the state. Nazism, however, also incorporated a belief in the racial destiny of the Germans and the necessity of destroying their racial enemy, the Jews. These beliefs, combined with the total control Hitler and the Nazis gained over Germany, led them to kill 6 million Jews during World War II, as well as millions of other people whom they deemed racially unfit.

Stalin, on the other hand, was not a nationalist or a racist; he claimed to be a communist and to be serving the will of the working people of the Soviet Union. In reality, however, Stalin's Soviet Union was closer in spirit to Nazi Germany than it was to the ideas of Karl Marx. Like Hitler, Stalin, who ruled the Soviet Union from the 1920s until his death in 1953, used his secret police to hunt down enemies—or people he thought might be enemies—herd them into camps, and kill millions of them.

HUMAN RIGHTS SIGNIFICANCE

At the beginning of the twenty-first century, it is difficult to point out many true totalitarian states. North Korea almost certainly qualifies; Saddam Hussein's Iraq may; and many would also call Fidel Castro's Cuba totalitarian. However, even though totalitarianism is not the threat that it once was, its ideas are constantly being borrowed by other oppressive regimes to enforce their rule and abuse their people.

Perhaps the most important element in totalitarian systems is the secret police, and the twenty-first century is still filled with countries who use secret police to enforce government control. The use of torture also

Giant mural glorifying Saddam Hussein at the Saddam Airport in Baghdad.

remains widespread, and not just in dictatorships. Democracies like Israel have been accused of torturing prisoners in the name of state security. Others, like the United States, in the name of fighting against terrorism or high crime rates, have passed laws reducing the defense of individuals against state prosecutions and death penalty convictions. An element of totalitarianism exists anywhere the state begins to excessively intrude into the lives of its citizens.

George Orwell, the British novelist, wrote in his novel *1984* that if totalitarianism took over our world, the future would look like "a boot stamping on a human face—forever." Reality might be more prosaic; rather than being dominated by evil dictators, there is the risk that we might gradually allow the state to take away our human rights out of our fear of other dangers. In the 1950s and 1960s, Americans looked the other way as the FBI and other federal agencies used illegal methods to track people they considered subversive. In South Africa, well-behaved middle-class whites pretended not to know what the police were doing to black prisoners in the name of apartheid—just as well-behaved, middle-class Germans looked the other way when Hitler's police took away Jews to be murdered. This was all done in the name of the state, and few people, even democracies, wish to oppose the power of the state. After all, when U.S. President John F. Kennedy said in his inaugural address in 1961, "Ask not what your country can do for you—ask what you can do for your country," the same words might have been twisted by the likes of Mussolini and other totalitarians, all by way of saying that the state is more important than the individual.

Carl Skutsch

See also: Freedom of Expression; Habeas Corpus; Torture.

Bibliography

Arendt, Hannah. *The Origins of Totalitarianism.* New York: Harcourt Brace, 1973.

Chirot, Daniel. *Modern Tyrants: The Power and Prevalence of Evil in Our Age.* New York: Free Press, 1994.

Kershaw, Ian, and Moshe Lewin. *Stalinism and Nazism: Dictatorships in Comparison.* Cambridge: Cambridge University Press, 1997.

Trade Unions

Unless human rights are fully respected, there will be no just, safe, and democratic world. Implementation of a comprehensive rights policy contributes to a social and economic world order that meets the basic needs of people, to world peace and security, and to equitable development. Free trade unions and democratic civil organizations can operate effectively and reinforce the fabric of civil society only in an environment in which fundamental human rights can be practiced. Trade union freedom is an inalienable human right.

Basic trade union rights are essential for trade unionists to do their jobs. The International Confederation of Free Trade Unions (ICFTU) has long insisted on the following rights in all countries:

"All workers, without distinction, must have the right to establish and, subject only to the rules of the organisation concerned, join organizations of their own choosing without prior authorisation.

"Trade unions must be able, without any interference from employers and the public authorities, to draw up their constitutions and rules, elect their representatives in full freedom, organize their administration and activities and formulate their programs."

"Trade unions must not be liable to dissolution or suspension by administrative action.

"Trade unions must be free to establish and join federations and confederations which, in turn, have the right to affiliate to international trade union organizations.

"Workers must have adequate protection against acts of anti-union discrimination regarding their employment, and trade unions must be protected against any acts of interference by employers in their establishment, functioning, or administration.

"Trade unions must be able to bargain collectively to regulate terms and conditions of employment and all other matters affecting workers' livelihoods.

"Workers and their trade unions must be able to take strike and other industrial action."

The variety of cases cited in the ICFTU's Annual Survey of Violations of Trade Union Rights shows that major attacks on trade union rights have increased in number in the past decade as a free market anti–trade union climate spreads through the post–cold war world. Unprecedented violations are taking place, both of individual workers' rights and those of the labor movement as a democratic institution. Long-established universal principles of freedom of association and collective bargaining contained in national and international jurisprudence are once more being challenged or merely ignored in an ever-widening number of countries on all continents. The number of violators in the 1990s expanded sharply, reaching nearly 120 states in the 1999 survey's analysis.

Just as the most repressive dictatorships appear to be on the decline, a new trend is generating a more subtle and often more effective repression of trade unions. This involves a growing transfer of influence to free-market forces and the large financial trusts that control them, often with the collaboration of local political elites. Labor is again becoming a commodity, workers are being denied basic rights, and trade unions are seen merely as obstacles to the free market.

Pressures resulting from politicians' chronic mismanagement of national economies are also taking a heavy toll on workers and their unions, as are the demands made by the World Bank and International Monetary Fund for socially unbalanced structural adjustment programs. However, far from being a barrier to development, strong trade unions are an essential counterweight to the power of capital contributing to balanced economic development and thus the growth of the international economy.

HUMAN AND TRADE UNION RIGHTS VIOLATIONS

Murder has become an all-too-frequent fate for trade unionists, with some 200 to 300 victims annually. In Colombia, workers are assassinated by leftist guerrilla groups and drug traffickers as well as by the authorities. In Algeria, blind terrorism strikes down workers' leaders, journalists, and many others in the population. Intimidation has recently cost the lives of unionists in numerous countries. In South Africa, long one of the worst cases, the rights situation has vastly improved since the introduction of majority rule.

The international free labor movement is combatting horrendous acts of violence occurring every day against individual unionists, including beatings, death threats, kidnappings, sexual harassment, arrests, imprisonment, and dismissals. Strikes and protests broken up by police and company thugs injure thousands of workers annually. These are common events in many parts of the world. Dismissal from employment is a frequently used means of intimidation, with at least 50,000 to 75,000 cases reported yearly.

In addition to these shocking violations of individuals' rights, a gravely disturbing trend is the upsurge of collective rights violations committed against trade unions. Workers' most basic right to organize in trade unions is still blatantly denied, often by law, in a number of countries, including Myanmar (formerly Burma), Saudi Arabia, Equatorial Guinea, Bahrain, Oman, Qatar, and the United Arab Emirates. In others, such as Cuba, Vietnam, Iran, Libya, Iraq, Syria, Sudan, North Korea, and China, so-called trade unions exist but serve merely to transmit the orders of the state to the workers. The shift toward democratization in Central and Eastern Europe and Africa has shortened this list of countries in recent years. Direct government interference violating trade union rights is common and on the increase. An even more threatening long-term danger to the labor movement is the growing tide of legal barriers that outlaw trade unionism.

Extensive restrictions on and violations of freedom of association contained in the ICFTU Annual Survey clearly illustrate the extent of the trade union rights struggle taking place in developing, transitional, and industrialized countries alike. The gravity and pervasiveness of threats to trade union rights underline the critical importance of the international labor movement's task for their defense and promotion. If left unchallenged, the erosion of basic workers' rights will lead to the decline and possible collapse of labor movements in many countries.

James R. Lewis

See also: Labor.

Bibliography

Barnes, Jack. *The Changing Face of U.S. Politics: Working Class Politics and the Trade Unions.* New York: Pathfinder Press, 1994.

Yates, Michael. *Why Unions Matter.* New York: Monthly Review Press, 1998.

Trials

Trials are at the center of the struggle for human rights. Most important, they are the arenas in which justice is served. Laws provide theoretical protection of justice and human rights; judges and the judicial systems organize this protection, but it is during trials that human rights are directly protected. And because many trials are open to the public, the degree of justice characterizing trials in a country is perhaps the best public evidence of the success or failure of human rights in that country.

Human rights issues and trials are linked in two areas. First, properly conducted trials are the best tools for defending the rights of a person indicted for a crime. Second, a trial is where the perpetrator of human rights abuses can be brought to justice. How effective a legal system is at achieving these twin goals in trials helps determine its effectiveness at protecting human rights.

PROTECTING THOSE ON TRIAL

The balance of power between the government and most individuals is inherently uneven. The state consists of the legislators

Three Kurds on trial, charged with speaking Kurdish during a meeting.

918

who make the laws, the courts who adjudicate them, the police who enforce them, and the prosecuting attorneys who defend them. If the state abuses this massive power, the individual is almost helpless. The best defense against state legal abuses is fair and open trials. International law clearly recognizes this. Article 11 of the United Nations Universal Declaration of Human Rights states that "everyone charged with a penal offense has the right to be presumed innocent until proved guilty according to law in a public trial at which he has had all the guarantees necessary for his defense."

The key elements in a fair trial are publicity, openness, and fairness. A public trial allows relatively impartial witnesses—the public and the press—to act as watchdogs to prevent abuses. Public scrutiny does not guarantee justice, but it makes government-sponsored injustice more difficult. Fairness requires that the accused be given access to legal representation, and fairness demands that, if he or she is unable to pay for such representation, the state will provide funds to pay for a defense attorney. Fairness also requires that trials be moderated by an impartial judge or panel of judges who ensure that a defendant's human rights are not being violated.

How well human rights are served in trials varies greatly from country to country. The legal systems in the democracies of Western Europe and North America provide generally fair trials, with some exceptions. Trials are almost always open to the public, most judges are presumed to be impartial, and defendants are provided with legal counsel. The rich can pay for better legal advice than the poor, and the prosecuting attorneys usually have more resources than their defense counterparts, but these inequities are not so great as to result in gross violations of human rights. (The United States has come under harsh attack in recent years for the poor legal defense given to many of those on trial in capital cases—a majority of whom are poor and black.)

In the rest of the world, trials are often much less fair. In many countries, defendants have no access to legal counsel; in others, such as China, defense attorneys are sometimes clearly on the side of the state, rather than the defendant. In many Third World countries, corruption is a constant problem during trials. Judges and juries can be bribed and bought, and justice goes to the highest bidder. In Indonesia, a Supreme Court clerk was caught on tape saying, "If you give us 50 million rupiah but your opponent gives us more, then the case will be won by your opponent." In Iran, many trials are kept entirely secret from the public, preventing any sort of outside criticism, and the legal aid provided to defendants is minimal.

PROSECUTING HUMAN RIGHTS ABUSERS

In addition to protecting the human rights of those indicted for crimes, trials can also be places where human rights abuses are prosecuted. Increasingly, since the 1990s, courts around the world have broadened the scope of their activities in attempts to bring human rights criminals to justice.

The modern tradition of human rights trials begins with the Nuremberg trials of Nazi war criminals following World War II. The Nazi leaders were accused of committing crimes against humanity, against the basic human rights that all people share. Because their acts were legal in Nazi Germany, their crimes—exterminations, deportations, and genocide—were judged according to a higher standard, above that of national law. The trials, which took place in 1945 and 1946, sentenced twelve of the Nazi leaders to death by hanging, three to life imprisonment, and four to moderate prison terms. The trials set the precedent that human rights criminals could and should be prosecuted. There was a higher law, above national law, to be obeyed.

More recently, war crimes trials have been convened in response to the Bosnian conflict, which resulted in the death of some 200,000 men, women, and children in the 1990s. In 1993, in response to reports of human rights crimes, the United Nations established an International Criminal Tribunal for the Former Yugoslavia (ICTY). Based in The Hague, Netherlands, the ICTY was authorized to indict leaders responsible for crimes against humanity. Many Bosnian leaders, mostly Serbs, were convicted of the crimes against humanity of genocide and "ethnic cleansing." During the 1999 Kosovo crisis, Yugoslavian president Slobodan Milosevic was indicted by the tribunal for human rights crimes against the Albanian people. Although it is unlikely that he (and other senior Serb leaders) will stand trial, the tribunal's work has gone some distance toward demonstrating that human rights crimes will be not be ignored.

CONCLUSION

Trials are the essential center of the struggle for human rights. In all countries, fairly and openly conducted trials are necessary to protect the rights of those indicted for crimes. In cases of war crimes and other human rights violations, trials can bring the guilty to justice, or, at least, bring injustice to the attention of the world.

Carl Skutsch

See also: Police and Law Enforcement; Prisons; Victims' Rights.

Bibliography

Ball, Howard. *Prosecuting War Crimes and Genocide: The Twentieth-Century Experience.* Lawrence: University Press of Kansas, 1999.

Pizzi, William T. *Trials Without Truth.* New York: New York University Press, 1999.

Scharf, Michael P. *Balkan Justice: The Story Behind the First International War Crimes Trial Since Nuremberg.* Durham, NC: Carolina Academic Press, 1997.

United Nations

The United Nations was founded in 1945 with two purposes in mind: first, to prevent another war like World War II, which had just ended; second, to attempt to make the world a better place for all of its citizens. Both goals have their roots in the assurance of human rights. War is perhaps the most lethal enemy of human rights: even when fought according to the laws of war, it results in horrors. But even without war, the world in 1945 was a far from perfect place, and the leaders who drew up the United Nations Charter hoped that the organization could play some role in spreading the idea and practice of human rights around the globe.

The idea of the United Nations grew out of the League of Nations. The League was established in 1919 in the aftermath of World War I. Its creators hoped that it would be a place where nations would gather to solve their problems and thus avoid war. Instead, the League, lacking the support of many of the world's largest countries (including the United States), watched helplessly as World War II broke out.

The United Nations was designed, its founders hoped, to avoid the mistakes of the League of Nations. It was created in discussions between the great powers—the United States, the Soviet Union, Great Britain, and China—and held its first meeting in San Francisco in April 1945. The UN Charter, unlike that of the League, actually gave it some power and authority to intervene when human rights were threatened. The decision to intervene was shared by two bodies: the General Assembly, in which each country gets one vote, and the Security Council, whose fifteen members decide, among other things, whether or not the United Nations should use force to stop a conflict or end a human rights catastrophe.

THE GENERAL ASSEMBLY

It is the UN General Assembly that has been most responsible for advancing the cause of human rights in international law. Over the years, the General Assembly has appointed subcommittees charged with discussing a particular issue and, when this was concluded, bringing a proclamation, statement, or declaration before the entire Assembly. The General Assembly then votes on the document, and if the document is accepted, it becomes a part of international law. The General Assembly, therefore, has been responsible for passing the various declarations that provide the legal defense of human rights in international law.

Of all the human rights documents passed by the General Assembly, the most important is the United Nations Universal Declaration of Human Rights. This document, passed by the General Assembly in 1948, grants all people of the world the same human rights and freedoms. Recognizing the historic nature of the Declaration, the Assembly called upon all nations "to cause it to be disseminated, displayed, read, and expounded principally in schools and other educational institutions." (This has not always been done, so there are

The General Assembly chamber at the United Nations.

schoolchildren all over the world who have never heard of the Universal Declaration of Human Rights or the rights that it grants them.) In the Declaration's preamble, the Assembly cites past "disregard and contempt for human rights [that] have resulted in barbarous acts which have outraged the conscience of mankind." This reference to the horrors of World War II—the Holocaust of European Jews and others being perhaps the most heinous—demonstrated the determination of the Declaration's framers to ensure that human rights would never again be so abused.

The body of the Universal Declaration of Human Rights defends the rights that had grown to be accepted in the Western world as universal: the right to life and liberty, the right to free speech, freedom from slavery and torture, the right to democratic representation, freedom from discrimination, and the right to a fair and open judicial process. All too often the words of the Declaration have been ignored.

In addition to the Universal Declaration of Human Rights, the General Assembly has passed other important and supplementary human rights documents. Among these documents are the Convention on the Prevention and Punishment of the Crime of Genocide (1948); the Declaration on the Rights of the Child (1959); the United Nations Declaration on the Elimination of All Forms of Racial Discrimination (1963); the

International Covenant on Economic, Social and Cultural Rights (1966); the International Covenant on Civil and Political Rights (1966); and the Declaration on the Elimination of Discrimination Against Women (1967).

INSTITUTIONS

There are a few UN institutions that make human rights their central focus. The most important of these is the United Nations Commission on Human Rights, established in 1946. The Commission is a leader in defining human rights and bringing human rights abuses to the attention of the General Assembly, the Security Council, and the world. Its leader, the High Commissioner for Human Rights, is usually the UN's spokesperson on human rights issues. The current High Commissioner, Mary Robinson, former president of Ireland, has been a strong human rights advocate, both before becoming High Commissioner and during her tenure in office. In 1999, speaking of the human rights horrors still being inflicted on civilians in war, Robinson said: "Civilians are no longer just victims of war—today they are regarded as instruments of war. Starving, terrorizing, murdering, raping civilians—all are seen as legitimate. Sex is no defense nor is age. . . . That is a strange, terrible state of affairs in the year after we commemorated the fiftieth anniversary of the Universal Declaration of Human Rights."

Also central to the UN's fight for human rights is the United Nations Educational, Scientific and Cultural Organization (UNESCO). UNESCO, as its name suggests, focuses on educational initiatives. It is therefore in the forefront of the fight against such human rights abuses as racism, discrimination against women, and the free flow of information (with a recent emphasis on access to the Internet).

THE SECURITY COUNCIL

If the United Nations consisted only of the General Assembly, the Commission on Human Rights, and UNESCO, human rights might be one of the institution's top priorities. But the United Nations was not created solely to defend human rights; it was also designed to be a diplomatic negotiating and problem-solving institution, and those roles are dominated by the Security Council, which is perhaps the most important and powerful body in the United Nations.

The Security Council has fifteen members, and five of them are permanent members: the United States, Russia, China, France, and the United Kingdom. Any of these five has the power to veto a Security Council decision. Since the Security Council is the part of the United Nations responsible for authorizing the use of force, no military action in defense of human rights can be taken without its agreement. That means that any one of the five permanent members can stop a United Nations–proposed human rights intervention.

This dynamic in the United Nations has prevented many military interventions for human rights purposes from occurring. Countries like Russia and China, in particular, are reluctant to authorize humanitarian interventions into other countries—even countries blatantly violating the Universal Declaration of Human Rights—because they have their own internal human rights problems (Russia in Chechnya, China in Tibet), and they do not wish to create a precedent that might encourage intervention and violation of their own sovereignty. For example, the United Nations was unable to reach a consensus on the use of military force to stop the genocidal behavior of the Serb militias in Bosnia, so the slaughter continued until the intervention of NATO forces in 1995. Similar Security Council reluctance was apparent in other recent human rights crises, including those in East Timor, Kosovo, and Iraq.

Although the United Nations as a whole is dedicated to protecting human rights, the five permanent members of the Security Council, who have a monopoly on military decision making, are also interested in protecting the interests of their own countries. And without the use of force, the only pressure the United Nations can bring to bear on governments that violate the human rights of their citizens is moral suasion. This is often not enough.

CONCLUSION

Some critics are extremely hostile to the United Nations. Books like William Jasper's *Global Tyranny* claim that the United Nations is bent on creating a world government that will take away all people's rights. They talk about secret airbases from which black helicopters roam the countryside preparing for a UN occupation of the United States. Those who believe these fantastic stories tend to cluster on the right of the political spectrum, but some of their suspicion has trickled into the mainstream, particularly in the United States. Some Americans remain suspicious of the United Nations and reluctant to support its ac-

A demonstration outside the United Nations calling for Sikh independence.

tions. In terms of its ability to achieve its goals of keeping the peace and spreading human rights, however, the United Nations is far less powerful than its opponents claim.

The United Nations is a symbol and a voice of morality, with the weight of world opinion standing behind its human rights proclamations. It gives human rights advocates around the world a standard to aspire to and an authoritative body to appeal to. But without the support of the world's largest nations, particularly the five permanent members of the Security Council, the UN's ability to protect human rights and prevent human rights abuses is quite limited.

Carl Skutsch

See also: International Law; Universal Declaration of Human Rights.

Bibliography

Baehr, P. R., and Leon Gordenker. *The United Nations in the 1990s.* New York: St. Martin's, 1992.

Meisler, Stanley. *United Nations: The First Fifty Years.* New York: Atlantic Monthly, 1995.

Universal Declaration of Human Rights

Passed unanimously by the General Assembly of the United Nations (UN) on December 10, 1948, the Universal Declaration of Human Rights (UDHR) is the foundation of contemporary international human rights law and the touchstone of the global human rights movement. The UDHR, which proclaims itself to be a "common standard of achievement for all peoples and all nations," consists of a Preamble together with thirty articles. It was intended to provide an authoritative interpretation of the clauses contained in the UN Charter (1945), under which member states commit to "take joint and separate action," to promote, "universal respect for, and observance of, human rights and fundamental freedoms for all without discrimination as to race, sex, language, or religion." While not legally binding on member states of the UN, the UDHR has attained the status of customary international law. The UDHR comprises the first part of the International Bill of Human Rights, along with the International Covenant on Civil and Political Rights and the International Covenant on Economic, Social and Cultural Rights, binding treaties that came into force in 1976. The UDHR has provided a model for many subsequent international and regional human rights treaties and conventions, and elements of the UDHR have been incorporated into the national constitutions of many nations. Hailed as the "international Magna Carta" by Eleanor Roosevelt, the former American First Lady who chaired the Human Rights Commission that drafted it, the UDHR is regarded as the twentieth century's most important human rights document. December 10 is celebrated internationally as Human Rights Day.

RIGHTS

The tradition of presenting the ethical and legal claims that citizens may lodge against their rulers in terms of declarations of rights began with the Magna Carta (1215), and continued through the English Bill of Rights (1689), the American Declaration of Independence (1776) and Bill of Rights (1791), and the French Declaration of the Rights of Man and of the Citizen (1789). Like these earlier documents, the UDHR presents a conception under which certain basic interests, powers, and liberties of individual persons are held to be inviolate in the face of state authority. While the idea of individual rights trumping government authority was not a new one when the UDHR was written, it did nevertheless incorporate significant differences in emphasis and treatment of rights than these earlier documents. In particular, the UDHR is more egalitarian and somewhat less individualistic than earlier standards; it eschews any culturally particular philosophical or religious underpinnings; it recognizes economic, social, and cultural rights not found in earlier statements of rights; and, most significantly, it was intended to provide an international standard by which to judge the performance of all governments, rather than just a national standard for a particular country.

The egalitarian and universal nature of the UDHR is seen clearly in Article 2, which

Rally at the United Nations to celebrate the fiftieth anniversary of the Universal Declaration of Human Rights, December 1998.

states: "Everyone is entitled to all of the rights and freedoms set forth in this Declaration, without distinction of any kind, such as race, color, sex, language, religion, political or other opinion, national or social origin, property, birth or other status." Nearly all of its thirty articles and their subclauses begin with words such as "All human beings," "Everyone, " or "No one." However, Article 16(3) departs from this pattern and states: "The family is the natural and fundamental group unit of society and is entitled to protection by society and the State." The Preamble speaks of the "inherent dignity and of the equal and inalienable rights of all members of the human family," but the UDHR carefully avoids any reference to the Enlightenment philosophical notions that human rights are "God-given" or that

they arise from any particular conception of the state of nature, natural law, reason, or contract. Instead, the Preamble alludes to "barbarous acts which have outraged the conscience of mankind," a reference to the Nazi Holocaust, and Article 1 simply states: "All human beings are born equal in dignity and rights. They are endowed with reason and conscience and should act toward one another in a spirit of brotherhood," without attempting to say exactly what "dignity" is or from whence these rights arise. Articles 3 through 21 codify traditional individual civil, judicial, and political rights, many of which can be found in earlier rights documents. However, Articles 22 through 27 represent a significant departure from earlier rights statements in that they recognize economic, social, and cultural rights, rights to economic security, to free choice of employment, and to education, among others. Article 28 states: "Everyone is entitled to a social and international order in which the rights and freedoms set forth in this Declaration can be fully realized," a clear indication of the international scope of the Declaration. The particular rights identified by the UDHR are stated in broad peremptory terms, and without significant qualification, however, Article 29(5) presents a general circumscription clause under which the exercise of the rights and freedoms set forth in the preceding clauses, "shall be subject only to such limitations as are determined by law solely for the purpose of securing due recognition and respect for the rights and freedoms of others and of meeting the just requirements of morality, public order and the general welfare in a democratic society." Part ethical standard, part legal code, and part political compromise, the UDHR represents the first serious attempt to cast the modern doctrine of human rights in terms that are truly universal.

HISTORICAL BACKGROUND

The UDHR was the culmination of seventy years of attempts to create a framework under which governments could be held accountable under international law for their performance in the field of human rights. In the nineteenth century, the states comprising the Concert of Europe signed the Congress of Berlin in 1878, which was intended to secure the peace in Europe and which also provided for diplomatic and, if needed, military intervention, in order to protect the religious freedom of the Christian minorities residing within the Ottoman Empire. The treaty, however, did not prevent the outbreak of World War I in Europe in 1914, nor did it prevent the genocide of the Armenians in 1915.

Despite this lesson, when the victorious powers set down the articles of the League of Nations Covenant in the Treaty of Versailles in 1919, the term *human rights* did not appear in it. The Treaty of Versailles did, however, contain two provisions that portended the later development of the international law of human rights: Article 22 established a mandate system, placed under the "guarantee of the League of Nations" to administer the former colonies for the defeated powers, which required their new governors "not to discriminate against protected minorities and to grant them special rights necessary for the preservation of their ethnic, religious, or linguistic integrity." Article 23 dealt with "fair and humane conditions of labor for men, women, and children" and established the International Labor Organization (ILO) to monitor compliance.

While the League of Nations did much good work during its early years and provided a model for the United Nations, it was undermined by the unwillingness of the great powers—including the United States, whose Senate never ratified the Treaty of Versailles—to relinquish sovereignty to an international organization. The "minorities system" envisioned by the League covenant did, however, plant the seed of the idea of international human rights, in particular, in the mind of a Russian jurist by the name of Andrei Nicolayevich Mandelstam (1869–1949). Mandelstam emigrated to Paris after the Bolshevik Revolution and in 1921 set up a commission to study the protection of minorities clauses. He was soon joined by Antoine Frangulis (1888–1975), a Greek jurist and diplomat, and together these two law professors began teaching and writing articles, arguing that the minority protection clauses of the 1919 Treaty should be generalized into a worldwide convention applying to all nations and all people whether they belong to a minority or a majority. On October 12, 1929, their Commission of International Law published a "Declaration of the International Rights of Man" consisting of a Preamble and six articles, but it attracted little notice. After Adolf Hitler came to power in 1933, Germany withdrew from the League. In 1936 Nazi Germany seized the Rhineland and denounced the Treaty of Versailles, and in 1938, when Hitler seized Austria and was appeased, the League of Nations collapsed. Shortly thereafter, with the Nazi invasion of Poland on September 1, 1939, World War II began.

WORLD WAR II

It was only weeks after the beginning of World War II that the idea of international human rights was revived and given new salience by the famous science fiction writer Herbert George Wells (1866–1946). On October 23, 1939, Wells wrote a letter to the *Times* of London in which he asked, "What are we fighting for?" and answered his own question by declaring it was for "the Rights of Man." Wells subsequently drew up his own "Declaration of Rights" and had it published in the *Daily Herald* from February 5 to 24, along with comments by distinguished persons, and the entire series was later turned into a Penguin Special Edition and translated into ten languages. Wells also sent correspondence about his Declaration of Rights to U.S. President Franklin D. Roosevelt (1882–1945), as well as to other world leaders, including Jan Masaryk, Chaim Weitzman, and Jan Christian Smuts.

In January 1941, President Roosevelt gave his famous "Four Freedoms" speech to Congress, in which he declared: "In future days, which we seek to make secure, we look forward to a world founded on four essential freedoms: freedom of speech and expression, freedom of worship, freedom from want, and freedom from fear." Roosevelt hoped that international solidarity and a concern for human rights would motivate the American people, and a Congress gripped by neoisolationist sentiments, to unite with the Allies against the forces of fascism in Europe. However, America only entered the war eleven months later, following the Japanese bombing of Pearl Harbor.

THE UNITED NATIONS

World War II provided abundant evidence of the need for an international security system to succeed the failed League of Nations. In January 1942, fifty-one nations signed the Declaration of the United Nations. As the war drew to a close, the "Big Four Powers" (the United States, the United Kingdom, the Soviet Union, and China) met at Dumbarton Oaks to work out an agreement on the shape of the proposed organization, and at Yalta in 1945, Roosevelt, Churchill, and Stalin worked out some remaining issues. During the war, Wells' idea that the protection of human rights was a major war aim had caught on; several commissions were set up, and new scholarship developed the idea further. In particular, the American Law Institute published a "Statement of Essential Human Rights" in 1944, which later became a principal source used by John P. Humphrey, when, in 1947, he drafted the Secretariat Outline that inspired the original text of the Universal Declaration of Human Rights. However, there was no mention of human rights in the Dumbarton Oaks proposal.

The fact that the final text of the UN Charter did contain language committing the new organization to the goal of promoting universal respect for, and observance of, human rights and fundamental freedoms is generally agreed to be the result of zealous lobbying by a determined group of unofficial people's delegates who attended the Charter conference in San Francisco in the spring of 1945. A group of these "consultants," representing various non-governmental organizations, including Clark Eichelberger of the American Association for the United Nations, Robert Watt of the American Federation of Labor, Joseph Proskauer of the American Jewish Committee, and Walter White and W. E. B. Du Bois of the National Association for the Advancement of Colored People, formed an ad hoc committee headed by James Shotwell of Columbia University and the Carnegie Endowment for International Peace and drew up a letter urging then U.S. Secretary of State John Stettinius to introduce amendments to the Charter concerning human rights. He agreed to do so on May 2, 1945, and then, during the next several days, the U.S. delegation persuaded the official delegates of the Soviet Union, China, and Britain to accept it. When the Charter conference concluded on June 26, 1945, in San Francisco, the Charter's Preamble stated: "We the peoples of the United Nations are determined to reaffirm faith in fundamental human rights, in the dignity and worth of the human person, in the equal rights of men and women of nations large and small." Article 1 of the Charter made "promoting and encouraging respect for human rights and fundamental freedoms for all without distinction as to race, sex, language, or religion" a principal goal of the UN.

However, the nations that met in San Francisco to draft the Charter were also concerned with guarding the prerogatives available to them under the traditional doctrine of national sovereignty. The language of the Charter stopped short of granting the UN or any other international body the authority to enforce and protect human rights standards against sovereign states. The government delegates assembled in San Francisco were willing to endorse the "promotion" of human rights, particularly when it applied to other countries, but were unwilling to accept international jurisdiction, particularly when it applied to their own governments. Fearing that broad language on human rights would threaten the principle of national sovereignty, the final version of the Charter also contained Article 2(7), which reads, "Nothing contained in the present Charter shall authorize the United Nations to intervene in matters which are essentially within the domestic jurisdiction of any state or shall require Members to submit such matters to settlement." This clause set up the essential contradiction within the UN system under which governments could profess to be committed to the international protection of human rights, while also claiming immunity from interference in their own internal affairs.

Once the formal commitment to promote (but not protect) human rights was accepted into the UN Charter, it became evident that there was no generally accepted definition or list of the human rights and fundamental freedoms that the organization was committed to promote. Mandated by the first General Assembly in 1946 to draft an international bill of rights, the Economic and Social Council established a Human Rights Commission that was charged with drafting a document on human rights that could accommodate the diverse political ideologies and cultures of the member states of the United Nations. In order to expedite the work of this Commission, a Human Rights Division was created within the Secretariat and a Canadian law professor, John Humphrey, was appointed as its head. Eleanor Roosevelt (1884–1962) was appointed to a special ad hoc preparatory commission charged with selecting members in the Human Rights Commission and was soon elected its chair. The preparatory commission set to work and held several meetings during late 1946. It was recommended that the Human Rights Commission should be a permanent body consisting of eighteen members acting in their personal capacities as experts in the field of human rights. However, the Economic and Social Council decided that its members should be government representatives and that its charge would be to draft an international bill of rights capable of universal acceptance.

THE HUMAN RIGIITS COMMISSION

The Human Rights Commission held its first session in January 1947. The members appointed to it included many distinguished scholars and diplomats, such as Dr. Peng-chun Chang of China, Dr. Charles Malik of Lebanon, Dr. René Cassin of France, Carlos Romulo of the Philippines, Hansa Mehta of India, Charles Duke of Great Britain, Don Felix Nieto del Rio of Chile, Dr. Richard Alfaro of Panama, Dr. Ghasseme Ghani of Iran, Dr. Don José A. Mora of Uruguay, Alexander Bogomolov of the Soviet Union, and Vladislav Ribnikar of Yugoslavia. The United States appointed Eleanor Roosevelt as its representative, and she was unanimously elected as the Commission's chair.

In carrying out its mandate, the Human Rights Commission (HRC) had to contend with a variety of vexing philosophical questions about the nature and scope of human rights, as well as some difficult political questions concerning what was politically feasible and likely to win the agreement of the governments represented in the General Assembly at the time. The members of the HRC struggled with these philosophical and political questions throughout 1947. They interviewed experts from various specialized agencies such as the ILO and the World Health Organization; they consulted international lawyers who had worked on the Nuremberg and Tokyo war crimes trials; and reviewed suggestions from numerous non-governmental organizations and distinguished individual scholars. The United Nations Educational, Scientific, and Cultural Organization (UNESCO) solicited the views of 150 distinguished thinkers from around the world. Among the luminaries who responded were Benedetto Croce of Italy, Lewis Mumford of the United States, J. M. Burgers of the Netherlands, and Jacques Maritain of France. In the summer of 1947, UNESCO convened a special Committee on the Philosophic Principles of the Rights of Man in Paris that sifted through the various submissions and concluded: "Human rights have become, and must remain, universal." It also concluded that it was not advisable to attempt to achieve doctrinal consensus on the philosophical and theological questions concerning the origin, nature, and ultimate justification of human rights, but rather that the HRC should seek common ground on specific human rights standards, and it went on to propose some specific civil, political, economic, and social rights.

The political difficulties facing the HRC were perhaps even more formidable. The language of the Charter had inspired the hope of thousands of oppressed people around the world, and soon the Commission was flooded with petitions from various quarters asking that the UN intervene on their behalf. These challenges to domestic jurisdiction were just what the governments had feared might happen, and the HRC had to put a stop to the practice by issuing a statement saying that it had no power to take action concerning individual allegations of human rights violations against governments. Disputes also arose within the HRC over issues such as labor rights and their relation to civil and political rights, the status of women, colonial peoples, and apartheid. Finally, Mrs. Roosevelt decided that a smaller group might be more effective, and an eight-member drafting committee consisting of herself and delegates from Australia, Chile, China, France, Lebanon, Britain, and the Soviet Union was appointed.

The drafting committee worked from a 400-page documented outline prepared by the Human Rights Division of the UN Secretariat led by John P. Humphrey. He prepared his Secretariat Outline from text supplied by many individuals and private organizations. The drafting committee was, however, still divided over the form that the document should take. One possibility was a multilateral treaty that would be binding international law; another was to have the language of the document incorporated into the UN Charter so that agreement to it would be a condition of membership in the UN; while yet another possibility was to make it a "Declaration" by the General Assembly carrying the force of only a non-binding recommendation. Some delegates wanted to include in it the right of individuals who believed that their human rights had been violated to petition the international court of justice, but others felt that having a binding Convention with powers of petition would violate the principle of national sovereignty. The Chinese delegate, P. C. Chang, finally proposed a compromise under which the HRC would first submit a non-binding Declaration, and then later introduce a binding Convention together with measures of implementation. A small working group headed by the French delegate, René Cassin, thereupon undertook the task of converting Humphrey's outline into a draft declaration.

A first draft of the International Declaration on Human Rights and a Draft International Covenant on Human Rights was completed by the end of 1947, and during the first half of 1948 copies of it were circulated for comment by governments and some private organizations. Some aspects of these drafts provoked strong objections while others met with wide agreement. In July 1948, the Human Rights Commission submitted its revised draft of the Declaration, consisting of a lengthy Preamble and twenty-eight articles, to the Economic and Social Council, which in turn submitted it to the General Assembly in September. The General Assembly devoted eighty-one meetings and considered 168 amendments before the final text was agreed to on December 6, 1948. In their final comments before the vote, many delegates made it clear that the knowledge of horrific atrocities committed during the Holocaust had provided the major impulse behind the Declaration. Some delegates thought it contained too many rights, while others worried that it contained too few. But finally, on the evening of December 10, 1948, in the Palais Chaillot, when the president of the General Assembly, Herbert Evatt of Australia, called for a vote, the resolution passed with forty-eight in favor, none opposed, and eight abstentions, whereupon Eleanor Roosevelt received a standing ovation from the Assembly.

TOWARD A BINDING AGREEMENT

While it had been the intention of the HRC to proceed expeditiously to the matter of drafting a binding convention, historical developments during the following years made this politically impossible: the Soviet Union exploded a thermonuclear device in early 1949, thus igniting the Cold War; the Korean War, the independence of Israel, and the process of de-colonization each played a role in transforming the politics of the United Nations. Only when the UN membership had greatly expanded to include the newly independent states of Africa and Asia was the body again able to act on this matter. The originally envisaged companion treaties, the International Covenant on Civil and Political Rights and the International Covenant on Economic, Social and Cultural Rights were passed by the General Assembly and opened for signature in 1966, and having secured the requisite number of ratifications, came into force in 1976.

Since 1948, the United Nations has produced more than seventy additional declarations, treaties, and covenants dealing with various human rights issues. Among the most important of these are: the International Convention for the Elimination of All Forms of Racial Discrimination (1969), the Convention on the Elimination of All Forms of Discrimination Against Women (1979), the Convention Against Torture and Other Cruel, Inhuman or Degrading Treatment or Punishment (1984), and the Convention on the Rights of the Child (1990). During that same period there have also been several regional human rights con-

ventions signed and ratified, including the European Convention on Human Rights (1951), the American Convention on Human Rights (1969), and the African Charter on Human and Peoples' Rights (1986). Several major international human rights conferences have been held, most recently in Vienna in 1993, that reaffirmed the basic principle of the universality of human rights laid down in the Universal Declaration.

The Universal Declaration of Human Rights began what was to become a "golden age" for standard setting in the field of human rights. Recent developments in the canon have extended and developed the contemporary conception of international human rights to include special protections for members of particularly vulnerable groups, for example, refugees, children, and indigenous peoples; a greatly expanded conception of women's rights; and the recognition of collective or "people's" rights to self-determination, development, and to a just international economic order. However, the current international system is still based on the notion of national sovereignty, and the contradiction inherent in the UN Charter between domestic jurisdiction and the international enforcement of human rights remains largely unresolved. In July 1998, a treaty creating an International Criminal Court with the universal jurisdiction to try persons accused of war crimes and crimes against humanity was approved and is pending ratification. In 1999, the war in Kosovo was viewed in some quarters as creating a "soft law" precedent under which the international community may intervene in the affairs of a sovereign nation in order to suppress genocide or other serious human rights violations. At the beginning of the twenty-first century, however, there was still no satisfactory solution to the problem of international human rights enforcement. The promise embodied in words of the Preamble of the UDHR that envisioned human rights becoming universally recognized and observed through "progressive measures, national and international," has not been broken, but it remains to be fully realized.

Morton E. Winston

See also: International Bill of Rights; United Nations.

Bibliography

Buergenthal, T. *International Human Rights in a Nutshell.* St. Paul, MN: West Publishing, 1988.

Humphrey, J. P. *Human Rights and the United Nations: A Great Adventure.* Dobbs Ferry, NY: Transnational, 1984.

Lauren, P. G. *The Evolution of International Human Rights: Visions Seen.* Philadelphia: University of Pennsylvania Press, 1998.

Morsink, J. *The Universal Declaration of Human Rights: Origins, Drafting and Intent.* Philadelphia: University of Pennsylvania Press, 1999.

Victims' Rights

The United Nations' commitment to victims' rights is outlined in the Declaration of Basic Principles of Justice for Victims of Crime and Abuse of Power, passed by the General Assembly in 1985. The Declaration states: "Victims should be treated with compassion and respect for their dignity. They are entitled to access to the mechanisms of justice and to prompt redress, as provided for by national legislation, for the harm that they have suffered." The passing of the Declaration was in response to a growing movement that believes that the victims of crime have been left out of the human rights equation.

Human rights documents, including the United Nations Universal Declaration of Human Rights, emphasize the rights of an accused criminal to a fair trial, fair treatment, and fair punishment, if convicted. In many countries, of course, these rights of the accused and convicted are loosely enforced, if they are enforced at all. But in those countries where accused criminals have fairly strong protection from police and judicial abuse (the United States, for example), there has been a growing outcry from the victims of crimes and their supporters that the rights of the victim have been ignored and that criminals have more rights than their victims.

However traumatized by the crimes committed against them, victims—unlike criminals—never face prosecution. In criminal trials, the prosecution almost always has more resources than the defense, and those accused of crime need their legal protections if trials are to have a semblance of fairness and equity. Nevertheless, it is true that the victim of a crime may be almost forgotten during the judicial process. Police focus on arrests, trials revolve around the maneuvers of attorneys moderated by judges, and the victim can be overlooked. For this reason, victims deserve to have certain rights guaranteed as basic human rights.

A key right allowed by the United Nations Declaration is the right to be heard. As the 1985 Declaration puts it: "Allowing the views and concerns of victims to be presented and considered at appropriate stages of the proceedings where their personal interests are affected, without prejudice to the accused and consistent with the relevant national criminal justice system" should be a human right. Usually this involves giving the victim a chance to speak during criminal sentencing, after the accused has already been convicted of the crime. (Allowing victims to speak freely during the trial, outside of the adversarial process, is usually considered too prejudicial to the rights of the accused.)

A second right granted by the United Nations Declaration requires "avoiding unnecessary delay in the disposition of cases and the execution of orders or decrees granting awards to victims." Victims should not have to wait excessively long to see a resolution of a case. This right can conflict directly with the interests of the accused criminal—sometimes it is to his or her advantage to delay a trial, hoping for a change of circumstances. How these conflicting rights are resolved varies from country to country.

Finally, the United Nations Declaration emphasizes the need to give victims proper

935

compensation for their suffering and loss: "Offenders or third parties responsible for their behavior should, where appropriate, make fair restitution to victims, their families or dependants. Such restitution should include the return of property or payment for the harm or loss suffered, reimbursement of expenses incurred as a result of the victimization, the provision of services and the restoration of rights." And if the person convicted of the crime is unable to provide compensation, or if no person is ever convicted of the crime, the state has an obligation to compensate victims. "When compensation is not fully available from the offender or other sources, States should endeavor to provide financial compensation to: (a) victims who have sustained significant bodily injury or impairment of physical or mental health as a result of serious crimes; (b) the family, in particular dependants of persons who have died or become physically or mentally incapacitated as a result of such victimization." The assumption here is that the state is responsible for civic safety, and it is the state's failure to protect the victim that made the crime possible, hence the state owes the crime victim compensation. This point of view seems quite reasonable—and usually does no harm

to the criminal's human rights—but it entails an expense that most countries are unwilling, or unable, to meet. Only in rich countries like the United States has state compensation for victims begun to occur, and then only in certain circumstances and with relatively small sums of money.

Victims' rights are a reasonable step along the progression of human rights, as long as they do not excessively conflict with the rights of the accused in a criminal trial. It would greatly advance human rights if police and courts could focus more concern on the suffering of the victim, rather than concentrating exclusively on convicting and incarcerating criminals.

Carl Skutsch

See also: Crime; Prisons; Trials.

Bibliography

Karmen, Andrew. *Crime Victims: An Introduction to Victimology.* Pacific Grove, CA: Brooks/Cole, 1990.

Moriarty, Laura J., and Robert A. Jerin. *Current Issues in Victimology Research.* Durham, NC: Carolina Academic Press, 1998.

War

War has significantly influenced the contemporary human rights movement in a number of different ways. Beyond the obvious fact that many of the more extreme human rights abuses take place in the context of armed conflict, it is the principles of international law underlying treaties and the laws of war that provide legal underpinnings for international human rights covenants. Nations have tried to build laws around war in order, in part, to lessen the damage caused to human rights by wars.

The laws of war arise out of the interplay between two major principles—necessity and humanity. The first principle is that whatever is necessary to defeat one's enemy is permissible, despite the death, pain, and destruction that arise out of the pursuit of victory. The second is that whatever causes unnecessary suffering is forbidden, either to soldiers or to civilians. Concretely, what the latter principle entails is that certain weapons regarded as particularly heinous may not be employed (e.g., poiso-

Colombian troops in gunboats hunt for guerrillas, July 1997.

nous gas), that prisoners of war must be treated humanely, and that civilian populations and non-military targets may not be attacked, robbed, and so on. Other concerns covered by the laws of war are such things as the misuse of flags of truce and of the symbols of the Red Cross and Red Crescent (as ruses for sneak attacks).

While the basic principles of necessity and humanity are easy to understand, in practice the dividing line between the two can be fuzzy. For example, why should expanding bullets be forbidden under modern laws of war, but nuclear weapons not be forbidden? And is attacking targets such as civilian oil storage facilities really necessary to defeat an enemy? While the human rights concerns over the laws of war are limited to actions taken against combatants and non-combatants of the opposing nation (thus Nazi Germany's liquidation of groups of its own citizens was not a violation of the laws of war but was a crime against humanity), it is readily apparent that the laws of war nevertheless supply many precedents for modern human rights law.

The laws of war are ancient. The ancient Greek historian Herodotus recounts an incident in which the Spartans murdered the Persian heralds in Sparta. Sparta tried to atone by sending to the court of King Xerxes Spartan men, who were to be killed as a way of paying for the lives of the Persian heralds. According to Herodotus, Xerxes responded by asserting that the Spartans "have broken what is customary usage among all mankind by killing the heralds, but I will not myself do what I rebuke them for." What is significant about this passage is that it indicates that even in the ancient world, there was a customary rule of war forbidding the killing of non-combatants—a custom the Spartans had broken, but that Xerxes refused to vio-

late. Other ancient peoples adhered to similar traditions. In Western medieval society, much the same attitude was expressed in certain rules of chivalry. The laws of war were eventually codified by Hugo Grotius, the father of international law, in 1625.

Modern laws of war began to be formulated in the nineteenth century. The first was a "Convention for the Amelioration of the Condition of the Wounded in Armies in the Field," signed in Geneva by twelve European nations in 1864. In 1899, at The Hague, a "Convention with Respect to the Laws and Customs of War on Land" brought together and formalized customary international law principles regarding prisoners of war and civilians. A number of other such agreements were signed between 1899 and the outbreak of World War II—The Hague Conference of 1907 and the Geneva Conventions of 1928 and 1929. These agreements formed the basis for the war crime trials that took place in Nuremberg and Tokyo following World War II. In 1949, a diplomatic conference meeting in Geneva, Switzerland, drafted a set of four treaties on the conduct of war that, like the conventions of 1928 and 1929, are also referred to as the Geneva Conventions.

It was the reaction to the atrocities associated with World War II (and, to a lesser extent, World War I) that led to the formation of the United Nations (UN) and to the initiation of the modern human rights movement. This concern is explicitly stated in the Preamble to the UN Charter.

Since its formation, the UN has sponsored a number of different conferences, studies, declarations and agreements addressing the conduct of war. In 1954, for example, the UN Educational, Scientific, and Cultural Organization sponsored a conference to protect cultural property dur-

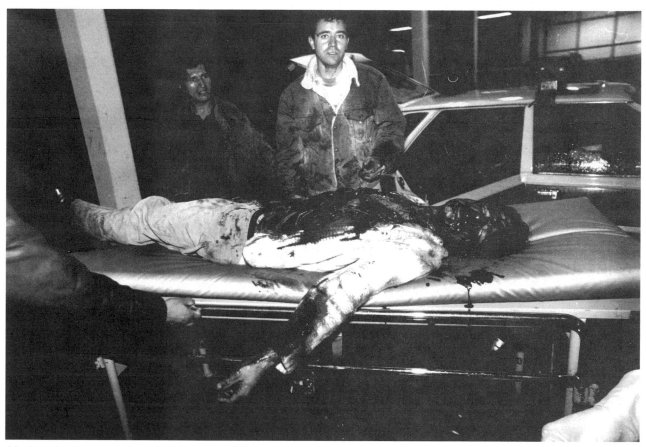

Victim of a guerrilla attack in Colombia, 1995.

ing war. This agreement, the "Convention for the Protection of Cultural Property in the Event of Armed Conflict," commonly referred to as the Hague Convention (a somewhat confusing appellation because of earlier Hague agreements), entered into force on August 7, 1956.

The International Conference on Human Rights, held in Teheran, Iran, in 1968, noted that the brutality of modern warfare eroded human rights and requested that the UN secretary-general address this matter. Accordingly, in 1970, the UN General Assembly affirmed eight basic principles for the protection of civilian populations in armed conflicts. In 1974, the United Nations also expressed particular concern for

the situation of women and children during war, a concern expressed in the Declaration on the Protection of Women and Children in Emergency Armed Conflict. More recently, in 1996, an expert appointed by the secretary-general submitted a report to the General Assembly on the impact of armed conflict on children.

Despite these efforts to reduce the damage to innocents caused by war, human rights continue to be the first casualty of most wars. In the late twentieth century, guerrilla wars were particularly damaging to the cause of human rights. When it is difficult to tell guerrillas from civilians, soldiers who are frustrated, poorly trained, or simply brutal may target civilians as well as guerrillas. Recent guerrilla conflicts in Colombia, Peru, and Sudan have all seen these kinds of human rights violations.

Conventional wars can also be responsible for human rights violations. Some human rights activists argued that the American 1999 air war against Yugoslavia was contrary to the laws of war because it targeted civilian installations—radio stations and power plants—in addition to military targets.

War, even when fought by democratic governments that generally respect human rights, remains the greatest threat to human rights.

James R. Lewis

See also: Conventional Weapons; Crimes Against Humanity; War Crimes.

Bibliography

Fisler, Lori, and David J. Scheffer, eds. *Law and Force in the New International Order.* Boulder, CO: Westview, 1991.

Neier, Aryeh. *War Crimes: Brutality, Genocide, Terror, and the Struggle for Justice.* New York: Times Books, 1998.

Steiner, Henry J., and Philip Alston, eds. *International Human Rights in Context: Law, Politics, Morals.* New York: Oxford University Press, 1996.

War Crimes

War crimes, which is a category one might easily imagine applies to all acts of savagery associated with warfare, actually has a more restricted definition. Most of the mayhem characteristic of armed conflict is not, in the technical sense of the term, a war crime. Although the range of actions covered by war crimes has gradually been refined and expanded, the specific focus of older, customary laws of war has been the treatment of prisoners and the treatment of the enemy's civilian population. The ancient civilizations of Greece, India, and China, for example, all acknowledged that one should not indiscriminately mistreat or kill prisoners of war or non-combatants.

Although the basic principle is thus thousands of years old, it was not until 1474 that anyone was ever actually tried in an international court for war crimes. In that year, twenty-seven judges of the Holy Roman Empire convicted and sentenced to death Peter van Hagenbach for allowing his troops to plunder, rape, and murder.

The notion of war crimes was gradually extended to cover the use of what were regarded as particularly heinous weapons and modes of warfare. It was a crime to cause destruction beyond what was necessary for the achievement of military objectives. Retrospectively, given the extreme destructiveness of contemporary weaponry, some of the earlier prohibitions now seem quaint. The 1899 Hague Conference, for example, prohibited the "launching of projectiles and explosives from balloons"—a mode of assault that seemed especially treacherous at the close of the nineteenth century. To have launched such an aerial assault after one's nation had signed the Hague Agreement would have violated one of the new laws of war, and hence constituted a war crime. Since then, of course, most of the world's wars have involved air bombardment. In fact, in NATO's conflict with the former Yugoslavia over Kosovo, the entire war was fought from the air. As war changes, the definitions of war crimes may also change.

War crimes overlap, and are sometimes confused with, a different category of violations that have come to be referred to as crimes against humanity. While war crimes can only, by definition, take place during an armed conflict, crimes against humanity can take place during times of international peace. Also, war crimes can only be committed against the soldiers and citizens of a nation with which one is at war, while crimes against humanity can include actions taken against segments of a nation's own population. Thus Nazi Germany's systematic murder of its own Jewish and Roma populations was not a war crime; rather, it was a crime against humanity.

The post-war Geneva Conventions of 1949 codified the laws of war—referred to as international humanitarian law—and included the new category of grave breaches of the conventions. These grave breaches include willful killing, torture, or inhuman treatment, including biological experiments; willfully causing great suffering or serious injury to a person's body or health; extensive destruction and appropriation of property not justified by military necessity and carried out unlawfully and wantonly; compelling a prisoner of war to serve in the forces of the hostile power; and willfully depriving a prisoner of war of the rights of a fair and regular trial prescribed in the Convention.

In 1977, the grave breaches of the Geneva Conventions were expanded by Protocol 1 to include such violations as situating civilians and undefended areas so as to make them the objects of attack by the enemy; misuse of the Red Cross or the Red Crescent emblem; the moving of segments of one's own population into areas of another country occupied by one's military; and assaults again historic monuments.

Another way in which the international law regulating war has changed is that individual soldiers may no longer defend themselves on the basis of the superior orders principle. Prior to the Nuremberg war crimes trials, soldiers could escape prosecution on the ground that they had been ordered to commit a war crime by a superior officer. This principle was rejected at Nuremberg. In a prominent example from the Vietnam War, the defense put forward by Lieutenant William Calley, that he was acting on orders from superiors when he massacred villagers at My Lai, was similarly rejected, and he was convicted on charges of war crimes.

James R. Lewis

See also: Crimes Against Humanity; Genocide; War.

Bibliography

Neier, Aryeh. *War Crimes: Brutality, Genocide, Terror, and the Struggle for Justice.* New York: Times Books, 1998.

Ratner, Steven R., and Jason S. Abrams. *Accountability for Human Rights Atrocities in International Law: Beyond the Nuremberg Legacy.* New York: Oxford University Press, 1997.

Steiner, Henry J., and Philip Alston, eds. *International Human Rights in Context: Law, Politics, Morals.* New York: Oxford University Press, 1996.

Elie Wiesel

Elie (Eliezer) Wiesel is known worldwide as a writer, academic, and human rights advocate. He lived the first fifteen years of his life in the closely knit Jewish community of Sighet, Transylvania (Romania), the only boy in a family of four children. In 1944, the Nazis occupied Sighet, and the Jews of Sighet, including Wiesel, his parents, and his sisters, were deported to the concentration camp at Auschwitz in Poland. His mother and younger sister died there. Wiesel and his father were transferred again, first to the concentration camp at Buna, and finally to Buchenwald, where his father died in January 1945, three months before the camp was liberated. Years later, Wiesel found that his two older sisters had also survived the Holocaust. The fact of his own survival, when so many had died, profoundly and irrevocably shaped the direction his life would take.

Immediately after being liberated, Wiesel was sent to France, where he eventually studied literature and philosophy at the Sor-

Elie Wiesel won the Nobel Peace Prize in 1986.

bonne and later worked as a journalist and teacher. Ten years after the end of the war, Wiesel was persuaded by Francois Mauriac, a well-known French writer, to break his self-imposed vow of silence and to write about his concentration camp experiences. The result was *Night*, an autobiographical account of the anguish, inhumanity, and degradation he both observed and endured in the camps. This slender book launched his writing career and his involvement in human rights causes.

In the years since then, Wiesel has written more than forty books, both fiction and non-fiction, several plays, and numerous essays. His earlier books, such as *Dawn* (1961) and *The Accident* (1962), deal with the profound and inescapable effects of their concentration camp experience on the lives of Holocaust survivors. Later books reflect his broadened commitment to basic human rights and his concerns for other persecuted groups. In addition, he has also written books on Hasidism and the Bible. Wiesel has received numerous literary awards, including the Prix Medicis, the Grand Prize in Literature from the City of Paris, and the Jewish Book Council Literary Award (twice).

Wiesel moved to the United States in the late 1950s and became a U.S. citizen in 1963. His academic career has included serving as Distinguished Professor of Judaic Studies at the City University of New York from 1972 to 1976; as the first Henry Luce Visiting Scholar in Humanities and Social Thought at Yale University from 1982 to 1983; and as the Andrew W. Mellon Professor in the Humanities at Boston University since 1976, where he is also a member of the faculty in the departments of religion and philosophy. In 1978, he was appointed by President Jimmy Carter as chairman of the President's Commission on the Holocaust, and two years later he became founding chairman of the United States Holocaust Memorial Council.

Over the years, Wiesel has supported widely divergent human rights campaigns. He has advocated for the cause of Jews in the Soviet Union, the victims of famine in Africa, the victims of forced disappearance in Argentina, and the victims of war in the former Yugoslavia. In recognition of his defense of human rights, he has received, among other awards, the Congressional Gold Medal, the Presidential Medal of Freedom, and the rank of Grand Officer in the French Legion of Honor. In 1986, he was awarded the Nobel Peace Prize.

Shortly after receiving the Nobel Prize, Wiesel and his wife established the Elie Wiesel Foundation for Humanity. The foundation's purpose is to provide a forum for scholars, politicians, artists, scientists, young people, and others to discuss the critical problems confronting the modern world and share their insights on achieving peaceful and humane solutions for them. The foundation also established a Humanitarian Award, which it gives annually to an individual whose accomplishments best exemplify the goals of the foundation. Past recipients have included Danielle Mitterrand of France for her work with children in Third World countries; King Juan Carlos of Spain for peacefully bringing democracy to his nation; and Hillary Rodham Clinton of the United States for her advocacy for children's issues. The foundation has also established educational centers in Israel for the purpose of assisting Ethiopian Jews to become fully participatory members of Israeli society.

Summarizing his passionate commitment to human rights, Elie Wiesel writes:

"Sometimes we must interfere. When human lives are endangered, when human dignity is in jeopardy, national borders and sensitivities become irrelevant. Whenever men or women are persecuted because of their race, religion, or political views, that place must—at that moment—become the center of the universe."

Donna J. Cook

See also: Genocide; Right to Life; Women's Rights.

Bibliography

Abrahamson, Irving. *Against Silence: The Voice and Vision of Elie Wiesel.* New York: Holocaust Library, 1985.

Brown, Robert McAfee. *Elie Wiesel: Messenger to All Humanity.* South Bend, IN: University of Notre Dame Press, 1984.

Wiesel, Elie. *All Rivers Run to the Sea: A Memoir.* New York: Alfred A. Knopf, 1995.

Women's Rights

If there is one message that echoes forth from this conference, let it be that human rights are women's rights and women's rights are human rights.

— HILLARY CLINTON, FOURTH WORLD CONFERENCE ON WOMEN, BEIJING, CHINA, 1995

This clarion call for women's human rights, initiated by women from around the world, echoed in the halls of power (including the United Nations and national governments) across the globe in the 1990s. What does this call mean for women? What has been its impact? What are the challenges that still remain?

The history of the international human rights movement has been one of neglect of women's human rights. It has taken many decades of local, regional, and international activism and networking to make women's human rights visible. Before the Universal Declaration of Human Rights by the United Nations in 1948, there were a number of international agreements safeguarding women's rights. For example, the Hague Conventions at the turn of the twentieth century dealt with conflicts of national laws concerning marriage, divorce, and guardianship of minors. International agreements adopted in 1904, 1910, 1921, and 1933 focused on preventing trafficking in women.

But after issuing the Universal Declaration, the international community put its faith in broad-based universal human rights to address women's issues as well as issues of other minorities. This general norm of non-discrimination is also the basis of the two main human rights covenants: the International Covenant on Civil and Political Rights and the International Covenant on Economic, Social, and Cultural Rights. But non-discrimination, while a laudable goal, may not go far enough to actively protect the rights of many women.

ORGANIZING FOR WOMEN'S RIGHTS

Given the consensus favoring more gender-neutral human rights proclamations, the only international body that specifically addressed women's rights was the United Nations Commission on the Status of Women, established in 1947. It was this body which initiated the International Women's Year in 1975, the International Women's Decade from 1975 to 1985, with world conferences in 1975 (Mexico City), 1980 (Copenhagen), 1985 (Nairobi), and 1995 (Beijing), and was instrumental in drafting the Convention on the Elimination of All Forms of Discrimination Against Women (CEDAW).

CEDAW's Preamble acknowledges that despite the UN's efforts to promote women's human rights, "extensive discrimination against women continues to exist." This discrimination violates "the principles of equality of rights and respect for human dignity, is an obstacle to the participation of women, on equal terms with men, in the political, social, economic, and cultural life of their countries, hampers the growth of the prosperity of society and the family and makes more difficult the full development of the potentialities of women in the service of their countries and of humanity."

CEDAW focuses on achieving substantive equality rather than simply guarantee-

946

ing equal protection under the law. It asks states to modify cultural patterns that perpetuate inequality and attempts to impose standards of equality in public and private life. Adopted by the UN General Assembly in 1979, by 1995 it was ratified by 139 countries and signed by 96 countries.

A GLOBAL CAMPAIGN

It was the solidarity forged over a decade that enabled women's organizations from around the world to have an important impact on the human rights discussions at the 1993 Second World Conference on Human Rights in Vienna. The announcement of the Conference sparked a worldwide mobilization by women to redefine the human rights framework. A Global Campaign for Women's Human Rights was initiated in 1991 by the Center for Women's Global Leadership at Rutgers University, the International Women's Tribune Center, and others.

The Global Campaign explored linkages between women's rights, violence against women, and human rights. Local action included marches, educational panels, exhibits, street theater, and protest rallies. The campaign also organized a worldwide petition drive, calling on the World Conference on Human Rights to "comprehensively address women's human rights at every level of its proceedings" and recognize gender-based violence "as a violation of human rights requiring immediate action."

In addition to the petition, the Global Campaign held local and regional hearings on women's human rights violations. Documents of these hearings were brought to the World Conference. Participants developed "satellite meetings" in which women from a region would gather to draft a report and make recommendations to the World Conference. Women in Latin America and Africa held several such meetings to create a platform to use for lobbying at the Conference. Finally, the Global Campaign sent women to the final preparatory meeting of the World Conference so their voices could be heard during the formulation of the Vienna Declaration and Platform of Action.

Thus, by effectively capitalizing on the networks and understanding gained during the various women's world conferences, and utilizing the resources from UN bodies and the human rights community, an international women's human rights movement was born. While this movement included particular critiques from various Third World women's movements, it also emphasized a universal solidarity among women. It was with this negotiated solidarity that the movement prepared for the World Conference in Vienna.

At Vienna, the international women's human rights movement cited the following major problems with existing human rights instruments: (1) Most human rights mechanisms seek enforcement of political rights only while leaving the protection of socio-economic, cultural, and collective rights—the rights which most affect women—to the discretion of individual states; (2) Most human rights instruments are state-focused and have no mechanisms to make non-state actors, the ones most often responsible for women's rights abuses, accountable for rights violations; (3) Current human rights documents emphasize rights in the public sphere, thereby overlooking the types of domestic and structural violence routinely inflicted on women. The women's lobby demonstrated that while claiming gender-neutrality, all instruments in fact assume men, particularly heterosexual men, to be the bearer of basic rights and do not adequately address women's realities. Women demanded a feminist transformation of human rights.

In addition to addressing the UN's limited interpretation of women's rights, the women's human rights movement also challenged religious fundamentalists and Asian governments that opposed women's human rights on the ground of cultural differences. Women argued that culture was used selectively, and in a rigid and ahistorical manner, by elites to maintain their hegemony at home. In the words of Hilary Bowker: "Women from every single culture and every part of the world are standing up and saying we won't accept cultural justification for abuses against us anymore. We are human, we have a right to have our human rights protected, and the world community must respond to that call and throw out any attempts to justify abuse on the grounds of culture."

At the end of the Conference, the movement sought to direct the momentum gathered at the Vienna Conference toward the upcoming World Conference on Women in Beijing. Dorothy Thomas, the founder-director of the Women's Rights Project of the Human Rights Watch, outlined three major challenges for the movement: to move from visibility of women's abuses to accountability for those violations; to avoid ghettoization of women's human rights, and to make them part of every level of the UN; and to continue to organize cross-culturally, remaining sensitive to the differences among women.

THE 1995 BEIJING CONFERENCE

At Beijing, one could witness the legacy of the women's human rights movement in Vienna and other UN world conferences in Cairo and Copenhagen. Many human rights organizations, such as the Center for Women's Global Leadership, Amnesty International, and Human Rights Watch, held workshops highlighting how women's groups could use the various human rights instruments for promoting education and achieving justice in their own countries. The focus was on getting legitimacy for women's perspectives in the human rights framework within communities worldwide.

Workshops held by different kinds of nongovernmental organizations—ranging from women's self-help groups working to prevent violence against women to development groups fighting structural adjustment policies and working for sustainable development—all highlighted the use of the human rights discourse in their work. As workshop organizer Rita Marin emphasized, the human rights framework can be seen as providing "power tools" that can be adapted for demanding justice and equality in almost any area. In addition to the important work of sharing information and networking with groups, the Global Campaign for Women's Human Rights held a Global Tribunal on Accountability of Women's Human Rights. This time the emphasis was not on making women's human rights abuses visible, but on demanding accountable changes. The judges recommended stronger, more concrete implementation of women's human rights. As one workshop organizer observed: "In Nairobi we were tentative, the emphasis was on that governments should support the international human rights treaties; in Beijing the demand is: governments must comply."

This assertive tone—a product of over two decades of organizing women around the world—was evident throughout the Conference. The Special Rapporteur on Violence Against Women, appointed as a re-

Women's rights rally in Algiers. The women are demonstrating in opposition to Islamic fundamentalists, January 1992.

sult of commitments made in Vienna, also noted the need to move from expressing grievances and demanding rights to seeking remedies. The resulting Beijing Declaration and Platform for Action reaffirmed the Vienna document in its commitment to the universality, inalienability, and interdependence of human rights; the need for governments to support women's human rights despite religious and cultural differences; and in its acknowledgment of violence against women in the home and in armed conflict as violations of human rights. That reaffirmation was especially heartening, representing triumph over renewed efforts by the Vatican and some governments to reverse gains won at Vienna.

The most significant new addition to the document is the acknowledgment of a kind of right to sexuality: "The human rights of women include their rights to have control over and decide freely and responsibly on matters related to their sexuality including sexual and reproductive health, free of coercion, discrimination, and violence." The document also, for the first time, acknowledged the significance of women's unpaid work in the home.

While the Beijing Declaration reaffirmed the commitment to provide new and additional resources toward implementing women's human rights, it did not indicate a willingness to reallocate existing resources to accomplish such a mission. Despite the theoretical and legal gains made in Vienna and Beijing, women's human rights are not a reality for most women around the world. Among the main obstacles noted by various scholars are the structures and practices of globalization, which have led to unjust economic policies and erosion of women's health and education. The human rights approach, based on apportioning blame and punishment to individuals, cannot address these violations adequately for international law, which itself is always applied selectively and can deal with the consequences but not with the causes of structural inequality.

Globalization has also weakened the role of the state, the main guarantor of human rights, and its ability to limit global flows of capital, goods, and markets that undermine the human rights of its citizens. Human rights for women is also challenged by the post–cold war rise of nationalism and religious fundamentalism. Particularly hostile to women's rights have been the fundamentalist Muslim regimes in countries like Iran, Afghanistan, and Saudi Arabia. In others places where fundamentalist movements have threatened to come to power, such as Algeria and Egypt, women have worked together to hold on to their rights.

For the international women's human rights community, there are several occasions for renewed action. Women from around the world need to continue building on the momentum from the world conferences and taking action at local and international levels to use the human rights framework to challenge the inequities of globalization, and, in the process, redefine the framework so that it becomes more achievable. This will require, in the words of one of the judges at the Beijing tribunal, "going with the spirits of the horse and the dragon." In Chinese cosmology, the horse symbolizes hard work, sacrifice, and patience while the dragon represents possibilities and power. Both are necessary to make women's human rights a reality.

Manisha Desai

See also: Abortion; Female Genital Mutilation; Reproductive Rights.

Bibliography

Bunch, Charlotte. "Organizing for Women's Human Rights Globally." In Joanna Kerr, ed., *Ours by Right: Women's Rights as Human Rights*. London: Zed, 1993.

Desai, Manisha. "From Vienna to Beijing: Women's Human Rights Activism and the Human Rights Community." In Peter Van Ness, ed., *Debating Human Rights: Critical Essays from the United States and Asia*. London: Routledge, 1999.

Friedman, Elisabeth. "Women's Human Rights: The Emergence of a Movement." In Julie Peters and Andrea Wolper, eds., *Women's Rights, Human Rights: International Feminist Perspectives*. New York: Routledge, 1995.

World Court

The international legal community's consideration for human rights is primarily focused on principles of humanitarianism, peaceful resolution of conflicts, and justice for all people. These fundamental principles define the rights of the individual to be free from harm and oppression.

These international principles led to the creation of the United Nations (UN). The UN has helped to mold the modern body of international law. The UN's Charter, declarations, and resolutions contribute to the body of legal materials that make up international human rights law. Unquestionably, of paramount importance is the Universal Declaration of Human Rights. This momentous document echoes the American Declaration of Independence when it proclaims in Article 1, "all human beings are born free and equal in dignity and rights," and in Article 7, "all are equal before the law and entitled without any discrimination to equal protection of the law."

In addition to UN documents, the international legal community relies on other sources to develop the rule of law. These are the customs and conventions that sovereign nations use in dealing with one another. Furthermore, special attention is paid to the opinions, commentaries, and discourses of leading jurists, legal academics, and authors of jurisprudence from all nations.

The international legal system comprises two entities. One is the World Court, whose permanent seat is in The Hague, in the Netherlands. This court is the legal organ of the United Nations. It primarily takes cases that derive from disputes between member states. Moreover, it can give advisory opinions on legal questions arising from debates between member states, other UN organs, and to specially authorized agencies outside the UN umbrella.

The second legal body is the International Criminal Court. Its concern is with international crimes perpetrated by individuals. More specifically, this court's mandate is to prosecute war crimes, crimes against humanity, and genocide.

Prior to the founding of a modern international court, a predecessor called the Permanent Court of International Justice (or PCIJ) was in place. This court had its inception in an Arbitration Court that came into being at the beginning of the twentieth century. This court still exists and has eighty-two participating countries.

The PCIJ took up residence at the Peace Palace in The Hague. Although this court had a fixed address, it never actually developed into a permanent court with full-time judges.

However, the agreement that was written by this international tribunal became the foundation of the World Court, also known as the International Court of Justice (ICJ). In 1946, the world saw the dissolution of the PCIJ and the election of the first members of the International Court of Justice at the first session of the UN General Assembly. Developed from principles found in the UN Charter, the primary objectives of the ICJ are to end conflict and achieve justice for all people.

A fifteen-member panel serves as judges for the International Court of Justice. These judges are elected by the UN Security Council and General Assembly. No two judges can come from the same nation. Each judge serves for a nine-year term, with elections every three years. The court can take jurisdiction over a argument only if all the states affected by the dispute have agreed.

From 1946 to 1996, the World Court dealt with forty-seven contentious cases between member states and delivered sixty-one judgments. It also gave twenty-three advisory opinions. The court looks at a multitude of international issues, such as fishery zones and national boundaries. Current cases pending before the ICJ dealing with human rights issues range from the right to self-determination to the legal use of force. The legality of the use of force was questioned in *Yugoslavia v. Belgium; Yugoslavia v. Canada; Yugoslavia v. France; Yugoslavia v. Germany; Yugoslavia v. Italy; Yugoslavia v. Netherlands; Yugoslavia v. Portugal;* and *Yugoslavia v. United Kingdom.* Moreover, current human rights cases involve armed activities on the territory of the the Congo in *Democratic Republic of the Congo v. Burundi; Democratic Republic of the Congo v. Uganda;* and *Democratic Republic of the Congo v. Rwanda.*

The fundamental purpose in establishing an international human rights legal system is to discourage future war criminals and criminal-like states. To do this takes a concordant effort by the global society. War criminals and nefarious states will expect their acts to go unpunished unless the judgment and opinions handed down by international jurists are taken as authoritative and binding. As Benjamin B. Ferencz, a former Nuremberg prosecutor, stated: "There can be no peace without justice, no justice without law and no meaningful law without a Court to decide what is just and lawful under any given circumstance."

Myra D. Mossman

See also: International Law.

Bibliography

McWhinney, Edward. *The International Court of Justice and the Western Tradition of International Law.* Boston: M. Nijhoff, 1987.

Xenophobia

Xenophobia means unreasonable fear of foreigners. Along with fear, it almost always includes hatred of foreigners. Xenophobia is one of the root causes of racism and discrimination. Xenophobia can also lead to acts of violence against people of different national origins.

The fear of foreigners is as old as humanity. A citizen of ancient Greece was distrustful of Greeks from other cities, even though they spoke the same language and worshipped the same gods. More recently, Europe's many wars were caused in part by suspicion of the foreigners who lived just on the other side of the border. Even the United States, a country that welcomes many immigrants every year, has a long tradition of xenophobia. During the nineteenth century, Americans formed anti-immigrant parties to oppose German and Irish immigration. The twentieth century witnessed the rise of right-wing groups that oppose immigration and are suspicious of treaties with former governments.

A number of different United Nations (UN) resolutions have mentioned xenopho-

Anti–United Nations rally called by the Michigan Militia. Suspicion of foreigners and foreign influences has led some Americans to form right-wing fringe groups.

bia, including a General Assembly resolution on December 12, 1960, that condemned racial, religious, and "national hatred" as violations of the UN Charter and the Universal Declaration of Human Rights. More recently, in 1993, the World Conference for Human Rights adopted the Vienna Declaration and Programme of Action, which explicitly mentioned xenophobia in Articles 15 and 30:

"Article 15. Respect for human rights and for fundamental freedoms without distinction of any kind is a fundamental rule of international human rights law. The speedy and comprehensive elimination of all forms of racism and racial discrimination, xenophobia and related intolerance is a priority task for the international community.

"Article 30. The World Conference on Human Rights also expresses its dismay and condemnation that gross and systematic violations and situations that constitute serious obstacles to the full enjoyment of all human rights continue to occur in different parts of the world. Such violations and obstacles include, as well as torture and cruel, inhuman and degrading treatment or punishment, summary and arbitrary executions, disappearances, arbitrary detentions, all forms of racism, racial discrimination and apartheid, foreign occupation and alien domination, xenophobia, poverty, hunger and other denials of economic, social and cultural rights, religious intolerance, terrorism, discrimination against women and lack of the rule of law."

Legal definitions and condemnations are laudable, but explaining and fighting xenophobia are more difficult. The origins of xenophobia are rooted somewhere deep in the human psyche. Throughout history, people have feared and hated those that are different themselves. In the twentieth century these fears and hatreds led to the slaughter

Thomas, a fifteen-year-old German neo-Nazi, 1992.

of millions. Nazi hatred of the Jews, Hutu hatred of the Tutsi, and German hatred of Turkish immigrant workers are not rational, and yet they persist. A sad sign of the persistence of xenophobia is the rebirth of a neo-nazi movement in the eastern provinces of Germany.

Xenophobia denies another person's essential humanity and thus is the first step toward denying his or her human rights.

James R. Lewis

See also: Racism.

Bibliography

Human Rights Watch. *"Germany for Germans": Xenophobia and Racist Violence in Germany.* New York: Human Rights Watch, 1995.

Appendix A
Human Rights Documents

It is generally agreed that the contemporary human rights movement came into being on December 10, 1948, when the Universal Declaration of Human Rights (UDHR) was formally adopted by the United Nations General Assembly. The UN Charter itself, however, is also an important foundational document. The Charter asserts that the protection and promotion of human rights is one of the principal purposes of the United Nations. The UDHR was adopted three years after the formation of the United Nations in order to make the UN's commitment to human rights more explicit.

Although the Universal Declaration of Human Rights has been widely cited as an authoritative document, it was not until the International Covenant on Civil and Political Rights (ICCPR) and the International Covenant on Economic, Social and Cultural Rights (ICESCR) entered into force that the international human rights movement really emerged into its own. These Covenants are treaties, meaning that, for the states that sign them, they have the binding force of international law. Collectively, these two Covenants, together with the UDHR, are referred to as the International Bill of Rights. While the UDHR provides a more specific delineation of the rights outlined in the UN Charter, the ICCPR and the ICESCR further elaborate the content of the UDHR.

Although many subsequent human rights resolutions and agreements have been promulgated, the UN Charter, the Universal Declaration of Human Rights, the International Covenant on Civil and Political Rights, and the International Covenant on Economic, Social and Cultural Rights are the foundation for everything else. All four of these documents are reproduced in full.

CHARTER OF THE UNITED NATIONS
June 26, 1945, 59 Stat. 1031, T.S. 993, 3 Bevans 1153, entered into force Oct. 24, 1945.

Preamble

WE THE PEOPLES OF THE UNITED NATIONS DETERMINED to save succeeding generations from the scourge of war, which twice in our lifetime has brought untold sorrow to mankind, and to reaffirm faith in fundamental human rights, in the dignity and worth of the human person, in the equal rights of men and women and of nations large and small, and to establish conditions under which justice and respect for the obligations aris-

ing from treaties and other sources of international law can be maintained, and to promote social progress and better standards of life in larger freedom,

AND FOR THESE ENDS to practice tolerance and live together in peace with one another as good neighbors, and to unite our strength to maintain international peace and security, and to ensure by the acceptance of principles and the institution of methods, that armed force shall not be used, save in the common interest, and to employ international machinery for the promotion of the economic and social advancement of all peoples,

HAVE RESOLVED TO COMBINE OUR EFFORTS TO ACCOMPLISH THESE AIMS. Accordingly, our respective Governments, through representatives assembled in the city of San Francisco, who have exhibited their full powers found to be in good and due form, have agreed to the present Charter of the United Nations and do hereby establish an international organization to be known as the United Nations.

Chapter I

Purposes and Principles

Article 1

The Purposes of the United Nations are:

1. To maintain international peace and security, and to that end: to take effective collective measures for the prevention and removal of threats to the peace, and for the suppression of acts of aggression or other breaches of the peace, and to bring about by peaceful means, and in conformity with the principles of justice and international law, adjustment or settlement of international disputes or situations which might lead to a breach of the peace;

2. To develop friendly relations among nations based on respect for the principle of equal rights and self-determination of peoples, and to take other appropriate measures to strengthen universal peace;

3. To achieve international cooperation in solving international problems of an economic, social, cultural, or humanitarian character, and in promoting and encouraging respect for human rights and for fundamental freedoms for all without distinction as to race, sex, language, or religion; and

4. To be a center for harmonizing the actions of nations in the attainment of these common ends.

Article 2

The Organization and its Members, in pursuit of the Purposes stated in Article 1, shall act in accordance with the following Principles:

1. The Organization is based on the principle of the sovereign equality of all its Members.

2. All Members, in order to ensure to all of them the rights and benefits resulting from membership, shall fulfill in good faith the obligations assumed by them in accordance with the present Charter.

3. All Members shall settle their international disputes by peaceful means in such a manner that international peace and security, and justice, are not endangered.

4. All Members shall refrain in their international relations from the threat or use of force against the territorial integrity or political independence of any state, or in any other manner inconsistent with the Purposes of the United Nations.

5. All Members shall give the United Nations every assistance in any action it takes in accordance with the present Charter, and shall refrain from giving assistance to any state against which the United Nations is taking preventive or enforcement action.

6. The Organization shall ensure that states which are not Members of the United Nations act in accordance with these Principles so far as may be necessary for the maintenance of international peace and security.

7. Nothing contained in the present Charter shall authorize the United Nations to intervene in matters which are essentially within the domestic jurisdiction of any state or shall require the Members to submit such matters to settlement under the present Charter; but this principle shall not prejudice the application of enforcement measures under Chapter VII.

Chapter II

Membership

Article 3

The original Members of the United Nations shall be the states which, having participated in the United Nations Conference on International Organization at San Francisco, or having previously signed the Declaration by United Nations of January 1, 1942, sign the present Charter and ratify it in accordance with Article 110.

Article 4

1. Membership in the United Nations is open to all other peace-loving states which accept the obligations contained in the present Charter and, in the judgment of the Organization, are able and willing to carry out these obligations.

2. The admission of any such state to membership in the United Nations will be effected by a decision of the General Assembly upon the recommendation of the Security Council.

Article 5

A member of the United Nations against which preventive or enforcement action has been taken by the Security Council may be suspended from the exercise of the rights and privileges of membership by the General Assembly upon the recommendation of the Security Council. The exercise of these rights and privileges may be restored by the Security Council.

Article 6

A Member of the United Nations which has persistently violated the Principles contained in the present Charter may be expelled from the Organization by the General Assembly upon the recommendation of the Security Council.

Chapter III

Organs

Article 7

1. There are established as the principal organs of the United Nations: a General Assembly, a Security Council, an Economic and Social Council, a Trusteeship Council, an International Court of Justice, and a Secretariat.

2. Such subsidiary organs as may be found necessary may be established in accordance with the present Charter.

Article 8

The United Nations shall place no restrictions on the eligibility of men and women to participate in any capacity and under conditions of equality in its principal and subsidiary organs.

Chapter IV

The General Assembly

Article 9

Composition

1. The General Assembly shall consist of all the Members of the United Nations.

2. Each member shall have not more than five representatives in the General Assembly.

Article 10

Functions and Powers

The General Assembly may discuss any questions or any matters within the scope of the present Charter or relating to the powers and functions of any organs provided for in the present Charter, and, except as provided in Article 12, may make recommendations to the Members of the United Nations or to the Security Council or to both on any such questions or matters.

Article 11

1. The General Assembly may consider the general principles of cooperation in the maintenance of international peace and security, including the principles governing disarmament and the regulation of armaments, and may make recommendations with regard to such principles to the Members or to the Security Council or to both.

2. The General Assembly may discuss any questions relating to the maintenance of international peace and security brought before it by any Member of the United Nations, or by the Security Council, or by a state which is not a Member of the United Nations in accordance with Article 35, paragraph 2, and, except as provided in Article 12, may make recommendations with regard to any such questions to the state or states concerned or to the Security Council or to both. Any such question on which action is necessary shall be referred to the Security Council by the General Assembly either before or after discussion.

3. The General Assembly may call the attention of the Security Council to situations which are likely to endanger international peace and security.

4. The powers of the General Assembly set forth in this Article shall not limit the general scope of Article 10.

Article 12

1. While the Security Council is exercising in respect of any dispute or situation the functions assigned to it in the present Charter, the General Assembly shall not make any recommendation with regard to that dispute or situation unless the Security Council so requests.

2. The Secretary-General, with the consent of the Security Council, shall notify the General Assembly at each session of any matters relative to the maintenance of international peace and security which are being dealt with by the Security Council and shall similarly notify the General Assembly, or the Members of the United Nations if the General Assembly is not in session, immediately the Security Council ceases to deal with such matters.

Article 13

1. The General Assembly shall initiate studies and make recommendations for the purpose of:

   a. promoting international cooperation in the political field and encouraging the progressive development of international law and its codification;

   b. promoting international cooperation in the economic, social, cultural, educational, and health fields, and assisting in the realization of human rights and fundamental freedoms for all without distinction as to race, sex, language, or religion.

2. The further responsibilities, functions and powers of the General Assembly with respect to matters mentioned in paragraph 1(b) above are set forth in Chapters IX and X.

Article 14

Subject to the provisions of Article 12, the General Assembly may recommend measures for the peaceful adjustment of any situation, regardless of origin, which it deems likely to impair the general welfare or friendly relations among nations, including situations resulting from a violation of the provisions of the present Charter setting forth the Purposes and Principles of the United Nations.

Article 15

1. The General Assembly shall receive and consider annual and special reports from the Security Council; these reports shall include an account of the measures that the Security Council has decided upon or taken to maintain international peace and security.

2. The General Assembly shall receive and consider reports from the other organs of the United Nations.

Article 16

The General Assembly shall perform such functions with respect to the international trusteeship system as are assigned to it under Chapters XII and XIII, including the approval of the trusteeship agreements for areas not designated as strategic.

Article 17

1. The General Assembly shall consider and approve the budget of the Organization.

2. The expenses of the Organization shall be borne by the Members as apportioned by the General Assembly.

3. The General Assembly shall consider and approve any financial and budgetary arrangements with specialized agencies referred to in Article 57 and shall examine the administrative budgets of such specialized agencies with a view to making recommendations to the agencies concerned.

Article 18

Voting

1. Each member of the General Assembly shall have one vote.

2. Decisions of the General Assembly on important questions shall be made by a two-thirds majority of the members

present and voting. These questions shall include: recommendations with respect to the maintenance of international peace and security, the election of the non-permanent members of the Security Council, the election of the members of the Economic and Social Council, the election of members of the Trusteeship Council in accordance with paragraph 1(c) of Article 86, the admission of new Members to the United Nations, the suspension of the rights and privileges of membership, the expulsion of Members, questions relating to the operation of the trusteeship system, and budgetary questions.

3. Decisions on other questions, Composition including the determination of additional categories of questions to be decided by a two-thirds majority, shall be made by a majority of the members present and voting.

Article 19

A Member of the United Nations which is in arrears in the payment of its financial contributions to the Organization shall have no vote in the General Assembly if the amount of its arrears equals or exceeds the amount of the contributions due from it for the preceding two full years. The General Assembly may, nevertheless, permit such a Member to vote if it is satisfied that the failure to pay is due to conditions beyond the control of the Member.

Article 20

Procedure

The General Assembly shall meet in regular annual sessions and in such special sessions as occasion may require. Special sessions shall be convoked by the Secretary-General at the request of the Security Council or of a majority of the Members of the United Nations.

Article 21

The General Assembly shall adopt its own rules of procedure. It shall elect its President for each session.

Article 22

The General Assembly may establish such subsidiary organs as it deems necessary for the performance of its functions.

Chapter V

The Security Council

Article 23

1. The Security Council shall consist of fifteen Members of the United Nations. The Republic of China, France, the Union of Soviet Socialist Republics, the United Kingdom of Great Britain and Northern Ireland, and the United States of America shall be permanent members of the Security Council. The General Assembly shall elect ten other Members of the United Nations to be non-permanent members of the Security Council, due regard being specially paid, in the first instance to the contribution of Members of the United Nations to the maintenance of international peace and security and to the other purposes of the Organization, and also to equitable geographical distribution. The non-permanent members of the Security Council shall be elected for a term of two years. In the first election of the non-permanent members after the increase of the membership of the Security Council from eleven to fifteen, two of the four additional members shall be chosen for a term of one year. A retiring member shall not be eligible for immediate re-election. Each member of the Security Council shall have one representative.

Article 24

Functions and Powers

1. In order to ensure prompt and effective action by the United Nations, its Members confer on the Security Council primary responsibility for the maintenance of international peace and security, and agree that in carrying out its duties under this responsibility the Security Council acts on their behalf.

2. In discharging these duties the Security Council shall act in accordance with the Purposes and Principles of the United Nations. The specific powers granted to the Security Council for the discharge of these duties are laid down in Chapters VI, VII, VIII, and XII.

3. The Security Council shall submit annual and, when necessary, special reports to the General Assembly for its consideration.

Article 25

The Members of the United Nations agree to accept and carry out the decisions of the Security Council in accordance with the present Charter.

Article 26

In order to promote the establishment and maintenance of international peace and security with the least diversion for armaments of the world's human and economic resources, the Security Council shall be responsible for formulating, with the assistance of the Military Staff Committee referred to in Article 47, plans to be submitted to the Members of the United Nations for the establishment of a system for the regulation of armaments.

Article 27

Voting

1. Each member of the Security Council shall have one vote.

2. Decisions of the Security Council on procedural matters shall be made by an affirmative vote of nine members.

3. Decisions of the Security Council on all other matters shall be made by an affirmative vote of nine members including the concurring votes of the permanent members; provided that, in decisions under Chapter VI, and under paragraph 3 of Article 52, a party to a dispute shall abstain from voting.

Article 28

Procedure

1. The Security Council shall be so organized as to be able to function continuously. Each member of the Security Council shall for this purpose be represented at all times at the seat of the Organization.

2. The Security Council shall hold periodic meetings at which each of its members may, if it so desires, be represented by a member of the government or by some other specially designated representative.

3. The Security Council may hold meetings at such places other than the seat of the Organization as in its judgment will best facilitate its work.

Article 29

The Security Council may establish such subsidiary organs as it deems necessary for the performance of its functions.

Article 30

The Security Council shall adopt its own rules of procedure, including the method of selecting its President.

Article 31

Any Member of the United Nations which is not a member of the Security Council may participate, without vote, in the discussion of any question brought before the Security Council whenever the latter considers that the interests of that Member are specially affected.

Article 32

Any Member of the United Nations which is not a member of the Security Council or any state which is not a Member of the United Nations, if it is a party to a dispute under consideration by the Security Council, shall be invited to participate, without vote, in the discussion relating to the dispute. The Security Council shall lay down such conditions as it deems just for the participation of a state which is not a Member of the United Nations.

Chapter VI

Pacific Settlement of Disputes

Article 33

1. The parties to any dispute, the continuance of which is likely to endanger the maintenance of international peace and security, shall, first of all, seek a solution by negotiation, en-

quiry, mediation, conciliation, arbitration, judicial settlement, resort to regional agencies or arrangements, or other peaceful means of their own choice.

2. The Security Council shall, when it deems necessary, call upon the parties to settle their dispute by such means.

Article 34

The Security Council may investigate any dispute, or any situation which might lead to international friction or give rise to a dispute, in order to determine whether the continuance of the dispute or situation is likely to endanger the maintenance of international peace and security.

Article 35

1. Any Member of the United Nations may bring any dispute, or any situation of the nature referred to in Article 34, to the attention of the Security Council or of the General Assembly.

2. A state which is not a Member of the United Nations may bring to the attention of the Security Council or of the General Assembly any dispute to which it is a party if it accepts in advance, for the purposes of the dispute, the obligations of pacific settlement provided in the present Charter.

3. The proceedings of the General Assembly in respect of matters brought to its attention under this Article will be subject to the provisions of Articles 11 and 12.

Article 36

1. The Security Council may, at any stage of a dispute of the nature referred to in Article 33 or of a situation of like nature, recommend appropriate procedures or methods of adjustment.

2. The Security Council should take into consideration any procedures for the settlement of the dispute which have already been adopted by the parties.

3. In making recommendations under this Article the Security Council should also take into consideration that legal disputes should as a general rule be referred by the parties to the International Court of Justice in accordance with the provisions of the Statute of the Court.

Article 37

1. Should the parties to a dispute of the nature referred to in Article 33 fail to settle it by the means indicated in that Article, they shall refer it to the Security Council.

2. If the Security Council deems that the continuance of the dispute is in fact likely to endanger the maintenance of

international peace and security, it shall decide whether to take action under Article 36 or to recommend such terms of settlement as it may consider appropriate.

Article 38

Without prejudice to the provisions of Articles 33 to 37, the Security Council may, if all the parties to any dispute so request, make recommendations to the parties with a view to a pacific settlement of the dispute.

Chapter VII

Action with Respect to Threats to the Peace, Breaches of the Peace, and Acts of Aggression

Article 39

The Security Council shall determine the existence of any threat to the peace, breach of the peace, or act of aggression and shall make recommendations, or decide what measures shall be taken in accordance with Articles 41 and 42, to maintain or restore international peace and security.

Article 40

In order to prevent an aggravation of the situation, the Security Council may, before making the recommendations or deciding upon the measures provided for in Article 39, call upon the parties concerned to comply with such provisional measures as it deems necessary or desirable. Such provisional measures shall be without prejudice to the rights, claims, or position of the parties concerned. The Security Council shall duly take account of failure to comply with such provisional measures.

Article 41

The Security Council may decide what measures not involving the use of armed force are to be employed to give effect to its decisions, and it may call upon the Members of the United Nations to apply such measures. These may include complete or partial interruption of economic relations and of rail, sea, air, postal, telegraphic, radio, and other means of communication, and the severance of diplomatic relations.

Article 42

Should the Security Council consider that measures provided for in Article 41 would be inadequate or have proved to be inadequate, it may take such action by air, sea, or land forces as may be necessary to maintain or restore international peace and security. Such action may include demonstrations, block-

ade, and other operations by air, sea, or land forces of Members of the United Nations.

Article 43

1. All Members of the United Nations, in order to contribute to the maintenance of international peace and security, undertake to make available to the Security Council, on its call and in accordance with a special agreement or agreements, armed forces, assistance, and facilities, including rights of passage, necessary for the purpose of maintaining international peace and security.

2. Such agreement or agreements shall govern the numbers and types of forces, their degree of readiness and general location, and the nature of the facilities and assistance to be provided.

3. The agreement or agreements shall be negotiated as soon as possible on the initiative of the Security Council. They shall be concluded between the Security Council and Members or between the Security Council and groups of Members and shall be subject to ratification by the signatory states in accordance with their respective constitutional processes.

Article 44

When the Security Council has decided to use force it shall, before calling upon a Member not represented on it to provide armed forces in fulfillment of the obligations assumed under Article 43, invite that Member, if the Member so desires, to participate in the decisions of the Security Council concerning the employment of contingents of that Member's armed forces.

Article 45

In order to enable the United Nations to take urgent military measures Members shall hold immediately available national air-force contingents for combined international enforcement action. The strength and degree of readiness of these contingents and plans for their combined action shall be determined, within the limits laid down in the special agreement or agreements referred to in Article 43, by the Security Council with the assistance of the Military Staff Committee.

Article 46

Plans for the application of armed force shall be made by the Security Council with the assistance of the Military Staff Committee.

Article 47

1. There shall be established a Military Staff Committee to advise and assist the Security Council on all questions relat-

ing to the Security Council's military requirements for the maintenance of international peace and security, the employment and command of forces placed at its disposal, the regulation of armaments, and possible disarmament.

2. The Military Staff Committee shall consist of the Chiefs of Staff of the permanent members of the Security Council or their representatives. Any Member of the United Nations not permanently represented on the Committee shall be invited by the Committee to be associated with it when the efficient discharge of the Committee's responsibilities requires the participation of that Member in its work.

3. The Military Staff Committee shall be responsible under the Security Council for the strategic direction of any armed forces placed at the disposal of the Security Council. Questions relating to the command of such forces shall be worked out subsequently.

4. The Military Staff Committee, with the authorization of the Security Council and after consultation with appropriate regional agencies, may establish regional subcommittees.

Article 48

1. The action required to carry out the decisions of the Security Council for the maintenance of international peace and security shall be taken by all the Members of the United Nations or by some of them, as the Security Council may determine.

2. Such decisions shall be carried out by the Members of the United Nations directly and through their action in the appropriate international agencies of which they are members.

Article 49

The Members of the United Nations shall join in affording mutual assistance in carrying out the measures decided upon by the Security Council.

Article 50

If preventive or enforcement measures against any state are taken by the Security Council, any other state, whether a Member of the United Nations or not, which finds itself confronted with special economic problems arising from the carrying out of those measures shall have the right to consult the Security Council with regard to a solution of those problems.

Article 51

Nothing in the present Charter shall impair the inherent right of individual or collective self-defense if an armed attack occurs against a Member of the United Nations, until the Secu-

rity Council has taken measures necessary to maintain international peace and security. Measures taken by Members in the exercise of this right of self-defense shall be immediately reported to the Security Council and shall not in any way affect the authority and responsibility of the Security Council under the present Charter to take at any time such action as it deems necessary in order to maintain or restore international peace and security.

Chapter VIII

Regional Arrangements

Article 52

1. Nothing in the present Charter precludes the existence of regional arrangements or agencies for dealing with such matters relating to the maintenance of international peace and security as are appropriate for regional action, provided that such arrangements or agencies and their activities are consistent with the Purposes and Principles of the United Nations.

2. The Members of the United Nations entering into such arrangements or constituting such agencies shall make every effort to achieve pacific settlement of local disputes through such regional arrangements or by such regional agencies before referring them to the Security Council.

3. The Security Council shall encourage the development of pacific settlement of local disputes through such regional arrangements or by such regional agencies either on the initiative of the states concerned or by reference from the Security Council.

4. This Article in no way impairs the application of Articles 34 and 35.

Article 53

1. The Security Council shall, where appropriate, utilize such regional arrangements or agencies for enforcement action under its authority. But no enforcement action shall be taken under regional arrangements or by regional agencies without the authorization of the Security Council, with the exception of measures against any enemy state, as defined in paragraph 2 of this Article, provided for pursuant to Article 107 or in regional arrangements directed against renewal of aggressive policy on the part of any such state, until such time as the Organization may, on request of the Governments concerned, be charged with the responsibility for preventing further aggression by such a state.

2. The term enemy state as used in paragraph 1 of this Article applies to any state which during the Second World War has been an enemy of any signatory of the present Charter.

Article 54

The Security Council shall at all times be kept fully informed of activities undertaken or in contemplation under regional arrangements or by regional agencies for the maintenance of international peace and security.

Chapter IX

International Economic and Social Co-operation

Article 55

With a view to the creation of conditions of stability and well-being which are necessary for peaceful and friendly relations among nations based on respect for the principle of equal rights and self-determination of peoples, the United Nations shall promote:

    a. higher standards of living, full employment, and conditions of economic and social progress and development;

    b. solutions of international economic, social, health, and related problems; and international cultural and educational co-operation; and

    c. universal respect for, and observance of, human rights and fundamental freedoms for all without distinction as to race, sex, language, or religion.

Article 56

All Members pledge themselves to take joint and separate action in cooperation with the Organization for the achievement of the purposes set forth in Article 55.

Article 57

1. The various specialized agencies, established by intergovernmental agreement and having wide international responsibilities, as defined in their basic instruments, in economic, social, cultural, educational, health, and related fields, shall be brought into relationship with the United Nations in accordance with the provisions of Article 63.

2. Such agencies thus brought into relationship with the United Nations are hereinafter referred to as specialized agencies.

Article 58

The Organization shall make recommendations for the coordination of the policies and activities of the specialized agencies.

Article 59

The Organization shall, where appropriate, initiate negotiations among the states concerned for the creation of any new specialized agencies required for the accomplishment of the purposes set forth in Article 55.

Article 60

Responsibility for the discharge of the functions of the Organization set forth in this Chapter shall be vested in the General Assembly and, under the authority of the General Assembly, in the Economic and Social Council, which shall have for this purpose the powers set forth in Chapter X.

Chapter X

The Economic and Social Council

Article 61

Composition

1. The Economic and Social Council shall consist of fifty-four Members of the United Nations elected by the General Assembly.

2. Subject to the provisions of paragraph 3, eighteen members of the Economic and Social Council shall be elected each year for a term of three years. A retiring member shall be eligible for immediate re-election.

3. At the first election after the increase in the membership of the Economic and Social Council from twenty-seven to fifty-four members, in addition to the members elected in place of the nine members whose term of office expires at the end of that year, twenty-seven additional members shall be elected. Of these twenty-seven additional members, the term of office of nine members so elected shall expire at the end of one year, and of nine other members at the end of two years, in accordance with arrangements made by the General Assembly.

4. Each member of the Economic and Social Council shall have one representative.

Article 62

Functions and Powers

1. The Economic and Social Council may make or initiate studies and reports with respect to international economic, social, cultural, educational, health, and related matters and may make recommendations with respect to any such matters to the General Assembly, to the Members of the United Nations, and to the specialized agencies concerned.

2. It may make recommendations for the purpose of promoting respect for, and observance of, human rights and fundamental freedoms for all.

3. It may prepare draft conventions for submission to the General Assembly, with respect to matters falling within its competence.

4. It may call, in accordance with the rules prescribed by the United Nations, international conferences on matters falling within its competence.

Article 63

1. The Economic and Social Council may enter into agreements with any of the agencies referred to in Article 57, defining the terms on which the agency concerned shall be brought into relationship with the United Nations. Such agreements shall be subject to approval by the General Assembly.

2. It may coordinate the activities of the specialized agencies through consultation with and recommendations to such agencies and through recommendations to the General Assembly and to the Members of the United Nations.

Article 64

1. The Economic and Social Council may take appropriate steps to obtain regular reports from the specialized agencies. It may make arrangements with the Members of the United Nations and with the specialized agencies to obtain reports on the steps taken to give effect to its own recommendations and to recommendations on matters falling within its competence made by the General Assembly.

2. It may communicate its observations on these reports to the General Assembly.

Article 65

The Economic and Social Council may furnish information to the Security Council and shall assist the Security Council upon its request.

Article 66

1. The Economic and Social Council shall perform such functions as fall within its competence in connection with the carrying out of the recommendations of the General Assembly.

2. It may, with the approval of the General Assembly, perform services at the request of Members of the United Nations and at the request of specialized agencies.

3. It shall perform such other functions as are specified elsewhere in the present Charter or as may be assigned to it by the General Assembly.

Article 67

1. Each member of the Economic and Social Council shall have one vote.

2. Decisions of the Economic and Social Council shall be made by a majority of the members present and voting.

Article 68

Procedure

The Economic and Social Council shall set up commissions in economic and social fields and for the promotion of human rights, and such other commissions as may be required for the performance of its functions.

Article 69

The Economic and Social Council shall invite any Member of the United Nations to participate, without vote, in its deliberations on any matter of particular concern to that Member.

Article 70

The Economic and Social Council may make arrangements for representatives of the specialized agencies to participate, without vote, in its deliberations and in those of the commissions established by it, and for its representatives to participate in the deliberations of the specialized agencies.

Article 71

The Economic and Social Council may make suitable arrangements for consultation with non-governmental organizations which are concerned with matters within its competence. Such arrangements may be made with international organizations and, where appropriate, with national organizations after consultation with the Member of the United Nations concerned.

Article 72

1. The Economic and Social Council shall adopt its own rules of procedure, including the method of selecting its President.

2. The Economic and Social Council shall meet as required in accordance with its rules, which shall include provision for the convening of meetings on the request of a majority of its members.

Chapter XI

Declaration Regarding Non-Self-Governing Territories

Article 73

Members of the United Nations which have or assume responsibilities for the administration of territories whose peoples have not yet attained a full measure of self-government recognize the principle that the interests of the inhabitants of these territories are paramount, and accept as a sacred trust the obligation to promote to the utmost, within the system of international peace and security established by the present Charter, the well-being of the inhabitants of these territories, and, to this end:

> a. to ensure, with due respect for the culture of the peoples concerned, their political, economic, social, and educational advancement, their just treatment, and their protection against abuses;

> b. to develop self-government, to take due account of the political aspirations of the peoples, and to assist them in the progressive development of their free political institutions, according to the particular circumstances of each territory and its peoples and their varying stages of advancement;

> c. to further international peace and security;

> d. to promote constructive measures of development, to encourage research, and to cooperate with one another and, when and where appropriate, with specialized international bodies with a view to the practical achievement of the social, economic, and scientific purposes set forth in this Article; and

> e. to transmit regularly to the Secretary-General for information purposes, subject to such limitation as security and constitutional considerations may require, statistical and other information of a technical nature relating to economic, social, and educational conditions in the territories for which they are respectively responsible other than those territories to which Chapter XII and XIII apply.

Article 74

Members of the United Nations also agree that their policy in respect of the territories to which this Chapter applies, no less than in respect of their metropolitan areas, must be based on the general principle of good-neighborliness, due account being taken of the interests and well-being of the rest of the world, in social, economic, and commercial matters.

Chapter XII

International Trusteeship System

Article 75

The United Nations shall establish under its authority an international trusteeship system for the administration and supervision of such territories as may be placed thereunder by subsequent individual agreements. These territories are hereinafter referred to as trust territories.

Article 76

The basic objectives of the trusteeship system, in accordance with the Purposes of the United Nations laid down in Article 1 of the present Charter, shall be:

> a. to further international peace and security;

> b. to promote the political, economic, social, and educational advancement of the inhabitants of the trust territories, and their progressive development towards self-government or independence as may be appropriate to the particular circumstances of each territory and its peoples and the freely expressed wishes of the peoples concerned, and as may be provided by the terms of each trusteeship agreement;

> c. to encourage respect for human rights and for fundamental freedoms for all without distinction as to race, sex, language, or religion, and to encourage recognition of the interdependence of the peoples of the world; and

> d. to ensure equal treatment in social, economic, and commercial matters for all Members of the United Nations and their nationals and also equal treatment for the latter in the administration of justice without prejudice to the attainment of the foregoing objectives and subject to the provisions of Article 80.

Article 77

1. The trusteeship system shall apply to such territories in the following categories as may be placed thereunder by means of trusteeship agreements:

> a. territories now held under mandate;

> b. territories which may be detached from enemy states as a result of the Second World War, and

> c. territories voluntarily placed under the system by states responsible for their administration.

2. It will be a matter for subsequent agreement as to which territories in the foregoing categories will be brought under the trusteeship system and upon what terms.

Article 78

The trusteeship system shall not apply to territories which have become Members of the United Nations, relationship among which shall be based on respect for the principle of sovereign equality.

Article 79

The terms of trusteeship for each territory to be placed under the trusteeship system, including any alteration or amendment, shall be agreed upon by the states directly concerned, including the mandatory power in the case of territories held under mandate by a Member of the United Nations, and shall be approved as provided for in Articles 83 and 85.

Article 80

1. Except as may be agreed upon in individual trusteeship agreements, made under Articles 77, 79, and 81, placing each territory under the trusteeship system, and until such agreements have been concluded, nothing in this Chapter shall be construed in or of itself to alter in any manner the rights whatsoever of any states or any peoples or the terms of existing international instruments to which Members of the United Nations may respectively be parties.

2. Paragraph 1 of this Article shall not be interpreted as giving grounds for delay or postponement of the negotiation and conclusion of agreements for placing mandated and other territories under the trusteeship system as provided for in Article 77.

Article 81

The trusteeship agreement shall in each case include the terms under which the trust territory will be administered and designate the authority which will exercise the administration of the trust territory. Such authority, hereinafter called the administering authority, may be one or more states or the Organization itself.

Article 82

There may be designated, in any trusteeship agreement, a strategic area or areas which may include part or all of the trust territory to which the agreement applies, without prejudice to any special agreement or agreements made under Article 43.

Article 83

1. All functions of the United Nations relating to strategic areas, including the approval of the terms of the trusteeship agreements and of their alteration or amendment, shall be exercised by the Security Council.

2. The basic objectives set forth in Article 76 shall be applicable to the people of each strategic area.

3. The Security Council shall, subject to the provisions of the trusteeship agreements and without prejudice to security considerations, avail itself of the assistance of the Trusteeship Council to perform those functions of the United Nations under the trusteeship system relating to political, economic, social, and educational matters in the strategic areas.

Article 84

It shall be the duty of the administering authority to ensure that the trust territory shall play its part in the maintenance of international peace and security. To this end the administering authority may make use of volunteer forces, facilities, and assistance from the trust territory in carrying out the obligations towards the Security Council undertaken in this regard by the administering authority, as well as for local defense and the maintenance of law and order within the trust territory.

Article 85

1. The functions of the United Nations with regard to trusteeship agreements for all areas not designated as strategic, including the approval of the terms of the trusteeship agreements and of their alteration or amendment, shall be exercised by the General Assembly.

2. The Trusteeship Council, operating under the authority of the General Assembly, shall assist the General Assembly in carrying out these functions.

Chapter XIII

The Trusteeship Council

Article 86

Composition

1. The Trusteeship Council shall consist of the following Members of the United Nations:

a. those Members administering trust territories;

b. such of those Members mentioned by name in Article 23 as are not administering trust territories; and

c. as many other Members elected for three-year terms by the General Assembly as may be necessary to ensure that the total number of members of the Trusteeship Council is equally divided between those Members of the United Nations which administer trust territories and those which do not.

2. Each member of the Trusteeship Council shall designate one specially qualified person to represent it therein.

Article 87

Functions and Powers

The General Assembly and, under its authority, the Trusteeship Council, in carrying out their functions, may:

> a. consider reports submitted by the administering authority;

> b. accept petitions and examine them in consultation with the administering authority;

> c. provide for periodic visits to the respective trust territories at times agreed upon with the administering authority; and

> d. take these and other actions in conformity with the terms of the trusteeship agreements.

Article 88

The Trusteeship Council shall formulate a questionnaire on the political, economic, social, and educational advancement of the inhabitants of each trust territory, and the administering authority for each trust territory within the competence of the General Assembly shall make an annual report to the General Assembly upon the basis of such questionnaire.

Article 89

Voting

1. Each member of the Trusteeship Council shall have one vote.

2. Decisions of the Trusteeship Council shall be made by a majority of the members present and voting.

Article 90

Procedure

1. The Trusteeship Council shall adopt its own rules of procedure, including the method of selecting its President.

2. The Trusteeship Council shall meet as required in accordance with its rules, which shall include provision for the convening of meetings on the request of a majority of its members.

Article 91

The Trusteeship Council shall, when appropriate, avail itself of the assistance of the Economic and Social Council and of the specialized agencies in regard to matters with which they are respectively concerned.

Chapter XIV

The International Court of Justice

Article 92

The International Court of Justice shall be the principal judicial organ of the United Nations. It shall function in accordance with the annexed Statute which is based upon the Statute of the Permanent Court of International Justice and forms an integral part of the present Charter.

Article 93

1. All Members of the United Nations are ipso facto parties to the Statute of the International Court of Justice.

2. A state which is not a Member of the United Nations may become a party to the Statute of the International Court of Justice on conditions to be determined in each case by the General Assembly upon the recommendation of the Security Council.

Article 94

1. Each Member of the United Nations undertakes to comply with the decision of the International Court of Justice in any case to which it is a party.

2. If any party to a case fails to perform the obligations incumbent upon it under a judgment rendered by the Court, the other party may have recourse to the Security Council, which may, if it deems necessary, make recommendations or decide upon measures to be taken to give effect to the judgment.

Article 95

Nothing in the present Charter shall prevent Members of the United Nations from entrusting the solution of their differences to other tribunals by virtue of agreements already in existence or which may be concluded in the future.

Article 96

1. The General Assembly or the Security Council may request the International Court of Justice to give an advisory opinion on any legal question.

2. Other organs of the United Nations and specialized agencies, which may at any time be so authorized by the General Assembly, may also request advisory opinions of the Court on legal questions arising within the scope of their activities.

Chapter XV

The Secretariat

Article 97

The Secretariat shall comprise a Secretary-General and such staff as the Organization may require. The Secretary-General shall be appointed by the General Assembly upon the recommendation of the Security Council. He shall be the chief administrative officer of the Organization.

Article 98

The Secretary-General shall act in that capacity in all meetings of the General Assembly, of the Security Council, of the Economic and Social Council, and of the Trusteeship Council, and shall perform such other functions as are entrusted to him by these organs. The Secretary-General shall make an annual report to the General Assembly on the work of the Organization.

Article 99

The Secretary-General may bring to the attention of the Security Council any matter which in his opinion may threaten the maintenance of international peace and security.

Article 100

1. In the performance of their duties the Secretary-General and the staff shall not seek or receive instructions from any government or from any other authority external to the Organization. They shall refrain from any action which might reflect on their position as international officials responsible only to the Organization.

2. Each Member of the United Nations undertakes to respect the exclusively international character of the responsibilities of the Secretary-General and the staff and not to seek to influence them in the discharge of their responsibilities.

Article 101

1. The staff shall be appointed by the Secretary-General under regulations established by the General Assembly.

2. Appropriate staffs shall be permanently assigned to the Economic and Social Council, the Trusteeship Council, and,

as required, to other organs of the United Nations. These staffs shall form a part of the Secretariat.

3. The paramount consideration in the employment of the staff and in the determination of the conditions of service shall be the necessity of securing the highest standards of efficiency, competence, and integrity. Due regard shall be paid to the importance of recruiting the staff on as wide a geographical basis as possible.

Chapter XVI

Miscellaneous Provisions

Article 102

1. Every treaty and every international agreement entered into by any Member of the United Nations after the present Charter comes into force shall as soon as possible be registered with the Secretariat and published by it.

2. No party to any such treaty or international agreement which has not been registered in accordance with the provisions of paragraph 1 of this Article may invoke that treaty or agreement before any organ of the United Nations.

Article 103

In the event of a conflict between the obligations of the Members of the United Nations under the present Charter and their obligations under any other international agreement, their obligations under the present Charter shall prevail.

Article 104

The Organization shall enjoy in the territory of each of its Members such legal capacity as may be necessary for the exercise of its functions and the fulfillment of its purposes.

Article 105

1. The Organization shall enjoy in the territory of each of its Members such privileges and immunities as are necessary for the fulfillment of its purposes.

2. Representatives of the Members of the United Nations and officials of the Organization shall similarly enjoy such privileges and immunities as are necessary for the independent exercise of their functions in connection with the Organization.

3. The General Assembly may make recommendations with a view to determining the details of the application of paragraphs 1 and 2 of this Article or may propose conventions to the Members of the United Nations for this purpose.

Chapter XVII

Transitional Security Arrangements

Article 106

Pending the coming into force of such special agreements referred to in Article 43 as in the opinion of the Security Council enable it to begin the exercise of its responsibilities under Article 42, the parties to the Four-Nation Declaration, signed at Moscow October 30, 1943, and France, shall, in accordance with the provisions of paragraph 5 of that Declaration, consult with one another and as occasion requires with other Members of the United Nations with a view to such joint action on behalf of the Organization as may be necessary for the purpose of maintaining international peace and security.

Article 107

Nothing in the present Charter shall invalidate or preclude action, in relation to any state which during the Second World War has been an enemy of any signatory to the present Charter, taken or authorized as a result of that war by the Governments having responsibility for such action.

Chapter XVIII

Amendments

Article 108

Amendments to the present Charter shall come into force for all Members of the United Nations when they have been adopted by a vote of two thirds of the members of the General Assembly and ratified in accordance with their respective constitutional processes by two thirds of the Members of the United Nations, including all the permanent members of the Security Council.

Article 109

1. A General Conference of the Members of the United Nations for the purpose of reviewing the present Charter may be held at a date and place to be fixed by a two-thirds vote of the members of the General Assembly and by a vote of any seven members of the Security Council. Each Member of the United Nations shall have one vote in the conference.

2. Any alteration of the present Charter recommended by a two-thirds vote of the conference shall take effect when ratified in accordance with their respective constitutional processes by two thirds of the Members of the United Nations including all the permanent members of the Security Council.

3. If such a conference has not been held before the tenth annual session of the General Assembly following the com-

ing into force of the present Charter, the proposal to call such a conference shall be placed on the agenda of that session of the General Assembly, and the conference shall be held if so decided by a majority vote of the members of the General Assembly and by a vote of any seven members of the Security Council.

Chapter XIX

Ratification and Signature

Article 110

1. The present Charter shall be ratified by the signatory states in accordance with their respective constitutional processes.

2. The ratifications shall be deposited with the Government of the United States of America, which shall notify all the signatory states of each deposit as well as the Secretary-General of the Organization when he has been appointed.

3. The present Charter shall come into force upon the deposit of ratifications by the Republic of China, France, the Union of Soviet Socialist Republics, the United Kingdom of Great Britain and Northern Ireland, and the United States of America, and by a majority of the other signatory states. A protocol of the ratifications deposited shall thereupon be drawn up by the Government of the United States of America which shall communicate copies thereof to all the signatory states.

4. The states signatory to the present Charter which ratify it after it has come into force will become original Members of the United Nations on the date of the deposit of their respective ratifications.

Article 111

The present Charter, of which the Chinese, French, Russian, English, and Spanish texts are equally authentic, shall remain deposited in the archives of the Government of the United States of America. Duly certified copies thereof shall be transmitted by that Government to the Governments of the other signatory states.

IN FAITH WHEREOF the representatives of the Governments of the United Nations have signed the present Charter.

DONE at the city of San Francisco the twenty-sixth day of June, one thousand nine hundred and forty-five.

THE UNIVERSAL DECLARATION OF HUMAN RIGHTS

On December 10, 1948, the General Assembly of the United Nations adopted and proclaimed the Universal Declaration of

Human Rights. Following this historic act the Assembly called upon all Member countries to publicize the text of the Declaration and "to cause it to be disseminated, displayed, read and expounded principally in schools and other educational institutions, without distinction based on the political status of countries or territories."

Preamble

Whereas recognition of the inherent dignity and of the equal and inalienable rights of all members of the human family is the foundation of freedom, justice and peace in the world,

Whereas disregard and contempt for human rights have resulted in barbarous acts which have outraged the conscience of mankind, and the advent of a world in which human beings shall enjoy freedom of speech and belief and freedom from fear and want has been proclaimed as the highest aspiration of the commonpeople,

Whereas it is essential, if man is not to be compelled to have recourse, as a last resort, to rebellion against tyranny and oppression, that human rights should be protected by the rule of law,

Whereas it is essential to promote the development of friendly relations between nations,

Whereas the peoples of the United Nations have in the Charter reaffirmed their faith in fundamental human rights, in the dignity and worth of the human person and in the equal rights of men and women and have determined to promote social progress and better standards of life in larger freedom,

Whereas Member States have pledged themselves to achieve, in co-operation with the United Nations, the promotion of universal respect for and observance of human rights and fundamental freedoms,

Whereas a common understanding of these rights and freedoms is of the greatest importance for the full realization of this pledge,

Now, Therefore,

THE GENERAL ASSEMBLY

proclaims

THIS UNIVERSAL DECLARATION OF HUMAN RIGHTS as a common standard of achievement for all peoples and all nations, to the end that every individual and every organ of society, keeping this Declaration constantly in mind, shall strive by teaching and education to promote respect for these rights and freedoms and by progressive measures, national and interna-

tional, to secure their universal and effective recognition and observance, both among the peoples of Member States themselves and among the peoples of territories under their jurisdiction.

Article 1

All human beings are born free and equal in dignity and rights. They are endowed with reason and conscience and should act towards one another in a spirit of brotherhood.

Article 2

Everyone is entitled to all the rights and freedoms set forth in this Declaration, without distinction of any kind, such as race, colour, sex, language, religion, political or other opinion, national or social origin, property, birth or other status. Furthermore, no distinction shall be made on the basis of the political, jurisdictional or international status of the country or territory to which a person belongs, whether it be independent, trust, non-self-governing or under any other limitation of sovereignty.

Article 3

Everyone has the right to life, liberty and security of person.

Article 4

No one shall be held in slavery or servitude; slavery and the slave trade shall be prohibited in all their forms.

Article 5

No one shall be subjected to torture or to cruel, inhuman or degrading treatment or punishment.

Article 6

Everyone has the right to recognition everywhere as a person before the law.

Article 7

All are equal before the law and are entitled without any discrimination to equal protection of the law. All are entitled to equal protection against any discrimination in violation of this Declaration and against any incitement to such discrimination.

Article 8

Everyone has the right to an effective remedy by the competent national tribunals for acts violating the fundamental rights granted him by the constitution or by law.

Article 9

No one shall be subjected to arbitrary arrest, detention or exile.

Article 10

Everyone is entitled in full equality to a fair and public hearing by an independent and impartial tribunal, in the determination of his rights and obligations and of any criminal charge against him.

Article 11

1. Everyone charged with a penal offence has the right to be presumed innocent until proved guilty according to law in a public trial at which he has had all the guarantees necessary for his defence.

2. No one shall be held guilty of any penal offence on account of any act or omission which did not constitute a penal offence, under national or international law, at the time when it was committed. Nor shall a heavier penalty be imposed than the one that was applicable at the time the penal offence was committed.

Article 12

No one shall be subjected to arbitrary interference with his privacy, family, home or correspondence, nor to attacks upon his honour and reputation. Everyone has the right to the protection of the law against such interference or attacks.

Article 13

1. Everyone has the right to freedom of movement and residence within the borders of each state.

2. Everyone has the right to leave any country, including his own, and to return to his country.

Article 14

1. Everyone has the right to seek and to enjoy in other countries asylum from persecution.

2. This right may not be invoked in the case of prosecutions genuinely arising from non-political crimes or from acts contrary to the purposes and principles of the United Nations.

Article 15

1. Everyone has the right to a nationality.

2. No one shall be arbitrarily deprived of his nationality nor denied the right to change his nationality.

Article 16

1. Men and women of full age, without any limitation due to race, nationality or religion, have the right to marry and to found a family. They are entitled to equal rights as to marriage, during marriage and at its dissolution.

2. Marriage shall be entered into only with the free and full consent of the intending spouses.

3. The family is the natural and fundamental group unit of society and is entitled to protection by society and the State.

Article 17

1. Everyone has the right to own property alone as well as in association with others.

2. No one shall be arbitrarily deprived of his property.

Article 18

Everyone has the right to freedom of thought, conscience and religion; this right includes freedom to change his religion or belief, and freedom, either alone or in community with others and in public or private, to manifest his religion or belief in teaching, practice, worship and observance.

Article 19

Everyone has the right to freedom of opinion and expression; this right includes freedom to hold opinions without interference and to seek, receive and impart information and ideas through any media and regardless of frontiers.

Article 20

1. Everyone has the right to freedom of peaceful assembly and association.

2. No one may be compelled to belong to an association.

Article 21

1. Everyone has the right to take part in the government of his country, directly or through freely chosen representatives.

2. Everyone has the right to equal access to public service in his country.

3. The will of the people shall be the basis of the authority of government; this shall be expressed in periodic and genuine elections which shall be by universal and equal suffrage and shall be held by secret vote or by equivalent free voting procedures.

Article 22

Everyone, as a member of society, has the right to social security and is entitled to realization, through national effort and international co-operation and in accordance with the organization and resources of each State, of the economic, social and cultural rights indispensable for his dignity and the free development of his personality.

Article 23

1. Everyone has the right to work, to free choice of employment, to just and favourable conditions of work and to protection against unemployment.

2. Everyone, without any discrimination, has the right to equal pay for equal work.

3. Everyone who works has the right to just and favourable remuneration ensuring for himself and his family an existence worthy of human dignity, and supplemented, if necessary, by other means of social protection.

4. Everyone has the right to form and to join trade unions for the protection of his interests.

Article 24

Everyone has the right to rest and leisure, including reasonable limitation of working hours and periodic holidays with pay.

Article 25

1. Everyone has the right to a standard of living adequate for the health and well-being of himself and of his family, including food, clothing, housing and medical care and necessary social services, and the right to security in the event of unemployment, sickness, disability, widowhood, old age or other lack of livelihood in circumstances beyond his control.

2. Motherhood and childhood are entitled to special care and assistance. All children, whether born in or out of wedlock, shall enjoy the same social protection.

Article 26

1. Everyone has the right to education. Education shall be free, at least in the elementary and fundamental stages. Elementary education shall be compulsory. Technical and professional education shall be made generally available and higher education shall be equally accessible to all on the basis of merit.

2. Education shall be directed to the full development of the human personality and to the strengthening of respect for human rights and fundamental freedoms. It shall promote understanding, tolerance and friendship among all nations, ra-cial or religious groups, and shall further the activities of the United Nations for the maintenance of peace.

3. Parents have a prior right to choose the kind of education that shall be given to their children.

Article 27

1. Everyone has the right freely to participate in the cultural life of the community, to enjoy the arts and to share in scientific advancement and its benefits.

2. Everyone has the right to the protection of the moral and material interests resulting from any scientific, literary or artistic production of which he is the author.

Article 28

Everyone is entitled to a social and international order in which the rights and freedoms set forth in this Declaration can be fully realized.

Article 29

1. Everyone has duties to the community in which alone the free and full development of his personality is possible.

2. In the exercise of his rights and freedoms, everyone shall be subject only to such limitations as are determined by law solely for the purpose of securing due recognition and respect for the rights and freedoms of others and of meeting the just requirements of morality, public order and the general welfare in a democratic society.

3. These rights and freedoms may in no case be exercised contrary to the purposes and principles of the United Nations.

Article 30

Nothing in this Declaration may be interpreted as implying for any State, group or person any right to engage in any activity or to perform any act aimed at the destruction of any of the rights and freedoms set forth herein.

THE INTERNATIONAL COVENANT ON CIVIL AND POLITICAL RIGHTS

G.A. res. 2200A (XXI), 21 U.N.GAOR Supp. (No. 16) at 49, U.N. Doc. A/6316 (1966), 993 U.N.T.S. 3, entered into force Jan. 3, 1976.

Preamble

The States Parties to the present Covenant, Considering that, in accordance with the principles proclaimed in the Charter of the

United Nations, recognition of the inherent dignity and of the equal and inalienable rights of all members of the human family is the foundation of freedom, justice and peace in the world,

Recognizing that these rights derive from the inherent dignity of the human person,

Recognizing that, in accordance with the Universal Declaration of Human Rights, the ideal of free human beings enjoying freedom from fear and want can only be achieved if conditions are created whereby everyone may enjoy his economic, social and cultural rights, as well as his civil and political rights,

Considering the obligation of States under the Charter of the United Nations to promote universal respect for, and observance of, human rights and freedoms,

Realizing that the individual, having duties to other individuals and to the community to which he belongs, is under a responsibility to strive for the promotion and observance of the rights recognized in the present Covenant,

Agree upon the following articles:

Part I

Article 1

1. All peoples have the right of self-determination. By virtue of that right they freely determine their political status and freely pursue their economic, social and cultural development.

2. All peoples may, for their own ends, freely dispose of their natural wealth and resources without prejudice to any obligations arising out of international economic co-operation, based upon the principle of mutual benefit, and international law. In no case may a people be deprived of its own means of subsistence.

3. The States Parties to the present Covenant, including those having responsibility for the administration of Non-Self-Governing and Trust Territories, shall promote the realization of the right of self-determination, and shall respect that right, in conformity with the provisions of the Charter of the United Nations.

Part II

Article 2

1. Each State Party to the present Covenant undertakes to take steps, individually and through international assistance and co-operation, especially economic and technical, to the maximum of its available resources, with a view to achieving progressively the full realization of the rights recognized in the present Covenant by all appropriate means, including particularly the adoption of legislative measures.

2. The States Parties to the present Covenant undertake to guarantee that the rights enunciated in the present Covenant will be exercised without discrimination of any kind as to race, colour, sex, language, religion, political or other opinion, national or social origin, property, birth or other status.

3. Developing countries, with due regard to human rights and their national economy, may determine to what extent they would guarantee the economic rights recognized in the present Covenant to non-nationals.

Article 3

The States Parties to the present Covenant undertake to ensure the equal right of men and women to the enjoyment of all economic, social and cultural rights set forth in the present Covenant.

Article 4

The States Parties to the present Covenant recognize that, in the enjoyment of those rights provided by the State in conformity with the present Covenant, the State may subject such rights only to such limitations as are determined by law only in so far as this may be compatible with the nature of these rights and solely for the purpose of promoting the general welfare in a democratic society.

Article 5

1. Nothing in the present Covenant may be interpreted as implying for any State, group or person any right to engage in any activity or to perform any act aimed at the destruction of any of the rights or freedoms recognized herein, or at their limitation to a greater extent than is provided for in the present Covenant.

2. No restriction upon or derogation from any of the fundamental human rights recognized or existing in any country in virtue of law, conventions, regulations or custom shall be admitted on the pretext that the present Covenant does not recognize such rights or that it recognizes them to a lesser extent.

Part III

Article 6

1. The States Parties to the present Covenant recognize the right to work, which includes the right of everyone to the opportunity to gain his living by work which he freely chooses or accepts, and will take appropriate steps to safeguard this right.

2. The steps to be taken by a State Party to the present Covenant to achieve the full realization of this right shall include technical and vocational guidance and training programmes, policies and techniques to achieve steady economic, social and cultural development and full and productive employment under conditions safeguarding fundamental political and economic freedoms to the individual.

Article 7

The States Parties to the present Covenant recognize the right of everyone to the enjoyment of just and favourable conditions of work which ensure, in particular:

(a) Remuneration which provides all workers, as a minimum, with:

(i) Fair wages and equal remuneration for work of equal value without distinction of any kind, in particular women being guaranteed conditions of work not inferior to those enjoyed by men, with equal pay for equal work;

(ii) A decent living for themselves and their families in accordance with the provisions of the present Covenant;

(b) Safe and healthy working conditions;

(c) Equal opportunity for everyone to be promoted in his employment to an appropriate higher level, subject to no considerations other than those of seniority and competence;

(d) Rest, leisure and reasonable limitation of working hours and periodic holidays with pay, as well as remuneration for public holidays.

Article 8

1. The States Parties to the present Covenant undertake to ensure:

(a) The right of everyone to form trade unions and join the trade union of his choice, subject only to the rules of the organization concerned, for the promotion and protection of his economic and social interests. No restrictions may be placed on the exercise of this right other than those prescribed by law and which are necessary in a democratic society in the interests of national security or public order or for the protection of the rights and freedoms of others;

(b) The right of trade unions to establish national federations or confederations and the right of the latter to form or join international trade-union organizations;

(c) The right of trade unions to function freely subject to no limitations other than those prescribed by law and which are necessary in a democratic society in the interests of national security or public order or for the protection of the rights and freedoms of others;

(d) The right to strike, provided that it is exercised in conformity with the laws of the particular country.

2. This article shall not prevent the imposition of lawful restrictions on the exercise of these rights by members of the armed forces or of the police or of the administration of the State.

3. Nothing in this article shall authorize States Parties to the International Labour Organisation Convention of 1948 concerning Freedom of Association and Protection of the Right to Organize to take legislative measures which would prejudice, or apply the law in such a manner as would prejudice, the guarantees provided for in that Convention.

Article 9

The States Parties to the present Covenant recognize the right of everyone to social security, including social insurance.

Article 10

The States Parties to the present Covenant recognize that:

1. The widest possible protection and assistance should be accorded to the family, which is the natural and fundamental group unit of society, particularly for its establishment and while it is responsible for the care and education of dependent children. Marriage must be entered into with the free consent of the intending spouses.

2. Special protection should be accorded to mothers during a reasonable period before and after childbirth. During such period working mothers should be accorded paid leave or leave with adequate social security benefits.

3. Special measures of protection and assistance should be taken on behalf of all children and young persons without any discrimination for reasons of parentage or other conditions. Children and young persons should be protected from economic and social exploitation. Their employment in work harmful to their morals or health or dangerous to life or likely to hamper their normal development should be punishable by law. States should also set age limits below which the paid employment of child labour should be prohibited and punishable by law.

Article 11

1. The States Parties to the present Covenant recognize the right of everyone to an adequate standard of living for himself

and his family, including adequate food, clothing and housing, and to the continuous improvement of living conditions. The States Parties will take appropriate steps to ensure the realization of this right, recognizing to this effect the essential importance of international co-operation based on free consent.

2. The States Parties to the present Covenant, recognizing the fundamental right of everyone to be free from hunger, shall take, individually and through international co-operation, the measures, including specific programmes, which are needed:

(a) To improve methods of production, conservation and distribution of food by making full use of technical and scientific knowledge, by disseminating knowledge of the principles of nutrition and by developing or reforming agrarian systems in such a way as to achieve the most efficient development and utilization of natural resources;

(b) Taking into account the problems of both food-importing and food-exporting countries, to ensure an equitable distribution of world food supplies in relation to need.

Article 12

1. The States Parties to the present Covenant recognize the right of everyone to the enjoyment of the highest attainable standard of physical and mental health.

2. The steps to be taken by the States Parties to the present Covenant to achieve the full realization of this right shall include those necessary for:

(a) The provision for the reduction of the stillbirth-rate and of infant mortality and for the healthy development of the child;

(b) The improvement of all aspects of environmental and industrial hygiene;

(c) The prevention, treatment and control of epidemic, endemic, occupational and other diseases;

(d) The creation of conditions which would assure to all medical service and medical attention in the event of sickness.

Article 13

1. The States Parties to the present Covenant recognize the right of everyone to education. They agree that education shall be directed to the full development of the human personality and the sense of its dignity, and shall strengthen the respect for human rights and fundamental freedoms. They further agree that education shall enable all persons to participate effectively in a free society, promote understanding, tolerance and friendship among all nations and all racial, ethnic or religious groups, and further the activities of the United Nations for the maintenance of peace.

2. The States Parties to the present Covenant recognize that, with a view to achieving the full realization of this right

(a) Primary education shall be compulsory and available free to all;

(b) Secondary education in its different forms, including technical and vocational secondary education, shall be made generally available and accessible to all by every appropriate means, and in particular by the progressive introduction of free education;

(c) Higher education shall be made equally accessible to all, on the basis of capacity, by every appropriate means, and in particular by the progressive introduction of free education;

(d) Fundamental education shall be encouraged or intensified as far as possible for those persons who have not received or completed the whole period of their primary education;

(e) The development of a system of schools at all levels shall be actively pursued, an adequate fellowship system shall be established, and the material conditions of teaching staff shall be continuously improved.

3. The States Parties to the present Covenant undertake to have respect for the liberty of parents and, when applicable, legal guardians to choose for their children schools, other than those established by the public authorities, which conform to such minimum educational standards as may be laid down or approved by the State and to ensure the religious and moral education of their children in conformity with their own convictions.

4. No part of this article shall be construed so as to interfere with the liberty of individuals and bodies to establish and direct educational institutions, subject always to the observance of the principles set forth in paragraph 1 of this article and to the requirement that the education given in such institutions shall conform to such minimum standards as may be laid down by the State.

Article 14

Each State Party to the present Covenant which, at the time of becoming a Party, has not been able to secure in its metropolitan territory or other territories under its jurisdiction compulsory primary education, free of charge, undertakes, within two years, to work out and adopt a detailed plan of action for the progressive implementation, within a reasonable number of years, to be fixed in the plan, of the principle of compulsory education free of charge for all.

Article 15

1. The States Parties to the present Covenant recognize the right of everyone: (a) To take part in cultural life; (b) To enjoy the benefits of scientific progress and its applications; (c) To benefit from the protection of the moral and material interests resulting from any scientific, literary or artistic production of which he is the author.

2. The steps to be taken by the States Parties to the present Covenant to achieve the full realization of this right shall include those necessary for the conservation, the development and the diffusion of science and culture.

3. The States Parties to the present Covenant undertake to respect the freedom indispensable for scientific research and creative activity.

4. The States Parties to the present Covenant recognize the benefits to be derived from the encouragement and development of international contacts and co-operation in the scientific and cultural fields.

Part IV

Article 16

1. The States Parties to the present Covenant undertake to submit in conformity with this part of the Covenant reports on the measures which they have adopted and the progress made in achieving the observance of the rights recognized herein.

2. (a) All reports shall be submitted to the Secretary-General of the United Nations, who shall transmit copies to the Economic and Social Council for consideration in accordance with the provisions of the present Covenant;

(b) The Secretary-General of the United Nations shall also transmit to the specialized agencies copies of the reports, or any relevant parts therefrom, from States Parties to the present Covenant which are also members of these specialized agencies in so far as these reports, or parts therefrom, relate to any matters which fall within the responsibilities of the said agencies in accordance with their constitutional instruments.

Article 17

1. The States Parties to the present Covenant shall furnish their reports in stages, in accordance with a programme to be established by the Economic and Social Council within one year of the entry into force of the present Covenant after consultation with the States Parties and the specialized agencies concerned.

2. Reports may indicate factors and difficulties affecting the degree of fulfilment of obligations under the present Covenant.

3. Where relevant information has previously been furnished to the United Nations or to any specialized agency by any State Party to the present Covenant, it will not be necessary to reproduce that information, but a precise reference to the information so furnished will suffice.

Article 18

Pursuant to its responsibilities under the Charter of the United Nations in the field of human rights and fundamental freedoms, the Economic and Social Council may make arrangements with the specialized agencies in respect of their reporting to it on the progress made in achieving the observance of the provisions of the present Covenant falling within the scope of their activities. These reports may include particulars of decisions and recommendations on such implementation adopted by their competent organs.

Article 19

The Economic and Social Council may transmit to the Commission on Human Rights for study and general recommendation or, as appropriate, for information the reports concerning human rights submitted by States in accordance with articles 16 and 17, and those concerning human rights submitted by the specialized agencies in accordance with article 18.

Article 20

The States Parties to the present Covenant and the specialized agencies concerned may submit comments to the Economic and Social Council on any general recommendation under article 19 or reference to such general recommendation in any report of the Commission on Human Rights or any documentation referred to therein.

Article 21

The Economic and Social Council may submit from time to time to the General Assembly reports with recommendations of a general nature and a summary of the information received from the States Parties to the present Covenant and the specialized agencies on the measures taken and the progress made in achieving general observance of the rights recognized in the present Covenant.

Article 22

The Economic and Social Council may bring to the attention of other organs of the United Nations, their subsidiary organs and specialized agencies concerned with furnishing technical assistance any matters arising out of the reports referred to in this part of the present Covenant which may assist such bodies in deciding, each within its field of competence, on the advisability of international measures likely to contribute to the effective progressive implementation of the present Covenant.

Article 23

The States Parties to the present Covenant agree that international action for the achievement of the rights recognized in the present Covenant includes such methods as the conclusion of conventions, the adoption of recommendations, the furnishing of technical assistance and the holding of regional meetings and technical meetings for the purpose of consultation and study organized in conjunction with the Governments concerned.

Article 24

Nothing in the present Covenant shall be interpreted as impairing the provisions of the Charter of the United Nations and of the constitutions of the specialized agencies which define the respective responsibilities of the various organs of the United Nations and of the specialized agencies in regard to the matters dealt with in the present Covenant.

Article 25

Nothing in the present Covenant shall be interpreted as impairing the inherent right of all peoples to enjoy and utilize fully and freely their natural wealth and resources.

Part V

Article 26

1. The present Covenant is open for signature by any State Member of the United Nations or member of any of its specialized agencies, by any State Party to the Statute of the International Court of Justice, and by any other State which has been invited by the General Assembly of the United Nations to become a party to the present Covenant.

2. The present Covenant is subject to ratification. Instruments of ratification shall be deposited with the Secretary-General of the United Nations.

3. The present Covenant shall be open to accession by any State referred to in paragraph 1 of this article.

4. Accession shall be effected by the deposit of an instrument of accession with the Secretary-General of the United Nations.

5. The Secretary-General of the United Nations shall inform all States which have signed the present Covenant or acceded to it of the deposit of each instrument of ratification or accession.

Article 27

1. The present Covenant shall enter into force three months after the date of the deposit with the Secretary-General of the United Nations of the thirty-fifth instrument of ratification or instrument of accession.

2. For each State ratifying the present Covenant or acceding to it after the deposit of the thirty-fifth instrument of ratification or instrument of accession, the present Covenant shall enter into force three months after the date of the deposit of its own instrument of ratification or instrument of accession.

Article 28

The provisions of the present Covenant shall extend to all parts of federal States without any limitations or exceptions.

Article 29

1. Any State Party to the present Covenant may propose an amendment and file it with the Secretary-General of the United Nations. The Secretary-General shall thereupon communicate any proposed amendments to the States Parties to the present Covenant with a request that they notify him whether they favour a conference of States Parties for the purpose of considering and voting upon the proposals. In the event that at least one third of the States Parties favours such a conference, the Secretary-General shall convene the conference under the auspices of the United Nations. Any amendment adopted by a majority of the States Parties present and voting at the conference shall be submitted to the General Assembly of the United Nations for approval.

2. Amendments shall come into force when they have been approved by the General Assembly of the United Nations and accepted by a two-thirds majority of the States Parties to the present Covenant in accordance with their respective constitutional processes.

3. When amendments come into force they shall be binding on those States Parties which have accepted them, other States Parties still being bound by the provisions of the present Covenant and any earlier amendment which they have accepted.

Article 30

Irrespective of the notifications made under article 26, paragraph 5, the Secretary-General of the United Nations shall inform all States referred to in paragraph 1 of the same article of the following particulars: (a) Signatures, ratifications and accessions under article 26; (b) The date of the entry into force of the present Covenant under article 27 and the date of the entry into force of any amendments under article 29.

Article 31

1. The present Covenant, of which the Chinese, English, French, Russian and Spanish texts are equally authentic, shall be deposited in the archives of the United Nations.

2. The Secretary-General of the United Nations shall transmit certified copies of the present Covenant to all States referred to in article 26.

FIRST OPTIONAL PROTOCOL TO THE INTERNATIONAL COVENANT ON CIVIL AND POLITICAL RIGHTS

G.A. res. 2200A (XXI), 21 U.N. GAOR Supp. (No. 16) at 59, U.N. Doc. A/6316 (1966), 999 U.N.T.S. 302, entered into force March 23, 1976.

The States Parties to the present Protocol,

Considering that in order further to achieve the purposes of the International Covenant on Civil and Political Rights (hereinafter referred to as the Covenant) and the implementation of its provisions it would be appropriate to enable the Human Rights Committee set up in part IV of the Covenant (hereinafter referred to as the Committee) to receive and consider, as provided in the present Protocol, communications from individuals claiming to be victims of violations of any of the rights set forth in the Covenant.

Have agreed as follows:

Article 1

A State Party to the Covenant that becomes a Party to the present Protocol recognizes the competence of the Committee to receive and consider communications from individuals subject to its jurisdiction who claim to be victims of a violation by that State Party of any of the rights set forth in the Covenant. No communication shall be received by the Committee if it concerns a State Party to the Covenant which is not a Party to the present Protocol.

Article 2

Subject to the provisions of article 1, individuals who claim that any of their rights enumerated in the Covenant have been violated and who have exhausted all available domestic remedies may submit a written communication to the Committee for consideration.

Article 3

The Committee shall consider inadmissible any communication under the present Protocol which is anonymous, or which it considers to be an abuse of the right of submission of such communications or to be incompatible with the provisions of the Covenant.

Article 4

1. Subject to the provisions of article 3, the Committee shall bring any communications submitted to it under the present Protocol to the attention of the State Party to the present Protocol alleged to be violating any provision of the Covenant.

2. Within six months, the receiving State shall submit to the Committee written explanations or statements clarifying the matter and the remedy, if any, that may have been taken by that State.

Article 5

1. The Committee shall consider communications received under the present Protocol in the light of all written information made available to it by the individual and by the State Party concerned.

2. The Committee shall not consider any communication from an individual unless it has ascertained that:

(a) The same matter is not being examined under another procedure of international investigation or settlement;

(b) The individual has exhausted all available domestic remedies. This shall not be the rule where the application of the remedies is unreasonably prolonged.

3. The Committee shall hold closed meetings when examining communications under the present Protocol.

4. The Committee shall forward its views to the State Party concerned and to the individual.

Article 6

The Committee shall include in its annual report under article 45 of the Covenant a summary of its activities under the present Protocol.

Article 7

Pending the achievement of the objectives of resolution 1514(XV) adopted by the General Assembly of the United Nations on 14 December 1960 concerning the Declaration on the Granting of Independence to Colonial Countries and Peoples, the provisions of the present Protocol shall in no way limit the right of petition granted to these peoples by the Charter of the United Nations and other international conventions and instruments under the United Nations and its specialized agencies.

Article 8

1. The present Protocol is open for signature by any State which has signed the Covenant.

2. The present Protocol is subject to ratification by any State which has ratified or acceded to the Covenant. Instruments of ratification shall be deposited with the Secretary-General of the United Nations.

3. The present Protocol shall be open to accession by any State which has ratified or acceded to the Covenant.

4. Accession shall be effected by the deposit of an instrument of accession with the Secretary-General of the United Nations.

5. The Secretary-General of the United Nations shall inform all States which have signed the present Protocol or acceded to it of the deposit of each instrument of ratification or accession.

Article 9

1. Subject to the entry into force of the Covenant, the present Protocol shall enter into force three months after the date of the deposit with the Secretary-General of the United Nations of the tenth instrument of ratification or instrument of accession.

2. For each State ratifying the present Protocol or acceding to it after the deposit of the tenth instrument of ratification or instrument of accession, the present Protocol shall enter into force three months after the date of the deposit of its own instrument of ratification or instrument of accession.

Article 10

The provisions of the present Protocol shall extend to all parts of federal States without any limitations or exceptions.

Article 11

1. Any State Party to the present Protocol may propose an amendment and file it with the Secretary-General of the United Nations. The Secretary-General shall thereupon communicate any proposed amendments to the States Parties to the present Protocol with a request that they notify him whether they favour a conference of States Parties for the purpose of considering and

voting upon the proposal. In the event that at least one third of the States Parties favours such a conference, the Secretary-General shall convene the conference under the auspices of the United Nations. Any amendment adopted by a majority of the States Parties present and voting at the conference shall be submitted to the General Assembly of the United Nations for approval.

2. Amendments shall come into force when they have been approved by the General Assembly of the United Nations and accepted by a two-thirds majority of the States Parties to the present Protocol in accordance with their respective constitutional processes.

3. When amendments come into force, they shall be binding on those States Parties which have accepted them, other States Parties still being bound by the provisions of the present Protocol and any earlier amendment which they have accepted.

Article 12

1. Any State Party may denounce the present Protocol at any time by written notification addressed to the Secretary-General of the United Nations. Denunciation shall take effect three months after the date of receipt of the notification by the Secretary-General.

2. Denunciation shall be without prejudice to the continued application of the provisions of the present Protocol to any communication submitted under article 2 before the effective date of denunciation.

Article 13

Irrespective of the notifications made under article 8, paragraph 5, of the present Protocol, the Secretary-General of the United Nations shall inform all States referred to in article 48, paragraph 1, of the Covenant of the following particulars:

(a) Signatures, ratifications and accessions under article 8;

(b) The date of the entry into force of the present Protocol under article 9 and the date of the entry into force of any amendments under article 11;

(c) Denunciations under article 12.

Article 14

1. The present Protocol, of which the Chinese, English, French, Russian and Spanish texts are equally authentic, shall be deposited in the archives of the United Nations.

2. The Secretary-General of the United Nations shall transmit certified copies of the present Protocol to all States referred to in article 48 of the Covenant.

SECOND OPTIONAL PROTOCOL TO THE INTERNATIONAL COVENANT ON CIVIL AND POLITICAL RIGHTS

Aiming at the abolition of the death penalty, G.A. res. 44/128, annex, 44 U.N. GAOR Supp. (No. 49) at 207, U.N. Doc. A/44/49 (1989), entered into force July 11, 1991.

The States Parties to the present Protocol, Believing that abolition of the death penalty contributes to enhancement of human dignity and progressive development of human rights,

Recalling article 3 of the Universal Declaration of Human Rights, adopted on 10 December 1948, and article 6 of the International Covenant on Civil and Political Rights, adopted on 16 December 1966,

Noting that article 6 of the International Covenant on Civil and Political Rights refers to abolition of the death penalty in terms that strongly suggest that abolition is desirable,

Convinced that all measures of abolition of the death penalty should be considered as progress in the enjoyment of the right to life,

Desirous to undertake hereby an international commitment to abolish the death penalty,

Have agreed as follows:

Article 1

1. No one within the jurisdiction of a State Party to the present Protocol shall be executed.

2. Each State Party shall take all necessary measures to abolish the death penalty within its jurisdiction.

Article 2

1. No reservation is admissible to the present Protocol, except for a reservation made at the time of ratification or accession that provides for the application of the death penalty in time of war pursuant to a conviction for a most serious crime of a military nature committed during wartime.

2. The State Party making such a reservation shall at the time of ratification or accession communicate to the Secretary-General of the United Nations the relevant provisions of its national legislation applicable during wartime.

3. The State Party having made such a reservation shall notify the Secretary-General of the United Nations of any beginning or ending of a state of war applicable to its territory.

Article 3

The States Parties to the present Protocol shall include in the reports they submit to the Human Rights Committee, in accordance with article 40 of the Covenant, information on the measures that they have adopted to give effect to the present Protocol.

Article 4

With respect to the States Parties to the Covenant that have made a declaration under article 41, the competence of the Human Rights Committee to receive and consider communications when a State Party claims that another State Party is not fulfilling its obligations shall extend to the provisions of the present Protocol, unless the State Party concerned has made a statement to the contrary at the moment of ratification or accession.

Article 5

With respect to the States Parties to the first Optional Protocol to the International Covenant on Civil and Political Rights adopted on 16 December 1966, the competence of the Human Rights Committee to receive and consider communications from individuals subject to its jurisdiction shall extend to the provisions of the present Protocol, unless the State Party concerned has made a statement to the contrary at the moment of ratification or accession.

Article 6

1. The provisions of the present Protocol shall apply as additional provisions to the Covenant.

2. Without prejudice to the possibility of a reservation under article 2 of the present Protocol, the right guaranteed in article 1, paragraph 1, of the present Protocol shall not be subject to any derogation under article 4 of the Covenant.

Article 7

1. The present Protocol is open for signature by any State that has signed the Covenant.

2. The present Protocol is subject to ratification by any State that has ratified the Covenant or acceded to it. Instruments of ratification shall be deposited with the Secretary-General of the United Nations.

3. The present Protocol shall be open to accession by any State that has ratified the Covenant or acceded to it.

4. Accession shall be effected by the deposit of an instrument of accession with the Secretary-General of the United Nations.

5. The Secretary-General of the United Nations shall inform all States that have signed the present Protocol or acceded to it of the deposit of each instrument of ratification or accession.

Article 8

1. The present Protocol shall enter into force three months after the date of the deposit with the Secretary-General of the United Nations of the tenth instrument of ratification or accession.

2. For each State ratifying the present Protocol or acceding to it after the deposit of the tenth instrument of ratification or accession, the present Protocol shall enter into force three months after the date of the deposit of its own instrument of ratification or accession.

Article 9

The provisions of the present Protocol shall extend to all parts of federal States without any limitations or exceptions.

Article 10

The Secretary-General of the United Nations shall inform all States referred to in article 48, paragraph 1, of the Covenant of the following particulars:

(a) Reservations, communications and notifications under article 2 of the present Protocol;

(b) Statements made under articles 4 or 5 of the present Protocol;

(c) Signatures, ratifications and accessions under article 7 of the present Protocol:

(d) The date of the entry into force of the present Protocol under article 8 thereof.

Article 11

1. The present Protocol, of which the Arabic, Chinese, English, French, Russian and Spanish texts are equally authentic, shall be deposited in the archives of the United Nations.

2. The Secretary-General of the United Nations shall transmit certified copies of the present Protocol to all States referred to in article 48 of the Covenant.

THE INTERNATIONAL COVENANT ON ECONOMIC, SOCIAL AND CULTURAL RIGHTS

G.A. res. 2200A (XXI), 21 U.N. GAOR Supp. (No. 16) at 52, U.N. Doc. A/6316 (1966), 999 U.N.T.S. 171, entered into force Mar. 23, 1976.

Preamble

The States Parties to the present Covenant,

Considering that, in accordance with the principles proclaimed in the Charter of the United Nations, recognition of the inherent dignity and of the equal and inalienable rights of all members of the human family is the foundation of freedom, justice and peace in the world,

Recognizing that these rights derive from the inherent dignity of the human person,

Recognizing that, in accordance with the Universal Declaration of Human Rights, the ideal of free human beings enjoying civil and political freedom and freedom from fear and want can only be achieved if conditions are created whereby everyone may enjoy his civil and political rights, as well as his economic, social and cultural rights,

Considering the obligation of States under the Charter of the United Nations to promote universal respect for, and observance of, human rights and freedoms,

Realizing that the individual, having duties to other individuals and to the community to which he belongs, is under a responsibility to strive for the promotion and observance of the rights recognized in the present Covenant,

Agree upon the following articles:

Part I

Article 1

1. All peoples have the right of self-determination. By virtue of that right they freely determine their political status and freely pursue their economic, social and cultural development.

2. All peoples may, for their own ends, freely dispose of their natural wealth and resources without prejudice to any obligations arising out of international economic co-operation, based upon the principle of mutual benefit, and international law. In no case may a people be deprived of its own means of subsistence.

3. The States Parties to the present Covenant, including those having responsibility for the administration of Non-Self-Governing and Trust Territories, shall promote the realization of the right of self-determination, and shall respect that right,

in conformity with the provisions of the Charter of the United Nations.

Part II

Article 2

1. Each State Party to the present Covenant undertakes to respect and to ensure to all individuals within its territory and subject to its jurisdiction the rights recognized in the present Covenant, without distinction of any kind, such as race, colour, sex, language, religion, political or other opinion, national or social origin, property, birth or other status.

2. Where not already provided for by existing legislative or other measures, each State Party to the present Covenant undertakes to take the necessary steps, in accordance with its constitutional processes and with the provisions of the present Covenant, to adopt such legislative or other measures as may be necessary to give effect to the rights recognized in the present Covenant.

3. Each State Party to the present Covenant undertakes:

(a) To ensure that any person whose rights or freedoms as herein recognized are violated shall have an effective remedy, notwithstanding that the violation has been committed by persons acting in an official capacity;

(b) To ensure that any person claiming such a remedy shall have his right thereto determined by competent judicial, administrative or legislative authorities, or by any other competent authority provided for by the legal system of the State, and to develop the possibilities of judicial remedy;

(c) To ensure that the competent authorities shall enforce such remedies when granted.

Article 3

The States Parties to the present Covenant undertake to ensure the equal right of men and women to the enjoyment of all civil and political rights set forth in the present Covenant.

Article 4

1. In time of public emergency which threatens the life of the nation and the existence of which is officially proclaimed, the States Parties to the present Covenant may take measures derogating from their obligations under the present Covenant to the extent strictly required by the exigencies of the situation, provided that such measures are not inconsistent with their other obligations under international law and do not in-

volve discrimination solely on the ground of race, colour, sex, language, religion or social origin.

2. No derogation from articles 6, 7, 8 (paragraphs 1 and 2), 11, 15, 16 and 18 may be made under this provision.

3. Any State Party to the present Covenant availing itself of the right of derogation shall immediately inform the other States Parties to the present Covenant, through the intermediary of the Secretary-General of the United Nations, of the provisions from which it has derogated and of the reasons by which it was actuated. A further communication shall be made, through the same intermediary, on the date on which it terminates such derogation.

Article 5

1. Nothing in the present Covenant may be interpreted as implying for any State, group or person any right to engage in any activity or perform any act aimed at the destruction of any of the rights and freedoms recognized herein or at their limitation to a greater extent than is provided for in the present Covenant.

2. There shall be no restriction upon or derogation from any of the fundamental human rights recognized or existing in any State Party to the present Covenant pursuant to law, conventions, regulations or custom on the pretext that the present Covenant does not recognize such rights or that it recognizes them to a lesser extent.

Part III

Article 6

1. Every human being has the inherent right to life. This right shall be protected by law. No one shall be arbitrarily deprived of his life.

2. In countries which have not abolished the death penalty, sentence of death may be imposed only for the most serious crimes in accordance with the law in force at the time of the commission of the crime and not contrary to the provisions of the present Covenant and to the Convention on the Prevention and Punishment of the Crime of Genocide. This penalty can only be carried out pursuant to a final judgement rendered by a competent court.

3. When deprivation of life constitutes the crime of genocide, it is understood that nothing in this article shall authorize any State Party to the present Covenant to derogate in any way from any obligation assumed under the provisions of the Convention on the Prevention and Punishment of the Crime of Genocide.

4. Anyone sentenced to death shall have the right to seek pardon or commutation of the sentence. Amnesty, pardon or commutation of the sentence of death may be granted in all cases.

5. Sentence of death shall not be imposed for crimes committed by persons below eighteen years of age and shall not be carried out on pregnant women.

6. Nothing in this article shall be invoked to delay or to prevent the abolition of capital punishment by any State Party to the present Covenant.

Article 7

No one shall be subjected to torture or to cruel, inhuman or degrading treatment or punishment. In particular, no one shall be subjected without his free consent to medical or scientific experimentation.

Article 8

1. No one shall be held in slavery; slavery and the slave-trade in all their forms shall be prohibited.

2. No one shall be held in servitude.

(a) No one shall be required to perform forced or compulsory labour;

(b) Paragraph 3 (a) shall not be held to preclude, in countries where imprisonment with hard labour may be imposed as a punishment for a crime, the performance of hard labour in pursuance of a sentence to such punishment by a competent court;

(c) For the purpose of this paragraph the term "forced or compulsory labour" shall not include:

(i) Any work or service, not referred to in subparagraph (b), normally required of a person who is under detention in consequence of a lawful order of a court, or of a person during conditional release from such detention;

(ii) Any service of a military character and, in countries where conscientious objection is recognized, any national service required by law of conscientious objectors;

(iii) Any service exacted in cases of emergency or calamity threatening the life or well-being of the community;

(iv) Any work or service which forms part of normal civil obligations.

Article 9

1. Everyone has the right to liberty and security of person. No one shall be subjected to arbitrary arrest or detention. No one shall be deprived of his liberty except on such grounds and in accordance with such procedure as are established by law.

2. Anyone who is arrested shall be informed, at the time of arrest, of the reasons for his arrest and shall be promptly informed of any charges against him.

3. Anyone arrested or detained on a criminal charge shall be brought promptly before a judge or other officer authorized by law to exercise judicial power and shall be entitled to trial within a reasonable time or to release. It shall not be the general rule that persons awaiting trial shall be detained in custody, but release may be subject to guarantees to appear for trial, at any other stage of the judicial proceedings, and, should occasion arise, for execution of the judgement.

4. Anyone who is deprived of his liberty by arrest or detention shall be entitled to take proceedings before a court, in order that court may decide without delay on the lawfulness of his detention and order his release if the detention is not lawful.

5. Anyone who has been the victim of unlawful arrest or detention shall have an enforceable right to compensation.

Article 10

1. All persons deprived of their liberty shall be treated with humanity and with respect for the inherent dignity of the human person.

(a) Accused persons shall, save in exceptional circumstances, be segregated from convicted persons and shall be subject to separate treatment appropriate to their status as unconvicted persons;

(b) Accused juvenile persons shall be separated from adults and brought as speedily as possible for adjudication.

3. The penitentiary system shall comprise treatment of prisoners the essential aim of which shall be their reformation and social rehabilitation. Juvenile offenders shall be segregated from adults and be accorded treatment appropriate to their age and legal status.

Article 11

No one shall be imprisoned merely on the ground of inability to fulfil a contractual obligation.

Article 12

1. Everyone lawfully within the territory of a State shall, within that territory, have the right to liberty of movement and freedom to choose his residence.

2. Everyone shall be free to leave any country, including his own.

3. The above-mentioned rights shall not be subject to any restrictions except those which are provided by law, are nec-

essary to protect national security, public order (ordre public), public health or morals or the rights and freedoms of others, and are consistent with the other rights recognized in the present Covenant.

4. No one shall be arbitrarily deprived of the right to enter his own country.

Article 13

An alien lawfully in the territory of a State Party to the present Covenant may be expelled therefrom only in pursuance of a decision reached in accordance with law and shall, except where compelling reasons of national security otherwise require, be allowed to submit the reasons against his expulsion and to have his case reviewed by, and be represented for the purpose before, the competent authority or a person or persons especially designated by the competent authority.

Article 14

1. All persons shall be equal before the courts and tribunals. In the determination of any criminal charge against him, or of his rights and obligations in a suit at law, everyone shall be entitled to a fair and public hearing by a competent, independent and impartial tribunal established by law. The press and the public may be excluded from all or part of a trial for reasons of morals, public order (ordre public) or national security in a democratic society, or when the interest of the private lives of the parties so requires, or to the extent strictly necessary in the opinion of the court in special circumstances where publicity would prejudice the interests of justice; but any judgement rendered in a criminal case or in a suit at law shall be made public except where the interest of juvenile persons otherwise requires or the proceedings concern matrimonial disputes or the guardianship of children.

2. Everyone charged with a criminal offence shall have the right to be presumed innocent until proved guilty according to law.

3. In the determination of any criminal charge against him, everyone shall be entitled to the following minimum guarantees, in full equality:

(a) To be informed promptly and in detail in a language which he understands of the nature and cause of the charge against him;

(b) To have adequate time and facilities for the preparation of his defence and to communicate with counsel of his own choosing;

(c) To be tried without undue delay;

(d) To be tried in his presence, and to defend himself in person or through legal assistance of his own choosing; to be informed, if he does not have legal assistance, of this right; and to have legal assistance assigned to him, in any case where the interests of justice so require, and without payment by him in any such case if he does not have sufficient means to pay for it;

(e) To examine, or have examined, the witnesses against him and to obtain the attendance and examination of witnesses on his behalf under the same conditions as witnesses against him;

(f) To have the free assistance of an interpreter if he cannot understand or speak the language used in court;

(g) Not to be compelled to testify against himself or to confess guilt.

4. In the case of juvenile persons, the procedure shall be such as will take account of their age and the desirability of promoting their rehabilitation.

5. Everyone convicted of a crime shall have the right to his conviction and sentence being reviewed by a higher tribunal according to law.

6. When a person has by a final decision been convicted of a criminal offence and when subsequently his conviction has been reversed or he has been pardoned on the ground that a new or newly discovered fact shows conclusively that there has been a miscarriage of justice, the person who has suffered punishment as a result of such conviction shall be compensated according to law, unless it is proved that the non-disclosure of the unknown fact in time is wholly or partly attributable to him.

7. No one shall be liable to be tried or punished again for an offence for which he has already been finally convicted or acquitted in accordance with the law and penal procedure of each country.

Article 15

1. No one shall be held guilty of any criminal offence on account of any act or omission which did not constitute a criminal offence, under national or international law, at the time when it was committed. Nor shall a heavier penalty be imposed than the one that was applicable at the time when the criminal offence was committed. If, subsequent to the commission of the offence, provision is made by law for the imposition of the lighter penalty, the offender shall benefit thereby.

2. Nothing in this article shall prejudice the trial and punishment of any person for any act or omission which, at the

time when it was committed, was criminal according to the general principles of law recognized by the community of nations.

Article 16

Everyone shall have the right to recognition everywhere as a person before the law.

Article 17

1. No one shall be subjected to arbitrary or unlawful interference with his privacy, family, home or correspondence, nor to unlawful attacks on his honour and reputation.

2. Everyone has the right to the protection of the law against such interference or attacks.

Article 18

1. Everyone shall have the right to freedom of thought, conscience and religion. This right shall include freedom to have or to adopt a religion or belief of his choice, and freedom, either individually or in community with others and in public or private, to manifest his religion or belief in worship, observance, practice and teaching.

2. No one shall be subject to coercion which would impair his freedom to have or to adopt a religion or belief of his choice.

3. Freedom to manifest one's religion or beliefs may be subject only to such limitations as are prescribed by law and are necessary to protect public safety, order, health, or morals or the fundamental rights and freedoms of others.

4. The States Parties to the present Covenant undertake to have respect for the liberty of parents and, when applicable, legal guardians to ensure the religious and moral education of their children in conformity with their own convictions.

Article 19

1. Everyone shall have the right to hold opinions without interference.

2. Everyone shall have the right to freedom of expression; this right shall include freedom to seek, receive and impart information and ideas of all kinds, regardless of frontiers, either orally, in writing or in print, in the form of art, or through any other media of his choice.

3. The exercise of the rights provided for in paragraph 2 of this article carries with it special duties and responsibilities. It may therefore be subject to certain restrictions, but these shall only be such as are provided by law and are necessary:

(a) For respect of the rights or reputations of others;

(b) For the protection of national security or of public order (ordre public), or of public health or morals.

Article 20

1. Any propaganda for war shall be prohibited by law.

2. Any advocacy of national, racial or religious hatred that constitutes incitement to discrimination, hostility or violence shall be prohibited by law.

Article 21

The right of peaceful assembly shall be recognized. No restrictions may be placed on the exercise of this right other than those imposed in conformity with the law and which are necessary in a democratic society in the interests of national security or public safety, public order (ordre public), the protection of public health or morals or the protection of the rights and freedoms of others.

Article 22

1. Everyone shall have the right to freedom of association with others, including the right to form and join trade unions for the protection of his interests.

2. No restrictions may be placed on the exercise of this right other than those which are prescribed by law and which are necessary in a democratic society in the interests of national security or public safety, public order (ordre public), the protection of public health or morals or the protection of the rights and freedoms of others. This article shall not prevent the imposition of lawful restrictions on members of the armed forces and of the police in their exercise of this right.

3. Nothing in this article shall authorize States Parties to the International Labour Organisation Convention of 1948 concerning Freedom of Association and Protection of the Right to Organize to take legislative measures which would prejudice, or to apply the law in such a manner as to prejudice, the guarantees provided for in that Convention.

Article 23

1. The family is the natural and fundamental group unit of society and is entitled to protection by society and the State.

2. The right of men and women of marriageable age to marry and to found a family shall be recognized.

3. No marriage shall be entered into without the free and full consent of the intending spouses.

4. States Parties to the present Covenant shall take appropriate steps to ensure equality of rights and responsibilities of spouses as to marriage, during marriage and at its dissolution. In the case of dissolution, provision shall be made for the necessary protection of any children.

Article 24

1. Every child shall have, without any discrimination as to race, colour, sex, language, religion, national or social origin, property or birth, the right to such measures of protection as are required by his status as a minor, on the part of his family, society and the State.

2. Every child shall be registered immediately after birth and shall have a name.

3. Every child has the right to acquire a nationality.

Article 25

Every citizen shall have the right and the opportunity, without any of the distinctions mentioned in article 2 and without unreasonable restrictions:

(a) To take part in the conduct of public affairs, directly or through freely chosen representatives;

(b) To vote and to be elected at genuine periodic elections which shall be by universal and equal suffrage and shall be held by secret ballot, guaranteeing the free expression of the will of the electors;

(c) To have access, on general terms of equality, to public service in his country.

Article 26

All persons are equal before the law and are entitled without any discrimination to the equal protection of the law. In this respect, the law shall prohibit any discrimination and guarantee to all persons equal and effective protection against discrimination on any ground such as race, colour, sex, language, religion, political or other opinion, national or social origin, property, birth or other status.

Article 27

In those States in which ethnic, religious or linguistic minorities exist, persons belonging to such minorities shall not be denied the right, in community with the other members of their group, to enjoy their own culture, to profess and practise their own religion, or to use their own language.

Part IV

Article 28

1. There shall be established a Human Rights Committee (hereafter referred to in the present Covenant as the Committee). It shall consist of eighteen members and shall carry out the functions hereinafter provided.

2. The Committee shall be composed of nationals of the States Parties to the present Covenant who shall be persons of high moral character and recognized competence in the field of human rights, consideration being given to the usefulness of the participation of some persons having legal experience.

3. The members of the Committee shall be elected and shall serve in their personal capacity.

Article 29

1. The members of the Committee shall be elected by secret ballot from a list of persons possessing the qualifications prescribed in article 28 and nominated for the purpose by the States Parties to the present Covenant.

2. Each State Party to the present Covenant may nominate not more than two persons. These persons shall be nationals of the nominating State.

3. A person shall be eligible for renomination.

Article 30

1. The initial election shall be held no later than six months after the date of the entry into force of the present Covenant.

2. At least four months before the date of each election to the Committee, other than an election to fill a vacancy declared in accordance with article 34, the Secretary-General of the United Nations shall address a written invitation to the States Parties to the present Covenant to submit their nominations for membership of the Committee within three months.

3. The Secretary-General of the United Nations shall prepare a list in alphabetical order of all the persons thus nominated, with an indication of the States Parties which have nominated them, and shall submit it to the States Parties to the present Covenant no later than one month before the date of each election.

4. Elections of the members of the Committee shall be held at a meeting of the States Parties to the present Covenant convened by the Secretary-General of the United Nations at the Headquarters of the United Nations. At that meeting, for which

two thirds of the States Parties to the present Covenant shall constitute a quorum, the persons elected to the Committee shall be those nominees who obtain the largest number of votes and an absolute majority of the votes of the representatives of States Parties present and voting.

Article 31

1. The Committee may not include more than one national of the same State.

2. In the election of the Committee, consideration shall be given to equitable geographical distribution of membership and to the representation of the different forms of civilization and of the principal legal systems.

Article 32

1. The members of the Committee shall be elected for a term of four years. They shall be eligible for re-election if renominated. However, the terms of nine of the members elected at the first election shall expire at the end of two years; immediately after the first election, the names of these nine members shall be chosen by lot by the Chairman of the meeting referred to in article 30, paragraph 4.

2. Elections at the expiry of office shall be held in accordance with the preceding articles of this part of the present Covenant.

Article 33

1. If, in the unanimous opinion of the other members, a member of the Committee has ceased to carry out his functions for any cause other than absence of a temporary character, the Chairman of the Committee shall notify the Secretary-General of the United Nations, who shall then declare the seat of that member to be vacant.

2. In the event of the death or the resignation of a member of the Committee, the Chairman shall immediately notify the Secretary-General of the United Nations, who shall declare the seat vacant from the date of death or the date on which the resignation takes effect.

Article 34

1. When a vacancy is declared in accordance with article 33 and if the term of office of the member to be replaced does not expire within six months of the declaration of the vacancy, the Secretary-General of the United Nations shall notify each of the States Parties to the present Covenant, which may within two months submit nominations in accordance with article 29 for the purpose of filling the vacancy.

2. The Secretary-General of the United Nations shall prepare a list in alphabetical order of the persons thus nominated and shall submit it to the States Parties to the present Covenant. The election to fill the vacancy shall then take place in accordance with the relevant provisions of this part of the present Covenant.

3. A member of the Committee elected to fill a vacancy declared in accordance with article 33 shall hold office for the remainder of the term of the member who vacated the seat on the Committee under the provisions of that article.

Article 35

The members of the Committee shall, with the approval of the General Assembly of the United Nations, receive emoluments from United Nations resources on such terms and conditions as the General Assembly may decide, having regard to the importance of the Committee's responsibilities.

Article 36

The Secretary-General of the United Nations shall provide the necessary staff and facilities for the effective performance of the functions of the Committee under the present Covenant.

Article 37

1. The Secretary-General of the United Nations shall convene the initial meeting of the Committee at the Headquarters of the United Nations.

2. After its initial meeting, the Committee shall meet at such times as shall be provided in its rules of procedure.

3. The Committee shall normally meet at the Headquarters of the United Nations or at the United Nations Office at Geneva.

Article 38

Every member of the Committee shall, before taking up his duties, make a solemn declaration in open committee that he will perform his functions impartially and conscientiously.

Article 39

1. The Committee shall elect its officers for a term of two years. They may be re-elected.

2. The Committee shall establish its own rules of procedure, but these rules shall provide, inter alia, that:

(a) Twelve members shall constitute a quorum;

(b) Decisions of the Committee shall be made by a majority vote of the members present.

Article 40

1. The States Parties to the present Covenant undertake to submit reports on the measures they have adopted which give effect to the rights recognized herein and on the progress made in the enjoyment of those rights:

> (a) Within one year of the entry into force of the present Covenant for the States Parties concerned;

> (b) Thereafter whenever the Committee so requests.

2. All reports shall be submitted to the Secretary-General of the United Nations, who shall transmit them to the Committee for consideration. Reports shall indicate the factors and difficulties, if any, affecting the implementation of the present Covenant.

3. The Secretary-General of the United Nations may, after consultation with the Committee, transmit to the specialized agencies concerned copies of such parts of the reports as may fall within their field of competence.

4. The Committee shall study the reports submitted by the States Parties to the present Covenant. It shall transmit its reports, and such general comments as it may consider appropriate, to the States Parties. The Committee may also transmit to the Economic and Social Council these comments along with the copies of the reports it has received from States Parties to the present Covenant.

5. The States Parties to the present Covenant may submit to the Committee observations on any comments that may be made in accordance with paragraph 4 of this article.

Article 41

1. A State Party to the present Covenant may at any time declare under this article that it recognizes the competence of the Committee to receive and consider communications to the effect that a State Party claims that another State Party is not fulfilling its obligations under the present Covenant. Communications under this article may be received and considered only if submitted by a State Party which has made a declaration recognizing in regard to itself the competence of the Committee. No communication shall be received by the Committee if it concerns a State Party which has not made such a declaration. Communications received under this article shall be dealt with in accordance with the following procedure:

> (a) If a State Party to the present Covenant considers that another State Party is not giving effect to the provisions of the present Covenant, it may, by written communication, bring the matter to the attention of that State Party. Within three months after the receipt of the communication the receiving State shall afford the State which sent the communication an explanation, or any other statement in writing clarifying the matter which should include, to the extent possible and pertinent, reference to domestic procedures and remedies taken, pending, or available in the matter;

> (b) If the matter is not adjusted to the satisfaction of both States Parties concerned within six months after the receipt by the receiving State of the initial communication, either State shall have the right to refer the matter to the Committee, by notice given to the Committee and to the other State;

> (c) The Committee shall deal with a matter referred to it only after it has ascertained that all available domestic remedies have been invoked and exhausted in the matter, in conformity with the generally recognized principles of international law. This shall not be the rule where the application of the remedies is unreasonably prolonged;

> (d) The Committee shall hold closed meetings when examining communications under this article;

> (e) Subject to the provisions of subparagraph (c), the Committee shall make available its good offices to the States Parties concerned with a view to a friendly solution of the matter on the basis of respect for human rights and fundamental freedoms as recognized in the present Covenant;

> (f) In any matter referred to it, the Committee may call upon the States Parties concerned, referred to in subparagraph (b), to supply any relevant information;

> (g) The States Parties concerned, referred to in subparagraph (b), shall have the right to be represented when the matter is being considered in the Committee and to make submissions orally and/or in writing;

> (h) The Committee shall, within twelve months after the date of receipt of notice under subparagraph (b), submit a report:

> > (i) If a solution within the terms of subparagraph (e) is reached, the Committee shall confine its report to a brief statement of the facts and of the solution reached;

> > (ii) If a solution within the terms of subparagraph (e) is not reached, the Committee shall confine its report to a brief statement of the facts; the written submissions and record of the oral submissions made by the

States Parties concerned shall be attached to the report. In every matter, the report shall be communicated to the States Parties concerned.

2. The provisions of this article shall come into force when ten States Parties to the present Covenant have made declarations under paragraph 1 of this article. Such declarations shall be deposited by the States Parties with the Secretary-General of the United Nations, who shall transmit copies thereof to the other States Parties. A declaration may be withdrawn at any time by notification to the Secretary-General. Such a withdrawal shall not prejudice the consideration of any matter which is the subject of a communication already transmitted under this article; no further communication by any State Party shall be received after the notification of withdrawal of the declaration has been received by the Secretary-General, unless the State Party concerned has made a new declaration.

Article 42

1. (a) If a matter referred to the Committee in accordance with article 41 is not resolved to the satisfaction of the States Parties concerned, the Committee may, with the prior consent of the States Parties concerned, appoint an ad hoc Conciliation Commission (hereinafter referred to as the Commission). The good offices of the Commission shall be made available to the States Parties concerned with a view to an amicable solution of the matter on the basis of respect for the present Covenant;

(b) The Commission shall consist of five persons acceptable to the States Parties concerned. If the States Parties concerned fail to reach agreement within three months on all or part of the composition of the Commission, the members of the Commission concerning whom no agreement has been reached shall be elected by secret ballot by a two-thirds majority vote of the Committee from among its members.

2. The members of the Commission shall serve in their personal capacity. They shall not be nationals of the States Parties concerned, or of a State not Party to the present Covenant, or of a State Party which has not made a declaration under article 41.

3. The Commission shall elect its own Chairman and adopt its own rules of procedure.

4. The meetings of the Commission shall normally be held at the Headquarters of the United Nations or at the United Nations Office at Geneva. However, they may be held at such other convenient places as the Commission may determine in consultation with the Secretary-General of the United Nations and the States Parties concerned.

5. The secretariat provided in accordance with article 36 shall also service the commissions appointed under this article.

6. The information received and collated by the Committee shall be made available to the Commission and the Commission may call upon the States Parties concerned to supply any other relevant information.

7. When the Commission has fully considered the matter, but in any event not later than twelve months after having been seized of the matter, it shall submit to the Chairman of the Committee a report for communication to the States Parties concerned:

(a) If the Commission is unable to complete its consideration of the matter within twelve months, it shall confine its report to a brief statement of the status of its consideration of the matter;

(b) If an amicable solution to the matter on tie basis of respect for human rights as recognized in the present Covenant is reached, the Commission shall confine its report to a brief statement of the facts and of the solution reached;

(c) If a solution within the terms of subparagraph (b) is not reached, the Commission's report shall embody its findings on all questions of fact relevant to the issues between the States Parties concerned, and its views on the possibilities of an amicable solution of the matter. This report shall also contain the written submissions and a record of the oral submissions made by the States Parties concerned;

(d) If the Commission's report is submitted under subparagraph (c), the States Parties concerned shall, within three months of the receipt of the report, notify the Chairman of the Committee whether or not they accept the contents of the report of the Commission.

8. The provisions of this article are without prejudice to the responsibilities of the Committee under article 41.

9. The States Parties concerned shall share equally all the expenses of the members of the Commission in accordance with estimates to be provided by the Secretary-General of the United Nations.

10. The Secretary-General of the United Nations shall be empowered to pay the expenses of the members of the Commission, if necessary, before reimbursement by the States Parties concerned, in accordance with paragraph 9 of this article.

Article 43

The members of the Committee, and of the ad hoc conciliation commissions which may be appointed under article 42, shall be entitled to the facilities, privileges and immunities of experts on mission for the United Nations as laid down in the relevant sections of the Convention on the Privileges and Immunities of the United Nations.

Article 44

The provisions for the implementation of the present Covenant shall apply without prejudice to the procedures prescribed in the field of human rights by or under the constituent instruments and the conventions of the United Nations and of the specialized agencies and shall not prevent the States Parties to the present Covenant from having recourse to other procedures for settling a dispute in accordance with general or special international agreements in force between them.

Article 45

The Committee shall submit to the General Assembly of the United Nations, through the Economic and Social Council, an annual report on its activities.

Part V

Article 46

Nothing in the present Covenant shall be interpreted as impairing the provisions of the Charter of the United Nations and of the constitutions of the specialized agencies which define the respective responsibilities of the various organs of the United Nations and of the specialized agencies in regard to the matters dealt with in the present Covenant.

Article 47

Nothing in the present Covenant shall be interpreted as impairing the inherent right of all peoples to enjoy and utilize fully and freely their natural wealth and resources.

Part VI

Article 48

1. The present Covenant is open for signature by any State Member of the United Nations or member of any of its specialized agencies, by any State Party to the Statute of the International Court of Justice, and by any other State which has been invited by the General Assembly of the United Nations to become a Party to the present Covenant.

2. The present Covenant is subject to ratification. Instruments of ratification shall be deposited with the Secretary-General of the United Nations.

3. The present Covenant shall be open to accession by any State referred to in paragraph 1 of this article.

4. Accession shall be effected by the deposit of an instrument of accession with the Secretary-General of the United Nations.

5. The Secretary-General of the United Nations shall inform all States which have signed this Covenant or acceded to it of the deposit of each instrument of ratification or accession.

Article 49

1. The present Covenant shall enter into force three months after the date of the deposit with the Secretary-General of the United Nations of the thirty-fifth instrument of ratification or instrument of accession.

2. For each State ratifying the present Covenant or acceding to it after the deposit of the thirty-fifth instrument of ratification or instrument of accession, the present Covenant shall enter into force three months after the date of the deposit of its own instrument of ratification or instrument of accession.

Article 50

The provisions of the present Covenant shall extend to all parts of federal States without any limitations or exceptions.

Article 51

1. Any State Party to the present Covenant may propose an amendment and file it with the Secretary-General of the United Nations. The Secretary-General of the United Nations shall thereupon communicate any proposed amendments to the States Parties to the present Covenant with a request that they notify him whether they favour a conference of States Parties for the purpose of considering and voting upon the proposals. In the event that at least one third of the States Parties favours such a conference, the Secretary-General shall convene the conference under the auspices of the United Nations. Any amendment adopted by a majority of the States Parties present and voting at the conference shall be submitted to the General Assembly of the United Nations for approval.

2. Amendments shall come into force when they have been approved by the General Assembly of the United Nations and accepted by a two-thirds majority of the States Parties to the present Covenant in accordance with their respective constitutional processes.

3. When amendments come into force, they shall be binding on those States Parties which have accepted them, other States Parties still being bound by the provisions of the present Covenant and any earlier amendment which they have accepted.

Article 52

Irrespective of the notifications made under article 48, paragraph 5, the Secretary-General of the United Nations shall inform all States referred to in paragraph 1 of the same article of the following particulars:

(a) Signatures, ratifications and accessions under article 48;

(b) The date of the entry into force of the present Covenant under article 49 and the date of the entry into force of any amendments under article 51.

Article 53

1. The present Covenant, of which the Chinese, English, French, Russian and Spanish texts are equally authentic, shall be deposited in the archives of the United Nations.

2. The Secretary-General of the United Nations shall transmit certified copies of the present Covenant to all States referred to in article 48.

CONVENTION ON THE PREVENTION AND PUNISHMENT OF THE CRIME OF GENOCIDE

Approved and proposed for signature and ratification or accession by General Assembly resolution 260 A (III) of 9 December 1948

Entered into force 12 January 1951, in accordance with article XIII

The Contracting Parties,

Having considered the declaration made by the General Assembly of the United Nations in its resolution 96 (I) dated 11 December 1946 that genocide is a crime under international law, contrary to the spirit and aims of the United Nations and condemned by the civilized world,

Recognizing that at all periods of history genocide has inflicted great losses on humanity, and

Being convinced that, in order to liberate mankind from such an odious scourge, international co-operation is required,

Hereby agree as hereinafter provided:

Article 1

The Contracting Parties confirm that genocide, whether committed in time of peace or in time of war, is a crime under international law which they undertake to prevent and to punish.

Article 2

In the present Convention, genocide means any of the following acts committed with intent to destroy, in whole or in part, a national, ethnical, racial or religious group, as such:

(a) Killing members of the group;

(b) Causing serious bodily or mental harm to members of the group;

(c) Deliberately inflicting on the group conditions of life calculated to bring about its physical destruction in whole or in part;

(d) Imposing measures intended to prevent births within the group;

(e) Forcibly transferring children of the group to another group.

Article 3

The following acts shall be punishable:

(a) Genocide;

(b) Conspiracy to commit genocide;

(c) Direct and public incitement to commit genocide;

(d) Attempt to commit genocide;

(e) Complicity in genocide.

Article 4

Persons committing genocide or any of the other acts enumerated in article 3 shall be punished, whether they are constitutionally responsible rulers, public officials or private individuals.

Article 5

The Contracting Parties undertake to enact, in accordance with their respective Constitutions, the necessary legislation to give effect to the provisions of the present Convention, and, in particular, to provide effective penalties for persons guilty of genocide or any of the other acts enumerated in article 3.

Article 6

Persons charged with genocide or any of the other acts enumerated in article 3 shall be tried by a competent tribunal of the State in the territory of which the act was committed, or by such international penal tribunal as may have jurisdiction with respect to those Contracting Parties which shall have accepted its jurisdiction.

Article 7

Genocide and the other acts enumerated in article 3 shall not be considered as political crimes for the purpose of extradition.

The Contracting Parties pledge themselves in such cases to grant extradition in accordance with their laws and treaties in force.

Article 8

Any Contracting Party may call upon the competent organs of the United Nations to take such action under the Charter of the United Nations as they consider appropriate for the prevention and suppression of acts of genocide or any of the other acts enumerated in article 3.

Article 9

Disputes between the Contracting Parties relating to the interpretation, application or fulfilment of the present Convention, including those relating to the responsibility of a State for genocide or for any of the other acts enumerated in article 3, shall be submitted to the International Court of Justice at the request of any of the parties to the dispute.

Article 10

The present Convention, of which the Chinese, English, French, Russian and Spanish texts are equally authentic, shall bear the date of 9 December 1948.

Article 11

The present Convention shall be open until 31 December 1949 for signature on behalf of any Member of the United Nations and of any nonmember State to which an invitation to sign has been addressed by the General Assembly.

The present Convention shall be ratified, and the instruments of ratification shall be deposited with the Secretary-General of the United Nations.

After 1 January 1950, the present Convention may be acceded to on behalf of any Member of the United Nations and of any non-member State which has received an invitation as aforesaid. Instruments of accession shall be deposited with the Secretary-General of the United Nations.

Article 12

Any Contracting Party may at any time, by notification addressed to the Secretary-General of the United Nations, ex-tend the application of the present Convention to all or any of the territories for the conduct of whose foreign relations that Contracting Party is responsible.

Article 13

On the day when the first twenty instruments of ratification or accession have been deposited, the Secretary-General shall draw up a proces-verbal and transmit a copy thereof to each Member of the United Nations and to each of the non-member States contemplated in article 11.

The present Convention shall come into force on the ninetieth day following the date of deposit of the twentieth instrument of ratification or accession.

Any ratification or accession effected, subsequent to the latter date shall become effective on the nineteenth day following the deposit of the instrument of ratification or accession.

Article 14

The present Convention shall remain in effect for a period of ten years as from the date of its coming into force.

It shall thereafter remain in force for successive periods of five years for such Contracting Parties as have not denounced it at least six months before the expiration of the current period.

Denunciation shall be effected by a written notification addressed to the Secretary-General of the United Nations.

Article 15

If, as a result of denunciations, the number of Parties to the present Convention should become less than sixteen, the Convention shall cease to be in force as from the date on which the last of these denunciations shall become effective.

Article 16

A request for the revision of the present Convention may be made at any time by any Contracting Party by means of a notification in writing addressed to the Secretary-General.

The General Assembly shall decide upon the steps, if any, to be taken in respect of such request.

Article 17

The Secretary-General of the United Nations shall notify all Members of the United Nations and the non-member States contemplated in article 11 of the following:

(a) Signatures, ratifications and accessions received in accordance with article 11;

(b) Notifications received in accordance with article 12;

(c) The date upon which the present Convention comes into force in accordance with article 13;

(d) Denunciations received in accordance with article 14;

(e) The abrogation of the Convention in accordance with article 15;

(f) Notifications received in accordance with article 16.

Article 18

The original of the present Convention shall be deposited in the archives of the United Nations.

A certified copy of the Convention shall be transmitted to each Member of the United Nations and to each of the non-member States contemplated in article 11.

Article 19

The present Convention shall be registered by the Secretary-General of the United Nations on the date of its coming into force.

INTERNATIONAL CONVENTION ON THE ELIMINATION OF ALL FORMS OF RACIAL DISCRIMINATION

Adopted and opened for signature and ratification by General Assembly resolution 2106 (XX) of 21 December 1965
Entered into force 4 January 1969, in accordance with Article 19

The States Parties to this Convention,

Considering that the Charter of the United Nations is based on the principles of the dignity and equality inherent in all human beings, and that all Member States have pledged themselves to take joint and separate action, in co-operation with the Organization, for the achievement of one of the purposes of the United Nations which is to promote and encourage universal respect for and observance of human rights and fundamental freedoms for all, without distinction as to race, sex, language or religion,

Considering that the Universal Declaration of Human Rights proclaims that all human beings are born free and equal in dignity and rights and that everyone is entitled to all the rights and freedoms set out therein, without distinction of any kind, in particular as to race, colour or national origin,

Considering that all human beings are equal before the law and are entitled to equal protection of the law against any discrimination and against any incitement to discrimination,

Considering that the United Nations has condemned colonialism and all practices of segregation and discrimination associated therewith, in whatever form and wherever they exist, and that the Declaration on the Granting of Independence to Colonial Countries and Peoples of 14 December 1960 (General Assembly resolution 1514 (XV)) has affirmed and solemnly proclaimed the necessity of bringing them to a speedy and unconditional end,

Considering that the United Nations Declaration on the Elimination of All Forms of Racial Discrimination of 20 November 1963 (General Assembly resolution 1904 [XVIII]) solemnly affirms the necessity of speedily eliminating racial discrimination throughout the world in all its forms and manifestations and of securing understanding of and respect for the dignity of the human person,

Convinced that any doctrine of superiority based on racial differentiation is scientifically false, morally condemnable, socially unjust and dangerous, and that there is no justification for racial discrimination, in theory or in practice, anywhere,

Reaffirming that discrimination between human beings on the grounds of race, colour or ethnic origin is an obstacle to friendly and peaceful relations among nations and is capable of disturbing peace and security among peoples and the harmony of persons living side by side even within one and the same State,

Convinced that the existence of racial barriers is repugnant to the ideals of any human society,

Alarmed by manifestations of racial discrimination still in evidence in some areas of the world and by governmental policies based on racial superiority or hatred, such as policies of apartheid, segregation or separation,

Resolved to adopt all necessary measures for speedily eliminating racial discrimination in all its forms and manifestations, and to prevent and combat racist doctrines and practices in order to promote understanding between races and to build an international community free from all forms of racial segregation and racial discrimination,

Bearing in mind the Convention concerning Discrimination in respect of Employment and Occupation adopted by the International Labour Organisation in 1958, and the Convention against Discrimination in Education adopted by the United Nations Educational, Scientific and Cultural Organization in 1960,

Desiring to implement the principles embodied in the United Nations Declaration on the Elimination of All Forms of Racial Discrimination and to secure the earliest adoption of practical measures to that end,

Have agreed as follows:

Part I

Article 1

1. In this Convention, the term "racial discrimination" shall mean any distinction, exclusion, restriction or preference based on race, colour, descent, or national or ethnic origin which has the purpose or effect of nullifying or impairing the recognition, enjoyment or exercise, on an equal footing, of human rights and fundamental freedoms in the political, economic, social, cultural or any other field of public life.

2. This Convention shall not apply to distinctions, exclusions, restrictions or preferences made by a State Party to this Convention between citizens and non-citizens.

3. Nothing in this Convention may be interpreted as affecting in any way the legal provisions of States Parties concerning nationality, citizenship or naturalization, provided that such provisions do not discriminate against any particular nationality.

4. Special measures taken for the sole purpose of securing adequate advancement of certain racial or ethnic groups or individuals requiring such protection as may be necessary in order to ensure such groups or individuals equal enjoyment or exercise of human rights and fundamental freedoms shall not be deemed racial discrimination, provided, however, that such measures do not, as a consequence, lead to the maintenance of separate rights for different racial groups and that they shall not be continued after the objectives for which they were taken have been achieved.

Article 2

1. States Parties condemn racial discrimination and undertake to pursue by all appropriate means and without delay a policy of eliminating racial discrimination in all its forms and promoting understanding among all races, and, to this end:

(a) Each State Party undertakes to engage in no act or practice of racial discrimination against persons, groups of persons or institutions and to ensure that all public authorities and public institutions, national and local, shall act in conformity with this obligation;

(b) Each State Party undertakes not to sponsor, defend or support racial discrimination by any persons or organizations;

(c) Each State Party shall take effective measures to review governmental, national and local policies, and to amend, rescind or nullify any laws and regulations which have the effect of creating or perpetuating racial discrimination wherever it exists;

(d) Each State Party shall prohibit and bring to an end, by all appropriate means, including legislation as required by circumstances, racial discrimination by any persons, group or organization;

(e) Each State Party undertakes to encourage, where appropriate, integrationist multiracial organizations and movements and other means of eliminating barriers between races, and to discourage anything which tends to strengthen racial division.

2. States Parties shall, when the circumstances so warrant, take, in the social, economic, cultural and other fields, special and concrete measures to ensure the adequate development and protection of certain racial groups or individuals belonging to them, for the purpose of guaranteeing them the full and equal enjoyment of human rights and fundamental freedoms. These measures shall in no case entail as a consequence the maintenance of unequal or separate rights for different racial groups after the objectives for which they were taken have been achieved.

Article 3

States Parties particularly condemn racial segregation and apartheid and undertake to prevent, prohibit and eradicate all practices of this nature in territories under their jurisdiction.

Article 4

States Parties condemn all propaganda and all organizations which are based on ideas or theories of superiority of one race or group of persons of one colour or ethnic origin, or which attempt to justify or promote racial hatred and discrimination in any form, and undertake to adopt immediate and positive measures designed to eradicate all incitement to, or acts of, such discrimination and, to this end, with due regard to the principles embodied in the Universal Declaration of Human Rights and the rights expressly set forth in article 5 of this Convention, inter alia:

(a) Shall declare an offence punishable by law all dissemination of ideas based on racial superiority or hatred, incitement to racial discrimination, as well as all acts of violence or incitement to such acts against any race or group of persons of another colour or ethnic origin, and also the provision of any assistance to racist activities, including the financing thereof;

(b) Shall declare illegal and prohibit organizations, and also organized and all other propaganda activities, which promote and incite racial discrimination, and shall recognize participation in such organizations or activities as an offence punishable by law;

(c) Shall not permit public authorities or public institutions, national or local, to promote or incite racial discrimination.

Article 5

In compliance with the fundamental obligations laid down in article 2 of this Convention, States Parties undertake to prohibit and to eliminate racial discrimination in all its forms and to guarantee the right of everyone, without distinction as to race, colour, or national or ethnic origin, to equality before the law, notably in the enjoyment of the following rights:

(a) The right to equal treatment before the tribunals and all other organs administering justice;

(b) The right to security of person and protection by the State against violence or bodily harm, whether inflicted by government officials or by any individual group or institution;

(c) Political rights, in particular the right to participate in elections—to vote and to stand for election—on the basis of universal and equal suffrage, to take part in the Government as well as in the conduct of public affairs at any level and to have equal access to public service;

(d) Other civil rights, in particular:

(i) The right to freedom of movement and residence within the border of the State;

(ii) The right to leave any country, including one's own, and to return to one's country;

(iii) The right to nationality;

(iv) The right to marriage and choice of spouse;

(v) The right to own property alone as well as in association with others;

(vi) The right to inherit;

(vii) The right to freedom of thought, conscience and religion;

(viii) The right to freedom of opinion and expression;

(ix) The right to freedom of peaceful assembly and association;

(e) Economic, social and cultural rights, in particular:

(i) The rights to work, to free choice of employment, to just and favourable conditions of work, to protection against unemployment, to equal pay for equal work, to just and favourable remuneration;

(ii) The right to form and join trade unions;

(iii) The right to housing;

(iv) The right to public health, medical care, social security and social services;

(v) The right to education and training;

(vi) The right to equal participation in cultural activities;

(f) The right of access to any place or service intended for use by the general public, such as transport hotels, restaurants, cafes, theatres and parks.

Article 6

States Parties shall assure to everyone within their jurisdiction effective protection and remedies, through the competent national tribunals and other State institutions, against any acts of racial discrimination which violate his human rights and fundamental freedoms contrary to this Convention, as well as the right to seek from such tribunals just and adequate reparation or satisfaction for any damage suffered as a result of such discrimination.

Article 7

States Parties undertake to adopt immediate and effective measures, particularly in the fields of teaching, education, culture and information, with a view to combating prejudices which lead to racial discrimination and to promoting understanding, tolerance and friendship among nations and racial or ethnical groups, as well as to propagating the purposes and principles of the Charter of the United Nations, the Universal Declaration of Human Rights, the United Nations Declaration on the Elimination of All Forms of Racial Discrimination, and this Convention.

Part II

Article 8

1. There shall be established a Committee on the Elimination of Racial Discrimination (hereinafter referred to as the Committee) consisting of eighteen experts of high moral stand-

ing and acknowledged impartiality elected by States Parties from among their nationals, who shall serve in their personal capacity, consideration being given to equitable geographical distribution and to the representation of the different forms of civilization as well as of the principal legal systems.

2. The members of the Committee shall be elected by secret ballot from a list of persons nominated by the States Parties. Each State Party may nominate one person from among its own nationals.

3. The initial election shall be held six months after the date of the entry into force of this Convention. At least three months before the date of each election the Secretary-General of the United Nations shall address a letter to the States Parties inviting them to submit their nominations within two months. The Secretary-General shall prepare a list in alphabetical order of all persons thus nominated, indicating the States Parties which have nominated them, and shall submit it to the States Parties.

4. Elections of the members of the Committee shall be held at a meeting of States Parties convened by the Secretary-General at United Nations Headquarters. At that meeting, for which two thirds of the States Parties shall constitute a quorum, the persons elected to the Committee shall be nominees who obtain the largest number of votes and an absolute majority of the votes of the representatives of States Parties present and voting.

5. (a) The members of the Committee shall be elected for a term of four years. However, the terms of nine of the members elected at the first election shall expire at the end of two years; immediately after the first election the names of these nine members shall be chosen by lot by the Chairman of the Committee;

(b) For the filling of casual vacancies, the State Party whose expert has ceased to function as a member of the Committee shall appoint another expert from among its nationals, subject to the approval of the Committee.

6. States Parties shall be responsible for the expenses of the members of the Committee while they are in performance of Committee duties. (amendment [see General Assembly resolution 47/111 of 16 December 1992]; status of ratification)

Article 9

1. States Parties undertake to submit to the Secretary-General of the United Nations, for consideration by the Committee, a report on the legislative, judicial, administrative or other measures which they have adopted and which give effect to the provisions of this Convention:

(a) within one year after the entry into force of the Convention for the State concerned; and

(b) thereafter every two years and whenever the Committee so requests. The Committee may request further information from the States Parties.

2. The Committee shall report annually, through the Secretary-General, to the General Assembly of the United Nations on its activities and may make suggestions and general recommendations based on the examination of the reports and information received from the States Parties. Such suggestions and general recommendations shall be reported to the General Assembly together with comments, if any, from States Parties.

Article 10

1. The Committee shall adopt its own rules of procedure.

2. The Committee shall elect its officers for a term of two years.

3. The secretariat of the Committee shall be provided by the Secretary-General of the United Nations.

4. The meetings of the Committee shall normally be held at United Nations Headquarters.

Article 11

1. If a State Party considers that another State Party is not giving effect to the provisions of this Convention, it may bring the matter to the attention of the Committee. The Committee shall then transmit the communication to the State Party concerned. Within three months, the receiving State shall submit to the Committee written explanations or statements clarifying the matter and the remedy, if any, that may have been taken by that State.

2. If the matter is not adjusted to the satisfaction of both parties, either by bilateral negotiations or by any other procedure open to them, within six months after the receipt by the receiving State of the initial communication, either State shall have the right to refer the matter again to the Committee by notifying the Committee and also the other State.

3. The Committee shall deal with a matter referred to it in accordance with paragraph 2 of this article after it has ascertained that all available domestic remedies have been invoked and exhausted in the case, in conformity with the generally recognized principles of international law. This shall not be the rule where the application of the remedies is unreasonably prolonged.

4. In any matter referred to it, the Committee may call upon the States Parties concerned to supply any other relevant information.

5. When any matter arising out of this article is being considered by the Committee, the States Parties concerned shall be entitled to send a representative to take part in the proceedings of the Committee, without voting rights, while the matter is under consideration.

Article 12

1. (a) After the Committee has obtained and collated all the information it deems necessary, the Chairman shall appoint an ad hoc Conciliation Commission (hereinafter referred to as the Commission) comprising five persons who may or may not be members of the Committee. The members of the Commission shall be appointed with the unanimous consent of the parties to the dispute, and its good offices shall be made available to the States concerned with a view to an amicable solution of the matter on the basis of respect for this Convention;

(b) If the States parties to the dispute fail to reach agreement within three months on all or part of the composition of the Commission, the members of the Commission not agreed upon by the States parties to the dispute shall be elected by secret ballot by a two-thirds majority vote of the Committee from among its own members.

2. The members of the Commission shall serve in their personal capacity. They shall not be nationals of the States parties to the dispute or of a State not Party to this Convention.

3. The Commission shall elect its own Chairman and adopt its own rules of procedure.

4. The meetings of the Commission shall normally be held at United Nations Headquarters or at any other convenient place as determined by the Commission.

5. The secretariat provided in accordance with article 10, paragraph 3, of this Convention shall also service the Commission whenever a dispute among States Parties brings the Commission into being.

6. The States parties to the dispute shall share equally all the expenses of the members of the Commission in accordance with estimates to be provided by the Secretary-General of the United Nations.

7. The Secretary-General shall be empowered to pay the expenses of the members of the Commission, if necessary, before reimbursement by the States parties to the dispute in accordance with paragraph 6 of this article.

8. The information obtained and collated by the Committee shall be made available to the Commission, and the Commission may call upon the States concerned to supply any other relevant information.

Article 13

1. When the Commission has fully considered the matter, it shall prepare and submit to the Chairman of the Committee a report embodying its findings on all questions of fact relevant to the issue between the parties and containing such recommendations as it may think proper for the amicable solution of the dispute.

2. The Chairman of the Committee shall communicate the report of the Commission to each of the States parties to the dispute. These States shall, within three months, inform the Chairman of the Committee whether or not they accept the recommendations contained in the report of the Commission.

3. After the period provided for in paragraph 2 of this article, the Chairman of the Committee shall communicate the report of the Commission and the declarations of the States Parties concerned to the other States Parties to this Convention.

Article 14

1. A State Party may at any time declare that it recognizes the competence of the Committee to receive and consider communications from individuals or groups of individuals within its jurisdiction claiming to be victims of a violation by that State Party of any of the rights set forth in this Convention. No communication shall be received by the Committee if it concerns a State Party which has not made such a declaration.

2. Any State Party which makes a declaration as provided for in paragraph 1 of this article may establish or indicate a body within its national legal order which shall be competent to receive and consider petitions from individuals and groups of individuals within its jurisdiction who claim to be victims of a violation of any of the rights set forth in this Convention and who have exhausted other available local remedies.

3. A declaration made in accordance with paragraph 1 of this article and the name of any body established or indicated in accordance with paragraph 2 of this article shall be deposited by the State Party concerned with the Secretary-General of the United Nations, who shall transmit copies thereof to the other States Parties. A declaration may be withdrawn at any time by notification to the Secretary-General, but such a withdrawal shall not affect communications pending before the Committee.

4. A register of petitions shall be kept by the body established or indicated in accordance with paragraph 2 of this ar-

ticle, and certified copies of the register shall be filed annually through appropriate channels with the Secretary-General on the understanding that the contents shall not be publicly disclosed.

5. In the event of failure to obtain satisfaction from the body established or indicated in accordance with paragraph 2 of this article, the petitioner shall have the right to communicate the matter to the Committee within six months.

6. (a) The Committee shall confidentially bring any communication referred to it to the attention of the State Party alleged to be violating any provision of this Convention, but the identity of the individual or groups of individuals concerned shall not be revealed without his or their express consent. The Committee shall not receive anonymous communications;

(b) Within three months, the receiving State shall submit to the Committee written explanations or statements clarifying the matter and the remedy, if any, that may have been taken by that State.

7. (a) The Committee shall consider communications in the light of all information made available to it by the State Party concerned and by the petitioner. The Committee shall not consider any communication from a petitioner unless it has ascertained that the petitioner has exhausted all available domestic remedies. However, this shall not be the rule where the application of the remedies is unreasonably prolonged;

(b) The Committee shall forward its suggestions and recommendations, if any, to the State Party concerned and to the petitioner.

8. The Committee shall include in its annual report a summary of such communications and, where appropriate, a summary of the explanations and statements of the States Parties concerned and of its own suggestions and recommendations.

9. The Committee shall be competent to exercise the functions provided for in this article only when at least ten States Parties to this Convention are bound by declarations in accordance with paragraph 1 of this article.

Article 15

1. Pending the achievement of the objectives of the Declaration on the Granting of Independence to Colonial Countries and Peoples, contained in General Assembly resolution 1514 (XV) of 14 December 1960, the provisions of this Convention shall in no way limit the right of petition granted to these peoples by other international instruments or by the United Nations and its specialized agencies.

2. (a) The Committee established under article 8, paragraph 1, of this Convention shall receive copies of the petitions from, and submit expressions of opinion and recommendations on these petitions to, the bodies of the United Nations which deal with matters directly related to the principles and objectives of this Convention in their consideration of petitions from the inhabitants of Trust and Non-Self-Governing Territories and all other territories to which General Assembly resolution 1514 (XV) applies, relating to matters covered by this Convention which are before these bodies;

(b) The Committee shall receive from the competent bodies of the United Nations copies of the reports concerning the legislative, judicial, administrative or other measures directly related to the principles and objectives of this Convention applied by the administering Powers within the Territories mentioned in subparagraph (a) of this paragraph, and shall express opinions and make recommendations to these bodies.

3. The Committee shall include in its report to the General Assembly a summary of the petitions and reports it has received from United Nations bodies, and the expressions of opinion and recommendations of the Committee relating to the said petitions and reports.

4. The Committee shall request from the Secretary-General of the United Nations all information relevant to the objectives of this Convention and available to him regarding the Territories mentioned in paragraph 2 (a) of this article.

Article 16

The provisions of this Convention concerning the settlement of disputes or complaints shall be applied without prejudice to other procedures for settling disputes or complaints in the field of discrimination laid down in the constituent instruments of, or conventions adopted by, the United Nations and its specialized agencies, and shall not prevent the States Parties from having recourse to other procedures for settling a dispute in accordance with general or special international agreements in force between them.

Part III

Article 17

1. This Convention is open for signature by any State Member of the United Nations or member of any of its specialized agencies, by any State Party to the Statute of the International Court of Justice, and by any other State which has been invited by the General Assembly of the United Nations to become a Party to this Convention.

2. This Convention is subject to ratification. Instruments of ratification shall be deposited with the Secretary-General of the United Nations.

Article 18

1. This Convention shall be open to accession by any State referred to in article 17, paragraph 1, of the Convention. 2. Accession shall be effected by the deposit of an instrument of accession with the Secretary-General of the United Nations.

Article 19

1. This Convention shall enter into force on the thirtieth day after the date of the deposit with the Secretary-General of the United Nations of the twenty-seventh instrument of ratification or instrument of accession.

2. For each State ratifying this Convention or acceding to it after the deposit of the twenty-seventh instrument of ratification or instrument of accession, the Convention shall enter into force on the thirtieth day after the date of the deposit of its own instrument of ratification or instrument of accession.

Article 20

1. The Secretary-General of the United Nations shall receive and circulate to all States which are or may become Parties to this Convention reservations made by States at the time of ratification or accession. Any State which objects to the reservation shall, within a period of ninety days from the date of the said communication, notify the Secretary-General that it does not accept it.

2. A reservation incompatible with the object and purpose of this Convention shall not be permitted, nor shall a reservation the effect of which would inhibit the operation of any of the bodies established by this Convention be allowed. A reservation shall be considered incompatible or inhibitive if at least two thirds of the States Parties to this Convention object to it.

3. Reservations may be withdrawn at any time by notification to this effect addressed to the Secretary-General. Such notification shall take effect on the date on which it is received.

Article 21

A State Party may denounce this Convention by written notification to the Secretary-General of the United Nations. Denunciation shall take effect one year after the date of receipt of the notification by the Secretary-General.

Article 22

Any dispute between two or more States Parties with respect to the interpretation or application of this Convention, which is not settled by negotiation or by the procedures expressly provided for in this Convention, shall, at the request of any of the parties to the dispute, be referred to the International Court of Justice for decision, unless the disputants agree to another mode of settlement.

Article 23

1. A request for the revision of this Convention may be made at any time by any State Party by means of a notification in writing addressed to the Secretary-General of the United Nations.

2. The General Assembly of the United Nations shall decide upon the steps, if any, to be taken in respect of such a request.

Article 24

The Secretary-General of the United Nations shall inform all States referred to in article 17, paragraph 1, of this Convention of the following particulars:

(a) Signatures, ratifications and accessions under articles 17 and 18;

(b) The date of entry into force of this Convention under article 19;

(c) Communications and declarations received under articles 14, 20 and 23;

(d) Denunciations under article 21.

Article 25

1. This Convention, of which the Chinese, English, French, Russian and Spanish texts are equally authentic, shall be deposited in the archives of the United Nations.

2. The Secretary-General of the United Nations shall transmit certified copies of this Convention to all States belonging to any of the categories mentioned in article 17, paragraph 1, of the Convention.

DECLARATION ON THE ELIMINATION OF ALL FORMS OF INTOLERANCE AND OF DISCRIMINATION BASED ON RELIGION OR BELIEF

Proclaimed by General Assembly resolution 36/55 of 25 November 1981

The General Assembly,

Considering that one of the basic principles of the Charter of the United Nations is that of the dignity and equality inherent in all human beings, and that all Member States have pledged themselves to take joint and separate action in co-operation with the

Organization to promote and encourage universal respect for and observance of human rights and fundamental freedoms for all, without distinction as to race, sex, language or religion,

Considering that the Universal Declaration of Human Rights and the International Covenants on Human Rights proclaim the principles of nondiscrimination and equality before the law and the right to freedom of thought, conscience, religion and belief,

Considering that the disregard and infringement of human rights and fundamental freedoms, in particular of the right to freedom of thought, conscience, religion or whatever belief, have brought, directly or indirectly, wars and great suffering to mankind, especially where they serve as a means of foreign interference in the internal affairs of other States and amount to kindling hatred between peoples and nations,

Considering that religion or belief, for anyone who professes either, is one of the fundamental elements in his conception of life and that freedom of religion or belief should be fully respected and guaranteed,

Considering that it is essential to promote understanding, tolerance and respect in matters relating to freedom of religion and belief and to ensure that the use of religion or belief for ends inconsistent with the Charter of the United Nations, other relevant instruments of the United Nations and the purposes and principles of the present Declaration is inadmissible,

Convinced that freedom of religion and belief should also contribute to the attainment of the goals of world peace, social justice and friendship among peoples and to the elimination of ideologies or practices of colonialism and racial discrimination,

Noting with satisfaction the adoption of several, and the coming into force of some, conventions, under the aegis of the United Nations and of the specialized agencies, for the elimination of various forms of discrimination,

Concerned by manifestations of intolerance and by the existence of discrimination in matters of religion or belief still in evidence in some areas of the world,

Resolved to adopt all necessary measures for the speedy elimination of such intolerance in all its forms and manifestations and to prevent and combat discrimination on the ground of religion or belief,

Proclaims this Declaration on the Elimination of All Forms of Intolerance and of Discrimination Based on Religion or Belief:

Article 1

1. Everyone shall have the right to freedom of thought, conscience and religion. This right shall include freedom to have a religion or whatever belief of his choice, and freedom, either individually or in community with others and in public or private, to manifest his religion or belief in worship, observance, practice and teaching.

2. No one shall be subject to coercion which would impair his freedom to have a religion or belief of his choice.

3. Freedom to manifest one's religion or belief may be subject only to such limitations as are prescribed by law and are necessary to protect public safety, order, health or morals or the fundamental rights and freedoms of others.

Article 2

1. No one shall be subject to discrimination by any State, institution, group of persons, or person on the grounds of religion or other belief.

2. For the purposes of the present Declaration, the expression "intolerance and discrimination based on religion or belief" means any distinction, exclusion, restriction or preference based on religion or belief and having as its purpose or as its effect nullification or impairment of the recognition, enjoyment or exercise of human rights and fundamental freedoms on an equal basis.

Article 3

Discrimination between human being on the grounds of religion or belief constitutes an affront to human dignity and a disavowal of the principles of the Charter of the United Nations, and shall be condemned as a violation of the human rights and fundamental freedoms proclaimed in the Universal Declaration of Human Rights and enunciated in detail in the International Covenants on Human Rights, and as an obstacle to friendly and peaceful relations between nations.

Article 4

1. All States shall take effective measures to prevent and eliminate discrimination on the grounds of religion or belief in the recognition, exercise and enjoyment of human rights and fundamental freedoms in all fields of civil, economic, political, social and cultural life.

2. All States shall make all efforts to enact or rescind legislation where necessary to prohibit any such discrimination, and to take all appropriate measures to combat intolerance on the grounds of religion or other beliefs in this matter.

Article 5

1. The parents or, as the case may be, the legal guardians of the child have the right to organize the life within the family in accordance with their religion or belief and bearing in mind the moral education in which they believe the child should be brought up.

2. Every child shall enjoy the right to have access to education in the matter of religion or belief in accordance with the wishes of his parents or, as the case may be, legal guardians, and shall not be compelled to receive teaching on religion or belief against the wishes of his parents or legal guardians, the best interests of the child being the guiding principle.

3. The child shall be protected from any form of discrimination on the ground of religion or belief. He shall be brought up in a spirit of understanding, tolerance, friendship among peoples, peace and universal brotherhood, respect for freedom of religion or belief of others, and in full consciousness that his energy and talents should be devoted to the service of his fellow men.

4. In the case of a child who is not under the care either of his parents or of legal guardians, due account shall be taken of their expressed wishes or of any other proof of their wishes in the matter of religion or belief, the best interests of the child being the guiding principle.

5. Practices of a religion or belief in which a child is brought up must not be injurious to his physical or mental health or to his full development, taking into account article 1, paragraph 3, of the present Declaration.

Article 6

In accordance with article 1 of the present Declaration, and subject to the provisions of article 1, paragraph 3, the right to freedom of thought, conscience, religion or belief shall include, inter alia, the following freedoms:

(a) To worship or assemble in connection with a religion or belief, and to establish and maintain places for these purposes;

(b) To establish and maintain appropriate charitable or humanitarian institutions;

(c) To make, acquire and use to an adequate extent the necessary articles and materials related to the rites or customs of a religion or belief;

(d) To write, issue and disseminate relevant publications in these areas;

(e) To teach a religion or belief in places suitable for these purposes;

(f) To solicit and receive voluntary financial and other contributions from individuals and institutions;

(g) To train, appoint, elect or designate by succession appropriate leaders called for by the requirements and standards of any religion or belief;

(h) To observe days of rest and to celebrate holidays and ceremonies in accordance with the precepts of one's religion or belief;

(i) To establish and maintain communications with individuals and communities in matters of religion and belief at the national and international levels.

Article 7

The rights and freedoms set forth in the present Declaration shall be accorded in national legislation in such a manner that everyone shall be able to avail himself of such rights and freedoms in practice.

Article 8

Nothing in the present Declaration shall be construed as restricting or derogating from any right defined in the Universal Declaration of Human Rights and the International Covenants on Human Rights.

DECLARATION ON THE RIGHTS OF PERSONS BELONGING TO NATIONAL OR ETHNIC, RELIGIOUS OR LINGUISTIC MINORITIES

Adopted by General Assembly resolution 47/135 of 18 December 1992

The General Assembly,

Reaffirming that one of the basic aims of the United Nations, as proclaimed in the Charter, is to promote and encourage respect for human rights and for fundamental freedoms for all, without distinction as to race, sex, language or religion,

Reaffirming faith in fundamental human rights, in the dignity and worth of the human person, in the equal rights of men and women and of nations large and small,

Desiring to promote the realization of the principles contained in the Charter, the Universal Declaration of Human Rights, the Convention on the Prevention and Punishment of the Crime of Genocide, the International Convention on the Elimination of All Forms of Racial Discrimination, the International Covenant on Civil and Political Rights, the International Covenant on Economic, Social and Cultural Rights, the Declaration on the Elimination of All Forms of Intolerance and of Discrimination Based on Religion or Belief, and the Convention on the Rights of the Child, as well as other relevant international instruments that have been adopted at the universal or regional level and those concluded between individual States Members of the United Nations,

Inspired by the provisions of article 27 of the International Covenant on Civil and Political Rights concerning the rights of persons belonging to ethnic, religious or linguistic minorities,

Considering that the promotion and protection of the rights of persons belonging to national or ethnic, religious and linguistic minorities contribute to the political and social stability of States in which they live,

Emphasizing that the constant promotion and realization of the rights of persons belonging to national or ethnic, religious and linguistic minorities, as an integral part of the development of society as a whole and within a democratic framework based on the rule of law, would contribute to the strengthening of friendship and cooperation among peoples and States,

Considering that the United Nations has an important role to play regarding the protection of minorities,

Bearing in mind the work done so far within the United Nations system, in particular by the Commission on Human Rights, the Subcommission on Prevention of Discrimination and Protection of Minorities and the bodies established pursuant to the International Covenants on Human Rights and other relevant international human rights instruments in promoting and protecting the rights of persons belonging to national or ethnic, religious and linguistic minorities,

Taking into account the important work which is done by intergovernmental and non-governmental organizations in protecting minorities and in promoting and protecting the rights of persons belonging to national or ethnic, religious and linguistic minorities,

Recognizing the need to ensure even more effective implementation of international human rights instruments with regard to the rights of persons belonging to national or ethnic, religious and linguistic minorities,

Proclaims this Declaration on the Rights of Persons Belonging to National or Ethnic, Religious and Linguistic Minorities:

Article 1

1. States shall protect the existence and the national or ethnic, cultural, religious and linguistic identity of minorities within their respective territories and shall encourage conditions for the promotion of that identity.

2. States shall adopt appropriate legislative and other measures to achieve those ends.

Article 2

1. Persons belonging to national or ethnic, religious and linguistic minorities (hereinafter referred to as persons belonging to minorities) have the right to enjoy their own culture, to profess and practise their own religion, and to use their own language, in private and in public, freely and without interference or any form of discrimination.

2. Persons belonging to minorities have the right to participate effectively in cultural, religious, social, economic and public life.

3. Persons belonging to minorities have the right to participate effectively in decisions on the national and, where appropriate, regional level concerning the minority to which they belong or the regions in which they live, in a manner not incompatible with national legislation.

4. Persons belonging to minorities have the right to establish and maintain their own associations.

5. Persons belonging to minorities have the right to establish and maintain, without any discrimination, free and peaceful contacts with other members of their group and with persons belonging to other minorities, as well as contacts across frontiers with citizens of other States to whom they are related by national or ethnic, religious or linguistic ties.

Article 3

1. Persons belonging to minorities may exercise their rights, including those set forth in the present Declaration, individually as well as in community with other members of their group, without any discrimination.

2. No disadvantage shall result for any person belonging to a minority as the consequence of the exercise or non-exercise of the rights set forth in the present Declaration.

Article 4

1. States shall take measures where required to ensure that persons belonging to minorities may exercise fully and effectively all their human rights and fundamental freedoms without any discrimination and in full equality before the law.

2. States shall take measures to create favourable conditions to enable persons belonging to minorities to express their characteristics and to develop their culture, language, religion, traditions and customs, except where specific practices are in violation of national law and contrary to international standards.

3. States should take appropriate measures so that, wherever possible, persons belonging to minorities may have adequate opportunities to learn their mother tongue or to have instruction in their mother tongue.

4. States should, where appropriate, take measures in the field of education, in order to encourage knowledge of the history, traditions, language and culture of the minorities existing within their territory. Persons belonging to minorities should have adequate opportunities to gain knowledge of the society as a whole.

5. States should consider appropriate measures so that persons belonging to minorities may participate fully in the economic progress and development in their country.

Article 5

1. National policies and programmes shall be planned and implemented with due regard for the legitimate interests of persons belonging to minorities.

2. Programmes of cooperation and assistance among States should be planned and implemented with due regard for the legitimate interests of persons belonging to minorities.

Article 6

States should cooperate on questions relating to persons belonging to minorities, inter alia, exchanging information and experiences, in order to promote mutual understanding and confidence.

Article 7

States should cooperate in order to promote respect for the rights set forth in the present Declaration.

Article 8

1. Nothing in the present Declaration shall prevent the fulfilment of international obligations of States in relation to persons belonging to minorities. In particular, States shall fulfil in good faith the obligations and commitments they have assumed under international treaties and agreements to which they are parties.

2. The exercise of the rights set forth in the present Declaration shall not prejudice the enjoyment by all persons of universally recognized human rights and fundamental freedoms.

3. Measures taken by States to ensure the effective enjoyment of the rights set forth in the present Declaration shall not prima facie be considered contrary to the principle of equality contained in the Universal Declaration of Human Rights.

4. Nothing in the present Declaration may be construed as permitting any activity contrary to the purposes and principles of the United Nations, including sovereign equality, territorial integrity and political independence of States.

Article 9

The specialized agencies and other organizations of the United Nations system shall contribute to the full realization of the rights and principles set forth in the present Declaration, within their respective fields of competence.

CONVENTION ON THE ELIMINATION OF ALL FORMS OF DISCRIMINATION AGAINST WOMEN

Adopted and opened for signature, ratification and accession by General Assembly resolution 34/180 of 18 December 1979

Entered into force 3 September 1981, in accordance with article 27(1)

The States Parties to the Present Convention,

Noting that the Charter of the United Nations reaffirms faith in fundamental human rights, in the dignity and worth of the human person and in the equal rights of men and women,

Noting that the Universal Declaration of Human Rights affirms the principle of the inadmissibility of discrimination and proclaims that all human beings are born free and equal in dignity and rights and that everyone is entitled to all the rights and freedoms set forth therein, without distinction of any kind, including distinction based on sex,

Noting that the States Parties to the International Covenants on Human Rights have the obligation to ensure the equal rights of men and women to enjoy all economic, social, cultural, civil and political rights,

Considering the international conventions concluded under the auspices of the United Nations and the specialized agencies promoting equality of rights of men and women,

Noting also the resolutions, declarations and recommendations adopted by the United Nations and the specialized agencies promoting equality of rights of men and women,

Concerned, however, that despite these various instruments extensive discrimination against women continues to exist,

Recalling that discrimination against women violates the principles of equality of rights and respect for human dignity, is an obstacle to the participation of women, on equal terms with men, in the political, social, economic and cultural life of their countries, hampers the growth of the prosperity of society and the family and makes more difficult the full development of the potentialities of women in the service of their countries and of humanity,

Concerned that in situations of poverty women have the least access to food, health, education, training and opportunities for employment and other needs,

Convinced that the establishment of the new international economic order based on equity and justice will contribute significantly towards the promotion of equality between men and women,

Emphasizing that the eradication of apartheid, all forms of racism, racial discrimination, colonialism, neo-colonialism, aggression, foreign occupation and domination and interference in the internal affairs of States is essential to the full enjoyment of the rights of men and women,

Affirming that the strengthening of international peace and security, the relaxation of international tension, mutual cooperation among all States irrespective of their social and economic systems, general and complete disarmament, in particular nuclear disarmament under strict and effective international control, the affirmation of the principles of justice, equality and mutual benefit in relations among countries and the realization of the right of peoples under alien and colonial domination and foreign occupation to self-determination and independence, as well as respect for national sovereignty and territorial integrity, will promote social progress and development and as a consequence will contribute to the attainment of full equality between men and women,

Convinced that the full and complete development of a country, the welfare of the world and the cause of peace require the maximum participation of women on equal terms with men in all fields,

Bearing in mind the great contribution of women to the welfare of the family and to the development of society, so far not fully recognized, the social significance of maternity and the role of both parents in the family and in the upbringing of children, and aware that the role of women in procreation should not be a basis for discrimination but that the upbringing of children requires a sharing of responsibility between men and women and society as a whole,

Aware that a change in the traditional role of men as well as the role of women in society and in the family is needed to achieve full equality between men and women,

Determined to implement the principles set forth in the Declaration on the Elimination of Discrimination against Women and, for that purpose, to adopt the measures required for the elimination of such discrimination in all its forms and manifestations,

Have agreed on the following:

Part I

Article 1

For the purposes of the present Convention, the term "discrimination against women" shall mean any distinction, exclusion or restriction made on the basis of sex which has the effect or purpose of impairing or nullifying the recognition, enjoyment or exercise by women, irrespective of their marital status, on a basis of equality of men and women, of human rights and fundamental freedoms in the political, economic, social, cultural, civil or any other field.

Article 2

States Parties condemn discrimination against women in all its forms, agree to pursue by all appropriate means and without delay a policy of eliminating discrimination against women and, to this end, undertake:

(a) To embody the principle of the equality of men and women in their national constitutions or other appropriate legislation if not yet incorporated therein and to ensure, through law and other appropriate means, the practical realization of this principle;

(b) To adopt appropriate legislative and other measures, including sanctions where appropriate, prohibiting all discrimination against women;

(c) To establish legal protection of the rights of women on an equal basis with men and to ensure through competent national tribunals and other public institutions the effective protection of women against any act of discrimination;

(d) To refrain from engaging in any act or practice of discrimination against women and to ensure that public authorities and institutions shall act in conformity with this obligation;

(e) To take all appropriate measures to eliminate discrimination against women by any person, organization or enterprise;

(f) To take all appropriate measures, including legislation, to modify or abolish existing laws, regulations, customs and practices which constitute discrimination against women;

(g) To repeal all national penal provisions which constitute discrimination against women.

Article 3

States Parties shall take in all fields, in particular in the political, social, economic and cultural fields, all appropriate measures, including legislation, to ensure the full development and advancement of women, for the purpose of guaranteeing them the exercise and enjoyment of human rights and fundamental freedoms on a basis of equality with men.

Article 4

1. Adoption by States Parties of temporary special measures aimed at accelerating de facto equality between men and women shall not be considered discrimination as defined in the present Convention, but shall in no way entail as a consequence the maintenance of unequal or separate standards; these measures shall be discontinued when the objectives of equality of opportunity and treatment have been achieved.

2. Adoption by States Parties of special measures, including those measures contained in the present Convention, aimed at protecting maternity shall not be considered discriminatory.

Article 5

States Parties shall take all appropriate measures:

(a) To modify the social and cultural patterns of conduct of men and women, with a view to achieving the elimination of prejudices and customary and all other practices which are based on the idea of the inferiority or the superiority of either of the sexes or on stereotyped roles for men and women;

(b) To ensure that family education includes a proper understanding of maternity as a social function and the recognition of the common responsibility of men and women in the upbringing and development of their children, it being understood that the interest of the children is the primordial consideration in all cases.

Article 6

States Parties shall take all appropriate measures, including legislation, to suppress all forms of traffic in women and exploitation of prostitution of women.

Part II

Article 7

States Parties shall take all appropriate measures to eliminate discrimination against women in the political and public life of the country and, in particular, shall ensure to women, on equal terms with men, the right:

(a) To vote in all elections and public referenda and to be eligible for election to all publicly elected bodies;

(b) To participate in the formulation of government policy and the implementation thereof and to hold public office and perform all public functions at all levels of government;

(c) To participate in non-governmental organizations and associations concerned with the public and political life of the country.

Article 8

States Parties shall take all appropriate measures to ensure to women, on equal terms with men and without any discrimination, the opportunity to represent their Governments at the international level and to participate in the work of international organizations.

Article 9

1. States Parties shall grant women equal rights with men to acquire, change or retain their nationality. They shall ensure in particular that neither marriage to an alien nor change of nationality by the husband during marriage shall automatically change the nationality of the wife, render her stateless or force upon her the nationality of the husband.

2. States Parties shall grant women equal rights with men with respect to the nationality of their children.

Part III

Article 10

States Parties shall take all appropriate measures to eliminate discrimination against women in order to ensure to them equal rights with men in the field of education and in particular to ensure, on a basis of equality of men and women:

(a) The same conditions for career and vocational guidance, for access to studies and for the achievement of diplomas in educational establishments of all categories in rural as well as in urban areas; this equality shall be ensured in pre-school, general, technical, professional and higher technical education, as well as in all types of vocational training;

(b) Access to the same curricula, the same examinations, teaching staff with qualifications of the same standard and school premises and equipment of the same quality;

(c) The elimination of any stereotyped concept of the roles of men and women at all levels and in all forms of education by encouraging coeducation and other types of education which will help to achieve this aim and, in particular, by the revision of textbooks and school programmes and the adaptation of teaching methods;

(d) The same opportunities to benefit from scholarships and other study grants;

(e) The same opportunities for access to programmes of continuing education, including adult and functional literacy programmes, particulary those aimed at reducing, at the earliest possible time, any gap in education existing between men and women;

(f) The reduction of female student drop-out rates and the organization of programmes for girls and women who have left school prematurely;

(g) The same Opportunities to participate actively in sports and physical education;

(h) Access to specific educational information to help to ensure the health and well-being of families, including information and advice on family planning.

Article 11

1. States Parties shall take all appropriate measures to eliminate discrimination against women in the field of employment in order to ensure, on a basis of equality of men and women, the same rights, in particular:

(a) The right to work as an inalienable right of all human beings;

(b) The right to the same employment opportunities, including the application of the same criteria for selection in matters of employment;

(c) The right to free choice of profession and employment, the right to promotion, job security and all benefits and conditions of service and the right to receive vocational training and retraining, including apprenticeships, advanced vocational training and recurrent training;

(d) The right to equal remuneration, including benefits, and to equal treatment in respect of work of equal value, as well as equality of treatment in the evaluation of the quality of work;

(e) The right to social security, particularly in cases of retirement, unemployment, sickness, invalidity and old age and other incapacity to work, as well as the right to paid leave;

(f) The right to protection of health and to safety in working conditions, including the safeguarding of the function of reproduction.

2. In order to prevent discrimination against women on the grounds of marriage or maternity and to ensure their effective right to work, States Parties shall take appropriate measures:

(a) To prohibit, subject to the imposition of sanctions, dismissal on the grounds of pregnancy or of maternity leave and discrimination in dismissals on the basis of marital status;

(b) To introduce maternity leave with pay or with comparable social benefits without loss of former employment, seniority or social allowances;

(c) To encourage the provision of the necessary supporting social services to enable parents to combine family obligations with work responsibilities and participation in public life, in particular through promoting the establishment and development of a network of child-care facilities;

(d) To provide special protection to women during pregnancy in types of work proved to be harmful to them.

3. Protective legislation relating to matters covered in this article shall be reviewed periodically in the light of scientific and technological knowledge and shall be revised, repealed or extended as necessary.

Article 12

1. States Parties shall take all appropriate measures to eliminate discrimination against women in the field of health care in order to ensure, on a basis of equality of men and women, access to health care services, including those related to family planning.

2. Notwithstanding the provisions of paragraph 1 of this article, States Parties shall ensure to women appropriate services in connection with pregnancy, confinement and the post-natal period, granting free services where necessary, as well as adequate nutrition during pregnancy and lactation.

Article 13

States Parties shall take all appropriate measures to eliminate discrimination against women in other areas of economic and social life in order to ensure, on a basis of equality of men and women, the same rights, in particular:

(a) The right to family benefits;

(b) The right to bank loans, mortgages and other forms of financial credit;

(c) The right to participate in recreational activities, sports and all aspects of cultural life.

Article 14

1. States Parties shall take into account the particular problems faced by rural women and the significant roles which rural women play in the economic survival of their families, including their work in the non-monetized sectors of the economy, and shall take all appropriate measures to ensure the application of the provisions of the present Convention to women in rural areas.

2. States Parties shall take all appropriate measures to eliminate discrimination against women in rural areas in order to ensure, on a basis of equality of men and women, that they participate in and benefit from rural development and, in particular, shall ensure to such women the right:

(a) To participate in the elaboration and implementation of development planning at all levels;

(b) To have access to adequate health care facilities, including information, counselling and services in family planning;

(c) To benefit directly from social security programmes;

(d) To obtain all types of training and education, formal and non-formal, including that relating to functional literacy, as well as, inter alia, the benefit of all community and extension services, in order to increase their technical proficiency;

(e) To organize self-help groups and co-operatives in order to obtain equal access to economic opportunities through employment or self employment;

(f) To participate in all community activities;

(g) To have access to agricultural credit and loans, marketing facilities, appropriate technology and equal treatment in land and agrarian reform as well as in land re-settlement schemes;

(h) To enjoy adequate living conditions, particularly in relation to housing, sanitation, electricity and water supply, transport and communications.

Part IV

Article 15

1. States Parties shall accord to women equality with men before the law.

2. States Parties shall accord to women, in civil matters, a legal capacity identical to that of men and the same opportunities to exercise that capacity. In particular, they shall give women equal rights to conclude contracts and to administer property and shall treat them equally in all stages of procedure in courts and tribunals.

3. States Parties agree that all contracts and all other private instruments of any kind with a legal effect which is directed at restricting the legal capacity of women shall be deemed null and void.

4. States Parties shall accord to men and women the same rights with regard to the law relating to the movement of persons and the freedom to choose their residence and domicile.

Article 16

1. States Parties shall take all appropriate measures to eliminate discrimination against women in all matters relating to marriage and family relations and in particular shall ensure, on a basis of equality of men and women:

(a) The same right to enter into marriage;

(b) The same right freely to choose a spouse and to enter into marriage only with their free and full consent;

(c) The same rights and responsibilities during marriage and at its dissolution;

(d) The same rights and responsibilities as parents, irrespective of their marital status, in matters relating to their children; in all cases the interests of the children shall be paramount;

(e) The same rights to decide freely and responsibly on the number and spacing of their children and to have access to the information, education and means to enable them to exercise these rights;

(f) The same rights and responsibilities with regard to guardianship, wardship, trusteeship and adoption of children, or similar institutions where these concepts exist in national legislation; in all cases the interests of the children shall be paramount;

(g) The same personal rights as husband and wife, including the right to choose a family name, a profession and an occupation;

(h) The same rights for both spouses in respect of the ownership, acquisition, management, administration, enjoyment and disposition of property, whether free of charge or for a valuable consideration.

2. The betrothal and the marriage of a child shall have no legal effect, and all necessary action, including legislation, shall be taken to specify a minimum age for marriage and to make the registration of marriages in an official registry compulsory.

Part V

Article 17

1. For the purpose of considering the progress made in the implementation of the present Convention, there shall be established a Committee on the Elimination of Discrimination against Women (hereinafter referred to as the Committee) consisting, at the time of entry into force of the Convention, of eighteen and, after ratification of or accession to the Convention by the thirty-fifth State Party, of twenty-three experts of high moral standing and competence in the field covered by the Convention. The experts shall be elected by States Parties from among their nationals and shall serve in their personal capacity, consideration being given to equitable geographical distribution and to the representation of the different forms of civilization as well as the principal legal systems.

2. The members of the Committee shall be elected by secret ballot from a list of persons nominated by States Parties. Each State Party may nominate one person from among its own nationals.

3. The initial election shall be held six months after the date of the entry into force of the present Convention. At least three months before the date of each election the Secretary-General of the United Nations shall address a letter to the States Parties inviting them to submit their nominations within two months. The Secretary-General shall prepare a list in alphabetical order of all persons thus nominated, indicating the States Parties which have nominated them, and shall submit it to the States Parties.

4. Elections of the members of the Committee shall be held at a meeting of States Parties convened by the Secretary-General at United Nations Headquarters. At that meeting, for which two thirds of the States Parties shall constitute a quorum, the persons elected to the Committee shall be those nominees who obtain the largest number of votes and an absolute majority of the votes of the representatives of States Parties present and voting.

5. The members of the Committee shall be elected for a term of four years. However, the terms of nine of the members elected at the first election shall expire at the end of two years; immediately after the first election the names of these nine members shall be chosen by lot by the Chairman of the Committee.

6. The election of the five additional members of the Committee shall be held in accordance with the provisions of paragraphs 2, 3 and 4 of this article, following the thirty-fifth ratification or accession. The terms of two of the additional members elected on this occasion shall expire at the end of two years, the names of these two members having been chosen by lot by the Chairman of the Committee.

7. For the filling of casual vacancies, the State Party whose expert has ceased to function as a member of the Committee shall appoint another expert from among its nationals, subject to the approval of the Committee.

8. The members of the Committee shall, with the approval of the General Assembly, receive emoluments from United Nations resources on such terms and conditions as the Assembly may decide, having regard to the importance of the Committee's responsibilities.

9. The Secretary-General of the United Nations shall provide the necessary staff and facilities for the effective performance of the functions of the Committee under the present Convention.

Article 18

1. States Parties undertake to submit to the Secretary-General of the United Nations, for consideration by the Committee, a report on the legislative, judicial, administrative or other measures which they have adopted to give effect to the provisions of the present Convention and on the progress made in this respect:

(a) Within one year after the entry into force for the State concerned;

(b) Thereafter at least every four years and further whenever the Committee so requests.

2. Reports may indicate factors and difficulties affecting the degree of fulfilment of obligations under the present Convention.

Article 19

1. The Committee shall adopt its own rules of procedure.

2. The Committee shall elect its officers for a term of two years.

Article 20

1. The Committee shall normally meet for a period of not more than two weeks annually in order to consider the reports submitted in accordance with article 18 of the present Convention.

2. The meetings of the Committee shall normally be held at United Nations Headquarters or at any other convenient place as determined by the Committee.

Article 21

1. The Committee shall, through the Economic and Social Council, report annually to the General Assembly of the United Nations on its activities and may make suggestions and general recommendations based on the examination of reports and information received from the States Parties. Such suggestions and general recommendations shall be included in the report of the Committee together with comments, if any, from States Parties.

2. The Secretary-General of the United Nations shall transmit the reports of the Committee to the Commission on the Status of Women for its information.

Article 22

The specialized agencies shall be entitled to be represented at the consideration of the implementation of such provisions of the present Convention as fall within the scope of their activities. The Committee may invite the specialized agencies to submit reports on the implementation of the Convention in areas falling within the scope of their activities.

Part VI

Article 23

Nothing in the present Convention shall affect any provisions that are more conducive to the achievement of equality between men and women which may be contained:

(a) In the legislation of a State Party; or

(b) In any other international convention, treaty or agreement in force for that State.

Article 24

States Parties undertake to adopt all necessary measures at the national level aimed at achieving the full realization of the rights recognized in the present Convention.

Article 25

1. The present Convention shall be open for signature by all States.

2. The Secretary-General of the United Nations is designated as the depositary of the present Convention.

3. The present Convention is subject to ratification. Instruments of ratification shall be deposited with the Secretary-General of the United Nations.

4. The present Convention shall be open to accession by all States. Accession shall be effected by the deposit of an instrument of accession with the Secretary-General of the United Nations.

Article 26

1. A request for the revision of the present Convention may be made at any time by any State Party by means of a notification in writing addressed to the Secretary-General of the United Nations.

2. The General Assembly of the United Nations shall decide upon the steps, if any, to be taken in respect of such a request.

Article 27

1. The present Convention shall enter into force on the thirtieth day after the date of deposit with the Secretary-General of the United Nations of the twentieth instrument of ratification or accession.

2. For each State ratifying the present Convention or acceding to it after the deposit of the twentieth instrument of ratification or accession, the Convention shall enter into force on the thirtieth day after the date of the deposit of its own instrument of ratification or accession.

Article 28

1. The Secretary-General of the United Nations shall receive and circulate to all States the text of reservations made by States at the time of ratification or accession.

2. A reservation incompatible with the object and purpose of the present Convention shall not be permitted.

3. Reservations may be withdrawn at any time by notification to this effect addressed to the Secretary-General of the United Nations, who shall then inform all States thereof. Such notification shall take effect on the date on which it is received.

Article 29

1. Any dispute between two or more States Parties concerning the interpretation or application of the present Convention which is not settled by negotiation shall, at the request of one of them, be submitted to arbitration. If within six months from the date of the request for arbitration the parties are unable to agree on the organization of the arbitration, any one of those parties may refer the dispute to the International Court of Justice by request in conformity with the Statute of the Court.

2. Each State Party may at the time of signature or ratification of the present Convention or accession thereto declare that it does not consider itself bound by paragraph 1 of this article. The other States Parties shall not be bound by that paragraph with respect to any State Party which has made such a reservation.

3. Any State Party which has made a reservation in accordance with paragraph 2 of this article may at any time withdraw that reservation by notification to the Secretary-General of the United Nations.

Article 30

The present Convention, the Arabic, Chinese, English, French, Russian and Spanish texts of which are equally authentic, shall be deposited with the Secretary-General of the United Nations.

IN WITNESS WHEREOF the undersigned, duly authorized, have signed the present Convention.

DECLARATION ON THE ELIMINATION OF VIOLENCE AGAINST WOMEN

Proclaimed by General Assembly resolution 48/104 of 20 December 1993

The General Assembly,

Recognizing the urgent need for the universal application to women of the rights and principles with regard to equality, security, liberty, integrity and dignity of all human beings,

Noting that those rights and principles are enshrined in international instruments, including the Universal Declaration of Human Rights, the International Covenant on Civil and Political Rights, the International Covenant on Economic, Social and Cultural Rights, the Convention on the Elimination of All Forms of Discrimination against Women and the Convention against Torture and Other Cruel, Inhuman or Degrading Treatment or Punishment,

Recognizing that effective implementation of the Convention on the Elimination of All Forms of Discrimination against Women would contribute to the elimination of violence against women and that the Declaration on the Elimination of Violence against Women, set forth in the present resolution, will strengthen and complement that process,

Concerned that violence against women is an obstacle to the achievement of equality, development and peace, as recognized in the Nairobi Forward-looking Strategies for the Advancement of Women, in which a set of measures to combat violence against women was recommended, and to the full implementation of the Convention on the Elimination of All Forms of Discrimination against Women,

Affirming that violence against women constitutes a violation of the rights and fundamental freedoms of women and impairs or nullifies their enjoyment of those rights and freedoms, and concerned about the long-standing failure to protect and promote those rights and freedoms in the case of violence against women,

Recognizing that violence against women is a manifestation of historically unequal power relations between men and women, which have led to domination over and discrimination against women by men and to the prevention of the full advancement of women, and that violence against women is one of the crucial social mechanisms by which women are forced into a subordinate position compared with men,

Concerned that some groups of women, such as women belonging to minority groups, indigenous women, refugee women, migrant women, women living in rural or remote communities, destitute women, women in institutions or in detention, female children, women with disabilities, elderly women and women in situations of armed conflict, are especially vulnerable to violence,

Recalling the conclusion in paragraph 23 of the annex to Economic and Social Council resolution 1990/15 of 24 May 1990 that the recognition that violence against women in the family and society was pervasive and cut across lines of income, class and culture had to be matched by urgent and effective steps to eliminate its incidence,

Recalling also Economic and Social Council resolution 1991/18 of 30 May 1991, in which the Council recommended the development of a framework for an international instrument that would address explicitly the issue of violence against women,

Welcoming the role that women's movements are playing in drawing increasing attention to the nature, severity and magnitude of the problem of violence against women,

Alarmed that opportunities for women to achieve legal, social, political and economic equality in society are limited, inter alia, by continuing and endemic violence,

Convinced that in the light of the above there is a need for a clear and comprehensive definition of violence against women, a clear statement of the rights to be applied to ensure the elimination of violence against women in all its forms, a commitment by States in respect of their responsibilities, and a commitment by the international community at large to the elimination of violence against women,

Solemnly proclaims the following Declaration on the Elimination of Violence against Women and urges that every effort be made so that it becomes generally known and respected:

Article 1

For the purposes of this Declaration, the term "violence against women" means any act of gender-based violence that results in, or is likely to result in, physical, sexual or psychological harm or suffering to women, including threats of such acts, coercion or arbitrary deprivation of liberty, whether occurring in public or in private life.

Article 2

Violence against women shall be understood to encompass, but not be limited to, the following:

(a) Physical, sexual and psychological violence occurring in the family, including battering, sexual abuse of female children in the household, dowry-related violence, marital rape, female genital mutilation and other traditional practices harmful to women, non-spousal violence and violence related to exploitation;

(b) Physical, sexual and psychological violence occurring within the general community, including rape, sexual abuse, sexual harassment and intimidation at work, in educational institutions and elsewhere, trafficking in women and forced prostitution;

(c) Physical, sexual and psychological violence perpetrated or condoned by the State, wherever it occurs.

Article 3

Women are entitled to the equal enjoyment and protection of all human rights and fundamental freedoms in the political,

economic, social, cultural, civil or any other field. These rights include, inter alia:

(a) The right to life;

(b) The right to equality;

(c) The right to liberty and security of person;

(d) The right to equal protection under the law;

(e) The right to be free from all forms of discrimination;

(f) The right to the highest standard attainable of physical and mental health;

(g) The right to just and favourable conditions of work;

(h) The right not to be subjected to torture, or other cruel, inhuman or degrading treatment or punishment.

Article 4

States should condemn violence against women and should not invoke any custom, tradition or religious consideration to avoid their obligations with respect to its elimination. States should pursue by all appropriate means and without delay a policy of eliminating violence against women and, to this end, should:

(a) Consider, where they have not yet done so, ratifying or acceding to the Convention on the Elimination of All Forms of Discrimination against Women or withdrawing reservations to that Convention;

(b) Refrain from engaging in violence against women;

(c) Exercise due diligence to prevent, investigate and, in accordance with national legislation, punish acts of violence against women, whether those acts are perpetrated by the State or by private persons;

(d) Develop penal, civil, labour and administrative sanctions in domestic legislation to punish and redress the wrongs caused to women who are subjected to violence; women who are subjected to violence should be provided with access to the mechanisms of justice and, as provided for by national legislation, to just and effective remedies for the harm that they have suffered; States should also inform women of their rights in seeking redress through such mechanisms;

(e) Consider the possibility of developing national plans of action to promote the protection of women against any form of violence, or to include provisions for that purpose in plans already existing, taking into account, as appropriate, such cooperation as can be provided by non-governmental organizations, particularly those concerned with the issue of violence against women;

(f) Develop, in a comprehensive way, preventive approaches and all those measures of a legal, political, administrative and cultural nature that promote the protection of women against any form of violence, and ensure that the re-victimization of women does not occur because of laws insensitive to gender considerations, enforcement practices or other interventions;

(g) Work to ensure, to the maximum extent feasible in the light of their available resources and, where needed, within the framework of international cooperation, that women subjected to violence and, where appropriate, their children have specialized assistance, such as rehabilitation, assistance in child care and maintenance, treatment, counselling, and health and social services, facilities and programmes, as well as support structures, and should take all other appropriate measures to promote their safety and physical and psychological rehabilitation;

(h) Include in government budgets adequate resources for their activities related to the elimination of violence against women;

(i) Take measures to ensure that law enforcement officers and public officials responsible for implementing policies to prevent, investigate and punish violence against women receive training to sensitize them to the needs of women;

(j) Adopt all appropriate measures, especially in the field of education, to modify the social and cultural patterns of conduct of men and women and to eliminate prejudices, customary practices and all other practices based on the idea of the inferiority or superiority of either of the sexes and on stereotyped roles for men and women;

(k) Promote research, collect data and compile statistics, especially concerning domestic violence, relating to the prevalence of different forms of violence against women and encourage research on the causes, nature, seriousness and consequences of violence against women and on the effectiveness of measures implemented to prevent and redress violence against women; those statistics and findings of the research will be made public;

(l) Adopt measures directed towards the elimination of violence against women who are especially vulnerable to violence;

(m) Include, in submitting reports as required under relevant human rights instruments of the United Nations, information pertaining to violence against women and measures taken to implement the present Declaration;

(n) Encourage the development of appropriate guidelines to assist in the implementation of the principles set forth in the present Declaration;

(o) Recognize the important role of the women's movement and non-governmental organizations world wide in raising awareness and alleviating the problem of violence against women;

(p) Facilitate and enhance the work of the women's movement and non-governmental organizations and cooperate with them at local, national and regional levels;

(q) Encourage intergovernmental regional organizations of which they are members to include the elimination of violence against women in their programmes, as appropriate.

Article 5

The organs and specialized agencies of the United Nations system should, within their respective fields of competence, contribute to the recognition and realization of the rights and the principles set forth in the present Declaration and, to this end, should, inter alia:

(a) Foster international and regional cooperation with a view to defining regional strategies for combating violence, exchanging experiences and financing programmes relating to the elimination of violence against women;

(b) Promote meetings and seminars with the aim of creating and raising awareness among all persons of the issue of the elimination of violence against women;

(c) Foster coordination and exchange within the United Nations system between human rights treaty bodies to address the issue of violence against women effectively;

(d) Include in analyses prepared by organizations and bodies of the United Nations system of social trends and problems, such as the periodic reports on the world social situation, examination of trends in violence against women;

(e) Encourage coordination between organizations and bodies of the United Nations system to incorporate the issue of violence against women into ongoing programmes, especially with reference to groups of women particularly vulnerable to violence;

(f) Promote the formulation of guidelines or manuals relating to violence against women, taking into account the measures referred to in the present Declaration;

(g) Consider the issue of the elimination of violence against women, as appropriate, in fulfilling their mandates with respect to the implementation of human rights instruments;

(h) Cooperate with non-governmental organizations in addressing the issue of violence against women.

Article 6

Nothing in the present Declaration shall affect any provision that is more conducive to the elimination of violence against women that may be contained in the legislation of a State or in any international convention, treaty or other instrument in force in a State.

CONVENTION ON THE RIGHTS OF THE CHILD

Adopted and opened for signature, ratification and accession by General Assembly resolution 44/25 of 20 November 1989

Entered into force 2 September 1990, in accordance with article 49

Preamble

The States Parties to the Present Convention,

Considering that, in accordance with the principles proclaimed in the Charter of the United Nations, recognition of the inherent dignity and of the equal and inalienable rights of all members of the human family is the foundation of freedom, justice and peace in the world,

Bearing in mind that the peoples of the United Nations have, in the Charter, reaffirmed their faith in fundamental human rights and in the dignity and worth of the human person, and have determined to promote social progress and better standards of life in larger freedom,

Recognizing that the United Nations has, in the Universal Declaration of Human Rights and in the International Covenants on Human Rights, proclaimed and agreed that everyone is entitled to all the rights and freedoms set forth therein, without distinction of any kind, such as race, colour, sex, language, religion, political or other opinion, national or social origin, property, birth or other status,

Recalling that, in the Universal Declaration of Human Rights, the United Nations has proclaimed that childhood is entitled to special care and assistance,

Convinced that the family, as the fundamental group of society and the natural environment for the growth and well-being of all its members and particularly children, should be afforded the necessary protection and assistance so that it can fully assume its responsibilities within the community,

Recognizing that the child, for the full and harmonious development of his or her personality, should grow up in a family environment, in an atmosphere of happiness, love and understanding,

Considering that the child should be fully prepared to live an individual life in society, and brought up in the spirit of the ideals proclaimed in the Charter of the United Nations, and in particular in the spirit of peace, dignity, tolerance, freedom, equality and solidarity,

Bearing in mind that the need to extend particular care to the child has been stated in the Geneva Declaration of the Rights of the Child of 1924 and in the Declaration of the Rights of the Child adopted by the General Assembly on 20 November 1959 and recognized in the Universal Declaration of Human Rights, in the International Covenant on Civil and Political Rights (in particular in articles 23 and 24), in the International Covenant on Economic, Social and Cultural Rights (in particular in article 10) and in the statutes and relevant instruments of specialized agencies and international organizations concerned with the welfare of children,

Bearing in mind that, as indicated in the Declaration of the Rights of the Child, "the child, by reason of his physical and mental immaturity, needs special safeguards and care, including appropriate legal protection, before as well as after birth,"

Recalling the provisions of the Declaration on Social and Legal Principles relating to the Protection and Welfare of Children, with Special Reference to Foster Placement and Adoption Nationally and Internationally; the United Nations Standard Minimum Rules for the Administration of Juvenile Justice (The Beijing Rules); and the Declaration on the Protection of Women and Children in Emergency and Armed Conflict,

Recognizing that, in all countries in the world, there are children living in exceptionally difficult conditions, and that such children need special consideration,

Taking due account of the importance of the traditions and cultural values of each people for the protection and harmonious development of the child,

Recognizing the importance of international co-operation for improving the living conditions of children in every country, in particular in the developing countries,

Have agreed as follows:

Part I

Article 1

For the purposes of the present Convention, a child means every human being below the age of eighteen years unless under the law applicable to the child, majority is attained earlier.

Article 2

1. States Parties shall respect and ensure the rights set forth in the present Convention to each child within their jurisdiction without discrimination of any kind, irrespective of the child's or his or her parent's or legal guardian's race, colour, sex, language, religion, political or other opinion, national, ethnic or social origin, property, disability, birth or other status.

2. States Parties shall take all appropriate measures to ensure that the child is protected against all forms of discrimination or punishment on the basis of the status, activities, expressed opinions, or beliefs of the child's parents, legal guardians, or family members.

Article 3

1. In all actions concerning children, whether undertaken by public or private social welfare institutions, courts of law, administrative authorities or legislative bodies, the best interests of the child shall be a primary consideration.

2. States Parties undertake to ensure the child such protection and care as is necessary for his or her well-being, taking into account the rights and duties of his or her parents, legal guardians, or other individuals legally responsible for him or her, and, to this end, shall take all appropriate legislative and administrative measures.

3. States Parties shall ensure that the institutions, services and facilities responsible for the care or protection of children shall conform with the standards established by competent authorities, particularly in the areas of safety, health, in the number and suitability of their staff, as well as competent supervision.

Article 4

States Parties shall undertake all appropriate legislative, administrative, and other measures for the implementation of the rights recognized in the present Convention. With regard to economic, social and cultural rights, States Parties shall undertake such measures to the maximum extent of their available resources and, where needed, within the framework of international co-operation.

Article 5

States Parties shall respect the responsibilities, rights and duties of parents or, where applicable, the members of the extended family or community as provided for by local custom, legal guardians or other persons legally responsible for the child, to provide, in a manner consistent with the evolving capacities of the child, appropriate direction and guidance in the exercise by the child of the rights recognized in the present Convention.

Article 6

1. States Parties recognize that every child has the inherent right to life.

2. States Parties shall ensure to the maximum extent possible the survival and development of the child.

Article 7

1. The child shall be registered immediately after birth and shall have the right from birth to a name, the right to acquire a nationality and, as far as possible, the right to know and be cared for by his or her parents.

2. States Parties shall ensure the implementation of these rights in accordance with their national law and their obligations under the relevant international instruments in this field, in particular where the child would otherwise be stateless.

Article 8

1. States Parties undertake to respect the right of the child to preserve his or her identity, including nationality, name and family relations as recognized by law without unlawful interference.

2. Where a child is illegally deprived of some or all of the elements of his or her identity, States Parties shall provide appropriate assistance and protection, with a view to re-establishing speedily his or her identity.

Article 9

1. States Parties shall ensure that a child shall not be separated from his or her parents against their will, except when competent authorities subject to judicial review determine, in accordance with applicable law and procedures, that such separation is necessary for the best interests of the child. Such determination may be necessary in a particular case such as one involving abuse or neglect of the child by the parents, or one where the parents are living separately and a decision must be made as to the child's place of residence.

2. In any proceedings pursuant to paragraph 1 of the present article, all interested parties shall be given an opportunity to participate in the proceedings and make their views known.

3. States Parties shall respect the right of the child who is separated from one or both parents to maintain personal relations and direct contact with both parents on a regular basis, except if it is contrary to the child's best interests.

4. Where such separation results from any action initiated by a State Party, such as the detention, imprisonment, exile, deportation or death (including death arising from any cause while the person is in the custody of the State) of one or both parents or of the child, that State Party shall, upon request, provide the parents, the child or, if appropriate, another member of the family with the essential information concerning the whereabouts of the absent member(s) of the family unless the provision of the information would be detrimental to the well-being of the child. States Parties shall further ensure that the submission of such a request shall of itself entail no adverse consequences for the person(s) concerned.

Article 10

1. In accordance with the obligation of States Parties under article 9, paragraph 1, applications by a child or his or her parents to enter or leave a State Party for the purpose of family reunification shall be dealt with by States Parties in a positive, humane and expeditious manner. States Parties shall further ensure that the submission of such a request shall entail no adverse consequences for the applicants and for the members of their family.

2. A child whose parents reside in different States shall have the right to maintain on a regular basis, save in exceptional circumstances personal relations and direct contacts with both parents. Towards that end and in accordance with the obligation of States Parties under article 9, paragraph 1, States Parties shall respect the right of the child and his or her parents to leave any country, including their own, and to enter their own country. The right to leave any country shall be subject only to such restrictions as are prescribed by law and which are necessary to protect the national security, public order (ordre public), public health or morals or the rights and freedoms of others and are consistent with the other rights recognized in the present Convention.

Article 11

1. States Parties shall take measures to combat the illicit transfer and non-return of children abroad.

2. To this end, States Parties shall promote the conclusion of bilateral or multilateral agreements or accession to existing agreements.

Article 12

1. States Parties shall assure to the child who is capable of forming his or her own views the right to express those views freely in all matters affecting the child, the views of the child being given due weight in accordance with the age and maturity of the child.

2. For this purpose, the child shall in particular be provided the opportunity to be heard in any judicial and administrative proceedings affecting the child, either directly, or through a representative or an appropriate body, in a manner consistent with the procedural rules of national law.

Article 13

1. The child shall have the right to freedom of expression; this right shall include freedom to seek, receive and impart information and ideas of all kinds, regardless of frontiers, either orally, in writing or in print, in the form of art, or through any other media of the child's choice.

2. The exercise of this right may be subject to certain restrictions, but these shall only be such as are provided by law and are necessary:

   (a) For respect of the rights or reputations of others; or

   (b) For the protection of national security or of public order (ordre public), or of public health or morals.

Article 14

1. States Parties shall respect the right of the child to freedom of thought, conscience and religion.

2. States Parties shall respect the rights and duties of the parents and, when applicable, legal guardians, to provide direction to the child in the exercise of his or her right in a manner consistent with the evolving capacities of the child.

3. Freedom to manifest one's religion or beliefs may be subject only to such limitations as are prescribed by law and are necessary to protect public safety, order, health or morals, or the fundamental rights and freedoms of others.

Article 15

1. States Parties recognize the rights of the child to freedom of association and to freedom of peaceful assembly.

2. No restrictions may be placed on the exercise of these rights other than those imposed in conformity with the law and which are necessary in a democratic society in the inter-

ests of national security or public safety, public order (ordre public), the protection of public health or morals or the protection of the rights and freedoms of others.

Article 16

1. No child shall be subjected to arbitrary or unlawful interference with his or her privacy, family, home or correspondence, nor to unlawful attacks on his or her honour and reputation.

2. The child has the right to the protection of the law against such interference or attacks.

Article 17

States Parties recognize the important function performed by the mass media and shall ensure that the child has access to information and material from a diversity of national and international sources, especially those aimed at the promotion of his or her social, spiritual and moral well-being and physical and mental health. To this end, States Parties shall:

(a) Encourage the mass media to disseminate information and material of social and cultural benefit to the child and in accordance with the spirit of article 29;

(b) Encourage international co-operation in the production, exchange and dissemination of such information and material from a diversity of cultural, national and international sources;

(c) Encourage the production and dissemination of children's books;

(d) Encourage the mass media to have particular regard to the linguistic needs of the child who belongs to a minority group or who is indigenous;

(e) Encourage the development of appropriate guidelines for the protection of the child from information and material injurious to his or her well-being, bearing in mind the provisions of articles 13 and 18.

Article 18

1. States Parties shall use their best efforts to ensure recognition of the principle that both parents have common responsibilities for the upbringing and development of the child. Parents or, as the case may be, legal guardians, have the primary responsibility for the upbringing and development of the child. The best interests of the child will be their basic concern.

2. For the purpose of guaranteeing and promoting the rights set forth in the present Convention, States Parties shall render appropriate assistance to parents and legal guardians in the performance of their child-rearing responsibilities and shall ensure the development of institutions, facilities and services for the care of children.

3. States Parties shall take all appropriate measures to ensure that children of working parents have the right to benefit from child-care services and facilities for which they are eligible.

Article 19

1. States Parties shall take all appropriate legislative, administrative, social and educational measures to protect the child from all forms of physical or mental violence, injury or abuse, neglect or negligent treatment, maltreatment or exploitation, including sexual abuse, while in the care of parent(s), legal guardian(s) or any other person who has the care of the child.

2. Such protective measures should, as appropriate, include effective procedures for the establishment of social programmes to provide necessary support for the child and for those who have the care of the child, as well as for other forms of prevention and for identification, reporting, referral, investigation, treatment and follow-up of instances of child maltreatment described heretofore, and, as appropriate, for judicial involvement.

Article 20

1. A child temporarily or permanently deprived of his or her family environment, or in whose own best interests cannot be allowed to remain in that environment, shall be entitled to special protection and assistance provided by the State.

2. States Parties shall in accordance with their national laws ensure alternative care for such a child.

3. Such care could include, inter alia, foster placement, kafalah of Islamic law, adoption or if necessary placement in suitable institutions for the care of children. When considering solutions, due regard shall be paid to the desirability of continuity in a child's upbringing and to the child's ethnic, religious, cultural and linguistic background.

Article 21

States Parties that recognize and/or permit the system of adoption shall ensure that the best interests of the child shall be the paramount consideration and they shall:

(a) Ensure that the adoption of a child is authorized only by competent authorities who determine, in accordance with applicable law and procedures and on the basis of all pertinent and reliable information, that the adoption is permissible in view of the child's status concerning parents, relatives and legal guardians and that, if required, the persons concerned have given their informed consent to the adoption on the basis of such counselling as may be necessary;

(b) Recognize that inter-country adoption may be considered as an alternative means of child's care, if the child cannot be placed in a foster or an adoptive family or cannot in any suitable manner be cared for in the child's country of origin;

(c) Ensure that the child concerned by inter-country adoption enjoys safeguards and standards equivalent to those existing in the case of national adoption;

(d) Take all appropriate measures to ensure that, in inter-country adoption, the placement does not result in improper financial gain for those involved in it;

(e) Promote, where appropriate, the objectives of the present article by concluding bilateral or multilateral arrangements or agreements, and endeavour, within this framework, to ensure that the placement of the child in another country is carried out by competent authorities or organs.

Article 22

1. States Parties shall take appropriate measures to ensure that a child who is seeking refugee status or who is considered a refugee in accordance with applicable international or domestic law and procedures shall, whether unaccompanied or accompanied by his or her parents or by any other person, receive appropriate protection and humanitarian assistance in the enjoyment of applicable rights set forth in the present Convention and in other international human rights or humanitarian instruments to which the said States are Parties.

2. For this purpose, States Parties shall provide, as they consider appropriate, co-operation in any efforts by the United Nations and other competent intergovernmental organizations or non-governmental organizations co-operating with the United Nations to protect and assist such a child and to trace the parents or other members of the family of any refugee child in order to obtain information necessary for reunification with his or her family. In cases where no parents or other members of the family can be found, the child shall be accorded the same protection as any other child permanently or temporarily deprived of his or her family environment for any reason, as set forth in the present Convention.

Article 23

1. States Parties recognize that a mentally or physically disabled child should enjoy a full and decent life, in condi-tions which ensure dignity, promote self-reliance and facilitate the child's active participation in the community.

2. States Parties recognize the right of the disabled child to special care and shall encourage and ensure the extension, subject to available resources, to the eligible child and those responsible for his or her care, of assistance for which application is made and which is appropriate to the child's condition and to the circumstances of the parents or others caring for the child.

3. Recognizing the special needs of a disabled child, assistance extended in accordance with paragraph 2 of the present article shall be provided free of charge, whenever possible, taking into account the financial resources of the parents or others caring for the child, and shall be designed to ensure that the disabled child has effective access to and receives education, training, health care services, rehabilitation services, preparation for employment and recreation opportunities in a manner conducive to the child's achieving the fullest possible social integration and individual development, including his or her cultural and spiritual development.

4. States Parties shall promote, in the spirit of international cooperation, the exchange of appropriate information in the field of preventive health care and of medical, psychological and functional treatment of disabled children, including dissemination of and access to information concerning methods of rehabilitation, education and vocational services, with the aim of enabling States Parties to improve their capabilities and skills and to widen their experience in these areas. In this regard, particular account shall be taken of the needs of developing countries.

Article 24

1. States Parties recognize the right of the child to the enjoyment of the highest attainable standard of health and to facilities for the treatment of illness and rehabilitation of health. States Parties shall strive to ensure that no child is deprived of his or her right of access to such health care services.

2. States Parties shall pursue full implementation of this right and, in particular, shall take appropriate measures:

(a) To diminish infant and child mortality;

(b) To ensure the provision of necessary medical assistance and health care to all children with emphasis on the development of primary health care;

(c) To combat disease and malnutrition, including within the framework of primary health care, through, inter alia, the application of readily available technology and through the provision of adequate nutritious foods and clean drinking-water, taking into consideration the dangers and risks of environmental pollution;

(d) To ensure appropriate pre-natal and post-natal health care for mothers;

(e) To ensure that all segments of society, in particular parents and children, are informed, have access to education and are supported in the use of basic knowledge of child health and nutrition, the advantages of breastfeeding, hygiene and environmental sanitation and the prevention of accidents;

(f) To develop preventive health care, guidance for parents and family planning education and services.

3. States Parties shall take all effective and appropriate measures with a view to abolishing traditional practices prejudicial to the health of children.

4. States Parties undertake to promote and encourage international co-operation with a view to achieving progressively the full realization of the right recognized in the present article. In this regard, particular account shall be taken of the needs of developing countries.

Article 25

States Parties recognize the right of a child who has been placed by the competent authorities for the purposes of care, protection or treatment of his or her physical or mental health, to a periodic review of the treatment provided to the child and all other circumstances relevant to his or her placement.

Article 26

1. States Parties shall recognize for every child the right to benefit from social security, including social insurance, and shall take the necessary measures to achieve the full realization of this right in accordance with their national law.

2. The benefits should, where appropriate, be granted, taking into account the resources and the circumstances of the child and persons having responsibility for the maintenance of the child, as well as any other consideration relevant to an application for benefits made by or on behalf of the child.

Article 27

1. States Parties recognize the right of every child to a standard of living adequate for the child's physical, mental, spiritual, moral and social development.

2. The parent(s) or others responsible for the child have the primary responsibility to secure, within their abilities and financial capacities, the conditions of living necessary for the child's development.

3. States Parties, in accordance with national conditions and within their means, shall take appropriate measures to assist parents and others responsible for the child to implement this right and shall in case of need provide material assistance and support programmes, particularly with regard to nutrition, clothing and housing.

4. States Parties shall take all appropriate measures to secure the recovery of maintenance for the child from the parents or other persons having financial responsibility for the child, both within the State Party and from abroad. In particular, where the person having financial responsibility for the child lives in a State different from that of the child, States Parties shall promote the accession to international agreements or the conclusion of such agreements, as well as the making of other appropriate arrangements.

Article 28

1. States Parties recognize the right of the child to education, and with a view to achieving this right progressively and on the basis of equal opportunity, they shall, in particular:

(a) Make primary education compulsory and available free to all;

(b) Encourage the development of different forms of secondary education, including general and vocational education, make them available and accessible to every child, and take appropriate measures such as the introduction of free education and offering financial assistance in case of need;

(c) Make higher education accessible to all on the basis of capacity by every appropriate means;

(d) Make educational and vocational information and guidance available and accessible to all children;

(e) Take measures to encourage regular attendance at schools and the reduction of drop-out rates.

2. States Parties shall take all appropriate measures to ensure that school discipline is administered in a manner consistent with the child's human dignity and in conformity with the present Convention.

3. States Parties shall promote and encourage international cooperation in matters relating to education, in particular with a view to contributing to the elimination of ignorance and illiteracy throughout the world and facilitating access to scientific and technical knowledge and modern teaching methods. In this regard, particular account shall be taken of the needs of developing countries.

Article 29

1. States Parties agree that the education of the child shall be directed to:

(a) The development of the child's personality, talents and mental and physical abilities to their fullest potential;

(b) The development of respect for human rights and fundamental freedoms, and for the principles enshrined in the Charter of the United Nations;

(c) The development of respect for the child's parents, his or her own cultural identity, language and values, for the national values of the country in which the child is living, the country from which he or she may originate, and for civilizations different from his or her own;

(d) The preparation of the child for responsible life in a free society, in the spirit of understanding, peace, tolerance, equality of sexes, and friendship among all peoples, ethnic, national and religious groups and persons of indigenous origin;

(e) The development of respect for the natural environment.

2. No part of the present article or article 28 shall be construed so as to interfere with the liberty of individuals and bodies to establish and direct educational institutions, subject always to the observance of the principle set forth in paragraph 1 of the present article and to the requirements that the education given in such institutions shall conform to such minimum standards as may be laid down by the State.

Article 30

In those States in which ethnic, religious or linguistic minorities or persons of indigenous origin exist, a child belonging to such a minority or who is indigenous shall not be denied the right, in community with other members of his or her group, to enjoy his or her own culture, to profess and practise his or her own religion, or to use his or her own language.

Article 31

1. States Parties recognize the right of the child to rest and leisure, to engage in play and recreational activities appropriate to the age of the child and to participate freely in cultural life and the arts.

2. States Parties shall respect and promote the right of the child to participate fully in cultural and artistic life and shall encourage the provision of appropriate and equal opportunities for cultural, artistic, recreational and leisure activity.

Article 32

1. States Parties recognize the right of the child to be protected from economic exploitation and from performing any work that is likely to be hazardous or to interfere with the child's education, or to be harmful to the child's health or physical, mental, spiritual, moral or social development.

2. States Parties shall take legislative, administrative, social and educational measures to ensure the implementation of the present article. To this end, and having regard to the relevant provisions of other international instruments, States Parties shall in particular:

(a) Provide for a minimum age or minimum ages for admission to employment;

(b) Provide for appropriate regulation of the hours and conditions of employment;

(c) Provide for appropriate penalties or other sanctions to ensure the effective enforcement of the present article.

Article 33

States Parties shall take all appropriate measures, including legislative, administrative, social and educational measures, to protect children from the illicit use of narcotic drugs and psychotropic substances as defined in the relevant international treaties, and to prevent the use of children in the illicit production and trafficking of such substances.

Article 34

States Parties undertake to protect the child from all forms of sexual exploitation and sexual abuse. For these purposes, States Parties shall in particular take all appropriate national, bilateral and multilateral measures to prevent:

(a) The inducement or coercion of a child to engage in any unlawful sexual activity;

(b) The exploitative use of children in prostitution or other unlawful sexual practices;

(c) The exploitative use of children in pornographic performances and materials.

Article 35

States Parties shall take all appropriate national, bilateral and multilateral measures to prevent the abduction of, the sale of or traffic in children for any purpose or in any form.

Article 36

States Parties shall protect the child against all other forms of exploitation prejudicial to any aspects of the child's welfare.

Article 37

States Parties shall ensure that:

(a) No child shall be subjected to torture or other cruel, inhuman or degrading treatment or punishment. Neither capital punishment nor life imprisonment without possibility of release shall be imposed for offences committed by persons below eighteen years of age;

(b) No child shall be deprived of his or her liberty unlawfully or arbitrarily. The arrest, detention or imprisonment of a child shall be in conformity with the law and shall be used only as a measure of last resort and for the shortest appropriate period of time;

(c) Every child deprived of liberty shall be treated with humanity and respect for the inherent dignity of the human person, and in a manner which takes into account the needs of persons of his or her age. In particular, every child deprived of liberty shall be separated from adults unless it is considered in the child's best interest not to do so and shall have the right to maintain contact with his or her family through correspondence and visits, save in exceptional circumstances;

(d) Every child deprived of his or her liberty shall have the right to prompt access to legal and other appropriate assistance, as well as the right to challenge the legality of the deprivation of his or her liberty before a court or other competent, independent and impartial authority, and to a prompt decision on any such action.

Article 38

1. States Parties undertake to respect and to ensure respect for rules of international humanitarian law applicable to them in armed conflicts which are relevant to the child.

2. States Parties shall take all feasible measures to ensure that persons who have not attained the age of fifteen years do not take a direct part in hostilities.

3. States Parties shall refrain from recruiting any person who has not attained the age of fifteen years into their armed forces. In recruiting among those persons who have attained the age of fifteen years but who have not attained the age of eighteen years, States Parties shall endeavour to give priority to those who are oldest.

4. In accordance with their obligations under international humanitarian law to protect the civilian population in armed conflicts, States Parties shall take all feasible measures to ensure protection and care of children who are affected by an armed conflict.

Article 39

States Parties shall take all appropriate measures to promote physical and psychological recovery and social reintegration of a child victim of: any form of neglect, exploitation, or abuse; torture or any other form of cruel, inhuman or degrading treatment or punishment; or armed conflicts. Such recovery and reintegration shall take place in an environment which fosters the health, self-respect and dignity of the child.

Article 40

1. States Parties recognize the right of every child alleged as, accused of, or recognized as having infringed the penal law to be treated in a manner consistent with the promotion of the child's sense of dignity and worth, which reinforces the child's respect for the human rights and fundamental freedoms of others and which takes into account the child's age and the desirability of promoting the child's reintegration and the child's assuming a constructive role in society.

2. To this end, and having regard to the relevant provisions of international instruments, States Parties shall, in particular, ensure that:

(a) No child shall be alleged as, be accused of, or recognized as having infringed the penal law by reason of acts or omissions that were not prohibited by national or international law at the time they were committed;

(b) Every child alleged as or accused of having infringed the penal law has at least the following guarantees:

(i) To be presumed innocent until proven guilty according to law;

(ii) To be informed promptly and directly of the charges against him or her, and, if appropriate, through his or her parents or legal guardians, and to have legal or other appropriate assistance in the preparation and presentation of his or her defence;

(iii) To have the matter determined without delay by a competent, independent and impartial authority or judicial body in a fair hearing according to law, in the presence of legal or other appropriate assistance and, unless it is considered not to be in the best interest of the child, in particular, taking into account his or her age or situation, his or her parents or legal guardians;

(iv) Not to be compelled to give testimony or to confess guilt; to examine or have examined adverse witnesses and to obtain the participation and examination of witnesses on his or her behalf under conditions of equality;

(v) If considered to have infringed the penal law, to have this decision and any measures imposed in consequence thereof reviewed by a higher competent, independent and impartial authority or judicial body according to law;

(vi) To have the free assistance of an interpreter if the child cannot understand or speak the language used;

(vii) To have his or her privacy fully respected at all stages of the proceedings.

3. States Parties shall seek to promote the establishment of laws, procedures, authorities and institutions specifically applicable to children alleged as, accused of, or recognized as having infringed the penal law, and, in particular:

(a) The establishment of a minimum age below which children shall be presumed not to have the capacity to infringe the penal law;

(b) Whenever appropriate and desirable, measures for dealing with such children without resorting to judicial proceedings, providing that human rights and legal safeguards are fully respected.

4. A variety of dispositions, such as care, guidance and supervision orders; counselling; probation; foster care; education and vocational training programmes and other alternatives to institutional care shall be available to ensure that children are dealt with in a manner appropriate to their well-being and proportionate both to their circumstances and the offence.

Article 41

Nothing in the present Convention shall affect any provisions which are more conducive to the realization of the rights of the child and which may be contained in:

(a) The law of a State party; or

(b) International law in force for that State.

Part II

Article 42

States Parties undertake to make the principles and provisions of the Convention widely known, by appropriate and active means, to adults and children alike.

Article 43

1. For the purpose of examining the progress made by States Parties in achieving the realization of the obligations undertaken in the present Convention, there shall be established a Committee on the Rights of the Child, which shall carry out the functions hereinafter provided.

2. The Committee shall consist of ten experts of high moral standing and recognized competence in the field covered by this Convention. The members of the Committee shall be elected by States Parties from among their nationals and shall serve in their personal capacity, consideration being given to equitable geographical distribution, as well as to the principal legal systems. (amendment)

3. The members of the Committee shall be elected by secret ballot from a list of persons nominated by States Parties. Each State Party may nominate one person from among its own nationals.

4. The initial election to the Committee shall be held no later than six months after the date of the entry into force of the present Convention and thereafter every second year. At least four months before the date of each election, the Secretary-General of the United Nations shall address a letter to States Parties inviting them to submit their nominations within two months. The Secretary-General shall subsequently prepare a list in alphabetical order of all persons thus nominated, indicating States Parties which have nominated them, and shall submit it to the States Parties to the present Convention.

5. The elections shall be held at meetings of States Parties convened by the Secretary-General at United Nations Headquarters. At those meetings, for which two thirds of States Parties shall constitute a quorum, the persons elected to the Committee shall be those who obtain the largest number of votes and an absolute majority of the votes of the representatives of States Parties present and voting.

6. The members of the Committee shall be elected for a term of four years. They shall be eligible for re-election if renominated. The term of five of the members elected at the first election shall expire at the end of two years; immediately after the first election, the names of these five members shall be chosen by lot by the Chairman of the meeting.

7. If a member of the Committee dies or resigns or declares that for any other cause he or she can no longer perform the duties of the Committee, the State Party which nominated the member shall appoint another expert from among its nationals to serve for the remainder of the term, subject to the approval of the Committee.

8. The Committee shall establish its own rules of procedure.

9. The Committee shall elect its officers for a period of two years.

10. The meetings of the Committee shall normally be held at United Nations Headquarters or at any other convenient place as determined by the Committee. The Committee shall normally meet annually. The duration of the meetings of the Committee shall be determined, and reviewed, if necessary, by a meeting of the States Parties to the present Convention, subject to the approval of the General Assembly.

11. The Secretary-General of the United Nations shall provide the necessary staff and facilities for the effective performance of the functions of the Committee under the present Convention.

12. With the approval of the General Assembly, the members of the Committee established under the present Convention shall receive emoluments from United Nations resources on such terms and conditions as the Assembly may decide.

Article 44

1. States Parties undertake to submit to the Committee, through the Secretary-General of the United Nations, reports on the measures they have adopted which give effect to the rights recognized herein and on the progress made on the enjoyment of those rights:

(a) Within two years of the entry into force of the Convention for the State Party concerned;

(b) Thereafter every five years.

2. Reports made under the present article shall indicate factors and difficulties, if any, affecting the degree of fulfilment of the obligations under the present Convention. Reports shall also contain sufficient information to provide the Committee with a comprehensive understanding of the implementation of the Convention in the country concerned.

3. A State Party which has submitted a comprehensive initial report to the Committee need not, in its subsequent reports submitted in accordance with paragraph 1 (b) of the present article, repeat basic information previously provided.

4. The Committee may request from States Parties further information relevant to the implementation of the Convention.

5. The Committee shall submit to the General Assembly, through the Economic and Social Council, every two years, reports on its activities.

6. States Parties shall make their reports widely available to the public in their own countries.

Article 45

In order to foster the effective implementation of the Convention and to encourage international co-operation in the field covered by the Convention:

(a) The specialized agencies, the United Nations Children's Fund, and other United Nations organs shall be entitled to be represented at the consideration of the implementation of such provisions of the present Convention as fall within the scope of their mandate. The Committee may invite the specialized agencies, the United Nations Children's Fund and other competent bodies as it may consider appropriate to provide expert advice on the implementation of the Convention in areas falling within the scope of their respective mandates. The Committee may invite the specialized agencies, the United Nations Children's Fund, and other United Nations organs to submit reports on the implementation of the Convention in areas falling within the scope of their activities;

(b) The Committee shall transmit, as it may consider appropriate, to the specialized agencies, the United Nations Children's Fund and other competent bodies, any reports from States Parties that contain a request, or indicate a need, for technical advice or assistance, along with the Committee's observations and suggestions, if any, on these requests or indications;

(c) The Committee may recommend to the General Assembly to request the Secretary-General to undertake on its behalf studies on specific issues relating to the rights of the child;

(d) The Committee may make suggestions and general recommendations based on information received pursuant to articles 44 and 45 of the present Convention. Such suggestions and general recommendations shall be transmitted to any State Party concerned and reported to the General Assembly, together with comments, if any, from States Parties.

Part III

Article 46

The present Convention shall be open for signature by all States.

Article 47

The present Convention is subject to ratification. Instruments of ratification shall be deposited with the Secretary-General of the United Nations.

Article 48

The present Convention shall remain open for accession by any State. The instruments of accession shall be deposited with the Secretary-General of the United Nations.

Article 49

1. The present Convention shall enter into force on the thirtieth day following the date of deposit with the Secretary-General of the United Nations of the twentieth instrument of ratification or accession.

2. For each State ratifying or acceding to the Convention after the deposit of the twentieth instrument of ratification or accession, the Convention shall enter into force on the thirtieth day after the deposit by such State of its instrument of ratification or accession.

Article 50

1. Any State Party may propose an amendment and file it with the Secretary-General of the United Nations. The Secretary-General shall thereupon communicate the proposed amendment to States Parties, with a request that they indicate whether they favour a conference of States Parties for the purpose of considering and voting upon the proposals. In the event that, within four months from the date of such communication, at least one third of the States Parties favour such a conference, the Secretary-General shall convene the conference under the auspices of the United Nations. Any amendment adopted by a majority of States Parties present and voting at the conference shall be submitted to the General Assembly for approval.

2. An amendment adopted in accordance with paragraph 1 of the present article shall enter into force when it has been approved by the General Assembly of the United Nations and accepted by a two-thirds majority of States Parties.

3. When an amendment enters into force, it shall be binding on those States Parties which have accepted it, other States Parties still being bound by the provisions of the present Convention and any earlier amendments which they have accepted.

Article 51

1. The Secretary-General of the United Nations shall receive and circulate to all States the text of reservations made by States at the time of ratification or accession.

2. A reservation incompatible with the object and purpose of the present Convention shall not be permitted.

3. Reservations may be withdrawn at any time by notification to that effect addressed to the Secretary-General of the United Nations, who shall then inform all States. Such notification shall take effect on the date on which it is received by the Secretary-General.

Article 52

A State Party may denounce the present Convention by written notification to the Secretary-General of the United Nations. Denunciation becomes effective one year after the date of receipt of the notification by the Secretary-General.

Article 53

The Secretary-General of the United Nations is designated as the depositary of the present Convention.

Article 54

The original of the present Convention, of which the Arabic, Chinese, English, French, Russian and Spanish texts are equally authentic, shall be deposited with the Secretary-General of the United Nations.

IN WITNESS THEREOF the undersigned plenipotentiaries, being duly authorized thereto by their respective governments, have signed the present Convention.

DECLARATION ON THE RIGHTS OF DISABLED PERSONS

Proclaimed by General Assembly resolution 3447 (XXX) of 9 December 1975

The General Assembly,

Mindful of the pledge made by Member States, under the Charter of the United Nations to take joint and separate action in co-operation with the Organization to promote higher standards of living, full employment and conditions of economic and social progress and development,

Reaffirming its faith in human rights and fundamental freedoms and in the principles of peace, of the dignity and worth of the human person and of social justice proclaimed in the Charter,

Recalling the principles of the Universal Declaration of Human Rights, the International Covenants on Human Rights, the Declaration of the Rights of the Child and the Declaration on the Rights of Mentally Retarded Persons, as well as the standards already set for social progress in the constitutions, conventions, recommendations and resolutions of the International Labour Organisation, the United Nations Educational, Scientific and Cultural Organization, the World Health Organization, the United Nations Children's Fund and other organizations concerned,

Recalling also Economic and Social Council resolution 1921 (LVIII) of 6 May 1975 on the prevention of disability and the rehabilitation of disabled persons,

Emphasizing that the Declaration on Social Progress and Development has proclaimed the necessity of protecting the rights and assuring the welfare and rehabilitation of the physically and mentally disadvantaged,

Bearing in mind the necessity of preventing physical and mental disabilities and of assisting disabled persons to develop their abilities in the most varied fields of activities and of promoting their integration as far as possible in normal life,

Aware that certain countries, at their present stage of development, can devote only limited efforts to this end,

Proclaims this Declaration on the Rights of Disabled Persons and calls for national and international action to ensure that it will be used as a common basis and frame of reference for the protection of these rights:

1. The term "disabled person" means any person unable to ensure by himself or herself, wholly or partly, the necessities of a normal individual and/or social life, as a result of deficiency, either congenital or not, in his or her physical or mental capabilities.

2. Disabled persons shall enjoy all the rights set forth in this Declaration. These rights shall be granted to all disabled persons without any exception whatsoever and without distinction or discrimination on the basis of race, colour, sex, language, religion, political or other opinions, national or social origin, state of wealth, birth or any other situation applying either to the disabled person himself or herself or to his or her family.

3. Disabled persons have the inherent right to respect for their human dignity. Disabled persons, whatever the origin, nature and seriousness of their handicaps and disabilities, have the same fundamental rights as their fellow-citizens of the same age, which implies first and foremost the right to enjoy a decent life, as normal and full as possible.

4. Disabled persons have the same civil and political rights as other human beings; paragraph 7 of the Declaration on the Rights of Mentally Retarded Persons applies to any possible limitation or suppression of those rights for mentally disabled persons.

5. Disabled persons are entitled to the measures designed to enable them to become as self-reliant as possible.

6. Disabled persons have the right to medical, psychological and functional treatment, including prosthetic and orthetic appliances, to medical and social rehabilitation, education, voca-

tional training and rehabilitation, aid, counselling, placement services and other services which will enable them to develop their capabilities and skills to the maximum and will hasten the processes of their social integration or reintegration.

7. Disabled persons have the right to economic and social security and to a decent level of living. They have the right, according to their capabilities, to secure and retain employment or to engage in a useful, productive and remunerative occupation and to join trade unions.

8. Disabled persons are entitled to have their special needs taken into consideration at all stages of economic and social planning.

9. Disabled persons have the right to live with their families or with foster parents and to participate in all social, creative or recreational activities. No disabled person shall be subjected, as far as his or her residence is concerned, to differential treatment other than that required by his or her condition or by the improvement which he or she may derive therefrom. If the stay of a disabled person in a specialized establishment is indispensable, the environment and living conditions therein shall be as close as possible to those of the normal life of a person of his or her age.

10. Disabled persons shall be protected against all exploitation, all regulations and all treatment of a discriminatory, abusive or degrading nature.

11. Disabled persons shall be able to avail themselves of qualified legal aid when such aid proves indispensable for the protection of their persons and property. If judicial proceedings are instituted against them, the legal procedure applied shall take their physical and mental condition fully into account.

12. Organizations of disabled persons may be usefully consulted in all matters regarding the rights of disabled persons.

13. Disabled persons, their families and communities shall be fully informed, by all appropriate means, of the rights contained in this Declaration.

BASIC PRINCIPLES ON THE INDEPENDENCE OF THE JUDICIARY

Adopted by the Seventh United Nations Congress on the Prevention of Crime and the Treatment of Offenders held at Milan from 26 August to 6 September 1985 and endorsed by General Assembly resolutions 40/32 of 29 November 1985 and 40/146 of 13 December 1985

Whereas in the Charter of the United Nations the peoples of the world affirm, inter alia, their determination to establish conditions under which justice can be maintained to achieve international co-operation in promoting and encouraging respect for human rights and fundamental freedoms without any discrimination,

Whereas the Universal Declaration of Human Rights enshrines in particular the principles of equality before the law, of the presumption of innocence and of the right to a fair and public hearing by a competent, independent and impartial tribunal established by law,

Whereas the International Covenants on Economic, Social and Cultural Rights and on Civil and Political Rights both guarantee the exercise of those rights, and in addition, the Covenant on Civil and Political Rights further guarantees the right to be tried without undue delay,

Whereas frequently there still exists a gap between the vision underlying those principles and the actual situation,

Whereas the organization and administration of justice in every country should be inspired by those principles, and efforts should be undertaken to translate them fully into reality,

Whereas rules concerning the exercise of judicial office should aim at enabling judges to act in accordance with those principles,

Whereas judges are charged with the ultimate decision over life, freedoms, rights, duties and property of citizens,

Whereas the Sixth United Nations Congress on the Prevention of Crime and the Treatment of Offenders, by its resolution 16, called upon the Committee on Crime Prevention and Control to include among its priorities the elaboration of guidelines relating to the independence of judges and the selection, professional training and status of judges and prosecutors,

Whereas it is, therefore, appropriate that consideration be first given to the role of judges in relation to the system of justice and to the importance of their selection, training and conduct,

The following basic principles, formulated to assist Member States in their task of securing and promoting the independence of the judiciary should be taken into account and respected by Governments within the framework of their national legislation and practice and be brought to the attention of judges, lawyers, members of the executive and the legislature and the public in general. The principles have been formulated principally with professional judges in mind, but they apply equally, as appropriate, to lay judges, where they exist.

Independence of The Judiciary

1. The independence of the judiciary shall be guaranteed by the State and enshrined in the Constitution or the law of the country. It is the duty of all governmental and other institutions to respect and observe the independence of the judiciary.

2. The judiciary shall decide matters before them impartially, on the basis of facts and in accordance with the law, without any restrictions, improper influences, inducements, pressures, threats or interferences, direct or indirect, from any quarter or for any reason.

3. The judiciary shall have jurisdiction over all issues of a judicial nature and shall have exclusive authority to decide whether an issue submitted for its decision is within its competence as defined by law.

4. There shall not be any inappropriate or unwarranted interference with the judicial process, nor shall judicial decisions by the courts be subject to revision. This principle is without prejudice to judicial review or to mitigation or commutation by competent authorities of sentences imposed by the judiciary, in accordance with the law.

5. Everyone shall have the right to be tried by ordinary courts or tribunals using established legal procedures. Tribunals that do not use the duly established procedures of the legal process shall not be created to displace the jurisdiction belonging to the ordinary courts or judicial tribunals.

6. The principle of the independence of the judiciary entitles and requires the judiciary to ensure that judicial proceedings are conducted fairly and that the rights of the parties are respected.

7. It is the duty of each Member State to provide adequate resources to enable the judiciary to properly perform its functions.

Freedom of Expression and Association

8. In accordance with the Universal Declaration of Human Rights, members of the judiciary are like other citizens entitled to freedom of expression, belief, association and assembly; provided, however, that in exercising such rights, judges shall always conduct themselves in such a manner as to preserve the dignity of their office and the impartiality and independence of the judiciary.

9. Judges shall be free to form and join associations of judges or other organizations to represent their interests, to promote their professional training and to protect their judicial independence.

Qualifications, Selection and Training

10. Persons selected for judicial office shall be individuals of integrity and ability with appropriate training or qualifications in law. Any method of judicial selection shall safeguard against judicial appointments for improper motives. In the selection of judges, there shall be no discrimination against a person on the grounds of race, colour, sex, religion, political or other opinion, national or social origin, property, birth or status, except that a requirement, that a candidate for judicial office must be a national of the country concerned, shall not be considered discriminatory.

Conditions of Service and Tenure

11. The term of office of judges, their independence, security, adequate remuneration, conditions of service, pensions and the age of retirement shall be adequately secured by law.

12. Judges, whether appointed or elected, shall have guaranteed tenure until a mandatory retirement age or the expiry of their term of office, where such exists.

13. Promotion of judges, wherever such a system exists, should be based on objective factors, in particular ability, integrity and experience.

14. The assignment of cases to judges within the court to which they belong is an internal matter of judicial administration, professional secrecy and immunity.

15. The judiciary shall be bound by professional secrecy with regard to their deliberations and to confidential information acquired in the course of their duties other than in public proceedings, and shall not be compelled to testify on such matters.

16. Without prejudice to any disciplinary procedure or to any right of appeal or to compensation from the State, in accordance with national law, judges should enjoy personal immunity from civil suits for monetary damages for improper acts or omissions in the exercise of their judicial functions.

Discipline, Suspension and Removal

17. A charge or complaint made against a judge in his/her judicial and professional capacity shall be processed expeditiously and fairly under an appropriate procedure. The judge shall have the right to a fair hearing. The examination of the matter at its initial stage shall be kept confidential, unless otherwise requested by the judge.

18. Judges shall be subject to suspension or removal only for reasons of incapacity or behaviour that renders them unfit to discharge their duties.

19. All disciplinary, suspension or removal proceedings shall be determined in accordance with established standards of judicial conduct.

20. Decisions in disciplinary, suspension or removal proceedings should be subject to an independent review. This principle may not apply to the decisions of the highest court and those of the legislature in impeachment or similar proceedings.

CODE OF CONDUCT FOR LAW ENFORCEMENT OFFICIALS

Adopted by General Assembly resolution 34/169 of 17 December 1979

Article 1

Law enforcement officials shall at all times fulfil the duty imposed upon them by law, by serving the community and by protecting all persons against illegal acts, consistent with the high degree of responsibility required by their profession.

Commentary:

(a) The term "law enforcement officials,' includes all officers of the law, whether appointed or elected, who exercise police powers, especially the powers of arrest or detention.

(b) In countries where police powers are exercised by military authorities, whether uniformed or not, or by State security forces, the definition of law enforcement officials shall be regarded as including officers of such services.

(c) Service to the community is intended to include particularly the rendition of services of assistance to those members of the community who by reason of personal, economic, social or other emergencies are in need of immediate aid.

(d) This provision is intended to cover not only all violent, predatory and harmful acts, but extends to the full range of prohibitions under penal statutes. It extends to conduct by persons not capable of incurring criminal liability.

Article 2

In the performance of their duty, law enforcement officials shall respect and protect human dignity and maintain and uphold the human rights of all persons.

Commentary:

(a) The human rights in question are identified and protected by national and international law. Among the relevant international instruments are the Universal Declaration of Human Rights, the International Covenant on Civil and Political Rights, the Declaration on the Protection of All Persons from Being Subjected to Torture and Other Cruel, Inhuman or Degrading Treatment or Punishment, the United Nations Declaration on the Elimination of All Forms of Racial Discrimination, the International Convention on the Elimination of All Forms of Racial Discrimination, the International Convention on the Suppression and Punishment of the Crime of Apartheid, the Convention on the Prevention and Punishment of the Crime of Genocide, the Standard Minimum Rules for the Treatment of Prisoners and the Vienna Convention on Consular Relations.

(b) National commentaries to this provision should indicate regional or national provisions identifying and protecting these rights.

Article 3

Law enforcement officials may use force only when strictly necessary and to the extent required for the performance of their duty.

Commentary:

(a) This provision emphasizes that the use of force by law enforcement officials should be exceptional; while it implies that law enforcement officials may be authorized to use force as is reasonably necessary under the circumstances for the prevention of crime or in effecting or assisting in the lawful arrest of offenders or suspected offenders, no force going beyond that may be used.

(b) National law ordinarily restricts the use of force by law enforcement officials in accordance with a principle of proportionality. It is to be understood that such national principles of proportionality are to be respected in the interpretation of this provision. In no case should this provision be interpreted to authorize the use of force which is disproportionate to the legitimate objective to be achieved.

(c) The use of firearms is considered an extreme measure. Every effort should be made to exclude the use of firearms, especially against children. In general, firearms should not be used except when a suspected offender offers armed resistance or otherwise jeopardizes the lives of others and less extreme measures are not sufficient to restrain or apprehend the suspected offender. In every instance in which a firearm is discharged, a report should be made promptly to the competent authorities.

Article 4

Matters of a confidential nature in the possession of law enforcement officials shall be kept confidential, unless the performance of duty or the needs of justice strictly require otherwise.

Commentary:

By the nature of their duties, law enforcement officials obtain information which may relate to private lives or be potentially harmful to the interests, and especially the reputation, of others. Great care should be exercised in safeguarding and using such information, which should be disclosed only in the performance of duty or to serve the needs of justice. Any disclosure of such information for other purposes is wholly improper.

Article 5

No law enforcement official may inflict, instigate or tolerate any act of torture or other cruel, inhuman or degrading treatment or punishment, nor may any law enforcement official invoke superior orders or exceptional circumstances such as a state of war or a threat of war, a threat to national security, internal political instability or any other public emergency as a justification of torture or other cruel, inhuman or degrading treatment or punishment.

Commentary:

(a) This prohibition derives from the Declaration on the Protection of All Persons from Being Subjected to Torture and Other Cruel, Inhuman or Degrading Treatment or Punishment, adopted by the General Assembly, according to which: "[Such an act is] an offence to human dignity and shall be condemned as a denial of the purposes of the Charter of the United Nations and as a violation of the human rights and fundamental freedoms proclaimed in the Universal Declaration of Human Rights [and other international human rights instruments]."

(b) The Declaration defines torture as follows:

". . . torture means any act by which severe pain or suffering, whether physical or mental, is intentionally inflicted by or at the instigation of a public official on a person for such purposes as obtaining from him or a third person information or confession, punishing him for an act he has committed or is suspected of having committed, or intimidating him or other persons. It does not include pain or suffering arising only from, inherent in or incidental to, lawful sanctions to the extent consistent with the Standard Minimum Rules for the Treatment of Prisoners."

(c) The term "cruel, inhuman or degrading treatment or punishment" has not been defined by the General Assembly but should be interpreted so as to extend the widest possible protection against abuses, whether physical or mental.

Article 6

Law enforcement officials shall ensure the full protection of the health of persons in their custody and, in particular, shall take immediate action to secure medical attention whenever required.

Commentary:

(a) "Medical attention," which refers to services rendered by any medical personnel, including certified medical practitioners and paramedics, shall be secured when needed or requested.

(b) While the medical personnel are likely to be attached to the law enforcement operation, law enforcement officials must take into account the judgement of such personnel when they recommend providing the person in custody with appropriate treatment through, or in consultation with, medical personnel from outside the law enforcement operation.

(c) It is understood that law enforcement officials shall also secure medical attention for victims of violations of law or of accidents occurring in the course of violations of law.

Article 7

Law enforcement officials shall not commit any act of corruption. They shall also rigorously oppose and combat all such acts.

Commentary:

(a) Any act of corruption, in the same way as any other abuse of authority, is incompatible with the profession of law enforcement officials. The law must be enforced fully with respect to any law enforcement official who commits an act of corruption, as Governments cannot expect to enforce the law among their citizens if they cannot, or will not, enforce the law against their own agents and within their agencies.

(b) While the definition of corruption must be subject to national law, it should be understood to encompass the commission or omission of an act in the performance of or in connection with one's duties, in response to gifts, promises or incentives demanded or accepted, or the wrongful receipt of these once the act has been committed or omitted.

(c) The expression "act of corruption" referred to above should be understood to encompass attempted corruption.

Article 8

Law enforcement officials shall respect the law and the present Code. They shall also, to the best of their capability, prevent and rigorously oppose any violations of them.

Law enforcement officials who have reason to believe that a violation of the present Code has occurred or is about to occur shall report the matter to their superior authorities and, where necessary, to other appropriate authorities or organs vested with reviewing or remedial power.

Commentary:

(a) This Code shall be observed whenever it has been incorporated into national legislation or practice. If legislation or practice contains stricter provisions than those of the present Code, those stricter provisions shall be observed.

(b) The article seeks to preserve the balance between the need for internal discipline of the agency on which public safety is largely dependent, on the one hand, and the need for dealing with violations of basic human rights, on the other. Law enforcement officials shall report violations within the chain of command and take other lawful action outside the chain of command only when no other remedies are available or effective. It is understood that law enforcement officials shall not suffer administrative or other penalties because they have reported that a violation of this Code has occurred or is about to occur.

(c) The term "appropriate authorities or organs vested with reviewing or remedial power" refers to any authority or organ existing under national law, whether internal to the law enforcement agency or independent thereof, with statutory, customary or other power to review grievances and complaints arising out of violations within the purview of this Code.

(d) In some countries, the mass media may be regarded as performing complaint review functions similar to those described in subparagraph (c) above. Law enforcement officials may, therefore, be justified if, as a last resort and in accordance with the laws and customs of their own countries and with the provisions of article 4 of the present Code, they bring violations to the attention of public opinion through the mass media.

(e) Law enforcement officials who comply with the provisions of this Code deserve the respect, the full support and the co-operation of the community and of the law enforcement agency in which they serve, as well as the law enforcement profession.

CONVENTION AGAINST TORTURE AND OTHER CRUEL, INHUMAN OR DEGRADING TREATMENT OR PUNISHMENT

Adopted and opened for signature, ratification and accession by General Assembly resolution 39/46 of 10 December 1984

Entered into force 26 June 1987, in accordance with article 27 (1)

The States Parties to this Convention,

Considering that, in accordance with the principles proclaimed in the Charter of the United Nations, recognition of the equal and inalienable rights of all members of the human family is the foundation of freedom, justice and peace in the world,

Recognizing that those rights derive from the inherent dignity of the human person,

Considering the obligation of States under the Charter, in particular Article 55, to promote universal respect for, and observance of, human rights and fundamental freedoms,

Having regard to article 5 of the Universal Declaration of Human Rights and article 7 of the International Covenant on Civil and Political Rights, both of which provide that no one shall be subjected to torture or to cruel, inhuman or degrading treatment or punishment,

Having regard also to the Declaration on the Protection of All Persons from Being Subjected to Torture and Other Cruel, Inhuman or Degrading Treatment or Punishment, adopted by the General Assembly on 9 December 1975,

Desiring to make more effective the struggle against torture and other cruel, inhuman or degrading treatment or punishment throughout the world,

Have agreed as follows:

Part I

Article 1

1. For the purposes of this Convention, the term "torture" means any act by which severe pain or suffering, whether physical or mental, is intentionally inflicted on a person for such purposes as obtaining from him or a third person information or a confession, punishing him for an act he or a third person has committed or is suspected of having committed, or intimidating or coercing him or a third person, or for any reason based on discrimination of any kind, when such pain or suffering is inflicted by or at the instigation of or with the consent or acquiescence of a public official or other person acting in an official capacity. It does not include pain or suffering arising only from, inherent in or incidental to lawful sanctions.

2. This article is without prejudice to any international instrument or national legislation which does or may contain provisions of wider application.

Article 2

1. Each State Party shall take effective legislative, administrative, judicial or other measures to prevent acts of torture in any territory under its jurisdiction.

2. No exceptional circumstances whatsoever, whether a state of war or a threat of war, internal political instability or any other public emergency, may be invoked as a justification of torture.

3. An order from a superior officer or a public authority may not be invoked as a justification of torture.

Article 3

1. No State Party shall expel, return ("refouler") or extradite a person to another State where there are substantial grounds for believing that he would be in danger of being subjected to torture.

2. For the purpose of determining whether there are such grounds, the competent authorities shall take into account all relevant considerations including, where applicable, the existence in the State concerned of a consistent pattern of gross, flagrant or mass violations of human rights.

Article 4

1. Each State Party shall ensure that all acts of torture are offences under its criminal law. The same shall apply to an attempt to commit torture and to an act by any person which constitutes complicity or participation in torture.

2. Each State Party shall make these offences punishable by appropriate penalties which take into account their grave nature.

Article 5

1. Each State Party shall take such measures as may be necessary to establish its jurisdiction over the offences referred to in article 4 in the following cases:

(a) When the offences are committed in any territory under its jurisdiction or on board a ship or aircraft registered in that State;

(b) When the alleged offender is a national of that State;

(c) When the victim is a national of that State if that State considers it appropriate.

2. Each State Party shall likewise take such measures as may be necessary to establish its jurisdiction over such offences in cases where the alleged offender is present in any territory under its jurisdiction and it does not extradite him pursuant to article 8 to any of the States mentioned in paragraph 1 of this article.

3. This Convention does not exclude any criminal jurisdiction exercised in accordance with internal law.

Article 6

1. Upon being satisfied, after an examination of information available to it, that the circumstances so warrant, any State Party in whose territory a person alleged to have committed any offence referred to in article 4 is present shall take him into custody or take other legal measures to ensure his presence. The custody and other legal measures shall be as provided in the law of that State but may be continued only for such time as is necessary to enable any criminal or extradition proceedings to be instituted.

2. Such State shall immediately make a preliminary inquiry into the facts.

3. Any person in custody pursuant to paragraph 1 of this article shall be assisted in communicating immediately with the nearest appropriate representative of the State of which he is a national, or, if he is a stateless person, with the representative of the State where he usually resides.

4. When a State, pursuant to this article, has taken a person into custody, it shall immediately notify the States referred to in article 5, paragraph 1, of the fact that such person is in custody and of the circumstances which warrant his detention. The State which makes the preliminary inquiry contemplated in paragraph 2 of this article shall promptly report its findings to the said States and shall indicate whether it intends to exercise jurisdiction.

Article 7

1. The State Party in the territory under whose jurisdiction a person alleged to have committed any offence referred to in article 4 is found shall in the cases contemplated in article 5, if it does not extradite him, submit the case to its competent authorities for the purpose of prosecution.

2. These authorities shall take their decision in the same manner as in the case of any ordinary offence of a serious nature under the law of that State. In the cases referred to in article 5, paragraph 2, the standards of evidence required for prosecution and conviction shall in no way be less stringent than those which apply in the cases referred to in article 5, paragraph 1.

3. Any person regarding whom proceedings are brought in connection with any of the offences referred to in article 4 shall be guaranteed fair treatment at all stages of the proceedings.

Article 8

1. The offences referred to in article 4 shall be deemed to be included as extraditable offences in any extradition treaty existing between States Parties. States Parties undertake to include such offences as extraditable offences in every extradition treaty to be concluded between them.

2. If a State Party which makes extradition conditional on the existence of a treaty receives a request for extradition from another State Party with which it has no extradition treaty, it may consider this Convention as the legal basis for extradition in respect of such offences. Extradition shall be subject to the other conditions provided by the law of the requested State.

3. States Parties which do not make extradition conditional on the existence of a treaty shall recognize such offences as extraditable offences between themselves subject to the conditions provided by the law of the requested State.

4. Such offences shall be treated, for the purpose of extradition between States Parties, as if they had been committed not only in the place in which they occurred but also in the territories of the States required to establish their jurisdiction in accordance with article 5, paragraph 1.

Article 9

1. States Parties shall afford one another the greatest measure of assistance in connection with criminal proceedings brought in respect of any of the offences referred to in article 4, including the supply of all evidence at their disposal necessary for the proceedings.

2. States Parties shall carry out their obligations under paragraph 1 of this article in conformity with any treaties on mutual judicial assistance that may exist between them.

Article 10

1. Each State Party shall ensure that education and information regarding the prohibition against torture are fully included in the training of law enforcement personnel, civil or military, medical personnel, public officials and other persons who may be involved in the custody, interrogation or treat-

ment of any individual subjected to any form of arrest, detention or imprisonment.

2. Each State Party shall include this prohibition in the rules or instructions issued in regard to the duties and functions of any such person.

Article 11

Each State Party shall keep under systematic review interrogation rules, instructions, methods and practices as well as arrangements for the custody and treatment of persons subjected to any form of arrest, detention or imprisonment in any territory under its jurisdiction, with a view to preventing any cases of torture.

Article 12

Each State Party shall ensure that its competent authorities proceed to a prompt and impartial investigation, wherever there is reasonable ground to believe that an act of torture has been committed in any territory under its jurisdiction.

Article 13

Each State Party shall ensure that any individual who alleges he has been subjected to torture in any territory under its jurisdiction has the right to complain to, and to have his case promptly and impartially examined by, its competent authorities. Steps shall be taken to ensure that the complainant and witnesses are protected against all ill-treatment or intimidation as a consequence of his complaint or any evidence given.

Article 14

1. Each State Party shall ensure in its legal system that the victim of an act of torture obtains redress and has an enforceable right to fair and adequate compensation, including the means for as full rehabilitation as possible. In the event of the death of the victim as a result of an act of torture, his dependants shall be entitled to compensation.

2. Nothing in this article shall affect any right of the victim or other persons to compensation which may exist under national law.

Article 15

Each State Party shall ensure that any statement which is established to have been made as a result of torture shall not be invoked as evidence in any proceedings, except against a person accused of torture as evidence that the statement was made.

Article 16

1. Each State Party shall undertake to prevent in any territory under its jurisdiction other acts of cruel, inhuman or degrading treatment or punishment which do not amount to torture as defined in article 1, when such acts are committed by or at the instigation of or with the consent or acquiescence of a public official or other person acting in an official capacity. In particular, the obligations contained in articles 10, 11, 12 and 13 shall apply with the substitution for references to torture of references to other forms of cruel, inhuman or degrading treatment or punishment.

2. The provisions of this Convention are without prejudice to the provisions of any other international instrument or national law which prohibits cruel, inhuman or degrading treatment or punishment or which relates to extradition or expulsion.

Part II

Article 17

1. There shall be established a Committee against Torture (hereinafter referred to as the Committee) which shall carry out the functions hereinafter provided. The Committee shall consist of ten experts of high moral standing and recognized competence in the field of human rights, who shall serve in their personal capacity. The experts shall be elected by the States Parties, consideration being given to equitable geographical distribution and to the usefulness of the participation of some persons having legal experience.

2. The members of the Committee shall be elected by secret ballot from a list of persons nominated by States Parties. Each State Party may nominate one person from among its own nationals. States Parties shall bear in mind the usefulness of nominating persons who are also members of the Human Rights Committee established under the International Covenant on Civil and Political Rights and who are willing to serve on the Committee against Torture.

3. Elections of the members of the Committee shall be held at biennial meetings of States Parties convened by the Secretary-General of the United Nations. At those meetings, for which two thirds of the States Parties shall constitute a quorum, the persons elected to the Committee shall be those who obtain the largest number of votes and an absolute majority of the votes of the representatives of States Parties present and voting.

4. The initial election shall be held no later than six months after the date of the entry into force of this Convention. At least four months before the date of each election, the Secretary-General of the United Nations shall address a letter

to the States Parties inviting them to submit their nominations within three months. The Secretary-General shall prepare a list in alphabetical order of all persons thus nominated, indicating the States Parties which have nominated them, and shall submit it to the States Parties.

5. The members of the Committee shall be elected for a term of four years. They shall be eligible for re-election if renominated. However, the term of five of the members elected at the first election shall expire at the end of two years; immediately after the first election the names of these five members shall be chosen by lot by the chairman of the meeting referred to in paragraph 3 of this article.

6. If a member of the Committee dies or resigns or for any other cause can no longer perform his Committee duties, the State Party which nominated him shall appoint another expert from among its nationals to serve for the remainder of his term, subject to the approval of the majority of the States Parties. The approval shall be considered given unless half or more of the States Parties respond negatively within six weeks after having been informed by the Secretary-General of the United Nations of the proposed appointment.

7. States Parties shall be responsible for the expenses of the members of the Committee while they are in performance of Committee duties. (amendment [see General Assembly resolution 47/111 of 16 December 1992]; status of ratification)

Article 18

1. The Committee shall elect its officers for a term of two years. They may be re-elected.

2. The Committee shall establish its own rules of procedure, but these rules shall provide, inter alia, that:

(a) Six members shall constitute a quorum;

(b) Decisions of the Committee shall be made by a majority vote of the members present.

3. The Secretary-General of the United Nations shall provide the necessary staff and facilities for the effective performance of the functions of the Committee under this Convention.

4. The Secretary-General of the United Nations shall convene the initial meeting of the Committee. After its initial meeting, the Committee shall meet at such times as shall be provided in its rules of procedure.

5. The States Parties shall be responsible for expenses incurred in connection with the holding of meetings of the States Parties and of the Committee, including reimburse-

ment to the United Nations for any expenses, such as the cost of staff and facilities, incurred by the United Nations pursuant to paragraph 3 of this article. (amendment [see General Assembly resolution 47/111 of 16 December 1992]; status of ratification)

Article 19

1. The States Parties shall submit to the Committee, through the Secretary-General of the United Nations, reports on the measures they have taken to give effect to their undertakings under this Convention, within one year after the entry into force of the Convention for the State Party concerned. Thereafter the States Parties shall submit supplementary reports every four years on any new measures taken and such other reports as the Committee may request.

2. The Secretary-General of the United Nations shall transmit the reports to all States Parties.

3. Each report shall be considered by the Committee which may make such general comments on the report as it may consider appropriate and shall forward these to the State Party concerned. That State Party may respond with any observations it chooses to the Committee.

4. The Committee may, at its discretion, decide to include any comments made by it in accordance with paragraph 3 of this article, together with the observations thereon received from the State Party concerned, in its annual report made in accordance with article 24. If so requested by the State Party concerned, the Committee may also include a copy of the report submitted under paragraph 1 of this article.

Article 20

1. If the Committee receives reliable information which appears to it to contain well-founded indications that torture is being systematically practised in the territory of a State Party, the Committee shall invite that State Party to co-operate in the examination of the information and to this end to submit observations with regard to the information concerned.

2. Taking into account any observations which may have been submitted by the State Party concerned, as well as any other relevant information available to it, the Committee may, if it decides that this is warranted, designate one or more of its members to make a confidential inquiry and to report to the Committee urgently.

3. If an inquiry is made in accordance with paragraph 2 of this article, the Committee shall seek the co-operation of the State Party concerned. In agreement with that State Party, such an inquiry may include a visit to its territory.

4. After examining the findings of its member or members submitted in accordance with paragraph 2 of this article, the Commission shall transmit these findings to the State Party concerned together with any comments or suggestions which seem appropriate in view of the situation.

5. All the proceedings of the Committee referred to in paragraphs 1 to 4 of this article shall be confidential, and at all stages of the proceedings the co-operation of the State Party shall be sought. After such proceedings have been completed with regard to an inquiry made in accordance with paragraph 2, the Committee may, after consultations with the State Party concerned, decide to include a summary account of the results of the proceedings in its annual report made in accordance with article 24.

Article 21

1. A State Party to this Convention may at any time declare under this article that it recognizes the competence of the Committee to receive and consider communications to the effect that a State Party claims that another State Party is not fulfilling its obligations under this Convention. Such communications may be received and considered according to the procedures laid down in this article only if submitted by a State Party which has made a declaration recognizing in regard to itself the competence of the Committee. No communication shall be dealt with by the Committee under this article if it concerns a State Party which has not made such a declaration. Communications received under this article shall be dealt with in accordance with the following procedure:

(a) If a State Party considers that another State Party is not giving effect to the provisions of this Convention, it may, by written communication, bring the matter to the attention of that State Party. Within three months after the receipt of the communication the receiving State shall afford the State which sent the communication an explanation or any other statement in writing clarifying the matter, which should include, to the extent possible and pertinent, reference to domestic procedures and remedies taken, pending or available in the matter;

(b) If the matter is not adjusted to the satisfaction of both States Parties concerned within six months after the receipt by the receiving State of the initial communication, either State shall have the right to refer the matter to the Committee, by notice given to the Committee and to the other State;

(c) The Committee shall deal with a matter referred to it under this article only after it has ascertained that all domestic remedies have been invoked and exhausted in the matter, in conformity with the generally recognized principles of international law. This shall not be the rule where the application of the remedies is unreasonably prolonged or is unlikely to bring effective relief to the person who is the victim of the violation of this Convention;

(d) The Committee shall hold closed meetings when examining communications under this article;

(e) Subject to the provisions of subparagraph (c), the Committee shall make available its good offices to the States Parties concerned with a view to a friendly solution of the matter on the basis of respect for the obligations provided for in this Convention. For this purpose, the Committee may, when appropriate, set up an ad hoc conciliation commission;

(f) In any matter referred to it under this article, the Committee may call upon the States Parties concerned, referred to in subparagraph (b), to supply any relevant information;

(g) The States Parties concerned, referred to in subparagraph (b), shall have the right to be represented when the matter is being considered by the Committee and to make submissions orally and/or in writing;

(h) The Committee shall, within twelve months after the date of receipt of notice under subparagraph (b), submit a report:

(i) If a solution within the terms of subparagraph (e) is reached, the Committee shall confine its report to a brief statement of the facts and of the solution reached;

(ii) If a solution within the terms of subparagraph (e) is not reached, the Committee shall confine its report to a brief statement of the facts; the written submissions and record of the oral submissions made by the States Parties concerned shall be attached to the report.

In every matter, the report shall be communicated to the States Parties concerned.

2. The provisions of this article shall come into force when five States Parties to this Convention have made declarations under paragraph 1 of this article. Such declarations shall be deposited by the States Parties with the Secretary-General of the United Nations, who shall transmit copies thereof to the other States Parties. A declaration may be withdrawn at any time by notification to the Secretary-General. Such a withdrawal shall not prejudice the consideration of any matter which is the subject of a communication already transmitted under this article; no further communication by any State Party

shall be received under this article after the notification of withdrawal of the declaration has been received by the Secretary-General, unless the State Party concerned has made a new declaration.

Article 22

1. A State Party to this Convention may at any time declare under this article that it recognizes the competence of the Committee to receive and consider communications from or on behalf of individuals subject to its jurisdiction who claim to be victims of a violation by a State Party of the provisions of the Convention. No communication shall be received by the Committee if it concerns a State Party which has not made such a declaration.

2. The Committee shall consider inadmissible any communication under this article which is anonymous or which it considers to be an abuse of the right of submission of such communications or to be incompatible with the provisions of this Convention.

3. Subject to the provisions of paragraph 2, the Committee shall bring any communications submitted to it under this article to the attention of the State Party to this Convention which has made a declaration under paragraph 1 and is alleged to be violating any provisions of the Convention. Within six months, the receiving State shall submit to the Committee written explanations or statements clarifying the matter and the remedy, if any, that may have been taken by that State.

4. The Committee shall consider communications received under this article in the light of all information made available to it by or on behalf of the individual and by the State Party concerned.

5. The Committee shall not consider any communications from an individual under this article unless it has ascertained that:

(a) The same matter has not been, and is not being, examined under another procedure of international investigation or settlement;

(b) The individual has exhausted all available domestic remedies; this shall not be the rule where the application of the remedies is unreasonably prolonged or is unlikely to bring effective relief to the person who is the victim of the violation of this Convention.

6. The Committee shall hold closed meetings when examining communications under this article.

7. The Committee shall forward its views to the State Party concerned and to the individual.

8. The provisions of this article shall come into force when five States Parties to this Convention have made declarations under paragraph 1 of this article. Such declarations shall be deposited by the States Parties with the Secretary-General of the United Nations, who shall transmit copies thereof to the other States Parties. A declaration may be withdrawn at any time by notification to the Secretary-General. Such a withdrawal shall not prejudice the consideration of any matter which is the subject of a communication already transmitted under this article; no further communication by or on behalf of an individual shall be received under this article after the notification of withdrawal of the declaration has been received by the Secretary-General, unless the State Party has made a new declaration.

Article 23

The members of the Committee and of the ad hoc conciliation commissions which may be appointed under article 21, paragraph 1 (e), shall be entitled to the facilities, privileges and immunities of experts on mission for the United Nations as laid down in the relevant sections of the Convention on the Privileges and Immunities of the United Nations.

Article 24

The Committee shall submit an annual report on its activities under this Convention to the States Parties and to the General Assembly of the United Nations.

Part III

Article 25

1. This Convention is open for signature by all States.

2. This Convention is subject to ratification. Instruments of ratification shall be deposited with the Secretary-General of the United Nations.

Article 26

This Convention is open to accession by all States. Accession shall be effected by the deposit of an instrument of accession with the Secretary-General of the United Nations.

Article 27

1. This Convention shall enter into force on the thirtieth day after the date of the deposit with the Secretary-General of the United Nations of the twentieth instrument of ratification or accession.

2. For each State ratifying this Convention or acceding to it after the deposit of the twentieth instrument of ratification or accession, the Convention shall enter into force on the thirtieth day after the date of the deposit of its own instrument of ratification or accession.

Article 28

1. Each State may, at the time of signature or ratification of this Convention or accession thereto, declare that it does not recognize the competence of the Committee provided for in article 20.

2. Any State Party having made a reservation in accordance with paragraph 1 of this article may, at any time, withdraw this reservation by notification to the Secretary-General of the United Nations.

Article 29

1. Any State Party to this Convention may propose an amendment and file it with the Secretary-General of the United Nations. The Secretary-General shall thereupon communicate the proposed amendment to the States Parties with a request that they notify him whether they favour a conference of States Parties for the purpose of considering and voting upon the proposal. In the event that within four months from the date of such communication at least one third of the States Parties favours such a conference, the Secretary-General shall convene the conference under the auspices of the United Nations. Any amendment adopted by a majority of the States Parties present and voting at the conference shall be submitted by the Secretary-General to all the States Parties for acceptance.

2. An amendment adopted in accordance with paragraph 1 of this article shall enter into force when two thirds of the States Parties to this Convention have notified the Secretary-General of the United Nations that they have accepted it in accordance with their respective constitutional processes.

3. When amendments enter into force, they shall be binding on those States Parties which have accepted them, other States Parties still being bound by the provisions of this Convention and any earlier amendments which they have accepted.

Article 30

1. Any dispute between two or more States Parties concerning the interpretation or application of this Convention which cannot be settled through negotiation shall, at the request of one of them, be submitted to arbitration. If within six months from thc date of the request for arbitration the Parties are unable to agree on the organization of the arbitration, any one of those Parties may refer the dispute to the International Court of Justice by request in conformity with the Statute of the Court.

2. Each State may, at the time of signature or ratification of this Convention or accession thereto, declare that it does not consider itself bound by paragraph 1 of this article. The other States Parties shall not be bound by paragraph 1 of this article with respect to any State Party having made such a reservation.

3. Any State Party having made a reservation in accordance with paragraph 2 of this article may at any time withdraw this reservation by notification to the Secretary-General of the United Nations.

Article 31

1. A State Party may denounce this Convention by written notification to the Secretary-General of the United Nations. Denunciation becomes effective one year after the date of receipt of the notification by the Secretary-General.

2. Such a denunciation shall not have the effect of releasing the State Party from its obligations under this Convention in regard to any act or omission which occurs prior to the date at which the denunciation becomes effective, nor shall denunciation prejudice in any way the continued consideration of any matter which is already under consideration by the Committee prior to the date at which the denunciation becomes effective.

3. Following the date at which the denunciation of a State Party becomes effective, the Committee shall not commence consideration of any new matter regarding that State.

Article 32

The Secretary-General of the United Nations shall inform all States Members of the United Nations and all States which have signed this Convention or acceded to it of the following:

(a) Signatures, ratifications and accessions under articles 25 and 26;

(b) The date of entry into force of this Convention under article 27 and the date of the entry into force of any amendments under article 29;

(c) Denunciations under article 31.

Article 33

1. This Convention, of which the Arabic, Chinese, English, French, Russian and Spanish texts are equally authentic, shall be deposited with the Secretary-General of the United Nations.

2. The Secretary-General of the United Nations shall transmit certified copies of this Convention to all States.

UNIVERSAL DECLARATION ON THE ERADICATION OF HUNGER AND MALNUTRITION

Adopted on 16 November 1974 by the World Food Conference convened under General Assembly resolution 3180

(XXVIII) of 17 December 1973; and endorsed by General Assembly resolution 3348 (XXIX) of 17 December 1974

The World Food Conference,

Convened by the General Assembly of the United Nations and entrusted with developing ways and means whereby the international community, as a whole, could take specific action to resolve the world food problem within the broader context of development and international economic co-operation,

Adopts the following Declaration:

Universal Declaration on the Eradication of Hunger and Malnutrition

Recognizing that:

(a) The grave food crisis that is afflicting the peoples of the developing countries where most of the world's hungry and ill-nourished live and where more than two thirds of the world's population produce about one third of the world's food—an imbalance which threatens to increase in the next 10 years—is not only fraught with grave economic and social implications, but also acutely jeopardizes the most fundamental principles and values associated with the right to life and human dignity as enshrined in the Universal Declaration of Human Rights;

(b) The elimination of hunger and malnutrition, included as one of the objectives in the United Nations Declaration on Social Progress and Development, and the elimination of the causes that determine this situation are the common objectives of all nations;

(c) The situation of the peoples afflicted by hunger and malnutrition arises from their historical circumstances, especially social inequalities, including in many cases alien and colonial domination, foreign occupation, racial discrimination, apartheid and neo-colonialism in all its forms, which continue to be among the greatest obstacles to the full emancipation and progress of the developing countries and all the peoples involved;

(d) This situation has been aggravated in recent years by a series of crises to which the world economy has been subjected, such as the deterioration in the international monetary system, the inflationary increase in import costs, the heavy burdens imposed by external debt on the balance of payments of many developing countries, a rising food demand partly due to demographic pressure, speculation, and a shortage of, and increased costs for, essential agricultural inputs;

(e) These phenomena should be considered within the framework of the on-going negotiations on the Charter of Economic Rights and Duties of States, and the General Assembly of the United Nations should be urged unanimously to agree upon, and to adopt, a Charter that will be an effective instrument for the establishment of new international economic relations based on principles of equity and justice;

(f) All countries, big or small, rich or poor, are equal. All countries have the full right to participate in the decisions on the food problem;

(g) The well-being of the peoples of the world largely depends on the adequate production and distribution of food as well as the establishment of a world food security system which would ensure adequate availability of, and reasonable prices for, food at all times, irrespective of periodic fluctuations and vagaries of weather and free of political and economic pressures, and should thus facilitate, amongst other things, the development process of developing countries;

(h) Peace and justice encompass an economic dimension helping the solution of the world economic problems, the liquidation of under-development, offering a lasting and definitive solution of the food problem for all peoples and guaranteeing to all countries the right to implement freely and effectively their development programmes. To this effect, it is necessary to eliminate threats and resort to force and to promote peaceful co-operation between States to the fullest extent possible, to apply the principles of non-interference in the internal affairs of other States, full equality of rights and respect of national independence and sovereignty, as well as to encourage the peaceful co-operation between all States, irrespective of their political, social and economic systems. The further improvement of international relations will create better conditions for international co-operation in all fields which should make possible large financial and material resources to be used, inter alia, for developing agricultural production and substantially improving world food security;

(i) For a lasting solution of the food problem all efforts should be made to eliminate the widening gaps which today separate developed and developing countries and to bring about a new international economic order. It should be possible for all countries to participate actively and effectively in the new international economic relations by the establishment of suitable international systems, where appropriate, capable of producing adequate action in order to establish just and equitable relations in international economic co-operation;

(j) Developing countries reaffirm their belief that the primary responsibility for ensuring their own rapid development rests with themselves. They declare, therefore, their readiness to continue to intensify their individual and collective efforts with a view to expanding their mutual co-operation in the field of agricultural development and food production, including the eradication of hunger and malnutrition;

(k) Since, for various reasons, many developing countries are not yet always able to meet their own food needs, urgent and effective international action should be taken to assist them, free of political pressures.

Consistent with the aims and objectives of the Declaration on the Establishment of a New International Economic Order and the Programme of Action adopted by the General Assembly at its sixth special session,

The Conference consequently solemnly proclaims:

1. Every man, woman and child has the inalienable right to be free from hunger and malnutrition in order to develop fully and maintain their physical and mental faculties. Society today already possesses sufficient resources, organizational ability and technology and hence the competence to achieve this objective. Accordingly, the eradication of hunger is a common objective of all the countries of the international community, especially of the developed countries and others in a position to help.

2. It is a fundamental responsibility of Governments to work together for higher food production and a more equitable and efficient distribution of food between countries and within countries. Governments should initiate immediately a greater concerted attack on chronic malnutrition and deficiency diseases among the vulnerable and lower income groups. In order to ensure adequate nutrition for all, Governments should formulate appropriate food and nutrition policies integrated in overall socio-economic and agricultural development plans based on adequate knowledge of available as well as potential food resources. The importance of human milk in this connection should be stressed on nutritional grounds.

3. Food problems must be tackled during the preparation and implementation of national plans and programmes for economic and social development, with emphasis on their humanitarian aspects.

4. It is a responsibility of each State concerned, in accordance with its sovereign judgement and internal legislation, to remove the obstacles to food production and to provide proper incentives to agricultural producers. Of prime importance for the attainment of these objectives are effective measures of socio-economic transformation by agrarian, tax, credit and investment policy reform and the reorganization of rural structures, such as the reform of the conditions of ownership,

the encouragement of producer and consumer co-operatives, the mobilization of the full potential of human resources, both male and female, in the developing countries for an integrated rural development and the involvement of small farmers, fishermen and landless workers in attaining the required food production and employment targets. Moreover, it is necessary to recognize the key role of women in agricultural production and rural economy in many countries, and to ensure that appropriate education, extension programmes and financial facilities are made available to women on equal terms with men.

5. Marine and inland water resources are today becoming more important than ever as a source of food and economic prosperity. Accordingly, action should be taken to promote a rational exploitation of these resources, preferably for direct consumption, in order to contribute to meeting the food requirements of all peoples.

6. The efforts to increase food production should be complemented by every endeavour to prevent wastage of food in all its forms.

7. To give impetus to food production in developing countries and in particular in the least developed and most seriously affected among them, urgent and effective international action should be taken, by the developed countries and other countries in a position to do so, to provide them with sustained additional technical and financial assistance on favourable terms and in a volume sufficient to their needs on the basis of bilateral and multilateral arrangements. This assistance must be free of conditions inconsistent with the sovereignty of the receiving States.

8. All countries, and primarily the highly industrialized countries, should promote the advancement of food production technology and should make all efforts to promote the transfer, adaptation and dissemination of appropriate food production technology for the benefit of the developing countries and, to that end, they should inter alia make all efforts to disseminate the results of their research work to Governments and scientific institutions of developing countries in order to enable them to promote a sustained agricultural development.

9. To assure the proper conservation of natural resources being utilized, or which might be utilized, for food production, all countries must collaborate in order to facilitate the preservation of the environment, including the marine environment.

10. All developed countries and others able to do so should collaborate technically and financially with the developing countries in their efforts to expand land and water resources for agricultural production and to assure a rapid increase in the availability, at fair costs, of agricultural inputs such as fertilizers and other chemicals, high-quality seeds, credit and technology. Co-operation among developing countries, in this connection, is also important.

11. All States should strive to the utmost to readjust, where appropriate, their agricultural policies to give priority to food production, recognizing, in this connection the interrelationship between the world food problem and international trade. In the determination of attitudes towards farm support programmes for domestic food production, developed countries should take into account, as far as possible, the interest of the food-exporting developing countries, in order to avoid detrimental effect on their exports. Moreover, all countries should co-operate to devise effective steps to deal with the problem of stabilizing world markets and promoting equitable and remunerative prices, where appropriate through international arrangements, to improve access to markets through reduction or elimination of tariff and non-tariff barriers on the products of interest to the developing countries, to substantially increase the export earnings of these countries, to contribute to the diversification of their exports, and apply to them, in the multilateral trade negotiations, the principles as agreed upon in the Tokyo Declaration, including the concept of non-reciprocity and more favourable treatment.

12. As it is the common responsibility of the entire international community to ensure the availability at all times of adequate world supplies of basic food-stuffs by way of appropriate reserves, including emergency reserves, all countries should co-operate in the establishment of an effective system of world food security by:

> Participating in and supporting the operation of the Global Information and Early Warning System on Food and Agriculture;

> Adhering to the objectives, policies and guidelines of the proposed International Undertaking on World Food Security as endorsed by the World Food Conference;

> Earmarking, where possible, stocks or funds for meeting international emergency food requirements as envisaged in the proposed International Undertaking on World Food Security and developing international guidelines to provide for the co-ordination and the utilization of such stocks;

> Co-operating in the provision of food aid for meeting emergency and nutritional needs as well as for stimulating rural employment through development projects.

All donor countries should accept and implement the concept of forward planning of food aid and make all efforts to provide commodities and/or financial assistance that will ensure adequate quantities of grains and other food commodities.

Time is short. Urgent and sustained action is vital. The Conference, therefore, calls upon all peoples expressing their will as individuals, and through their Governments, and non-governmental organizations, to work together to bring about the end of the age-old scourge of hunger.

The Conference affirms:

The determination of the participating States to make full use of the United Nations system in the implementation of this Declaration and the other decisions adopted by the Conference.

CONVENTION RELATING TO THE STATUS OF REFUGEES

Adopted on 28 July 1951 by the United Nations Conference of Plenipotentiaries on the Status of Refugees and Stateless Persons convened under General Assembly resolution 429 (V) of 14 December 1950

Entered into force 22 April 1954, in accordance with article 43

Preamble

The High Contracting Parties,

Considering that the Charter of the United Nations and the Universal Declaration of Human Rights approved on 10 December 1948 by the General Assembly have affirmed the principle that human beings shall enjoy fundamental rights and freedoms without discrimination,

Considering that the United Nations has, on various occasions, manifested its profound concern for refugees and endeavoured to assure refugees the widest possible exercise of these fundamental rights and freedoms,

Considering that it is desirable to revise and consolidate previous international agreements relating to the status of refugees and to extend the scope of and the protection accorded by such instruments by means of a new agreement,

Considering that the grant of asylum may place unduly heavy burdens on certain countries, and that a satisfactory solution of a problem of which the United Nations has recognized the international scope and nature cannot therefore be achieved without international co-operation,

Expressing the wish that all States, recognizing the social and humanitarian nature of the problem of refugees, will do everything within their power to prevent this problem from becoming a cause of tension between States,

Noting that the United Nations High Commissioner for Refugees is charged with the task of supervising international conventions providing for the protection of refugees, and recognizing that the effective co-ordination of measures taken to deal with this problem will depend upon the co-operation of States with the High Commissioner,

Have agreed as follows:

Chapter I

General Provisions

Article 1. Definition of the Term "Refugee"

A. For the purposes of the present Convention, the term "refugee" shall apply to any person who:

(1) Has been considered a refugee under the Arrangements of 12 May 1926 and 30 June 1928 or under the Conventions of 28 October 1933 and 10 February 1938, the Protocol of 14 September 1939 or the Constitution of the International Refugee Organization;

Decisions of non-eligibility taken by the International Refugee Organization during the period of its activities shall not prevent the status of refugee being accorded to persons who fulfil the conditions of paragraph 2 of this section;

(2) As a result of events occurring before 1 January 1951 and owing to well-founded fear of being persecuted for reasons of race, religion, nationality, membership of a particular social group or political opinion, is outside the country of his nationality and is unable, or owing to such fear, is unwilling to avail himself of the protection of that country; or who, not having a nationality and being outside the country of his former habitual residence as a result of such events, is unable or, owing to such fear, is unwilling to return to it.

In the case of a person who has more than one nationality, the term "the country of his nationality" shall mean each of the countries of which he is a national, and a person shall not be deemed to be lacking the protection of the country of his nationality if, without any valid reason based on well-founded fear, he has not availed himself of the protection of one of the countries of which he is a national.

B. (1) For the purposes of this Convention, the words "events occurring before 1 January 1951" in article 1, section A, shall be understood to mean either (a) "events occurring in Europe before 1 January 1951"; or (b) "events occurring in Europe or elsewhere before 1 January 1951"; and each Contracting State shall make a declaration at the time of signature, ratification or accession, specifying which of these meanings it applies for the purpose of its obligations under this Convention.

(2) Any Contracting State which has adopted alternative (a) may at any time extend its obligations by adopting alternative (b) by means of a notification addressed to the Secretary-General of the United Nations.

C. This Convention shall cease to apply to any person falling under the terms of section A if:

(1) He has voluntarily re-availed himself of the protection of the country of his nationality; or

(2) Having lost his nationality, he has voluntarily reacquired it; or

(3) He has acquired a new nationality, and enjoys the protection of the country of his new nationality; or

(4) He has voluntarily re-established himself in the country which he left or outside which he remained owing to fear of persecution; or

(5) He can no longer, because the circumstances in connection with which he has been recognized as a refugee have ceased to exist, continue to refuse to avail himself of the protection of the country of his nationality; Provided that this paragraph shall not apply to a refugee falling under section A (1) of this article who is able to invoke compelling reasons arising out of previous persecution for refusing to avail himself of the protection of the country of nationality;

(6) Being a person who has no nationality he is, because the circumstances in connection with which he has been recognized as a refugee have ceased to exist, able to return to the country of his former habitual residence;

Provided that this paragraph shall not apply to a refugee falling under section A (1) of this article who is able to invoke compelling reasons arising out of previous persecution for refusing to return to the country of his former habitual residence.

D. This Convention shall not apply to persons who are at present receiving from organs or agencies of the United Nations other than the United Nations High Commissioner for Refugees protection or assistance.

When such protection or assistance has ceased for any reason, without the position of such persons being definitively settled in accordance with the relevant resolutions adopted by the General Assembly of the United Nations, these persons shall ipso facto be entitled to the benefits of this Convention.

E. This Convention shall not apply to a person who is recognized by the competent authorities of the country in which he has taken residence as having the rights and obligations which are attached to the possession of the nationality of that country.

F. The provisions of this Convention shall not apply to any person with respect to whom there are serious reasons for considering that

(a) He has committed a crime against peace, a war crime, or a crime against humanity, as defined in the international instruments drawn up to make provision in respect of such crimes;

(b) He has committed a serious non-political crime outside the country of refuge prior to his admission to that country as a refugee;

(c) He has been guilty of acts contrary to the purposes and principles of the United Nations.

Article 2. General Obligations

Every refugee has duties to the country in which he finds himself, which require in particular that he conform to its laws and regulations as well as to measures taken for the maintenance of public order.

Article 3. Non-Discrimination

The Contracting States shall apply the provisions of this Convention to refugees without discrimination as to race, religion or country of origin.

Article 4. Religion

The Contracting States shall accord to refugees within their territories treatment at least as favourable as that accorded to their nationals with respect to freedom to practise their religion and freedom as regards the religious education of their children.

Article 5. Rights Granted Apart from This Convention

Nothing in this Convention shall be deemed to impair any rights and benefits granted by a Contracting State to refugees apart from this Convention.

Article 6. The Term "In the Same Circumstances"

For the purposes of this Convention, the term "in the same circumstances, implies that any requirements (including requirements as to length and conditions of sojourn or residence) which the particular individual would have to fulfil for the enjoyment of the right in question, if he were not a refugee, must be fulfilled by him, with the exception of requirements which by their nature a refugee is incapable of fulfilling.

Article 7. Exemption from Reciprocity

1. Except where this Convention contains more favourable provisions, a Contracting State shall accord to refugees the same treatment as is accorded to aliens generally.

2. After a period of three years' residence, all refugees shall enjoy exemption from legislative reciprocity in the territory of the Contracting States.

3. Each Contracting State shall continue to accord to refugees the rights and benefits to which they were already entitled, in the absence of reciprocity, at the date of entry into force of this Convention for that State.

4. The Contracting States shall consider favourably the possibility of according to refugees, in the absence of reciprocity, rights and benefits beyond those to which they are entitled according to paragraphs 2 and 3, and to extending exemption from reciprocity to refugees who do not fulfil the conditions provided for in paragraphs 2 and 3.

5. The provisions of paragraphs 2 and 3 apply both to the rights and benefits referred to in articles 13, 18, 19, 21 and 22 of this Convention and to rights and benefits for which this Convention does not provide.

Article 8. Exemption from Exceptional Measures

With regard to exceptional measures which may be taken against the person, property or interests of nationals of a foreign State, the Contracting States shall not apply such measures to a refugee who is formally a national of the said State solely on account of such nationality. Contracting States which, under their legislation, are prevented from applying the general principle expressed in this article, shall, in appropriate cases, grant exemptions in favour of such refugees.

Article 9. Provisional Measures

Nothing in this Convention shall prevent a Contracting State, in time of war or other grave and exceptional circumstances, from taking provisionally measures which it considers to be essential to the national security in the case of a particular person, pending a determination by the Contracting State that that person is in fact a refugee and that the continuance of such measures is necessary in his case in the interests of national security.

Article 10. Continuity of Residence

1. Where a refugee has been forcibly displaced during the Second World War and removed to the territory of a Contracting State, and is resident there, the period of such enforced sojourn shall be considered to have been lawful residence within that territory.

2. Where a refugee has been forcibly displaced during the Second World War from the territory of a Contracting State and has, prior to the date of entry into force of this Conven-

tion, returned there for the purpose of taking up residence, the period of residence before and after such enforced displacement shall be regarded as one uninterrupted period for any purposes for which uninterrupted residence is required.

Article 11. Refugee Seamen

In the case of refugees regularly serving as crew members on board a ship flying the flag of a Contracting State, that State shall give sympathetic consideration to their establishment on its territory and the issue of travel documents to them or their temporary admission to its territory particularly with a view to facilitating their establishment in another country.

Chapter II

Juridical Status

Article 12. Personal Status

1. The personal status of a refugee shall be governed by the law of the country of his domicile or, if he has no domicile, by the law of the country of his residence.

2. Rights previously acquired by a refugee and dependent on personal status, more particularly rights attaching to marriage, shall be respected by a Contracting State, subject to compliance, if this be necessary, with the formalities required by the law of that State, provided that the right in question is one which would have been recognized by the law of that State had he not become a refugee.

Article 13. Movable and Immovable Property

The Contracting States shall accord to a refugee treatment as favourable as possible and, in any event, not less favourable than that accorded to aliens generally in the same circumstances, as regards the acquisition of movable and immovable property and other rights pertaining thereto, and to leases and other contracts relating to movable and immovable property.

Article 14. Artistic Rights and Industrial Property

In respect of the protection of industrial property, such as inventions, designs or models, trade marks, trade names, and of rights in literary, artistic and scientific works, a refugee shall be accorded in the country in which he has his habitual residence the same protection as is accorded to nationals of that country. In the territory of any other Contracting States, he shall be accorded the same protection as is accorded in that territory to nationals of the country in which he has his habitual residence.

Article 15. Right of Association

As regards non-political and non-profit-making associations and trade unions the Contracting States shall accord to refugees lawfully staying in their territory the most favourable treatment accorded to nationals of a foreign country, in the same circumstances.

Article 16. Access to Courts

1. A refugee shall have free access to the courts of law on the territory of all Contracting States.

2. A refugee shall enjoy in the Contracting State in which he has his habitual residence the same treatment as a national in matters pertaining to access to the courts, including legal assistance and exemption from cautio judicatum solvi.

3. A refugee shall be accorded in the matters referred to in paragraph 2 in countries other than that in which he has his habitual residence the treatment granted to a national of the country of his habitual residence.

Chapter III

Gainful Employment

Article 17. Wage-Earning Employment

1. The Contracting States shall accord to refugees lawfully staying in their territory the most favourable treatment accorded to nationals of a foreign country in the same circumstances, as regards the right to engage in wage-earning employment.

2. In any case, restrictive measures imposed on aliens or the employment of aliens for the protection of the national labour market shall not be applied to a refugee who was already exempt from them at the date of entry into force of this Convention for the Contracting State concerned, or who fulfils one of the following conditions:

    (a) He has completed three years' residence in the country;

    (b) He has a spouse possessing the nationality of the country of residence. A refugee may not invoke the benefit of this provision if he has abandoned his spouse;

    (c) He has one or more children possessing the nationality of the country of residence.

3. The Contracting States shall give sympathetic consideration to assimilating the rights of all refugees with regard to wage-earning employment to those of nationals, and in par-

ticular of those refugees who have entered their territory pursuant to programmes of labour recruitment or under immigration schemes.

Article 18. Self-Employment

The Contracting States shall accord to a refugee lawfully in their territory treatment as favourable as possible and, in any event, not less favourable than that accorded to aliens generally in the same circumstances, as regards the right to engage on his own account in agriculture, industry, handicrafts and commerce and to establish commercial and industrial companies.

Article 19. Liberal Professions

1. Each Contracting State shall accord to refugees lawfully staying in their territory who hold diplomas recognized by the competent authorities of that State, and who are desirous of practising a liberal profession, treatment as favourable as possible and, in any event, not less favourable than that accorded to aliens generally in the same circumstances.

2. The Contracting States shall use their best endeavours consistently with their laws and constitutions to secure the settlement of such refugees in the territories, other than the metropolitan territory, for whose international relations they are responsible.

Chapter IV

Welfare

Article 20. Rationing

Where a rationing system exists, which applies to the population at large and regulates the general distribution of products in short supply, refugees shall be accorded the same treatment as nationals.

Article 21. Housing

As regards housing, the Contracting States, in so far as the matter is regulated by laws or regulations or is subject to the control of public authorities, shall accord to refugees lawfully staying in their territory treatment as favourable as possible and, in any event, not less favourable than that accorded to aliens generally in the same circumstances.

Article 22. Public Education

1. The Contracting States shall accord to refugees the same treatment as is accorded to nationals with respect to elementary education.

2. The Contracting States shall accord to refugees treatment as favourable as possible, and, in any event, not less favourable than that accorded to aliens generally in the same circumstances, with respect to education other than elementary education and, in particular, as regards access to studies, the recognition of foreign school certificates, diplomas and degrees, the remission of fees and charges and the award of scholarships.

Article 23. Public Relief

The Contracting States shall accord to refugees lawfully staying in their territory the same treatment with respect to public relief and assistance as is accorded to their nationals.

Article 24. Labour Legislation and Social Security

1. The Contracting States shall accord to refugees lawfully staying in their territory the same treatment as is accorded to nationals in respect of the following matters:

(a) In so far as such matters are governed by laws or regulations or are subject to the control of administrative authorities: remuneration, including family allowances where these form part of remuneration, hours of work, overtime arrangements, holidays with pay, restrictions on home work, minimum age of employment, apprenticeship and training, women's work and the work of young persons, and the enjoyment of the benefits of collective bargaining;

(b) Social security (legal provisions in respect of employment injury, occupational diseases, maternity, sickness, disability, old age, death, unemployment, family responsibilities and any other contingency which, according to national laws or regulations, is covered by a social security scheme), subject to the following limitations:

(i) There may be appropriate arrangements for the maintenance of acquired rights and rights in course of acquisition;

(ii) National laws or regulations of the country of residence may prescribe special arrangements concerning benefits or portions of benefits which are payable wholly out of public funds, and concerning allowances paid to persons who do not fulfil the contribution conditions prescribed for the award of a normal pension.

2. The right to compensation for the death of a refugee resulting from employment injury or from occupational disease shall not be affected by the fact that the residence of the beneficiary is outside the territory of the Contracting State.

3. The Contracting States shall extend to refugees the benefits of agreements concluded between them, or which may be concluded between them in the future, concerning the maintenance of acquired rights and rights in the process of acquisition in regard to social security, subject only to the conditions which apply to nationals of the States signatory to the agreements in question.

4. The Contracting States will give sympathetic consideration to extending to refugees so far as possible the benefits of similar agreements which may at any time be in force between such Contracting States and non-contracting States.

Chapter V

Administrative Measures

Article 25. Administrative Assistance

1. When the exercise of a right by a refugee would normally require the assistance of authorities of a foreign country to whom he cannot have recourse, the Contracting States in whose territory he is residing shall arrange that such assistance be afforded to him by their own authorities or by an international authority.

2. The authority or authorities mentioned in paragraph 1 shall deliver or cause to be delivered under their supervision to refugees such documents or certifications as would normally be delivered to aliens by or through their national authorities.

3. Documents or certifications so delivered shall stand in the stead of the official instruments delivered to aliens by or through their national authorities, and shall be given credence in the absence of proof to the contrary.

4. Subject to such exceptional treatment as may be granted to indigent persons, fees may be charged for the services mentioned herein, but such fees shall be moderate and commensurate with those charged to nationals for similar services.

5. The provisions of this article shall be without prejudice to articles 27 and 28.

Article 26. Freedom of Movement

Each Contracting State shall accord to refugees lawfully in its territory the right to choose their place of residence and to move freely within its territory subject to any regulations applicable to aliens generally in the same circumstances.

Article 27. Identity Papers

The Contracting States shall issue identity papers to any refugee in their territory who does not possess a valid travel document.

Article 28. Travel Documents

1. The Contracting States shall issue to refugees lawfully staying in their territory travel documents for the purpose of travel outside their territory, unless compelling reasons of national security or public order otherwise require, and the provisions of the Schedule to this Convention shall apply with respect to such documents. The Contracting States may issue such a travel document to any other refugee in their territory; they shall in particular give sympathetic consideration to the issue of such a travel document to refugees in their territory who are unable to obtain a travel document from the country of their lawful residence.

2. Travel documents issued to refugees under previous international agreements by Parties thereto shall be recognized and treated by the Contracting States in the same way as if they had been issued pursuant to this article.

Article 29. Fiscal Charges

1. The Contracting States shall not impose upon refugees duties, charges or taxes, of any description whatsoever, other or higher than those which are or may be levied on their nationals in similar situations.

2. Nothing in the above paragraph shall prevent the application to refugees of the laws and regulations concerning charges in respect of the issue to aliens of administrative documents including identity papers.

Article 30. Transfer of Assets

1. A Contracting State shall, in conformity with its laws and regulations, permit refugees to transfer assets which they have brought into its territory, to another country where they have been admitted for the purposes of resettlement.

2. A Contracting State shall give sympathetic consideration to the application of refugees for permission to transfer assets wherever they may be and which are necessary for their resettlement in another country to which they have been admitted.

Article 31. Refugees Unlawfully in the Country of Refuge

1. The Contracting States shall not impose penalties, on account of their illegal entry or presence, on refugees who,

coming directly from a territory where their life or freedom was threatened in the sense of article 1, enter or are present in their territory without authorization, provided they present themselves without delay to the authorities and show good cause for their illegal entry or presence.

2. The Contracting States shall not apply to the movements of such refugees restrictions other than those which are necessary and such restrictions shall only be applied until their status in the country is regularized or they obtain admission into another country. The Contracting States shall allow such refugees a reasonable period and all the necessary facilities to obtain admission into another country.

Article 32. Expulsion

1. The Contracting States shall not expel a refugee lawfully in their territory save on grounds of national security or public order.

2. The expulsion of such a refugee shall be only in pursuance of a decision reached in accordance with due process of law. Except where compelling reasons of national security otherwise require, the refugee shall be allowed to submit evidence to clear himself, and to appeal to and be represented for the purpose before competent authority or a person or persons specially designated by the competent authority.

3. The Contracting States shall allow such a refugee a reasonable period within which to seek legal admission into another country. The Contracting States reserve the right to apply during that period such internal measures as they may deem necessary.

Article 33. Prohibition of Expulsion or Return ("refoulement")

1. No Contracting State shall expel or return ("refouler") a refugee in any manner whatsoever to the frontiers of territories where his life or freedom would be threatened on account of his race, religion, nationality, membership of a particular social group or political opinion.

2. The benefit of the present provision may not, however, be claimed by a refugee whom there are reasonable grounds for regarding as a danger to the security of the country in which he is, or who, having been convicted by a final judgement of a particularly serious crime, constitutes a danger to the community of that country.

Article 34. Naturalization

The Contracting States shall as far as possible facilitate the assimilation and naturalization of refugees. They shall in par-

ticular make every effort to expedite naturalization proceedings and to reduce as far as possible the charges and costs of such proceedings.

Chapter VI

Executory and Transitory Provisions

Article 35. Co-operation of the National Authorities with the United Nations

1. The Contracting States undertake to co-operate with the Office of the United Nations High Commissioner for Refugees, or any other agency of the United Nations which may succeed it, in the exercise of its functions, and shall in particular facilitate its duty of supervising the application of the provisions of this Convention.

2. In order to enable the Office of the High Commissioner or any other agency of the United Nations which may succeed it, to make reports to the competent organs of the United Nations, the Contracting States undertake to provide them in the appropriate form with information and statistical data requested concerning:

   (a) The condition of refugees,

   (b) The implementation of this Convention, and

   (c) Laws, regulations and decrees which are, or may hereafter be, in force relating to refugees.

Article 36. Information on National Legislation

The Contracting States shall communicate to the Secretary-General of the United Nations the laws and regulations which they may adopt to ensure the application of this Convention.

Article 37. Relation to Previous Conventions

Without prejudice to article 28, paragraph 2, of this Convention, this Convention replaces, as between Parties to it, the Arrangements of 5 July 1922, 31 May 1924, 12 May 1926, 30 June 1928 and 30 July 1935, the Conventions of 28 October 1933 and 10 February 1938, the Protocol of 14 September 1939 and the Agreement of 15 October 1946.

Chapter VII

Final Clauses

Article 38. Settlement of Disputes

Any dispute between Parties to this Convention relating to its interpretation or application, which cannot be settled by other means, shall be referred to the International Court of Justice at the request of any one of the parties to the dispute.

Article 39. Signature, Ratification and Accession

1. This Convention shall be opened for signature at Geneva on 28 July 1951 and shall thereafter be deposited with the Secretary-General of the United Nations. It shall be open for signature at the European Office of the United Nations from 28 July to 31 August 1951 and shall be re-opened for signature at the Headquarters of the United Nations from 17 September 1951 to 31 December 1952.

2. This Convention shall be open for signature on behalf of all States Members of the United Nations, and also on behalf of any other State invited to attend the Conference of Plenipotentiaries on the Status of Refugees and Stateless Persons or to which an invitation to sign will have been addressed by the General Assembly. It shall be ratified and the instruments of ratification shall be deposited with the Secretary-General of the United Nations.

3. This Convention shall be open from 28 July 1951 for accession by the States referred to in paragraph 2 of this article. Accession shall be effected by the deposit of an instrument of accession with the Secretary-General of the United Nations.

Article 40. Territorial Application Clause

1. Any State may, at the time of signature, ratification or accession, declare that this Convention shall extend to all or any of the territories for the international relations of which it is responsible. Such a declaration shall take effect when the Convention enters into force for the State concerned.

2. At any time thereafter any such extension shall be made by notification addressed to the Secretary-General of the United Nations and shall take effect as from the ninetieth day after the day of receipt by the Secretary- General of the United Nations of this notification, or as from the date of entry into force of the Convention for the State concerned, whichever is the later.

3. With respect to those territories to which this Convention is not extended at the time of signature, ratification or accession, each State concerned shall consider the possibility of taking the necessary steps in order to extend the application of this Convention to such territories, subject, where necessary for constitutional reasons, to the consent of the Governments of such territories.

Article 41. Federal Cause

In the case of a Federal or non-unitary State, the following provisions shall apply:

(a) With respect to those articles of this Convention that come within the legislative jurisdiction of the federal legislative authority, the obligations of the Federal Government shall to this extent be the same as those of parties which are not Federal States;

(b) With respect to those articles of this Convention that come within the legislative jurisdiction of constituent States, provinces or cantons which are not, under the constitutional system of the Federation, bound to take legislative action, the Federal Government shall bring such articles with a favourable recommendation to the notice of the appropriate authorities of States, provinces or cantons at the earliest possible moment;

(c) A Federal State Party to this Convention shall, at the request of any other Contracting State transmitted through the Secretary-General of the United Nations, supply a statement of the law and practice of the Federation and its constituent units in regard to any particular provision of the Convention showing the extent to which effect has been given to that provision by legislative or other action.

Article 42. Reservations

1. At the time of signature, ratification or accession, any State may make reservations to articles of the Convention other than to articles 1, 3, 4, 16 (1), 33, 36–46 inclusive.

2. Any State making a reservation in accordance with paragraph 1 of this article may at any time withdraw the reservation by a communication to that effect addressed to the Secretary-General of the United Nations.

Article 43. Entry into Force

1. This Convention shall come into force on the ninetieth day following the day of deposit of the sixth instrument of ratification or accession.

2. For each State ratifying or acceding to the Convention after the deposit of the sixth instrument of ratification or accession, the Convention shall enter into force on the ninetieth day following the date of deposit by such State of its instrument of ratification or accession.

Article 44. Denunciation

1. Any Contracting State may denounce this Convention at any time by a notification addressed to the Secretary-General of the United Nations.

2. Such denunciation shall take effect for the Contracting State concerned one year from the date upon which it is received by the Secretary-General of the United Nations.

3. Any State which has made a declaration or notification under article 40 may, at any time thereafter, by a notification to the Secretary-General of the United Nations, declare that the Convention shall cease to extend to such territory one year after the date of receipt of the notification by the Secretary-General.

Article 45. Revision

1. Any Contracting State may request revision of this Convention at any time by a notification addressed to the Secretary-General of the United Nations.

2. The General Assembly of the United Nations shall recommend the steps, if any, to be taken in respect of such request.

Article 46. Notifications by the Secretary-General of the United Nations

The Secretary-General of the United Nations shall inform all Members of the United Nations and non-member States referred to in article 39:

(a) Of declarations and notifications in accordance with section B of article 1;

(b) Of signatures, ratifications and accessions in accordance with article 39;

(c) Of declarations and notifications in accordance with article 40;

(d) Of reservations and withdrawals in accordance with article 42;

(e) Of the date on which this Convention will come into force in accordance with article 43;

(f) Of denunciations and notifications in accordance with article 44;

(g) Of requests for revision in accordance with article 45.

IN FAITH WHEREOF the undersigned, duly authorized, have signed this Convention on behalf of their respective Governments.

DONE at Geneva, this twenty-eighth day of July, one thousand nine hundred and fifty-one, in a single copy, of which the English and French texts are equally authentic and which shall remain deposited in the archives of the United Nations, and certified true copies of which shall be delivered to all Members of the United Nations and to the non-member States referred to in article 39.

DECLARATION ON TERRITORIAL ASYLUM

Adopted by General Assembly resolution 2312 (XXII) of 14 December 1967

The General Assembly,

Recalling its resolutions 1839 (XVII) of 19 December 1962, 2100 (XX) of 20 December 1965 and 2203 (XXI) of 16 December 1966 concerning a declaration on the right of asylum,

Considering the work of codification to be undertaken by the International Law Commission in accordance with General Assembly resolution 1400 (XIV) of 21 November 1959,

Adopts the following Declaration:

The General Assembly,

Noting that the purposes proclaimed in the Charter of the United Nations are to maintain international peace and security, to develop friendly relations among all nations and to achieve international co-operation in solving international problems of an economic, social, cultural or humanitarian character and in promoting and encouraging respect for human rights and for fundamental freedoms for all without distinction as to race, sex, language or religion,

Mindful of the Universal Declaration of Human Rights, which declares in article 14 that:

"1. Everyone has the right to seek and to enjoy in other countries asylum from persecution.

"2. This right may not be invoked in the case of prosecutions genuinely arising from non-political crimes or from acts contrary to the purposes and principles of the United Nations,"

Recalling also article 13, paragraph 2, of the Universal Declaration of Human Rights, which states:

"Everyone has the right to leave any country, including his own, and to return to his country,"

Recognizing that the grant of asylum by a State to persons entitled to invoke article 14 of the Universal Declaration of Human Rights is a peaceful and humanitarian act and that, as such, it cannot be regarded as unfriendly by any other State,

Recommends that, without prejudice to existing instruments dealing with asylum and the status of refugees and stateless persons, States should base themselves in their practices relating to territorial asylum on the following principles:

Article 1

1. Asylum granted by a State, in the exercise of its sovereignty, to persons entitled to invoke article 14 of the Universal Declaration of Human Rights, including persons struggling against colonialism, shall be respected by all other States.

2. The right to seek and to enjoy asylum may not be invoked by any person with respect to whom there are serious reasons for considering that he has committed a crime against peace, a war crime or a crime against humanity, as defined in the international instruments drawn up to make provision in respect of such crimes.

3. It shall rest with the State granting asylum to evaluate the grounds for the grant of asylum.

Article 2

1. The situation of persons referred to in article 1, paragraph 1, is, without prejudice to the sovereignty of States and the purposes and principles of the United Nations, of concern to the international community.

2. Where a State finds difficulty in granting or continuing to grant asylum, States individually or jointly or through the United Nations shall consider, in a spirit of international solidarity, appropriate measures to lighten the burden on that State.

Article 3

1. No person referred to in article 1, paragraph 1, shall be subjected to measures such as rejection at the frontier or, if he has already entered the territory in which he seeks asylum, expulsion or compulsory return to any State where he may be subjected to persecution.

2. Exception may be made to the foregoing principle only for overriding reasons of national security or in order to safeguard the population, as in the case of a mass influx of persons.

3. Should a State decide in any case that exception to the principle stated in paragraph 1 of this article would be justified, it shall consider the possibility of granting to the persons concerned, under such conditions as it may deem appropriate, an opportunity, whether by way of provisional asylum or otherwise, of going to another State.

Article 4

States granting asylum shall not permit persons who have received asylum to engage in activities contrary to the purposes and principles of the United Nations.

Appendix B
Human Rights Organizations

Compiled by Laurie Wiseberg

At the present time, there are thousands of human rights organizations worldwide operating at the local (grassroots), national, regional, and international levels. These groups may be operating with a broad mandate encompassing the entire spectrum of civil, cultural, economic, political, and social rights, or they may be narrowly focused on certain specific rights (freedom from torture, freedom of the press, the right to housing); they may focus on the rights of certain groups—women, children, refugees, internally displaced persons, workers, prisoners, persons with disabilities, minorities or indigenous peoples—or they may be differentiated with respect to the strategies they adopt and the activities they undertake, such as fact-finding, lobbying, education, litigation, or humanitarian assistance to victims.

This listing of Nongovernmental Organizations (NGOs) has been compiled from the database of organizations concerned with human rights and social justice maintained by Human Rights Internet (HRI). The database has approximately 8,000 entries and is now available on-line at <www.hri.ca>. HRI recognizes, however, that even this is simply the tip of the iceberg, given the dramatic expansion in NGOs engaged in human rights work in almost every country in the world during the past decades. What is presented in this encyclopedia is, therefore, a sampling from the extremely rich universe of human rights NGOs. In selecting the approximately 200 NGOs for inclusion in this volume, an attempt was made to focus on NGOs working at the international or regional levels, but also to provide examples of strong national-level NGOs from all regions. In the selection process, attention was also paid to providing a sample that would highlight the enormous diversity of the issues and concerns engaging the attention of human rights NGOs. It is important to note, however, that there was no attempt to evaluate the work of the NGOs and that inclusion or exclusion from this listing should in no way be taken as endorsement or criticism of the work of an organization. Moreover, the descriptions rely heavily on what the organizations say about their own objectives and activities.

Two organizations—Amnesty International and Human Rights Watch—stand out as human rights advocates, and so we decided to place them first, ahead of the alphabetical list. By placing them there we do not suggest that they are perfect, but only that their size and maturity as organizations mean that they tend to be more effective at informing the world of the human rights problems that beset it. If you begin your research with these two, you are not likely to go wrong.

Name: Amnesty International
Other Name: Amnistie internationale; Amnestia Internacional
Acronyms: AI
Languages: English, French, Spanish, Arabic
Address: International Secretariat
        1 Easton St.
        London WC1X 8DJ, UK
Telephone Number: (44–171) 413–5500
Fax Number: (44–171) 956–1157
Email: amnestyis@amnesty.org
Web Page: www.amnesty.org

Amnesty International (AI), founded in 1961, is a worldwide campaigning movement to promote all the human rights enshrined in the Universal Declaration of Human Rights and other international standards. In particular, AI campaigns to free all prisoners of conscience: ensure fair and prompt trials for political prisoners, abolish the death penalty, torture, and other cruel treatment of prisoners, to end political killings and "disappearances" as well as to oppose human rights abuses by opposition groups. It has 54 National Sections and local groups in over 150 countries.

Name: Human Rights Watch
Acronyms: HRW
Language: English
Address: 350 Fifth Avenue
        34th Floor
        New York, NY 10118–3299, USA
Telephone Number: (1–212) 290–4700
Fax Number: (1–212) 736–1300
Email: hrwnyc@hrw.org
Web Page: http://www.hrw.org

Human Rights Watch (HRW), founded in 1978, through its regional divisions (Africa, the Americas, Asia, the Middle East, and Europe and Central Asia) conducts regular, systematic investigations of human rights abuses in countries around the world. It addresses the human rights practices of governments of all political stripes, of all geopolitical alignments, and of all ethnic and religious persuasions. In internal wars it documents violations by both governments and rebel groups. HRW defends freedom of thought and expression, due process, and equal protection of the law; it documents and denounces murders, disappearances, torture, arbitrary imprisonment, exile, censorship, and other abuses of internationally recognized human rights.

Name: Abo Akademin—Ihmisoikeusinstutuutti
Other Name: Abo Akademi—Institutet for Manskliga
   Rattigheter; Abo Academy—Institute for Human Rights
Acronyms: AA
Language: Finnish; English
Address: Abo Akademi University
          Gezeliusgatan 2
          SF-20500 Turku, Finland
Telephone Number: (358–2) 215–4713 (courses); 215–4324
   (publications); 215–4325 (databases)
Fax Number: (358–2) 215–4699 (courses)
Email: johanna.bondas@abo.fi (courses)
Web Page: http://www.abo.fi/instut/imr/

The Institute for Human Rights of Åbo Akademi University (AA), founded in 1985, is an integrated unit of the Department of Law. AA focuses on research in the field of the international protection of human rights. The Institute also offers lectures, courses, and seminars, and organizes international meetings and symposia. The expertise and the library of the Institute and the databases FINDOC and DOMBASE are at the disposal of other universities, national and international organizations, and other bodies. It also has a close cooperation with the human rights institutes in the other Nordic countries.

Name: Academia Mexicana de Derechos Humanos
Other Name: Mexican Academy of Human Rights;
   l'Academie mexicaine des droits de l'homme
Acronyms: AMDH
Languages: Spanish; English; French
Address: Filosofia y Letras 88
          Colonia Copilco-Universidad
          Apdo. Postal 70–473
          04360 Mexico DF, Mexico
Telephone Number: (52–5) 659–4980; 659–8764
Fax Number: (52–5) 658–7279
Email: amdh@laneta.apc.org;
      acmedehu@servidor.unam.mx
Web Page: http://lanic.utexas.edu/la/region/news/arc/amdh

The Mexican Academy for Human Rights (AMDH), founded in 1984, works to train local groups and individuals to promote and defend human rights. AMDH also produces material for groups working in other areas related to human rights

to use in incorporating human rights issues into their work. And it documents and analyzes human rights abuses and networks with other human rights organizations.

Name: African Centre for Democracy and Human Rights
   Studies
Other Name: Centre africain pour la démocratie et les
   études des droits de l'homme
Acronyms: ACDHRS
Languages: English; French
Address: Kairaba Avenue
          Kombo St. Mary's Division
          Gambia
Telephone Number: (220) 39–45–25; 39–49–61
Fax Number: (220) 39–49–62
Email: acdhrs@acdhrs.gm
Web Page: http://www.acdhrs.gm

The African Centre for Democracy and Human Rights Studies (ACDHRS), established in 1989, promotes the observance of human and peoples' rights and democratic principles throughout Africa as an independent pan-African NGO. ACDHRS researches; produces publications; undertakes education, training, documentation; and disseminates and collects information.

Name: African Women's Development and Communication
   Network
Acronyms: FEMNET
Languages: English; French
Address: P.O. Box 54562
          Nairobi, Kenya
Telephone Number: (254–2) 741–301/20
Fax Number: (254–2) 742–927
Email: femnet@africaonline.co.ke
Web Page: http://www.co.ke/femnet

The African Women's Development and Communication Network (FEMNET), founded in 1985, works to strengthen the role and contribution of NGOs focusing on women's development in Africa and to lobby African governments to put in place policies that reflect gender sensitivity. FEMNET also initiates, develops, provides, and maintains channels and means of communication on matters relating to African women's development. It publishes pamphlets, articles, and books on human rights and maintains a documentation center. It also advises and assists other organizations on matters pertaining to African women.

Name: Agencia Latinoamericana de Información
Other Name: Agence Latino-Américaine d'Information;
   Latin American Information Agency
Acronyms: ALAI
Languages: Spanish; English; French

Address: Casilla 17–12–877
Av. 12 Octubre N18–24
Of 53
Quito, ECUADOR
Telephone Number: (593–2) 50–50–74; 22–15–70
Fax Number: (593–2) 50–50–73
Email: info@alai.ecuanex.net.ec
Web Page: http://alainet.org

The Latin America Information Agency (ALAI), founded in 1976, is an organization for communication and vigilance based on human rights and the participation of social movements in the community of Latin America. Its actions are based on the battle for democracy and the basic requirement for social justice and democratic life.

Name: Aide à toute détresse quart monde
Other Name: Mouvement ATD Quart Monde; ATD Fourth World Movement; ATD Bewegung Vierte Welt
Language: French
Address: 107 av. de General Leclerc
95480 Pierrelaye, France
Telephone Number: (33–1) 037–1111
Email: information@atd-quartmonde.org
Web Page: http://www.atd-quartmonde.org/accueil-fr.html

The International Movement ATD Fourth World, founded in 1957, fights against poverty and social exclusion. The Movement works to gain recognition for society's most deprived individuals and groups—the "Fourth World"—and to include them as full and free participants in social, economic, cultural and political life. It also seeks to promote human rights for those on the lowest level of the social scale: the right to work, housing, health, education, and culture, and the right to social and political representation.

Name: Al-Haq
Other Name: Law in the Service of Man
Languages: Arabic; English
Address: P.O. Box 1413
Ramallah
West Bank, Palestine
Telephone Number: (972–2) 295–6421; 295–4646
Fax Number: (972–2) 295–4903
Email: haq@alhaq.org
Web Page: http://www.alhaq.org

Al-Haq, founded in 1979, works for the protection and promotion of the principles of human rights and the rule of law. It monitors, documents, and investigates human rights violations. It researches issues pertaining to the rule of law in occupied territories. Al-Haq publishes studies on various aspects of the legal and human rights situation in the Israeli-occupied West Bank and Gaza Strip. It tries, through direct intervention and other means, to bring specific abuses to an end. Al-Haq also seeks to provide consultative and educational services to the Palestinian community concerning individual and collective rights in an effort to realize and protect these rights.

Name: Aliran Kesedaran Negara
Acronyms: ALIRAN
Languages: Malay; English
Address: 103 Medan Penaga
11600 Jelutong
Penang, Malaysia
Telephone Number: (60–4) 658–5251
Fax Number: (60–4) 658–5197
Email: alirankn@hotmail.com
Web Page: www.malaysia.net/aliran

The Aliran Kesedaran Negara (ALIRAN), founded in 1977, is dedicated to justice, freedom, and solidarity. It raises public awareness on important issues affecting Malaysians. It issues media releases, which analyze various issues related to its quest for an alternative order, and responds to both local and international human rights appeals. It also acts as a coordinating body or secretariat for appeals and campaigns on specific social and human rights issues. ALIRAN is an important source of independent information on Malaysia for political analysts, academics, and others interested in what is really happening in the country.

Name: All Africa Conference of Churches
Other Name: Conférence des églises de toute l'Afrique; Conferencia de Igrejas de Toda Africa
Acronyms: AACC; CETA; CITA
Languages: English; French; Portugese
Address: P.O. Box 14205
Nairobi, Kenya
Telephone Number: (254–2) 441–483; 441–338; 441–339; 445–827
Fax Number: (254–2) 443–241
Email: aacc-Infodesk@maf.org

The All African Conference of Churches (AACC) Commission on Human and Peoples' Rights, founded in 1963, works on matters relating to human and peoples' rights and international affairs, and acts or renders advice to the AACC on these matters; promotes and protects human and peoples' rights, and monitors their implementation; assists and encourages member churches and organizations to be concerned with and to promote and protect said rights in their countries and elsewhere; collects documents, undertakes studies and research, disseminates information, organizes seminars, symposia, and conferences, and renders advisory services on national and international affairs and matters relating to human and peoples' rights; lobbies for the ratification of the African Charter on Human and Peoples' Rights; communicates and cooperates with other African and international organizations with similar objectives; and provides assistance to persons whose rights have been violated.

Name: American Association for the Advancement of Science
Other Name: Science and Human Rights Program
Acronyms: AAAS
Language: English
Address: 1200 New York Ave. NW
　　　　　Washington, DC 20005, USA
Telephone Number: (1–202) 326–6790
Fax Number: (1–202) 289–4950
Email: shrp@aaas.org
Web Page: http://shr.aaas.org

The American Association for the Advancement of Science and Human Rights Program (AAAS), founded in 1976, works on the premise that to be consistent with the principles of scientific freedom and responsibility, scientific societies should encourage international respect for the human rights standards. AAAS conducts casework on behalf of scientists, engineers, and health professionals whose human rights have been violated, prepares statements and reports, and convenes meetings on human rights issues of special concern to scientists. It also organizes humanitarian and fact-finding missions and assists affiliates in dealing with cases and issues of special importance to the scientific community. It also works training NGOs in scientific human rights investigations and information management.

Name: American Friends Service Committee
Acronyms: AFSC
Language: English
Address: 1501 Cherry St.
　　　　　Philadelphia, PA 19102, USA
Telephone Number: (1–215) 241–7000
Fax Number: (1–215) 241–7275
Email: afscinfo@afsc.org
Web Page: www.afsc.org

The American Friends Service Committee (AFSC), founded in 1917, is a Quaker organization that includes people of various faiths who are committed to social justice, peace, and humanitarian service. AFSC has programs that focus on issues related to economic justice, peace-building, and demilitarization, social justice, and youth in the United States, Africa, Asia, Latin America, and the Middle East. Its work is based on the belief in the worth of every person, and faith in the power of love to overcome violence and injustice.

Name: Anti-Slavery International
Acronyms: AS
Language: English
Address: Thomas Clarkson House, The Stableyard
　　　　　Broomgrove Road
　　　　　London SW9 9TL, UK
Telephone Number: (44–0207) 501–8920

Fax Number: (44–0207) 738–4110
Email: admin@antislavery.org
Web Page: www.antislavery.org

Anti-Slavery (AS), founded in 1839, promotes the eradication of slavery, slavery-like practices, and freedom for everyone who is subjected to them. AS focuses on the rights of people who are particularly vulnerable to exploitation of their labor, notably women, children, migrant workers, and indigenous peoples. It collects information about abuses, raises public awareness, and promotes action to end them and influences policy-makers in governments or other institutions at national and international level to take action accordingly. AS also supports victims and works with organizations campaigning on their behalf.

Name: Arab Organization for Human Rights
Other Name: Organisation arabe des droits de l'homme
Acronyms: AOHR; OADH
Languages: Arabic; English; French
Address: 91, Marghani Ave.
　　　　　Massr al Jadida
　　　　　Cairo 11341, Egypt
Telephone Number: (20–2) 418–1396; 418–8378
Fax Number: (20–2) 418–5346
Email: aohr@link.com.eg

The Arab Organization for Human Rights (AOHR), founded in 1983, works for the respect of human rights and fundamental freedoms of all citizens and residents of the Arab world. AOHR defends any individual whose human rights are violated. It endeavors, regardless of political considerations, to obtain release of detained or imprisoned persons, and seeks relief and assistance for persons whose freedom is restricted in any way or who are subject to coercion of any kind because of their beliefs and political convictions, or for reasons of race, sex, labor, or language. AOHR provides legal assistance where necessary and possible, calls for improvements in conditions of prisoners of conscience and works for amnesty of persons sentenced for political reasons.

Name: ARTICLE 19: International Centre Against
　　　　Censorship
Acronyms: Article 19
Address: Lancaster House
　　　　　33 Islington High St.
　　　　　London N1 9LH, UK
Telephone Number: (44–20) 72–78–92–92
Fax Number: (44–20) 77–13–13–56
Email: info@article19.org
Web Page: http://www.article19.org

Article 19: International Centre Against Censorship (Article 19), founded in 1986, works worldwide to combat censorship by promoting freedom of expression and access to official information. It monitors, researches, publishes, lobbies, campaigns, and litigates on behalf of freedom of expression wherever it is threatened. Article 19 works to develop standards to advance media freedom, assist individuals to speak out and campaign for the free flow of information—within countries and internationally, and works to strengthen the local capacity to monitor and protest censorship.

Name: Asamblea Permanente por los Derechos Humanos
Other Name: Permanent Assembly for Human Rights
Acronyms: APDH
Address: Callao 569
           3er Cuerpo
           Buenos Aires 1022, Argentina
Telephone Number: (54–1) 374–4382; 476–2061;
   373–0397; 373–6073
Fax Number: (54–1) 814–3714
Email: apdh@mail.misiones.org.ar
Web Page: http://www.misiones.org.ar/apdh

The Permanent Assembly for Human Rights (APDH), created in 1975, addresses the systemic violations of human rights in Argentina. APDH works to promote truth and justice. It lobbies for internal human rights legislation and educates the public on past human rights abuses. It also runs programs on juvenile justice; the prison system; the lack of independence in the judiciary; economic, social, and cultural rights; freedom of press; and the rights to information and self-determination.

Name: Asia Monitor Resource Center
Acronyms: AMRC
Languages: English; Cantonese
Address: 444 Nathan Road, 8B
           Kowloon, Hong Kong
Telephone Number: (852)23–32–13–46
Fax Number: (852) 23–85–53–19
Email: amrc@pacific.net.hk/AMRC@HK.SUPER.NET
Web Page: http://www.pacific.net.hk/~amrc

The Asia Monitor Resource Center (AMRC), founded in 1976, focuses on Asian labor concerns. AMRC supports democratic and independent labor movements in Asia by providing information, tools, and skills as well as the opportunity for the exchange of experiences and ideas. AMRC provides services in training programs, campaigns, and other organizing strategies to grassroots NGOs and labor organizations that focus on women workers, labor issues, and development.

Name: Asia Pacific Forum on Women, Law and
   Development
Acronyms: APWLD
Language: English
Address: 9th floor, APDC Building
           Pesiaran Duta
           P.O. Box 12224
           50480 Kuala Lumpur, Malaysia

Telephone Number: (60–3) 651–0648
Fax Number: (60–3) 654–1371
Email: apwld@pactok.peg.apc.org

The Asia Pacific Forum on Women, Law and Development (APWLD), founded in 1986, works to advance the cause of women by creating an environment of social equality. APWLD works to develop a moral value code for equality and justice, and ratification and implementation of the UN Convention on the Elimination of All Forms of Discrimination Against Women. It also facilitates an information exchange to further individual and collective action and promotion of equality and political and economic rights for women, including their participation in policy planning.

Name: Asian Center for the Progress of Peoples
Acronyms: ACPP
Address: 52 Princess Margaret Road
           1/F, Kowloon, Hong Kong
Telephone Number: (852–2) 714–5123; 712–3989
Fax Number: (852–2) 711–3545
Email: acpp@hk.super.net

The Asian Center for the Progress of Peoples (ACPP), founded in 1979, is a religiously inspired (Catholic) organization. ACCP works by supporting national groups on justice and peace concerns and promotes international solidarity on justice issues. It tries to identify and address the root causes of injustice in Asia and cooperates with other groups in research, advocacy, and training. ACCP also maintains a documentation center and publishes educational aids. ACCP administers the Hotline Asia-Oceania, a project of the Justice and Peace Coordinating Committee for Asia. Hotline Asia-Oceania provides an urgent alert on cases of human rights violations involving members of grassroots organizations and justice and peace advocates. ACPP commits itself to a number of projects especially on labor, church response, and evangelization, and development issues.

Name: Asian Centre for Women's Human Rights
Acronyms: ASCENT
Language: English
Address: P.O. Box AC 662 Cubao
           1135 Quezon City, Philippines
Telephone Number: (63–2) 928–4973; 410–1512
Fax Number: (63–2) 533–0452; 928–4973; 911–0513
Email: ascent@csi.com.ph
Web Page: http://www.whrnet.org/partners.html

The Asian Center for Women's Rights (ASCENT) works to train women's organizations in Asia on human rights standards. It monitors, investigates, documents, and reports on violations of women's human rights. ASCENT's Women's Human Rights Defenders Program focuses on training women's rights activists on how to document, monitor, investigate, campaign, and make interventions on the different human rights violations perpetrated on women. ASCENT's Women in Armed Conflict Defenders Program assists, documents, and monitors women's human rights violations in war and armed conflict situations in Asia.

Name: Asian Coalition for Housing Rights
Other Name: Habitat International Coalition—Asia
Language: English
Address: P.O. Box 24–74
          Klongchan Bangkapi
          Bangkok 10240, Thailand
Telephone Number: (66–2) 538–0919
Fax Number: (66–2) 539–9950
Email: achrsec@mail.ksc.net

The Asian Coalition for Housing Rights was formed in 1988. The Coalition hopes to encourage more Asian groups to participate and work on regional actions in order to create a process of change in their struggle for housing rights. It also works to encourage governments in the region to recognize the human right to housing and to limit evictions and the impact of displacing people.

Name: Asian Cultural Forum on Development
Acronyms: ACFOD
Address: P.O. Box 26
          Bungthonglang
          Bangkok 10240, Thailand
Telephone Number: (66–2) 377–9357; (66–2) 370–2701
Fax Number: (66–2) 374–0464
Email:acfod@ksc15.th.com
Web Page: http://ksc11.th.com/acfodbkk

The Asian Cultural Forum on Development (ACFOD), founded in 1975, promotes integral development within the region. ACFOD has members in some thirty countries in Asia Pacific. It works to advocate integral development and counteract destructive/dehumanized development. It promotes peace, harmony, human rights, gender justice, and equity, as well as participatory democracy, sustainable development and provides a platform for grassroots exchanges and action.

Name: Asian Human Rights Commission
Acronyms: AHRC
Language: English
Address: Unit D, 7th Floor
          16 Argyle St., Mongkok Commercial Centre
          Kowloon, Hong Kong SAR
Telephone Number: (852–2) 698–6339
Fax Number: (852–2) 698–6367
Email: ahrchk@ahrchk.org
Web Page: http://www.ahrchk.net

The Asian Human Rights Commission (AHRC) was formed

in 1984 and works to provide an avenue for creating greater awareness and realization about human rights in the Asian region. It works to mobilize Asian and international public opinion to obtain relief and redress for the victims of human rights violations. AHRC prepares reports and takes appropriate action to prevent anticipated or continuing human rights violations. At the same time that the AHRC was formally constituted, it created the Asian Legal Resource Center (ALRC) to develop effective legal resources for the poor and disadvantaged of Asia. The two organizations collaborate closely. The AHRC monitors the regional human rights situation, does advocacy work and engages in research through its documentation program.

Name: Asian Regional Resource Center for Human Rights
      Education
Acronyms: ARRC
Language: English
Address: P.O. Box 26
          Bungthonglang P.O.
          Bangkok 10242, Thailand
Telephone Number: (66–2) 377–9357; 370–2701
Fax Number: (66–2) 731–2216
Email: arrc@ksc.th.com

The Asian Regional Resource Center for Human Rights Education (ARRC), founded in 1992, collects, exchanges, and distributes human rights education material. It also translates/adapts available materials, and produces new ones into regional languages, and provides training in human rights education and sharing of skills and methods at regional and national levels.

Name: Asociacion pro Derechos Humanos
Other Name: Association for Human Rights
Acronyms: APRODEH
Languages: Spanish; English
Address: Jr. Pachacutec 980
          Jesus Maria, Lima 11, Peru
Telephone Number: (51–1) 431–0482; 424–7057;
      431–4837
Fax Number: (51–14) 431–0477
Email: E-mail: webmaster@aprodeh.org.pe
Web Page: http://ekeko.rcp.net.pe/aprodeh/primera.htm

The Asociacion Pro Derechos Humanos (APRODEH), founded in September 1983, is dedicated to the defense, protection, promotion, and teaching of human rights in Peru. It documents and investigates human rights abuses, runs programs of legal assistance and training in the popular sector, provides humanitarian and legal assistance to the victims of human rights violations, and advocates for solidarity and cooperation without discrimination.

Name: Association des femmes africaines pour la recherche
      sur le développement

Other Name: Association of African Women for Research and Development
Acronyms: AFARD; AAWORD
Address: c/o CODESRIA
          B.P. 3304
          Dakar, Senegal
Telephone Number: (221) 825–9822; 825–9823
Fax Number: (221) 824–1289
Email: codesria@Sonatel.senent.net

The Association of African Women for Research and Development (AAWORD), founded in 1977, organizes different research working groups that members can join in accordance with their area of specialization and research interests. It undertakes research on issues relating to women, particularly the impact on women of economic development, health, and reproductive issues, and creates regional and international networks, both for African women researchers and for those concerned with development in Africa. AAWORD also encourages the formation of research working groups nationally in Africa.

Name: Association for Civil Rights in Israel
Acronyms: ACRI
Address: P.O. Box 35401
          Jerusalem 91352, Israel
Telephone Number: (972–2) 652–1218
Fax Number: (972–2) 652–1219
Email: acri@actcom.co.il
Web Page: http://nif.org/acri/

The Association for Civil Rights in Israel (ACRI), founded in 1972, is modeled after the American Civil Liberties Union. ACRI works to promote and defend civil and human rights in Israel through litigation, legislation, lobbying, and education. It takes civil rights cases to court to establish precedents that will prevent future abuse. ACRI has four offices in major Israeli cities, and provides advice and counsels victims of human rights abuse. Violations are brought to the attention of responsible authorities, and corrective action is called for. It also prepares teaching materials for use in Arab and Jewish schools, and conducts seminars for teachers on methods of raising civil rights awareness. It also takes part in police and paramilitary border police training programs.

Name: Association malienne des droits de l'homme
Other Name: Malian Association for Human Rights
Acronyms: AMDH
Language: French
Address: BP 3129
          Bamako, Mali
Telephone Number: (223) 22–34–62
Fax Number: (223) 22–93–77
Email: amdh@malinet.ml

The Malian Association for Human Rights (AMDH), formed in 1988, works to promote the respect of human rights in Mali by the government, the legal system, and the general public. It encourages research and compiles documentation on human rights in general, and Africa and Mali in particular, disseminates information, and organizes seminars and conferences to better promote human rights.

Name: Association pour la prevention de la torture
Other Name: Association for the Prevention of Torture;
    Asociacion para la Prevencion de la Tortura
Acronyms: APT
Languages: French; English; Spanish
Address: Case Postale 2267
          1211 Geneva 2 Depot, Switzerland
Telephone Number: (41–22) 734–2088
Fax Number: (41–22) 734–5649
Email: apt@apt.ch; webmaster@apt.ch
Web Page: http://www.apt.ch

The Association for the Prevention of Torture (APT), founded in 1977, works to prevent torture and treatment contrary to human dignity. It seeks to ensure the implementation of international laws and principles forbidding torture and to reinforce mechanisms—such as visits to places of detention—for the prevention of ill-treatment.

Name: Australian Human Rights Information Centre
Acronyms: AHRIC
Language: English
Address: Faculty of Law
          University of New South Wales
          Sydney 2052, NSW, Australia
Telephone Number: (61–2) 93–85–15–25
Fax Number: (61–2) 93–85–11–75
Email: ahric@unsw.edu.au
Web Page: http://www.austlii.edu.au/ahric/

The Australian Human Rights Information Centre (AHRIC) was formed as a body of the Human Rights Centre at the University of NSW. AHRIC seeks to increase public awareness about human rights procedures, standards, and issues within the Asia-Pacific region. It provides accessible information on human rights to the general public and to NGOs, government departments, human rights advocates, community legal centers, journalists, educators, researchers, and students. It also maintains a comprehensive collection of human rights documentation and runs an on-line database service. AHRIC also undertakes research and prepares publications, organizes educational activities, and responds to requests for technical advice in the area of human rights.

Name: Bangladesh Manobadhikar Samonnoy Parishad
Other Name: Coordinating Council for Human Rights in Bangladesh

Acronyms: BMSP; CCHRB
Languages: Bengali; English
Address: House 5/4 (First Floor)
          Block-F, Lalmatia
          Dhaka-1207, Bangladesh
Telephone Number:
Fax Number: (880–2) 81–72–11

The Coordinating Council for Human Rights in Bangladesh (CCHRB) was launched in 1986 as an initiative of Hotline, itself a project of the Commission for Justice and Peace, to link human rights organizations, organizations operating for social development and any organization having a human rights program or supporting oppressed groups. CCHRB works to raise public consciousness about human rights violations and the coordination of human rights activities of member organizations. It provides training for human rights workers and works for the ratification of important human rights instruments by the Bangladesh government. CCHRB also investigates and analyzes human rights situations; provides legal education, legal aid, and mediation for disadvantaged groups and individuals; and operates a documentation center.

Name: B'Tselem—Hamerkaz Hamayd'a Hayisraeli
    Lizehooyot Ha-Adam Ba-Shetahim
Other Name: B'Tselem—Israeli Information Center for
    Human Rights in the Occupied Territories
Languages: Hebrew; English; Arabic
Address: 43 Emek Refaim St.
          Second Floor
          Jerusalem 93141, Israel
Telephone Number: (972–2) 561–7271
Fax Number: (972–2) 561–0756
Email: btselem@btselem.org/mail@btselem.org
Web Page: http://www.btselem.org

B'Tselem–Israeli Information Center for Human Rights in the Occupied Territories (B'Tselem), founded in 1989, works to protect, monitor, document, and improve human rights in the Occupied Territories. B'Tselem provides information on human rights in the territories. Quantitative and qualitative data is compiled and regular data summaries are distributed to the media and other interested parties. In addition, B'Tselem responds to queries from Knesset members, government committees, researchers, students, and the media. It also provides human rights briefings to visiting foreign delegations and members of the diplomatic community. B'Tselem also conducts public education and organizes advocacy campaigns.

Name: Cairo Institute for Human Rights Studies
Acronyms: CIHRS
Languages: English; Arabic
Address: P.O. Box 117
          (Maglis el-Shaab)
          Cairo, Egypt

Telephone Number: (20–2) 354–3715; 355–1112; 594–1913
Fax Number: (20–2) 355–4200
Email: cihrs@idsc.gov.eg

The Cairo Institute for Human Rights Studies (CIHRS), formed in 1993, is a research center specializing in the study of human rights in the Arab world. It works to gain a deeper understanding of the structural problems that impede the implementation of international human rights law in Arab societies. It explores innovative approaches to the dissemination of human rights values and standards in Arab societies and provides channels of intellectual interaction between Arab and foreign research communities interested in promoting and implementing human rights at the regional and global levels. CIHRS also generates ideas relevant to peaceful solutions to the main problems of transition to democratic systems in Arab countries with special emphasis on human rights implementation. CIHRS's activities include conceptual and applied research, educational programs, seminars, courses, periodical, and nonperiodical publications, as well as providing research facilities and consultation to interested researchers.

Name: Cambodian Human Rights and Development
    Association
Acronyms: ADHOC
Languages: Khmer; English
Address: House No. 1, Street 158
          Oukghna Troeung Kang, Sangkat Beng Raing
          Khan Daun, Phnom Penh, Cambodia
Telephone Number: (855–23) 218–653
Fax Number: (855–23) 217–229
Email: adhoc@forum.org.kh
Web Page: http://cambodia-hr.org/adhoc/home.htm

The Cambodian Human Rights Association (ADHOC), established in 1992, promotes human rights in Cambodia. ADHOC focuses on human rights education and training. It publishes and distributes a magazine with information on the association's work and other human rights material. Its training includes providing basic information about international human rights standards and imparting skills in human rights monitoring. It also assists victims of human rights abuses and works to improve conditions in prisons. It has a documentation center and conducts research.

Name: Canadian Human Rights Foundation
Other Name: Fondation canadienne des droits de la
    personne
Acronyms: CHRF
Languages: English; French
Address: 1425 Rene-Levesque Blvd. West
          Suite 307
          Montreal, Quebec H3G 1T7, Canada
Telephone Number: (1–514) 954–0382
Fax Number: (1–514) 954–0659

Email: chrf@chrf.ca
Web Page: http://www.chrf.ca

The Canadian Human Rights Foundation (CHRF), founded in 1967, works for the defense and promotion of human rights through education, in Canada and around the world. CHRF runs training programs, initiates dialogue, and fosters research through conferences on emerging human rights issues, as well as offers a series of publications that include educational materials.

Name: Carter Center
Other Name: Carter-Menil Foundation
Language: English
Address: One Copenhill
     453 Freedom Parkway
     Atlanta, GA 30307, USA
Telephone Number: (1–404) 420–5151; Human Rights: 420–5183
Fax Number: (1–404) 420–5196; 420–5196; 420–5145
Web Page: www.cartercenter.org

The Carter Center, founded in conjunction with Emory University in 1982, strives to advance peace and health in neighborhoods and nations around the globe. The Center, guided by a fundamental commitment to human rights, wages peace by bringing warring parties to the negotiating table, monitoring elections, safeguarding human rights, and building strong democracies through economic development. It also conducts research and collaborates with other organizations, public or private, in carrying out its mission. The goal is to help create a world where every man, woman, and child has the opportunity to enjoy good health and live in peace.

Name: Casa Alianza
Other Name: Covenant House Latin America
Languages: Spanish; English
Address: SJO 1039
     P.O. Box 025216
     Miami, Florida 33102–5216, USA
Telephone Number: (506) 253–5439
Fax Number: (506) 224–5689
Email: info@casa-alianza.org
Web Page: http://www.casa-alianza.org

Casa Alianza, founded in 1981, is dedicated to the defense and rehabilitation of street children in Guatemala, Honduras, México, and Nicaragua. Casa Alianza is the Latin American branch of the New York–based Covenant House, and advocates for children's rights in the region. Casa Alianza provides legal aid and defense to street children, and investigates, denounces, and prosecutes violators of children's rights in both local and international courts. It also provides direct program assistance to street children.

Name: Center for Civil and Human Rights, University of Notre Dame
Acronyms: CCHR
Language: English
Address: Notre Dame
     IN 46556–0535, USA
Telephone Number: (1–219) 631–8555
Fax Number: (1–219) 631–8702
Email: law.cchr.1@nd.edu
Web Page: http://www.nd.edu/~cchr/

The Center for Civil and Human Rights at the Law School of Notre Dame (CCHR), founded in 1973, is an institute for advanced research and teaching. It focuses on international human rights and undertakes various research projects and maintains archives with a variety of materials from human rights organizations throughout the world. It is involved not only in the education of law students and lawyers but also in the education of the community at large concerning human rights issues throughout the world, through teaching programs, publications, and research projects. CCHR has a program where young lawyers from around the world spend a year together studying international human rights law so that they, in turn, may become teachers and advocates for the cause of human rights.

Name: Center for Economic and Social Rights
Other Name: Centro para Derechos Economicos y Sociales
Acronyms: CESR
Languages: English; Spanish
Address: 25 Ann St., 6th Floor
     New York, NY 10038, USA
Telephone Number: (1–212) 634–3424
Fax Number: (1–212) 634–3425
Email: mgreen@cesr.org/rights@cesr.org
Web Page: www.cesr.org

The Center for Economic and Social Rights (CESR) is one of the first U.S.-based human rights organizations to develop a practical program of fact-finding, education, and advocacy in the area of economic and social rights. CESR works to promote sustainable human development through human rights activism. It works with scientists and community and social justice organizations to build public awareness and advocate for policy change. To demonstrate the viability of this new human rights model, CESR restricts its focus to countries in which the government is actively involved in egregious violation, communities are organized and request support, and remedies are feasible. CESR has three major program areas: Health and Environment, Global Economic Justice, and Education and Outreach.

Name: Centre for Applied Legal Studies
Acronyms: CALS
Address: University of the Witwatersrand

P.O. WITS 2050
South Africa
Telephone Number: (27–11) 403–6918; 403–6922
Fax Number: (27–11) 403–2431
Email: 125ta2ti@solon.law.wits.ac.za

The Centre for Applied Legal Studies (CALS), established in 1978, studies and monitors the South African legal system and works for changes that will eliminate discrimination and injustice.

Name: Center for Human Rights and Humanitarian Law of
    American University
Address: Washington College of Law
          4801 Massachusetts Ave., Suite 310
          Washington, DC 20016–8181, USA
Telephone Number: (1–202) 274–4180
Fax Number: (1–202) 274–4130
Email: humlaw@wcl.american.edu
Web Page: http://www.wcl.american.edu/pub/humright

The Center for Human Rights and Humanitarian Law was established at the Washington College of Law of American University in 1990. The Center sponsors conferences with international organizations and NGOs. It also assists in developing human rights and humanitarian materials, and trains lawyers in the theory and practice of human rights and humanitarian law. As well, the Center is a home for U.S. and foreign human rights monitors and scholars to study and pursue research in these areas.

Name: Centre for International and Comparative Human
    Rights Law, Queens University of Belfast
Language: English
Address: School of Law
          Belfast BT7 1NN
          Northern Ireland
Telephone Number: (44–1232) 245–133
Fax Number: (44–1232) 325–590
Web Page: http://www.law.qub.ac.uk/

The Centre for International and Comparative Human Rights Law, of Queen's University, Belfast, supports a community of researchers in the area of human rights and promotes cooperation with other academic and human rights institutions, so as to produce scholarship of excellence in the field.

Name: Center for the Study of Human Rights, Columbia
    University
Acronyms: CSHR
Language: English
Address: 1108 International Affairs Building
          420 West 118th St.
          New York, NY 10027, USA

Telephone Number: (1–212) 854–2479
Fax Number: (1–212) 316–4578
Email: cshr@columbia.edu
Web Page: http://www.columbia.edu/cu/humanrights

The Center for the Study of Human Rights (CSHR), established in 1978, works to promote human rights research and education on a multidisciplinary basis at Columbia University and overseas. It seeks to integrate human rights education and research into the fields of law, the social sciences, the humanities, international and public affairs, public health, and social work. Overseas it promotes the research and educational capacities of educational institutions and human rights NGOs.

Name: Center for Women's Global Leadership
Language: English
Address: Rutgers, The State University of New Jersey
          160 Ryders Lane
          New Brunswick, NJ 08901–8555, USA
Telephone Number: (1–908) 932–8782
Fax Number: (1–908) 932–1180
Email: cwgl@igc.org;
Web Page: http://www.cwgl.rutgers.edu

The Center for Women's Global Leadership (Global Center), founded in 1989, is part of the Institute for Women's Leadership at Rutgers University. The Global Center's programs promote the leadership of women and advance feminist perspectives in policy-making processes in local, national, and international arenas. It also fosters women's leadership in the area of human rights through women's global leadership institutes, strategic planning activities, international mobilization campaigns, UN monitoring, global education endeavors, publications, and is also a resource center. The Global Center works from a human rights perspective with an emphasis on violence against women, sexual and reproductive health, and socioeconomic well-being. The Global Center's programs are in two broad areas of policy and advocacy: leadership development and global education.

Name: Centre on Housing Rights and Evictions,
    International Secretariat
Acronyms: COHRE
Languages: English; French; Spanish
Address: 83, rue de Montbrillant
          1202 Geneva, Switzerland
Telephone Number: (41–22) 734–1028
Fax Number: (41–22) 734–1028
Email: sleckie@ibm.net

The Centre on Housing Rights and Evictions (COHRE), established in 1991, is committed to ensuring the full enjoyment of economic, social, and cultural rights for everyone, everywhere, with a particular focus on the right to adequate housing and preventing forced evictions. It promotes practical legal and other solutions to the problem of homelessness, inadequate housing, and forced evictions. COHRE facilitates interaction between local community-based organizations and NGOs and the international human rights system by raising awareness of housing rights and promoting the application of international human rights law and mechanisms to protect such rights.

Name: Centro de Derechos Humanos "Fray Bartolome de las Casas"
Other Name: Fray Bartolome de las Casas Center for Human Rights
Acronyms: CDHFBC
Language: Spanish
Address: Centro de Derechos Humanos
     "Fray Bartolomé de las Casas"
     Apartado Postal 178
     San Cristóbal de Las Casas, Chiapas, México
Telephone Number: (52–9) 678–7396; 678–7395
Fax Number: (52–9) 67–88–35–51
Email: cdhbcasas@laneta.apc.org
Web Page: http://www.laneta.apc.org/cdhbcasas/

The "Fray Bartolomé de Las Casas" Human Rights Center (CDHFBC), founded in 1989, works to promote and defend human rights without distinction of creed or political orientation, giving preference to those victims who are socially marginalized by their poverty. A Christian organization, the Center carries out its work in the spirit of the evangelical teachings. CDHFBC verifies and documents abuses, examines national and international legislation, asks the corresponding authorities to comply with and respect recognized human rights norms, and promotes such legal norms. CDHFBC provides materials, courses, and workshops to facilitate an understanding of human rights and the mechanisms for defending and promoting them.

Name: Civicus: World Alliance for Citizen Participation
Acronyms: CIVICUS
Language: English
Address: 919 18th St. NW, 3rd Floor
     Washington, DC 20006, USA
Telephone Number: (1–202) 331–8518
Fax Number: (1–202) 331–8774
Email: info@civicus.org
Web Page: http://www.civicus.org

The World Alliance for Citizen Participation (CIVICUS), founded in 1993, is dedicated to strengthening citizen action and civil society throughout the world. CIVICUS works to help nurture the foundation, growth, protection and resourcing of citizen action throughout the world, and especially in areas where participatory democracy, freedom of association of citizens, and their funds for public benefit are threatened.

CIVICUS also has programs to promote leadership roles of women in civil society, youth participation in civil society, and corporate philanthropy and corporate citizenship.

Name: Civil Liberties Organisation
Acronyms: CLO
Address: 1A, Hussey St.
     Jibowu-Yaba
     Lagos, Nigeria
Telephone Number: (234–1) 774–6694; 584–0288
Fax Number: (234–1) 584–0288
Email: clo@gacom.net
Web Page: http://www.clo.org.ng

The Civil Liberties Organisation (CLO), established in 1987, promotes the principles and practices of fundamental human rights in Nigeria as enshrined in the constitution of Nigeria and in accordance with the African Charter on Human and Peoples' Rights and the UN Declaration on Human Rights. CLO provides legal aid in cases involving gross abuse or violation of human rights and conducts research on human rights issues, including conditions in Nigerian prisons and police. It also mounts campaigns to expose governmental abuses.

Name: Comision Andina de Juristas
Other Name: Andean Commission of Jurists
Acronyms: ACJ
Address: Los Sauces 285
     San Isidro
     Lima, Peru
Telephone Number: (511) 440–7907; 442–8094
Fax Number: (511) 442–6468
Email: postmast@cajpe.org.pe
Web Page: www.cajpe.org.pe

The Andean Commission of Jurists (ACJ), founded in 1982, carries out its activities in the six countries of the Andean region. It supports the creation and spread of democratic institutions and the reform and modernization of the State from a democratic perspective and encourages respect for human rights. ACJ carries out comparative analysis of the Andean region. Its work promotes the creation of spaces for pluralistic dialogue, the formulation of specialized and reliable opinions, detailed and systematized information, and demonstrates a versatile use of opportunities to comment on and directly influence political decision-making. It promotes the domestic application of the international law of human rights and systematically follows up the situation of human rights in the region, including the promotion and protection of women's rights, and the rights of indigenous peoples.

Name: Comision Chilena de Derechos Humanos
Other Name: Chilean Commission for Human Rights
Acronyms: CCHDH

Language: Spanish
Address: Santa Lucia 162
              Santiago, Chile
Telephone Number: (56–2) 633–3995; 633–3041
Fax Number: (56–2) 633–5562

The Chilean Commission for Human Rights (CCHDH), established in 1978, works for the protection and promotion of human rights in Chile as defined by the Universal Declaration of Human Rights and other international human rights covenants and treaties. CCHDH denounces all individual, civil, political, or social violations of human rights of Chileans, at home or abroad; provides legal assistance to victims of human rights violations, and collects information on human rights violations for presentation to national and international bodies. It also promotes international solidarity with the victims of human rights violations in Chile, and struggles for the derogation of legislation that facilitates the violation of those rights guaranteed by the Chilean constitution and by international instruments.

Name: Comision de Derechos Humanos de El Salvador
          (No-Gubernamental)
Other Name: Human Rights Commission of El Salvador
          (Nongovernmental)
Acronyms: CDHES
Address: Colonia Miralvalle
              Calle Genova No. 383
              San Salvador, El Salvador
Telephone Number: (503) 229–5750
Fax Number: (503) 228–0316

The Human Rights Commission of El Salvador (CDHES), founded in 1978, works to promote observance of human rights in El Salvador. CDHES documents cases of human rights violations, prepares official denunciations, using both domestic and international legal resources and investigates complaints as well as gathers testimony from on-site visits. It compiles statistical data on different aspects of human rights violations and provides psychological counseling to victims of human rights abuses, particularly to children and their relatives.

Name: Comision Ecumenica de Derechos Humanos
Other Name: Ecumenical Commission for Human Rights
Acronyms: CEDHU
Address: Casilla 17–03–720
              Quito, Ecuador
Telephone Number: (593–2) 570–619
Fax Number: (593–2) 580–825
Email: cedhu@ecuanex.net.ec
Web Page: www.derechos.net/cedhu/index.htm

The Comision Ecumenico de Derechos Humanos (CEDHU),

founded in 1978, promotes awareness of basic rights and develops educational programs especially among popular organizations and investigates and systematizes complaints of human rights violations in Ecuador. CEDHU also provides legal assistance to persons and groups whose rights are violated and provides teachers, students, and other groups with human rights documentation and materials, as well as coordinates activities with other human rights groups through the Frente Ecuatoriano por la Defensa de los Derechos Humanos. It participates in campaigns of solidarity with other Latin American countries.

Name: Comision para la Defensa de los Derechos Humanos
          en Centroamerica
Other Name: Commission for the Defense of Human Rights
          in Central America
Acronyms: CODEHUCA
Address: Apartado Postal 189
              Paseo de los Estudiantes
              San José 1002, Costa Rica
Telephone Number: (506) 224–5970; 225–0270;
          253–7827
Fax Number: (506) 234–2935
Email: secop@codehuca.or.cr
Web Page: http://www.codehuca.or.cr/

The Commission for the Defense of Human Rights in Central America (CODEHUCA), formed in 1978, researches and analyzes the civil and political rights; economic, social, and cultural rights; and the rights of peoples (peace, self-determination, a healthy and safe environment, development, and sovereignty). CODEHUCA fights vigorously for the human rights of Central Americans through its twelve member human rights organizations in Belize, Guatemala, Honduras, El Salvador, Nicaragua, Costa Rica, and Panama.

Name: Comite de Familiares de victima de las Violaciones
          de Derechos Humanos de El Salvador "Marianella
          Garcia Villas"
Other Name: Committee of Relatives for the Liberation of
          Political Prisoners and Disappeared "Marianella Garcia
          Villas"
Acronyms: CODEFAM
Language: Spanish
Address: Calle Gabriela Mistral
              No. 614
              Colonia Centroamérica
              San Salvador, El Salvador
Telephone Number: (503) 226–7989
Fax Number: (503) 226–7989
Email: emendozaz@navegante.com.sv

The Comite de Familiares Pro-Libertad de Presos y Desaparecidos Politicos de El Salvador (CODEFAM) "Marianella

Garcia Villas," established in 1981, works to liberate political prisoners and to discover the fate of those who have disappeared. CODEFAM works to promote and defend human rights and raise public awareness of the issues. It investigates prison conditions, allegations of torture, and disappearances.

Name: Comite Latinoamericano para la Defensa de los
    Derechos de la Mujer
Other Name: Latin American Committee for the Defense of
    Women's Rights
Acronyms: CLADEM
Languages: Spanish; English
Address: Jr. Estados Unidos 1295
            Jesús Maria
            Lima 11, PERU
Telephone Number: (51–1) 463–9237
Fax Number: (51–1) 463–5898
Email: cladem@chavin.rcp.net.pe
Web Page: http://www.derechos.org/cladem

The Comite Latinoamericano para la Defensa de los Derechos de la Mujer (CLADEM) is a regionwide network of women's organizations founded in 1987. It has 17 national offices. CLADEM plans strategies for regional actions to encourage the defense and exercise of women's rights in Latin America. It promotes exchanges of experiences in women's defense work within the region, consolidates links of solidarity among women at the national, regional, and interregional levels, and creates mechanisms for immediate response to emergencies. CLADEM works for greater participation by women from their perspective and interests in the discussion and decision-making on national and regional issues. It also works to develop an alternative concept of law that will contribute to the elimination of all forms of discrimination.

Name: Commonwealth Human Rights Initiative
Acronyms: CHRI
Language: English
Address: F1/12A Hauz Khas Enclave
            New Delhi 110 016, India
Telephone Number: (91–11) 686–4678; 685–9823;
    652–8152
Fax Number: (91–11) 686–4688
Email: chriall@nda.vsnl.net.in

The Commonwealth Human Rights Initiative (CHRI), established in 1987, is a joint undertaking of five nongovernmental Commonwealth organizations. CHRI's purpose is to make human rights a higher priority for the Commonwealth, and a reality for citizens in all 54 Commonwealth countries. It tries to persuade governments to pay more attention to human rights and has set up an expert group on intergovernmental

cooperation in the field. CHRI also serves as a link with over 250 NGO and watchdog groups in the Commonwealth.

Name: Coordinating Committee of Human Rights
    Organizations in Thailand
Acronyms: CCHROT
Languages: Thai; English
Address: c/o UCL
            109 Shuthisanwinijchai Rd.
            Samsen-Nok, Huaykwang
            Bangkok 10310, Thailand
Telephone Number: (66–2) 276–9846 to 7
Fax Number: (66–2) 693–4939

The Coordinating Committee of Human Rights Organizations in Thailand (CCHROT), founded in 1983, coordinates the work of human rights organizations in Thailand. It works with member organizations to develop common policies and strategies, and helps link NGOs with relevant government organizations in Thailand and abroad. CCHROT has a documentation and information system for use in public awareness campaigns on such issues as farmers' rights and prostitution. CCHROT also helps coordinate urgent action campaigns and assists with the annual human rights commemoration held during Human Rights Week.

Name: Cultural Survival
Acronyms: CS
Languages: English; Spanish; Portuguese; Danish
Address: Center for Cultural Survival
            96 Mt. Auburn St.
            Cambridge, MA 02138, USA
Telephone Number: (1–617) 441–5400
Fax Number: (1–617) 441–5417
Email: csinc@cs.org
Web Page: www.cs.org

Cultural Survival (CS), founded in 1972, works in educational and communication forums that advocate the rights, voice, and vision of indigenous peoples. CS draws attention to issues confronting indigenous peoples through its publications, student conferences, and educational outreach. It promotes the cause of self-determination and provides important and carefully analyzed information that is used by indigenous and non-indigenous peoples.

Name: Danske Center for Menneskerettigheder
Other Name: Danish Centre of Human Rights
Acronyms: DCHR
Languages: Danish; English
Address: 38 Studiestraede
            1455 Copenhagen, Denmark
Telephone Number: (45–33) 30–88–88
Fax Number: (45–33) 30–88–00

Email: hb@humanrights.dk; center@humanrights.dk
Web Page: http://www.humanrights.dk

The Danish Centre for Human Rights (DCHR), established in 1987, undertakes research, information, education, and documentation relating to Danish, European, and international human rights conditions. DCHR considers human rights work to be interdisciplinary, including law, anthropology, sociology, economics, humanities, journalism, and pedagogy. It cooperates with organizations and public authorities in Denmark, and with human rights centers and humanitarian organizations in other countries.

Name: Defence for Children International
Other Name: Defensa de los Ninos Internacional; Defense des Enfants International
Acronyms: DCI; DNI; DEI
Languages: English; French; Spanish
Address: C.P. 88
           CH-1211
           Geneva 20, Switzerland
Telephone Number: (41–22) 734–0550
Fax Number: (41–22) 740–1145
Email: dci-hq@pingnet.ch, dci-juv.justice@pingnet.ch
Web Page: http://www.defence-for-children.org

Defence for Children International (DCI), founded in 1979, works through its branches in over 60 countries to ensure ongoing, practical, systematic, and concerted international action specially directed toward promoting and protecting the rights of the child. DCI publishes information on all aspects of children's rights, investigates cases of violations, monitors and evaluates the practical implementation of children's rights, and works to stimulate international cooperation and action nationally, regionally, and internationally to improve the response to children's rights problems.

Name: Derechos Human Rights
Acronyms: DERECHOS
Languages: English; Spanish
Address: P.O. Box 2516
           El Cerrito, CA 94530–5516, USA
Telephone Number: (1–510) 528–7794
Fax Number: (1–510) 528–9710
Email: hr@derechos.org
Web Page: http://www.derechos.org

Derechos Human Rights (DERECHOS), founded in 1996, works for the respect and promotion of human rights all over the world. DERECHOS uses the Internet as its primary tool and focuses on public education of human rights and human rights violations. DERECHOS also investigates human rights abuses, including their causes and consequences and contributes to the development of international and national human rights law and the rule of law. It fights against the impunity of human rights violators and assists human rights NGOs, activists, and victims of human rights or humanitarian law violations.

Name: Diplomacy Training Program
Acronyms: DTP
Language: English
Address: DTP, Faculty of Law
           University of New South Wales
           Sydney, 2052, Australia
Telephone Number: (61–2) 93–85–28–07; 93–85–22–77
Fax Number: (61–2) 93–85–17–78; 93–85–11–75
Email: dtp@unsw.edu.au
Web Page: http://www.law.unsw.edu.au/centres/dtp

The Diplomacy Training Program (DTP), established in 1989, is affiliated with the University of New South Wales providing human rights training in the Asia-Pacific region. A specialized program in the region that trains in human rights and "people's diplomacy" skills to NGOs and other sectors of civil society. DPT has developed specialized teaching materials and participatory skill-building methods. It provides an introduction to international human rights standards and procedures, and practical skills for human rights education, lobbying, peace-building, working with the media, and good governance.

Name: Disabled Peoples' International
Other Name: Organisation mondiale des personnes handicapées; Organizacion Mundial de Personas Impedidas
Acronyms: DPI; OMPH; OMPI
Languages: English; French; Spanish
Address: 101–7 Evergreen Place
           Winnipeg
           Manitoba R3L 2T3, Canada
Telephone Number: (1–204) 287–8010
Fax Number: (1–204) 453–1367
Email: dpi@dpi.org, kiwanuka@dpi.org
Web Page: www.dpi.org

The Disabled Peoples' International (DPI), founded in 1980, speaks to governments, NGOs, and others on issues that affect disabled people. DPI also addresses issues of justice, human rights, peace, and international development through the development of partnerships and linkages with government, business, and the academic world wherever they might be mutually beneficial.

Name: Droits de l'homme sans frontierès
Other Name: Human Rights Without Frontiers
Languages: French; English
Address: Ave. Winston Churchill 11/33
           1180 Brussels, Belgium

Telephone Number: (32–2) 345–6145
Fax Number: (32–2) 343–7491
Email: info@hrwf.net

Human Rights Without Frontiers (HRWF) works to promote democracy, the rule of law, and the rights of the individual—man, woman, and child—everywhere in the world, by every appropriate means.

Name: ECPAT International
Other Name: End Child Prostitution, Child Pornography
    and Trafficking of Children for Sexual Purposes
Acronyms: ECPAT
Language: English
Address: 328 Phayathai Rd.
          Bangkok 10400, Thailand
Telephone Number: (66–2) 519–2794
Fax Number: (66–2) 519–2794
Email: ecpatbkk@ksc15.th.com
Web Page: http://www.ecpat.net

ECPAT, founded in 1990, is a global network of organizations and individuals working together for the elimination of commercial sexual exploitation of children: child prostitution, child pornography, and the trafficking of children for sexual purposes. It seeks to encourage the world community to ensure that children everywhere enjoy their fundamental rights free and secure from all forms of commercial sexual exploitation. It motivates local communities to find strategies that will protect children and works closely with NGOs, IGOs, and other individuals and groups. ECPAT provides training for personnel working to rehabilitate child victims and seeks ways to control the flow of child pornography. It works with young people to develop solutions and the tourist industry to prevent child sex tourism.

Name: Egyptian Organization for Human Rights
Acronyms: EOHR
Languages: Arabic; English
Address: 8/10 Matahaf El-Manyal Street
          10th Floor
          Manyal El Roda, Cairo, Egypt
Telephone Number: (20–2) 363–6811; 362–0467
Fax Number: (20–2) 362–1613
Email: eohr@link.com.eg, eohr@idsc.gov.eg
Web Page: http://www.eohr.org.eg

The Egyptian Organization for Human Rights (EOHR), founded in 1985, works for the support and defense of human rights in Egypt. EOHR monitors the human rights situation in Egypt and defends the rights of Egyptian citizens against human rights violations, regardless of the identity or the affiliation of the victim(s) or of the violator(s). It acts against both governmental and nongovernmental human rights violations. EOHR reports human rights violations and tries to create a

strong popular understanding and support for human rights principles. EOHR urges the authorities to revise all laws that are not in line with international human rights standards, and calls upon the government to stop all practices that disregard Egypt's international commitments. EOHR also tries to encourage national and international civil institutions to take steps to stop human rights abuses. EOHR has seventeen provincial branches located throughout Egypt.

Name: Ethiopian Human Rights Council
Acronyms: EHRCO
Languages: English; Amharic
Address: P.O. Box 2432
          Addis Ababa, Ethiopia
Telephone Number: (251–1) 51–44–89
Fax Number: (251–1) 41–45–39
Email: ehrco@telecom.net.et

The Ethiopian Human Rights Council (EHRCO), established in 1991, works to promote human rights, democracy, and the rule of law in Ethiopia. EHRCO monitors the human rights situation in the country, documents violations, and publishes reports that are disseminated nationally and internationally. It receives individual complaints of violations, intercedes with the authorities on behalf of victims, and provides legal assistance to those whose rights have been violated.

Name: European Consultation on Refugees and Exiles
Other Name: Consultation européenne sur les réfugiés et les
    exiles; Consulta Europea sobre Refugiados and
    Exiliados
Acronyms: ECRE; CERE; CERE
Languages: English; French; Spanish
Address: Bondway Hous
          3/9 Bondway
          London SW8 1SJ, United Kingdom
          Stapleton Ho., Clifton Centre
          Unit 22, 110 Clifton St.
          London EC2A, 4HT UK
Telephone Number: (44–20) 77–29–51–52
Fax Number: (44–20) 77–29–51–41
Email: ecre@ecre.org
Web Page: http://www.ecre.org

The European Consultation on Refugees and Exiles (ECRE), founded in 1976, is an umbrella for member agencies in 25 countries working toward fair and humane policies for the treatment of asylum seekers and refugees. It provides member agencies with accurate and detailed information on all aspects of the European refugee situation through monitoring and collecting information. ECRE also undertakes advocacy work, through its member organizations to improve the situation of refugees in Europe. It also runs a forum for legal practitioners to discuss issues facing them on a daily basis. ECRE also works to develop policies that will demonstrate the mutual realization of refugee and host states' interests and needs.

Name: European Legal Network on Asylum and Exiles
Acronyms: ELENA
Languages: English; French; Spanish
Address: c/o France Terre d'Asile
          425 rue Ganneron
          75018 Paris, France
Telephone Number: (33–1) 53–04–39–99
Fax Number: (33–1) 53–04–02–40
Email: E-mail: 100753.1030@compuserve.com
Web Page: http://www.ecre.org

ELENA is a forum, as part of the ECRE's work, for legal practitioners who aim to promote the highest human rights standards for the treatment of refugees, asylum seekers, and other persons in need of international protection in their daily counseling and advocacy work. The ELENA network extends across 25 central and western European states and involves some 2,000 lawyers and legal counselors.

Name: European Roma Rights Center
Other Name:
Acronyms: ERRC
Language: English
Address: P.O. Box 10/24
          H-1525 Budapest 114, Hungary
Telephone Number: (36–1) 428–2351
Fax Number: (36–1) 428–2356
Email: attila@errc.org
Web Page: http://www.errc.org

The European Roma Rights Center (ERRC), founded in 1995, is an international public interest law organization that monitors the situation of Roma in Europe and provides legal defense to victims of human rights violations. The ERRC acts to combat racism and discrimination against Roma and to empower Roma to their own defense by engaging in activities, which include monitoring the human rights situation of Roma in Europe; publishing information on human rights abuse of Roma and news about the Romani civil rights movement in the form of press releases; reports on the situation of Roma in various countries; legal defense by providing and supporting legal services to Romani victims of human rights violations; conducting seminars aimed at the dissemination of information concerning Roma rights and the promotion of change-oriented litigation and law reform; advocating Roma rights in domestic and international governmental and nongovernmental settings; maintaining a documentation center of Roma-related human rights and legal material; awarding grants to nongovernmental organizations that defend the rights of Roma; offering scholarships and stipends to Romani students of law and public administration.

Name: Federacion Latinoamericana de Asociaciones
      Familiares de Detenidos-Desaparecidos
Other Name: Latin American Federation of Associations of
      Families of the Detained-Disappeared
Acronyms: FEDEFAM
Languages: Spanish; English
Address: Apartado 2444
          Carmelitas 1010–A
          Caracas, Venezuela
Telephone Number: (58–2) 564–0503; 564–2746
Fax Number: (58–2) 564–2746
Email: fedefam@true.net

The Latin American Federation of Associations of Families of the Detained-Disappeared (FEDEFAM), founded in 1981, works on problems of the detained-disappeared in Latin America and the Caribbean. It is made up of the Asociaciones de Familiares of the countries of Latin America and the Caribbean in which there are forced disappearances. FEDEFAM works to rescue the detained-disappeared alive and to bring before justice those responsible for these crimes. It also works for the enactment of national and international legal norms that will define forced disappearance as a crime against humanity and that will prevent its occurrence and the return of the children of the detained-disappeared to their proper homes.

Name: Fédération internationale de l'action des chrétiens
      pour l'abolition de la torture
Other Name: International Federation of Christian Action
      for the Abolition of Torture
Acronyms: FIACAT
Address: 7, rue Georges Lardennois
          75019 Paris, France
Telephone Number: (33–1) 40–40–42–43
Fax Number: (33–1) 40–40–42–44
Email: acat-fr@worldnet.fr
Web Page: http://home.worldnet.fr/acatfr/

The International Federation of Christian Action for the Abolition of Torture (FIACAT), established in 1974, works to mobilize the Christian community in the struggle against torture, the mistreatment of individuals, and the incarceration of political prisoners and dissidents in psychiatric hospitals. It also campaigns for the respect of human rights covenants and other international instruments concerned with human rights.

Name: Fédération internationale des ligues des droits de
      l'homme
Other Name: International Federation of Human Rights
      Leagues; Federacion Internacional de Liguas de
      Derechos Humanos
Acronyms: FIDH
Languages: French; English; Spanish
Address: 17, Passage de la Main d'Or
          75011 Paris, France

Telephone Number: (33–1) 43–55–25–18
Fax Number: (33–1) 43–55–18–80
Email: fidh@csi.com
Web Page: www.fidh.imaginet.fr

The International Federation of Human Rights Leagues (FIDH), founded in 1922, works to promote the implementation of the Universal Declaration of Human Rights and other international instruments of human rights protection. It conducts interventions, public awareness campaigns, missions, training, and supports human rights activists through judicial cooperation programs. FIDH also lobbies international authorities on human rights issues.

Name: Foundation for Human Rights Initiative
Acronyms: FHRI
Language: English
Address: P.O. Box 11027
          Kampala, Uganda
Telephone Number: (256–41) 530–095/6
Fax Number: (256–41) 540–561
Email: fhri@starcom.co.ug
Web Page: http://www.hri.ca/parnters/fhri/

The Foundation for Human Rights Initiative (FHRI), formed in 1992, works to provide better formulation and understanding of human rights strategies and programs, and advocates for just and humane laws. It also encourages sharing of information and experience among human rights workers and supports paralegal training, conferences, and meetings. FHRI also provides legal advice, counseling, and referrals.

Name: François-Xavier Bagnoud Center for Health and
      Human Rights
Acronyms: FXB Center
Language: English
Address: 651 Huntington Ave.
          7th Floor
          Boston, MA 02115, USA
Telephone Number: (1–617) 432–0656; 432–4315;
      432–4611
Fax Number: (1–617) 432–4310
Email: fxbcenter@igc.apc.org
Web Page: http://www.hri.ca/partners/fxbcenter

The François-Xavier Bagnoud Center for Health and Human Rights (FXB Center), established in 1993, focuses exclusively on health and human rights, combines the academic strengths of research and teaching with a strong commitment to service and advocacy. The FXB Center works at international and national levels through collaboration and partnerships with health and human rights practitioners, governmental and NGOs, academic institutions, and international agencies to catalyze the health and human rights movement. It also works

to influence policies and practices and expand the knowledge about linkages between health and human rights in specific contexts such as HIV/AIDS, children's rights and health, and women's health and rights.

Name: Freedom House
Languages: English; Capabilities in Russian; Ukrainian;
      French; English
Address: 120 Wall Street
          Floor 26
          New York, NY 10005, USA
Telephone Number: (1–212) 514–8040
Fax Number: (1–212) 514–8050
Email: fh@freedomhouse.org; kguida@freedomhouse.org;
      freedomhs2@aol.com freedom
Web Page: http://www.freedomhouse.org

Freedom House, founded in 1941, champions the rights of democratic activists, religious believers, trade unionists, journalists, and proponents of free markets. It is an advocate for the world's young democracies and it conducts research, education, and training initiatives that promote human rights, democracy, free market economics, the rule of law, independent media, and U.S. engagement in international affairs.

Name: Gesellschaft fur Bedrohte Volker
Other Name: Society for Threatened Peoples
Acronyms: GfbV
Address: Postfach 2024
          D-37010 Goettingen, Germany
Telephone Number: (49–551) 49–90–60
Fax Number: (49–551) 58–0–28
Email: info@gfbv.de
Web Page: http://www.gfbv.de

The Society for Threatened Peoples (GfbV), founded in 1970, works to protect and toward the realization of human rights of groups worldwide. The main focus of GfbV includes continuous distribution of information about the situation of persecuted and threatened peoples through press releases and conferences, appeals, demonstrations, and protest actions. It also advises journalists, publishers, publishing houses, solicitors, and relief agencies and supports political refugees and members of minorities in applying for political asylum status, and gives background information for solicitors and courts.

Name: Global Alliance Against Traffic in Women
Acronyms: GAATW
Language: English
Address: P.O. Box 1281
          Bangkrak Post Office
          Bangkok 10500, Thailand
Telephone Number: (66–2) 864–1427
Fax Number: (66–2) 864–1637

Email: GAATW@mozart.inet.co.th
Web Page: http://www.inet.co.th/org/gaatw

The Global Alliance Against Traffic in Women (GAATW), founded in 1994, works to ensure that the human rights of trafficked women are respected and protected by authorities and agencies. GAATW involves grassroots women in all work to improve practical support to trafficked persons and advocacy work at all levels. It trains antitrafficking activists to apply a human rights framework for promoting and protecting the rights of trafficked persons. It also builds alliances with international organizations at all levels in enforcing and utilizing the existing human rights instruments to address trafficking issues. GAATW campaigns for a new definition of trafficking in persons and promotes and facilitates action research on issues relating to traffic in women.

Name: Global Sisterhood Network
Acronyms: GSN
Language: English
Address: University of Melbourne
                 Parkville, Victoria 3052, Australia
Telephone Number: (61–3) 93–44–6556
Fax Number: (61–3) 93–44–7959
Email: globalsisterhood@onelist.com
Web Page: http://home.vicnet.net.au/~globalsn

The Global Sisterhood Network (GSN), founded in 1996, monitors electronic and print media for developments in agriculture, economics, employment, environment, health, law, militarism, politics, technology, trade, and science that have a direct impact on the realities of women's lives. GSN provides regularly updated information and helps in projects that work to improve the quality of lives of women and children as well as protect their rights.

Name: Groupe d'études et de recherches sur la démocratie
             et le développement économique et social—Afrique
Other Name: Study and Research Group on Democracy and
             on Economic and Social Development—Africa
Acronyms: GERDDES; ICRD
Languages: English; French; Portuguese
Address: BP 1258
                 Cotonou, Benin
Telephone Number: (229) 334–333
Fax Number: (229) 334–499; 334–332

The Study and Research Group on Democracy and on Economic and Social Development—Africa (GERDDES-Africa), founded in 1990, works to advance the course of democracy with a view to accelerating the development process in African countries. The International Centre for Research and Democracy and Development (ICRD), which is the research and executive organ of GERDDES-Africa, opened in 1994. ICRD

conducts studies, research, and training on issues relating to democracy and development in Africa, and proposes or undertakes actions to promote, defend, and consolidate democracy in Africa, particularly election observation and free press issues.

Name: Guyana Human Rights Association
Acronyms: GHRA
Language: English
Address: P.O. Box 10653
                 Georgetown, Guyana
Telephone Number: (592–2) 61789; 74911
Fax Number: (592–2) 74948
Email: ghra.guy@solutions2000.net

The Guyana Human Rights Association (GHRA), founded in 1979, works to monitor and defend civil and political rights, especially those relating to the administration of justice, freedom of expression, and democracy. GHRA also works to secure the economic, social, and cultural rights of vulnerable sectors of society, especially women, indigenous people, people with disabilities, children, minorities, HIV/AIDS carriers, and prisoners. It promotes a human rights culture free from inequality and discrimination. GHRA makes available documentation about human rights violations, especially violations against the integrity of the person and due process of law.

Name: Handicap International
Language: French
Address: 14, Avenue Berthelot
                 Lyon Cedex 07
                 Paris 69361, France
Telephone Number: (33) 478–69–79–79; Minitel 3615
     HANDICA
Fax Number: (33) 478–69–79–94
Email: handicap-international@infonie.fr
Web Page: http://www.handicap-international.org

Handicap International, founded in 1982, intervenes in favor of the handicapped and the most vulnerable populations wherever and whenever armed conflict has destroyed existing systems of assistance and solidarity. Similar assistance is also made available in countries where there are severe economic problems, or where its expertise in prevention and socioeconomic development is requested. It conducts projects in rehabilitation, prevention, rural development, and emergency programs.

Name: Human Rights Advocates
Acronyms: HRA
Languages: English; Spanish
Address: P.O. Box 5675
                 Berkeley, CA 94705, USA
Telephone Number: (1–650) 341–2585
Fax Number: (1–650) 341–1395

Email: cindy@mcglashan.com
Web Page: http://www.humanrightsadvocates.org

Human Rights Advocates (HRA), founded in 1978, works to promote the development and effective use of international law through study, education, and practice. It provides education concerning the application of international human rights law in domestic forums and promotes this body of law domestically and internationally. HRA works to protect the fundamental human rights of individuals such as migrant workers and asylum seekers in California, administrative detainees in Asia, and people without food in Ethiopia. It also works to direct needed emphasis to rights frequently neglected: the rights of civilian victims and prisoners of war, and the interrelationship between armed conflict and human rights violations. HRA works to draw attention to the issue of population transfer as a violation of human rights. It also works to bring international attention to the growing problem of environmental refugees, persons displaced by widespread pollution of streams and lands and by development projects. HRA provides its legal expertise and assistance to lawyers involved in lawsuits in which international human rights law can be used effectively.

Name: Human Rights Centre, University of Essex
Language: English
Address: Wivenhoe Park
          Colchester
          Essex C04 3SQ, UK
Telephone Number: (44–1206) 87–25–58
Fax Number: (44–1206) 87–36–27
Email: hrc@essex.ac.uk
Web Page: http://www2.essex.ac.uk/human_rights_centre/

The Human Rights Centre, established in 1983, coordinates the university's interdisciplinary human rights teaching program as well as its program of research, training, external consultancy and publication on international, comparative, and national aspects of human rights. The Centre brings academics from across the world to share their knowledge of their country and region.

Name: Human Rights Commission of Pakistan
Acronyms: HRCP
Address: Aiwan-i-Jamhoor
          107 Tipu Block
          New Garden Town
          Lahore, Pakistan
Telephone Number: (92–42) 583–8341; 586–4994;
          586–5969
Fax Number: (92–42) 571–3078

The Human Rights Commission of Pakistan, formed in 1986, works for the implementation of the Universal Declaration of Human Rights and for the ratification and implementation of other UN charters, covenants, and protocols on human rights. It promotes studies in the field of human rights and mobilizes public opinion through different media. It cooperates with and aids national and international organizations and individuals engaged in the promotion of human rights. It provides legal aid to victims and to persons striving to protect human rights.

Name: Human Rights Council of Australia
Acronyms: HRCA
Language: English
Address: P.O. Box 841
          Marrickville
          NSW, Australia 1475
Telephone Number: (61–02) 95–59–22–69
Fax Number: (61–02) 95–59–22–69
Email: agf@peg.apc.org; andref@mpx.com.au
Web Page: http://www.ozemail.com.au/~hrca

The Human Rights Council of Australia (HRCA), founded in 1978, promotes understanding of and respect for human rights for all persons without discrimination through adherence to the International Bill of Rights, and other human rights instruments, internationally and within Australia. It carries out research and advocacy on a human rights approach to development assistance and participates in continued advocacy on the rights of indigenous Australians. HRCA also conducts campaigns and holds conferences on a wide variety of topics.

Name: Human Rights Documentation Centre, University of
      Namibia
Address. Faculty of Law
          New Campus
          P/Bag 13301
          Windhoek, Namibia
Telephone Number: (264–61) 206–3664
Fax Number: (264–61) 206–3293
Email: cmchombu@mail.unam.na; hrdc@unam.na

The Human Rights and Documentation Centre was established as part of the Faculty of Law of the University of Namibia in July 1993. It conducts research on human rights and promotes human rights in Namibia. It pays special attention to the rights of women, and works to educate Namibians on human rights issues.

Name: Human Rights in China
Acronyms: HRIC
Language: English
Address: 350 Fifth Ave., Suite 3309
          New York, NY 10118, USA
Telephone Number: (1–212) 239–4495
Fax Number: (1–212) 239–2561
Email: Email: hrichina@hrichina.org
Web Page: http://www.hrichina.org

Human Rights in China (HRIC), founded in 1989, monitors the implementation of international human rights standards in the People's Republic of China and carries out human rights advocacy and education among Chinese people inside and outside the country. HRIC's work includes documenting and publicizing human rights abuses in China, informing Chinese people about international human rights standards and the methods by which they are enforced and assisting those persecuted and imprisoned in China for the nonviolent exercise of their rights. The primary focus of all of HRIC's work is to encourage and empower the nascent grassroots human rights movement in China.

Name: Human Right Internet
Other Name: Internet: International Human Rights Documentation Network; Internet: Réseau international de documentation sur les droits humains; Internet: Red Internacional de Documentación sobre los Derechos Humanos
Acronyms: HRI
Languages: English; French; Spanish
Address: 8 York St.
             Suite 302
             Ottawa, ON K1N 5S6, Canada
Telephone Number: (1–613) 789–7407
Fax Number: (1–613) 789–7414
Email: hri@hri.ca
Web Page: http://www.hri.ca

Human Rights Internet (HRI), founded in 1976, works to support the work of global NGOs in their struggle to obtain human rights for all. HRI works as an international communications network and clearinghouse on human rights with universal coverage, to make information on the human rights community easily available. HRI promotes human rights education, stimulates research, encourages the sharing of information, and builds international solidarity among those committed to the principles enshrined in the International Bill of Human Rights.

Name: Human Rights Program—Harvard Law School
Acronyms: HRP
Address: Pound Hall, Room 401
             Harvard Law School
             Cambridge, MA 02138, USA
Telephone Number: (1–617) 495–9362
Fax Number: (1–617) 495–1110
Email: hrp@law.harvard.edu
Web Page: http://www.law.harvard.edu/Programs/HRP

The Human Rights Program (HRP), founded in 1985, gives impetus and direction to international human rights work at Harvard Law School. It fosters course work, the participation of students in human rights activities, clinical work, and re-

search and scholarship. Through its student internships, speaker series, visiting fellowships, clinical work, and applied research, the Program forges cooperative links with a range of human rights organizations in this country and abroad, and works with other Harvard faculties and programs engaged in human rights work. HRP also plans and directs international conferences on human rights issues, and publishes reports and scholarship resulting from them.

Name: Index on Censorship
Other Name: Writers and Scholars Educational Trust
Acronyms: WSET
Address: Lancaster House
             33 Islington High St.
             London N1 9LH, UK
Telephone Number: (44–171) 278–2313
Fax Number: (44–171) 278–1878
Email: frank@indexoncensorship.org
Web Page: www.indexoncensorship.org

The Index on Censorship (WSET), founded in 1970, works to document the censorship and repression of writers, scholars, journalists, and others worldwide. It assists in the publication of banned writings and provides a platform for the discussion of problems of freedom of expression.

Name: Indian Law Resource Center
Other Name: Centro de Recursos sobre el Derecho Indigenista
Languages: English; Spanish
Address: 602 North Ewing St.
             Helena, MT 59601, USA
Telephone Number: (1–406) 449–2006
Fax Number: (1–406) 449–2031
Email: mt@indianlaw.org
Web Page: http://www.indianlaw.org/

The Indian Law Resource Center, founded in 1978, is dedicated to protecting the right of indigenous peoples to live with dignity and respect according to the ways of their ancestors. It works to ensure the survival of indigenous peoples, including protection of their land rights, environment, and right to self-determination. The Center provides legal and technical support to indigenous communities working on these issues, and works to reform national and international laws to recognize indigenous human rights.

Name: Informal Sector Service Centre
Acronyms: INSEC
Languages: Nepali; English
Address: P.O. Box 2726
             Kathmandu, Nepal
Nepal Telephone Number: (977–1) 270–770; 278–770
Fax Number: (977–1) 270–551

Email: insec@mos.com.np
Web Page: www.hri.ca/partners/insec

The Informal Sector Service Centre (INSEC), founded in 1988, works to bring human rights services to the grassroots and general public. INSEC has five regional centers that monitor human rights violations and programs at district levels. In general, INSEC works to protect and promote human rights through advocacy, lobbying, training, education, information, campaigns and projects at national, regional, and grassroots levels. It has developed a methodology for its grassroots activities. It conducts studies, does research and organizes seminars to accumulate knowledge for future action, which is then used for implementation of activities at the grassroots level.

Name: Institut arabe des droits de l'homme
Other Name: Arab Institute for Human Rights
Acronyms: IADH; AIHR
Languages: French; English
Address: 14, rue El Jahedh
             (via El Moez)
             El Menzah 1004, Tunisia
Telephone Number: (216–1) 767–003; 767–889
Fax Number: (216–1) 750–911
Email: aihr.infocenter@gnet.tn

The Arab Institute for Human Rights (AIHR) was founded in 1989 by three groups: the Arab Organization for Human Rights (AOHR), the Arab Lawyers' Union (ALU), and the Tunisian League for the Defense of Human Rights (TLDHR). AIHR disseminates information on human rights principles as elaborated in the Universal Declaration of Human Rights and promotes and defends human rights throughout the Arab world. It promotes knowledge of civil, political, cultural, social, and economic human rights, and runs training courses in human rights for members of NGOs and various civic associations. It also conducts research on the status of women in Arab countries and human rights/democracy education in the Arab region, and promotes a network of information and data concerning the state of human rights in the Arab region through AHRINET, the Reseau arabe de documentation et d'information en droits de l'homme and publishes pedagogical material on human rights documentation.

Name: Institut international des droits de l'homme
Other Name: International Institute of Human Rights
Acronyms: IIDH; IIHR
Address: 2, Allee René Cassin
             F-67000 Strasbourg, France
Telephone Number: (33–3) 88–45–84–45
Fax Number: (33–3) 88–45–84–50
Email: iidhiihr@mail.sdv.fr, iidhiihr@factorix.sdv.fr

The International Institute of Human Rights (IIDH), founded in 1969, works to promote and protect fundamental human rights through the study of human rights issues. It organizes international colloquia, seminars, and training courses; undertakes research work and encourages human rights education. IIDH also publishes books and periodicals, and collates and circulates documents.

Name: Institute for War and Peace Reporting
Acronyms: IWPR
Language: English
Address: Lancaster House
             33 Islington High St.
             London N1 9LH, UK
Telephone Number: (44–207) 713–7130
Fax Number: (44–207) 713–7140
Email: info@iwpr.net
Web Page: www.iwpr.net

The Institute for War and Peace Reporting (IWPR), founded in 1991, works to inform the international debate on conflict and supports the independent media development through collaborative journalistic projects and other forms of practical assistance in regions in transition. IWPR contributes to the resolution of conflict and to the strengthening of civil society, democracy, and the rule of law. It focuses on the Balkans, the Caucasus, and the Central Asian states, with additional projects elsewhere in Eastern Europe and the former Soviet Union. Comparative research projects consider the relationship between media and conflict in Africa, Asia, and Europe.

Name: Instituto Brasileiro de Analises Sociais e Economicas
Other Name: Instituto Brasileno de Analisis Socio
    Economico; Brazilian Institute for Social and Economic
    Analyses
Acronyms: IBASE
Languages: Portugese; Spanish; English
Address: Rua Visconde de Ouro Preto
             no.5—7o. andar—Botafogo 22250–180
             Rio de Janeiro RJ, Brasil
Telephone Number: (55–21) 553–0676
Fax Number: (55–21) 552–8796
Email: ibase@ax.apc.org
Web Page: http://www.ibase.br

The Brazilian Institute for Social and Economic Analyses (IBASE), founded in 1981, works to build a democratic society through the dissemination of information and knowledge. IBASE works with peoples' movements and devotes itself to defending human rights, the law, general welfare, and above all, the participation of all citizens (men and women) in developing democracy. IBASE encourages national and international networking between NGOs, and works to promote greater interaction between NGOs. It offers courses, consultancy, and training to other NGOs on software development, data processing, and communications. IBASE has also worked on projects for income generation, has created a database relevant to formulating policy in this area, and is working on a database to help evaluate the quality of life of Brazilians.

Name: Instituto de Defensa Legal
Other Name: Institute for Legal Defense
Acronyms: IDL; IDEELE
Languages: Spanish; English
Address: Toribio Polo 248
                Lima 18, Peru
Telephone Number: (51–1) 441–0192; 442–4037
Fax Number: (51–1) 441–6128; 221–1237
Email: ideele@idl.org.pe

The Instituto de Defensa Legal (IDL), organized in 1983, provides legal services to people whose rights have been violated as well as providing training to labor leaders. IDL also formulates legislation to promote the enforcement of peoples' rights. It provides legal assistance to political prisoners, and publishes and disseminates educational materials on human rights.

Name: Instituto Interamericano de Derechos Humanos
Other Name: Inter-American Institute of Human Rights
Acronyms: IIDH; IIHR
Language: Spanish
Address: Apartado 10.081–1000
                San José, Costa Rica
Telephone Number: (506) 234–0404
Fax Number: (506) 234–0955
Email: instituto@iidh.ed.cr, cediidh@sol.racsa.co.cr
Web Page: http://www.iidh.ed.cr

The Inter-American Institute of Human Rights (IIHR), founded in 1980, promotes and strengthens respect for human rights, and supports the consolidation of democracy through research, education, political mediation, technical assistance in the field of human rights, and through specialized publications.

Name: Instituto Latinoamericano de Servicios Legales
    Alternativos
Other Name: Latin American Institute for Alternative Legal
    Services
Acronyms: ILSA
Languages: Spanish; English
Address: ILSA, A.A. 077844
                Bogota, Colombia
Telephone Number: (57–1) 245–5955; 288–4437;
    288–4772; 288–3678; 288–0961; 288–0416
Fax Number: (57–1) 288–4854
Email: silsa@col1.telecom.com.co
Web Page: http://www.ilsa.org.co

The Instituto Latinoamericano de Servicios Legales Alternativos (ILSA), formed in 1978, supports and promotes a growing movement of innovative legal service agencies in Latin America and the Caribbean. ILSA serves as a point of encounter and reflection for NGOs from Mexico to Argentina that provide legal support services to community organizations in their struggle for social change. It promotes a comprehensive approach to the defense of human rights in the region and encourages the practice of law in the service of social change. ILSA runs programs in four areas: education for legal service agencies, communication, publication, and research. It maintains an extensive data bank on alternative legal practices and does research on issues relevant to the work of grassroots organizations and the legal services agencies that serve them.

Name: Institutt for Menneskerettigheter—Universitetet i
    Oslo
Other Name: Norwegian Institute of Human Rights—
    University of Oslo
Acronyms: NIHR
Languages: Norwegian; English
Address: Universitetsgaten 22/24
                N-0162 Oslo, Norway
Telephone Number: (47–22) 84–20–45
Fax Number: (47–22) 84–20–02
Email: betty.haugen@nihr.uio.no; admin@nihr.uio.no
Web Page: http://www.uio.no/www-misc/imr/index.html

The Norwegian Institute of Human Rights, founded in 1987, is a university institute devoted to research on human rights. The research activity is divided into four research programs: universalization of human rights with particular emphasis on the role of the UN; human rights and the Council of Europe; human rights and normative traditions; human rights and development. The Institute contributes to the realization of internationally recognized human rights worldwide, through research, teaching, advice and international activities, and documentation and information.

Name: InterAfrica Group: Centre for Dialogue on
    Humanitarian, Peace and Development Issues in the
    Horn of Africa
Language: English
Address: P.O. Box 1631
                Addis Ababa, Ethiopia
Telephone Number: (251–1) 518–790
Fax Number: (251–1) 517–554
Email: iag@telecom.net.et
Web Page: http://www.interafrica.org

The InterAfrica Group (IAG), established in 1991, is a center for dialogue on humanitarianism, peace, and development in the Horn of Africa. IAG is active with networks in the five countries of the Horn of Africa (Djibouti, Eritrea, Ethiopia, Somalia, and Sudan) IAG's three thematic areas of work are humanitarianism and peace-building, economic reform, and governance and democratic development. IAG also hosts the NGO Networking Service, a project dedicated to improving the flow of information between the North and South and to the enhanced capacity of indigenous civil society organizations in the Horn of Africa.

Name: Interights: The International Centre for the Legal
  Protection of Human Rights
Acronyms: INTERIGHTS
Language: English
Address: Lancaster House
  33 Islington High St.
  London N1 9LH, UK
Telephone Number: (44–171) 278–3230
Fax Number: (44–171) 278–4334
Email: ir@interights.org
Web Page: www.interights.org

The International Centre for the Legal Protection of Human Rights (INTERIGHTS), founded in 1982, provides leadership in the development of legal protection for human rights and freedoms through the effective use of international and comparative human rights law. INTERIGHTS helps judges, lawyers, practitioners, NGOs, and victims with the practical application of international and comparative human rights law in national, regional, and international courts and tribunals. It focuses on pursuing existing legal remedies to protect human rights.

Name: International Alert
Acronyms: IA
Address: 1 Glyn St.
  London SE11 5HT, UK
Telephone Number: (44–171) 793–8383
Fax Number: (44–171) 793–7975
Email: general@international-alert.org
Web Page: http://www.international-alert.org

International Alert (IA), founded in 1985, responds to violent conflict within countries and the subsequent abuse of individual and collective human rights in conflict situations by encouraging conflict resolution and peace-building efforts. IA works to identify and address the root causes of violence and contribute to the just and peaceful transformation of violent internal conflict. It seeks to strengthen the ability of people in conflict situations to make peace by facilitating dialogue at different levels and sectors of society in conflict; helping to develop and enhance local capacities—through, for example, funding or training, by facilitating peace-oriented development work amongst grassroots organizations and local peace-building initiatives; and, encouraging the international community to address the structural causes of conflict.

Name: International Centre for Human Rights and
  Democratic Development
Other Name: Centre international des droits de la personne
  et du developpement democratique; Centro Internacional
  de Derechos Humanos y Desarollo Democratico
Acronyms: ICHRDD; CIDPDD
Languages: English; French; Spanish
Address: 63, rue de Bresoles
  Suite 100
  Montreal, Quebec H2Y 1V7, Canada
Telephone Number: (1–514) 283–6073
Fax Number: (1–514) 283–3792
Email: ichrdd@ichrdd.ca
Web Page: http://www.ichrdd.ca

The International Centre for Human Rights and Democratic Development (ICHRDD), founded in 1988, is a Canadian institution with an international mandate. It works with citizens' groups and governments in Canada and abroad to promote human and democratic rights, as defined in the International Bill of Human Rights. ICHRDD's work emphasizes advocacy and capacity building. It provides political, financial, and technical support to many frontline human rights groups, indigenous peoples' groups, and democratic movements around the world. It advocates policy changes in national and international institutions, and strengthens the capacity of its partners to do the same. ICHRDD also assists the efforts of NGOs to gain access to multilateral institutions. It works to mainstream women's rights in human rights mechanisms. It brings together members of civil society and the State from different countries to discuss fundamental human rights and democratic development issues. It raises public awareness of human rights violations and sponsors research, publications, conferences, missions of enquiry, and other public events.

Name: International Centre for Trade Union Rights
Other Name: Centre international pour les droits syndicaux;
  Centro Internacional para los Derechos Sindicales
Acronyms: ICTUR; CIDS; CIDS
Languages: English; French; Spanish
Address: UCATT House
  177 Abbeville Road
  London SW4 9RL, UK
Telephone Number: (44–171) 498–4700
Fax Number: (44–171) 498–0611
Email: ictur@gn.apc.org
Web Page: http://www.ictur.labornet.org

The International Centre for Trade Union Rights (ICTUR), established in 1987, works to defend and extend the rights of trade unions and trade unionists around the world to collect information on and increase awareness of trade union rights and their violations. ICTUR carries out its activities in the spirit of the United Nations Charter, the Universal Declaration of Human Rights, the International Labor Organisation Conventions, and appropriate international treaties. It uses its influence to extend and strengthen the rights of trade unions in line with the above declarations.

Name: International Confederation of Free Trade Unions
Other Name: Confédération internationale des syndicats libres; Internationaler Bund Freier Gewerkschaften; Confederacion Internacional de Organizaciones Sindicales Libres
Acronyms: ICFTU; CISL; IBFG; CIOSL
Languages: English; French; German; Spanish
Address: 5 Boulevard du Roi Albert II
          Bte 1
          1210 Brussels, Belgium
Telephone Number: (32–2) 224–0211
Fax Number: (32–2) 201–5815
Email: internetpo@icftu.org, press@icftu.org, turigts@icftu.org
Web Page: http://www.icftu.org

The International Confederation of Free Trade Unions (ICFTU), founded in 1949, works to promote workers' rights through campaigns on issues such as the respect and defense of trade union and workers' rights, the eradication of forced and child labor, the promotion of equal rights for working women, the environment, education programs for trade unionists all over the world, and encouraging the organization of young workers. It also sends missions to investigate the trade union situation in many countries.

Name: International Commission of Jurists
Other Name: Commission internationale de juristes; Comision Internacional de Juristas; Centre for the Independence of Judges and Lawyers; Centre pour l'indépendance des magistrats et des avocats; Centro para la Independencia de Jueces y Abogados
Acronyms: ICJ; CIJ; CIJ; CIJL; CIMA; CIJA
Address: P.O. Box 216
          81 A Av. de Chatelaine
          CH-1219
          Chatelaine/Geneva Switzerland
Telephone Number: (41–22) 979–3800
Fax Number: (41–22) 979–3801; (41–22) 979–3824
Email: icjch@gn.apc.org, pandit@icj.org
Web Page: http://www.icj.org

The International Commission of Jurists (ICJ), founded in 1952, works to promote the understanding and observance of the rule of law, as well as the promotion and legal protection of human rights throughout the world. A special focus is the interdependence and interrelation of economic, social, cultural, civil, and political rights under the rule of law. The ICJ

has a network of independent national sections and affiliated legal organizations around the world. It created Centre for the Independence of Judges and Lawyers (CIJL) in 1978 to promote and protect the independence of the judiciary and the legal profession, and monitor and endeavor to protect the human rights of persons working in legal professions.

Name: International Committee of the Red Cross
Other Name: Comité international de la croix rouge; Comite Internacional de la Cruz Roja
Acronyms: ICRC; CICR; CICR
Languages: English; French; Spanish
Address: 19, avenue de la Paix
          CH-1202
          Geneva, Switzerland
Telephone Number: (41–22) 734–6001; 730–2529
Fax Number: (41–22) 734–8280; 733–2057; 730–2899; 730–2250
Email: mveuthey@icrc.org/webmaster.gva@gwn.icrc.org
Web Page: http://www.icrc.org/

The International Committee of the Red Cross (ICRC), founded in 1863, works to protect the lives and dignity of victims of war and internal violence, and to provide them with assistance. It directs and coordinates the international relief activities in situations of conflict. ICRC also endeavors to prevent suffering by promoting and strengthening humanitarian law and universal humanitarian principles.

Name: International Council on Human Rights Policy
Acronyms: ICHRP
Languages: English; French
Address: 48, chemin du Grand-Montfleury
          1290 Versoix, Switzerland
Telephone Number: (41–22) 775–3300
Fax Number: (41–22) 775–3303
Email: ichrp@international-council.org

The International Council on Human Rights Policy (ICHRP), founded in 1998, conducts applied research into current human rights issues. Its research is designed to be of practical relevance to policy-makers and practitioners in international and regional organizations, in governments and intergovernmental agencies, and in NGOs of all kinds.

Name: International Freedom of Expression Exchange
Other Name: Échange international de la liberté d'expression; Intercambio Internacional por la Libertad de Expresion
Acronyms: IFEX
Languages: English; French; Spanish
Address: IFEX
          489 College St., Suite 403
          Toronto, Ontario M6G 1A5, Canada
Telephone Number: (1–416) 515–9622

Fax Number: (1–416) 515–7879
Email: ifex@ifex.org
Web Page: http://www.ifex.org

The International Freedom of Expression exchange (IFEX), founded in 1992, works to link freedom of expression groups around the world, largely through the Internet. One of the central components of IFEX is the Action Alert Network (AAN), which reports free expression abuses in geographic regions or area of expertise to IFEX for circulation to other members and interested organizations all over the world. IFEX also supports and strengthens fledgling freedom of expression around the world.

Name: International Gay and Lesbian Human Rights
      Commission
Other Name: Comision Internacional Por Los Derechos
      Humanos de Gays y Lesbianas; Internationale
      Kommission fur Schwule & Lesbische Menschenrechte
Acronyms: IGLHRC
Languages: English; Spanish; French; Vietnamese; Portuguese; Russian; German
Address: 1360 Mission St., Suite 200
          San Francisco, CA 94103, USA
Telephone Number: (1–415) 255–8680
Fax Number: (1–415) 255–8662
Email: iglhrc@iglhrc.org
Web Page: http://www.iglhrc.org

The International Gay and Lesbian Human Rights Commission (IGLHRC), founded in 1990, works to protect and advance human rights of all people and communities subject to discrimination or abuse on the basis of sexual orientation, gender identity, or HIV status. IGLHRC responds to such human rights violations around the world through training and workshops, particularly for activists from the developing world and by providing legal documentation, referrals, and other types of support services to those fleeing persecution on the basis of sexual orientation, gender identity, or HIV sero-status. It also works to make governments and other human rights organizations more aware of the rights of their lesbian and gay citizens. IGLHRC also serves as an information clearinghouse on grassroots gay and lesbian and AIDS groups worldwide.

Name: International Helsinki Federation for Human Rights
Other Name: Fédération internationale Helsinki pour les
      droits de l'homme
Acronyms: IHF
Language: English
Address: Rummelhardtgasse 2/18
          A-1090 Vienna, Austria
Telephone Number: (43–1) 408–8822
Fax Number: (43–1) 408–8822–50
Email: office@ihf-hr.org, helsinki@ping.at
Web Page: http://www.ihf-hr.org/

The International Helsinki Federation for Human Rights (IHF), founded in 1982, seeks to promote compliance of the states participating in the Organization for Security and Cooperation in Europe with the human rights provisions to which they committed themselves in the Helsinki Final Act and its follow-up documents, as well as with relevant international law. The IHF provides a structure through which independent Helsinki committees support one another and strengthen the human rights movement by giving their efforts an international dimension. The IHF is involved in fact-finding missions, trial and election monitoring, briefings for international organizations and the media, and the production of reports based on the work of local civil organizations.

Name: International Indian Treaty Council
Other Name: Consejo Internacional de los Tratados Indios
Acronyms: IITC; CITI
Languages: English; Spanish
Address: Information Office
          2390 Mission St., Ste. 301
          San Francisco, CA 94110, USA
Telephone Number: (1–415) 641–4482
Fax Number: (1–415) 512–1507
Email: iitc@igc.apc.org
Web Page: http://www.treatycouncil.org/

The International Indian Treaty Council (IITC), founded in 1974, is an organization of Indigenous Peoples from North, Central, and South America and the Pacific working for the sovereignty and self-determination of Indigenous Peoples and the recognition and protection of Indigenous Rights, Traditional Cultures, and Sacred Lands. IITC supports grassroots indigenous struggles through information dissemination, networking, coalition building, technical assistance, organizing and facilitating the effective participation of traditional peoples in local, regional, national, and international fora, events, and gatherings. It also provides training and leadership development to representatives of Indigenous communities, including youth, and monitors human rights complaints filed on behalf of indigenous peoples facing violations of their freedom of religion, forced relocations, arbitrary detentions, and other crisis situations.

Name: International Institute for Democracy and Electoral
      Assistance
Acronyms: International IDEA
Language: English
Address: Strömsborg
          103 34 Stockholm, Sweden
Telephone Number: (46–8) 698–3700
Fax Number: (46–8) 20–24–22
Email: info@idea.int
Web Page: http://www.int-idea.se

The International Institute for Democracy and Electoral Assistance (International IDEA), created in 1995, promotes and advances sustainable democracy, and improves and consolidates electoral processes worldwide. It provides a forum for discussions and action among individuals and organizations involved in democracy promotion. Global in ownership and scope, it is independent of national interests. It works to promote and advance sustainable democracy worldwide by broadening the understanding and promoting the implementation of the norms, rules, and guidelines that apply to multiparty pluralism and democratic processes. It also undertakes election monitoring and works to ensure that gender equity is observed in election rules and regulations as well as practices.

Name: International Institute for Human Rights,
    Environment and Development
Acronyms: INHURED International
Languages: English; Nepali
Address: P.O. Box 12684
           Pulchowk
           Lalitpur, Nepal
Telephone Number: (977–1) 520054; 520042
Fax Number: (977–1) 520042; 521180
Email: info@inhured.wlink.com.np

The International Institute for Human Rights, Environment and Development (INHURED International) was established in 1987. INHURED International has a regional focus and promotes human rights education, research, and effective representation before international forums, and peaceful environment and sustainable development. It works to establish and strengthen national and regional human rights instruments in the Asia-Pacific region, and addresses the human rights concerns of women, children, refugees, the disabled, "untouchables," and indigenous peoples. It exposes the adverse impacts of international financial institutions' policies on civil, political, economic, social, and cultural rights and the right to development. INHURED International's activities include electoral observation, training, and monitoring; organizing special internship and fellowship programs for international and Nepali students and scholars; and initiating and organizing regional and international conferences and public hearings.

Name: International League for Human Rights
Acronyms: ILHR
Language: English
Address: 432 Park Avenue South, Rm. 1103
           New York, NY 10016, USA
Telephone Number: (1–212) 684–1221
Fax Number: (1–212) 684–1696
Email: info@ilhr.org
Web Page: http://ilhr.org

The International League for Human Rights (ILHR), founded in 1942, works to keep human rights at the forefront of inter-

national affairs and to give meaning and effect to the human rights values enshrined in international human rights treaties and conventions. ILHR defends individual human rights advocates who have risked their lives to promote the ideals of a just and civil society in their homelands. It also raises human rights issues and cases before the UN and other intergovernmental regional organizations in partnership with colleagues abroad, helping to amplify their voices and coordinate strategies for effective human rights protection.

Name: International Movement Against All Forms of
    Discrimination and Racism
Acronyms: IMADR
Language: English
Address: International Secretariat
           3–5–11 Roppongi, Minato-Ku
           Tokyo 106, Japan
Telephone Number: (81–3) 35–86–74–47
Fax Number: (81–3) 35–86–74–62
Email: imadris@imadr.org
Web Page: http://www.imadr.org

The International Movement Against All Forms of Discrimination and Racism (IMADR), founded in 1988, has a global network with regional committees devoted to eliminating all forms of discrimination around the world. It works to forge international solidarity among discriminated minorities and advance the international regime of human rights through networking and appeal campaigns, conferences, research, and publication, and international advocacy at the international, regional, and national levels.

Name: International Network for Girls
Acronyms: INfG
Language: English
Address: NGO Working Groups on Girls
           UNICEF—3 UN Plaza, TA 24A
           New York, NY 10017, USA
Telephone Number: (1–212) 824–6394
Fax Number: (1–212) 824–6482
Email: sfriedman@unicef.org
Web Page: http://www.girlsrights.org

The International Network for Girls (INfG), established in 1995 by the UN Working Group on Girls, works to bring together grassroots organizations from around the world who are working to promote and protect the rights of girls.

Name: International PEN
Other Name: Writers in Prison Committee
Acronyms: PEN
Address: 9/10 Charter House Buildings
           Goswell Road
           London, EC1M 7AT, UK
Telephone Number: (44–171) 253–4306

Fax Number: (44–171) 253–5711
Email: intpen@gn.apc.org

International PEN, founded in 1921, works to promote and maintain friendship and intellectual cooperation between men and women of letters in all countries in the interests of literature, freedom of expression, and international goodwill. PEN works to obtain the release of imprisoned writers and mobilize public opinion on issues of freedom of expression. The PEN Writers in Prison Committee was set up in 1960, with the aim of obtaining the release of imprisoned writers.

Name: International Women's Rights Action Watch
Acronyms: IWRAW
Languages: English; French; Spanish; Polish
Address: c/o Hubert Humphrey Institute of Public Affairs
        University of Minnesota
        301–19th Ave. South
        Minneapolis, MN 55455, USA
Telephone Number: (1–612) 625–5093
Fax Number: (1–612) 624–0068
Email: iwraw@hhh.umn.edu
Web Page: http://www.igc.org/iwraw/

The International Women's Rights Action Watch (IWRAW), organized in 1985, monitors the implementation of the Convention on the Elimination of All Forms of Discrimination Against Women (the CEDAW Convention). IWRAW is an international network that focuses on the advancement of women's human rights. It is served by a resource and communications center based at the University of Minnesota's Humphrey Institute of Public Affairs. It provides technical assistance and research support for women's human rights projects such as law reform, policy advocacy, and monitoring government performance under international human rights treaties, and establishes connections with others who share the concern of implementing women's human rights. IWRAW also concentrates on supporting NGOs, especially in developing countries, in their efforts to change law, culture, and society so that women can fully participate in their countries' development.

Name: International Women's Rights Action Watch—Asia
    Pacific
Acronyms: IWRAW
Language: English
Address: 2nd Floor
        Blk F, Anjung Felda, Jl. Maktab
        5400 Kuala Lumpur, Malaysia
Telephone Number: (60–3) 291–3292
Fax Number: (60–3) 292–4203
Email: iwraw@po.jaring.my
Web Page: http://www.womenasia.com/iwraw/index.htm

The International Women's Rights Action Watch—Asia Pa-

cific (IWRAW–Asia Pacific), was formed in 1993, to monitor the Convention on the Elimination of All Forms of Discrimination Against Women (the CEDAW Convention) implementation and provide training and public education on using the Convention effectively in policy-making in the Asia Pacific region. IWRAW-Asia Pacific is part of the international (IWRAW) network of activists, scholars, and organizations that focuses on the advancement of women's human rights that is based in the United States.

Name: International Women's Tribune Centre
Acronyms: IWTC
Languages: English; French; Spanish
Address: 777 United Nations Plaza
        New York, NY 10017, USA
Telephone Number: (1–212) 687–8633
Fax Number: (1–212) 661–2704
Email: iwtc@igc.apc.org
Web Page: http://www.womenink.org/iwtc.hmtl

The International Women's Tribune Centre (IWTC), founded in 1976, works by responding to requests from women in the Third World for information and technical assistance related to women and development activities. IWTC promotes increased participation of women in shaping and redefining a development process that is participatory, holistic, and inclusive. The four sector areas it concentrates on are information, communication, and networking; science, technology, and environment; community economic development; and organizing women (including women's human rights).

Name: Internationale Gesellschaft für Menschenrechte
Other Name: International Society for Human Rights;
    Societe internationale pour les droits de l'homme;
    Sociedad Internacional para los Derechos Humanos;
    Associazione Internazionale per i Diritti dell'Umo
Acronyms: IGFM; ISHR; SIDH; SEDH; AIDU
Languages: German; English; French; Spanish; Russian
Address: Borsigallee 16
        D-60388
        Frankfurt-am-Main, Germany
Telephone Number: (49–69) 420–1080
Fax Number: (49–69) 420–10829
Email: is@ishr.org
Web Page: http://www.ishr.org, http://www.igfm.de

The International Society for Human Rights (ISHR), founded in 1972, seeks to promote international understanding and tolerance in all areas of culture and society. ISHR was founded in order to support individuals who share this principle and, consequently, strive nonviolently for their rights. It does this through help with individual cases, creating public awareness through publications, and assisting with development projects and humanitarian aid.

Name: ISIS International-Manila
Acronyms: ISIS
Address: P.O. Box 1837
         Quezon City Main
         Quezon City 1100, Philippines
Telephone Number: (63–2) 435–3405; 435–3408;
    436–0312; 436–7863
Fax Number: (632) 924–1065
Email: isis@isiswomen.org
Web Page: http://www.isiswomen.org

ISIS International, founded in 1974, is dedicated to women's information and communication needs. ISIS works to document ideas and visions and create channels of communication. It collects and shares information. Through networking and building links, it focuses on advancing women's rights, leadership, and empowerment in Asia and the Pacific. With connections in over 150 countries, it also monitors changing trends and analyses concerning women worldwide.

Name: Isis: Women's International Cross-Cultural Exchange
Acronyms: ISIS-WICCE
Language: English
Address: P.O. Box 4934
         Kampala, Uganda
Telephone Number: (256–41) 543–953
Fax Number: (256–41) 543–954
Email: isis@starcom.co.ug
Web Page: http://www.isis.or.ug

Isis-Women's International Cross Culture Exchange (ISIS-WICCE) is an action oriented women's resource center, started in 1974 in Switzerland and relocated to Uganda in 1993 to better gather information concerning African women and make it more accessible and available to women worldwide. ISIS-WICCE works to communicate ideas, create solidarity networks, and share information to overcome gender-related inequalities. ISIS-WICCE is committed to the empowerment of women in order to promote equality, development, and peace through providing opportunities to women globally to share experiences and access to information, and to network with one another.

Name: Kenya Human Rights Commission
Acronyms: KHRC
Language: English
Address: P.O. Box 41079
         Nairobi, Kenya
Telephone Number: (254–2) 574–998; 574–999; 576–066
Fax Number: (254–2) 574–997
Email: khrc@AfricaOnline.Co.Ke
Web Page: http://www.hri.ca/partners/khrc/

The Kenya Human Rights Commission (KHRC), established in 1992, operates in Kenya as an advocacy and monitoring organization. It is based in both the USA and Kenya as an attempt to link Kenya fully in the international struggle for human rights. KHRC seeks to incorporate human rights ideals into institutions of governance. KHRC monitors the human rights situation in Kenya and the Kenyan government's observance of human rights. It promotes public awareness through dissemination of information, undertakes human rights litigation, and analyzes current and proposed legislation to ensure that human rights concerns are not undermined. KHRC also conducts research and organizes seminars and conferences, as well as maintaining a human rights library and resource center. It works as part of a legal/human rights NGO network.

Name: Korea Human Rights Network
Acronyms: KOHRNET
Language: Korean
Address: 592–7 Changshin 2–dong
         Jongro-gu
         Seoul 110–542, Korea
Telephone Number: (82–2) 763–2606
Fax Number: (82–2) 745–5604
Email: minbyun@jinbo.net; gyusum@chollian.net

The Korea Human Rights Network (KOHRNET), founded in 1994, is composed of nine local human rights organizations in South Korea. KOHRNET is committed to the realization of true democracy and human rights. Its objectives are to: coordinate and consult on current human rights issues, collect and distribute information on human rights, promote human rights education, and participate in international solidarity human rights work. KOHRNET provides NGOs in Korea with consultation services and advice in human rights matters, disseminates human rights information, engages in human rights educational work, and creates international linkages.

Name: Law and Society Trust
Acronyms: LST
Address: No. 3 Kynsey Terrace
         Colombo 8, Sri Lanka
Telephone Number: (94–1) 691–228; 684–845
Fax Number: (94–1) 686–843

The Law Society and Trust (LST), established in 1982, studies law and social change, particularly in the field of legal processes and institutions. LST researches, advocates, documents through fact-finding, media programs, and lectures as well as trains paralegals.

Name: Lawyers Committee for Human Rights
Acronyms: LCHR
Language: English
Address: Lawyers Committee for Human Rights
         333 Seventh Ave., 13th Floor
         New York, NY 10001–5004, USA

Telephone Number: (1–212) 845–5200
Fax Number: (1–212) 845–5299
Email. lclubin@lchr.org
Web Page: http://www.lchr.org

The Lawyers Committee for Human Rights (LCHR), founded in 1978, works to protect and promote fundamental human rights by building the legal institutions and structures that will guarantee human rights in the long term. LCHR supports independent human rights advocacy at the local level and seeks to influence the U.S. government to promote the rule of law in both its foreign and domestic policy, and presses for greater integration of human rights into the work of the UN and the World Bank. LCHR also works to protect refugees through the representation of asylum seekers and by challenging legal restrictions on the rights of refugees in the United States and around the world.

Name: Lawyers for Human Rights
Acronyms: LHR
Language: English
Address: Kutlwanong Democracy Centre
   357 Visagie Street
   cnr Visagie and Prinsloo Streets
   Pretoria 0002, South Africa
Telephone Number: (27–12) 320–2943/5, 622–5550
Fax Number: (27–12) 320–2949
Email: lhrpta@wn.apc.org
Web Page: http://www.lhr.org.za

Lawyers for Human Rights (LHR), established in 1979, works to ensure the creation of an independent and impartial judiciary in South Africa. It also monitors and prevents human rights violations in South Africa, eradicates all forms of discrimination, and promotes participatory democracy. LHR offers legal services to victims of human rights abuse. National projects include law reform, paralegal training, human rights education, disability rights, housing rights, and women's rights.

Name: Legal Assistance Centre
Acronyms: LAC
Language: English
Address: P.O. Box 604
   Windhoek 9000, Namibia
Telephone Number: (264–61) 22–33–56
Fax Number: (264–61) 23–49–53
Email: legal@iafrica.com.na

The Legal Assistance Centre (LAC), a public interest law firm, commenced operations in 1988, simultaneously with the opening of the Human Rights Documentation Centre (HRDC) a paralegal advice office in Northern Namibia. The LAC and HRDC provide services to persons who would otherwise have to travel hundreds of miles in order to obtain legal assistance. LAC and its affiliated advice offices take on cases in the public interest in which the outcome may have an impact on the rights of a group of people, rather than cases that merely benefit an individual. It runs a legal education project that educates communities about their rights in terms of the constitution and about various areas of law that affect them on a day-to-day basis. It is also involved in constitutional test cases, focusing on such areas as the equality clause in the constitution together with the affirmative action clause and the declared Principles of State Policy, which may be invoked in asserting the rights of women and redressing present imbalances. LAC provides litigation and advice and works to make the Labor Act accessible to the public. LAC is also engaged in police education and training, and on questions concerning the status of refugees, victims of HIV/AIDS, and reform of criminal law and justice.

Name: Legal Resources Centre
Acronyms: LRC
Language: English
Address: LRC
   P.O. Box 157
   WITS 2050, South Africa
Telephone Number: (27–11) 403–7694
Fax Number: (27–11) 403–1058
Email: bongani@lrc.org.za

The Legal Resources Centre (LRC), a public interest law firm/ NGO, was established in 1979. It concentrates on test case litigation, social and economic rights, and above all, land rights. The LRC runs a fellowship program for the training of candidate attorneys that aims to increase access to the legal profession by disadvantaged groups, as well as increasing the experience and commitment of the legal profession to public interest law.

Name: Legal Resources Foundation
Acronyms: LRF
Address: P.O. Box 918
   Harare, Zimbabwe
Telephone Number: (263–4) 728–212
Fax Number: (263–4) 728–213
Email: lrfhre@mail.pci.co.2w

The Legal Resources Foundation (LRF), founded in 1984, provides legal assistance to indigent victims and promotes human rights. It conducts a number of comprehensive training programs, particularly for human rights workers from around Africa and provides personnel to carry out in-country training programs for other groups. The LRF also conducts paralegal education and law enforcement programs. LRF publishes human rights materials, and contributes regularly to debates on legislation and other matters of a public interest nature. LRF has established branches in Bulawayo, Gweru, Masvingo, and Mutare.

Name: Lembaga Penelitian, Pendidikan dan Penerangan
    Ekonomi dan Sosial
Other Name: Institute for Economic and Social Research,
    Education and Information
Acronyms: LP3ES
Language: Bahasa Indonesia
Address: P.O. Box 493 JKT
        Jakarta 100002, Indonesia
Telephone Number: (62–21) 597–211

The Institute for Economic and Social Research, Education
and Information (LP3ES), established in 1971, encourages
development policies that emphasize equitable development
and widen the institutional base for participation. LP3ES promotes the advancement of economic and social sciences to
foster the sociocultural development and human rights of the
Indonesian people through research, education, and information activities. It works to improve the public's knowledge
and understanding about Indonesian development problems
and promote international cooperation with national and international organizations that have similar objectives. The
Institute conducts research on social problems related to the
development of human resources in regional, rural, and small
urban centers, and in marginal settlement areas. LP3ES also
publishes research and project reports, monographs, training
guidebooks, and other materials on sociocultural issues; holds
seminars and workshops for research workers, policy-makers,
action groups, and community leaders. The documentation,
library, and information services produce select bibliogra-
phies and documentation in such fields as small-scale industry, rural technology, and community development work.

Name: Liga Española Pro-Derechos Humanos
Other Name: Spanish League for Human Rights
Acronyms: LEPDDHH
Language: Spanish
Address: C/Hermosilla 114 Sótano A
        28009 Madrid, Spain
Telephone Number: (34–91) 401–9695
Fax Number: (34–91) 401–9695
Email: lepddhh@lander.es
Web Page: http://www.lander.es/~lepddhh/index.html

The Spanish League for Human Rights (LEPDDHH), founded
in 1913, works to defend and monitor human rights and fundamental freedoms in Spain and Latin America. It participates
in congresses and conferences, and publishes information on
abuses.

Name: Ligue internationale contre le racisme et
    l'antisémitisme
Other Name: International League Against Racism and
    Antisemitism
Acronyms: LICRA

Languages: French; Spanish; English
Address: 42, rue du Louvre
        F-15001 Paris, France
Telephone Number: (33–1) 45–08–08–08
Fax Number: (33–1) 45–08–18–18
Email: licra@club-internet.com
Web Page: http://www.licra.com

The International League Against Racism and Antisemitism
(LICRA), founded in 1927, works to oppose racism and anti-
Semitism, and defends the rights of victims to peace and ex-
istence around the world.

Name: Ligue mauritanienne des droits de l'homme
Other Name: Mauritanian League for Human Rights
Acronyms: LMDH
Address: Avenue Gamal Abdel Nasser
        B.P. 20023
        Nouakchott, Mauritania
Telephone Number: (22–22) 576–24
Fax Number: (22–22) 517–11

The Mauritanian League for Human Rights (LMDH), established in 1986, works to promote respect for human rights by
sensitizing public opinion on the human rights situation, de-
nouncing rights abuse, and working with the press.

Name: Ludwig Boltzmann Institut fur Menschenrechte
Other Name: Ludwig Boltzmann Institute of Human
    Rights
Acronyms: BIM
Languages: German; English
Address: Hessgasse 1
        A-1010 Vienna, Austria
Telephone Number: (43–1) 42–77; 27–420
Fax Number: (43–1) 42–77; 27–429
Email: bim.staatsrecht@univie.ac.at
Web Page: http://www.univie.ac.at/bim

The Ludwig Boltzmann Institute of Human Rights (BIM) was
founded in 1992 in Vienna as a center for documentation, research, and information services on human rights. BIM maintains databases on the legal systems and de facto human rights
situations in all countries of the world. In addition, it conducts
programming in a number of areas including actions against
torture, war crimes, and deportation issues. It also conducts
peacekeeping and peace-building training programs and university courses on human rights.

Name: Médecins sans frontières—International
Other Name: Doctors Without Borders—International
Acronyms: MSF
Languages: French; English
Address: 39, rue de la Tourelle
        B-1040 Brussels, Belgium

Telephone Number: (32–2) 280–1881
Fax Number: (32–2) 280–0173
Email: office-intnl@brussels.msf.org
Web Page: http://www.msf.org

Doctors Without Borders—International (MSF), founded in 1971, provides emergency medical assistance to populations in danger. Part of MSF's work is to address any violations of basic human rights encountered by field teams, violations perpetrated or sustained by political actors. It does so by confronting the responsible actors themselves, by putting pressure on them through mobilization of the international community, and by issuing information publicly.

Name: Memorial Human Rights Center
Other Name: Memorial Society for Public Historical
    Enlightenment, Human Rights and Charity
Language: Russian
Address: P.O. Box 552
              Moscow 125057, Russia
Telephone Number: (7–095) 200–6506; 209–7883
Fax Number: (7–095) 209–5779
Email: memhrcenter@gas.apc.org

The Memorial Human Rights Center (Memorial) began in 1987. Memorial has a broad humanitarian program. It works to overcome the effects of totalitarianism in Soviet consciousness; promote democratic, humanitarian views and traditions; and defend human rights. Memorial monitors and reports on human rights violations in Russia and throughout the former Soviet Union. It sends missions to "hot points" of interethnic conflict to observe and disseminate information about human rights violations. It participates in negotiation processes when invited to do so by parties to the conflict, and conducts other forms of third-party mediation. Memorial also does human rights education, provides assistance to political prisoners, and works in the rehabilitation of torture victims.

Name: Minnesota Advocates for Human Rights
Acronyms: MAHR
Language: English
Address: 310 Fourth Ave. South
              Suite 1000
              Minneapolis, MN, 55415–1012, USA
Telephone Number: (1–612) 341–3302
Fax Number: (1–612) 341–2971
Email: mnadvocates@igc.apc.org
Web Page: http://www.mnadvocates.org

Minnesota Advocates for Human Rights (MAHR), founded in 1983, is dedicated to the promotion and protection of internationally recognized human rights. MAHR is committed to enabling individuals and communities to realize their fundamental human rights and responsibilities through programs and projects that integrate human rights fact finding, advocacy, and education. It works locally, nationally, and internationally on human rights issues impacting children, women, refugees and immigrants, and marginalized populations. MHRA documents human rights abuses, advocates on behalf of individual victims, educates on human rights issues, and provides training and technical assistance to address and prevent human rights violations.

Name: Minority Rights Group International
Acronyms: MRG
Language: English
Address: 379 Brixton Road
              London SW9 7DE, UK
Telephone Number: (44–020) 7978–9498
Fax Number: (44–171) 738–6265
Email: minority.rights@mrgmail.org
Web Page: http://www.minorityrights.org

Minority Rights Group International (MRG), founded in 1965, works in four main areas to promote and further minority rights worldwide. It researches and publicizes information about minorities around the world; advocates for the rights of minorities at the United Nations (UN) and governments; educates children and teachers on minority issues to counter racism and prejudice; works with organizations and activists to build alliances, discusses ideas, and develops skills. MRG undertakes regional projects that promote the rights of ethnic, religious, and linguistic minority groups and foster intercommunity cooperation.

Name: Movimento de Justica e Direitos Humanos
Other Name: Movimiento de Justicia y Derechos Humanos;
    Movement for Justice and Human Rights
Acronyms: MJDH
Languages: Portugese; Spanish; English
Address: Rua Andrade Neves
              159/conjunto 102, Porto Alegre
              RS, 90010–210, Brasil
Telephone Number: (55–51) 221–9130
Fax Number: (55–51) 221–9130
Email: mjdh@hotmail.com
Web Page: http://www.direitoshumanos.org.br/

Movement for Justice and Human Rights (MJDH), founded in 1979, works to promote and protect fundamental human rights of Latin Americans. It works for community justice and returning disappeared children in the region. It also works to educate and protect journalists and academics on human rights issues.

Name: Movimento Nacional de Defesa dos Direitos
    Humanos
Other Name: Movimiento Nacional de Defensa de los
    Derechos Humanos; National Movement for the Defense
    of Human Rights
Acronyms: MNDDH

Languages: Portugese; Spanish; English
Address: SCS Ed. Oscar Niemeyer
         Quadra 02, Bloco D
         7031690 Brasilia D.F., Brasil
Telephone Number: (55–61) 225–3337
Fax Number: (55–61) 225–7157

The National Movement for Human Rights (MNDDH), founded in 1982, supports agrarian and urban reform, combats police violence, and reports on human rights developments. MNDDH works for cultural, economic, and social rights of the exploited majority and devastated minority of the Brazilian population by organizing and informing people to increase their awareness of the oppressed situation in which the majority of the population finds itself. It also works for the protection of human rights, including also the punishment of those responsible for human rights violations, and reparation payments to victims and to overcome institutional, partisan, and religious interests and all forms of discrimination. MNDDH has projects in the rural, indigenous, and urban areas, and deals with issues related to housing, transportation, health, education, communication, racism, and ecology. It also encourages political participation and human rights education.

Name: National Coalition for Haitian Rights
Acronyms: NCHR
Address: 275 7th Ave., 25th floor
         New York, NY 10001–6708, USA
Telephone Number: (1–212) 337–0005
Fax Number: (1–212) 337–0028
Email: insight@nchr.org
Web Page: www.nchr.org

The National Coalition for Haitian Rights (NCHR), founded in 1982, works to promote and protect the rights of Haitian refugees and Haitian Americans under U.S. and international law. NCHR also works to advance respect for human rights, rule of law, and the development of civil and democratic society in Haiti.

Name: National Council for Civil Liberties
Other Name: Liberty
Acronyms: NCCL
Language: English
Address: 21 Tabard St.
         London SE1 4LA, UK
Telephone Number: (44–171) 403–3888
Fax Number: (44–171) 407–5354
Email: Email: liberty@apc.org.uk
Web Page: http://www.liberty-human-rights.org.uk

The National Council for Civil Liberties (NCCL), founded in 1934, works to defend and extend the civil and political rights of people in Britain. ACCL provides advice and information on rights issues, analyzes implications of proposed changes to legislation. It also researches a wide range of rights issues, including the need for privacy laws, civil liberties issues in Europe, misuse of the criminal records system, the operation of the Prevention of Terrorism Act, the variations in sentencing in different courts, and proposals for a national identity card system.

Name: Network of East-West Women
Acronyms: NEWW
Language: English
Address: 1601 Connecticut Ave. NW
         Suite 701
         Washington, DC 20009, USA
Telephone Number: (1–202) 265–3585
Fax Number: (1–202) 265–3508
Email: eastwest@neww.org
Web Page: http://www.neww.org

The Network of East-West Women (NEWW), founded in 1990, links over 2,000 women's advocates in more than 40 countries who work in partnership to promote tolerance, democracy, nonviolence, health, and respect for institutions of a civil society. NEWW works to empower women and girls throughout the East (Central and Eastern Europe, the NIS, and the Russian Federation) and the West by dialogue, networking, campaigns, and educational and informational exchanges. NEWW supports action and joint projects inspired by feminist principles. It also coordinates ad hoc committees, training workshops, consultations, conferences, and informational exchanges.

Name: Observatoire international des prisons
Other Name: International Prison Watch; Observatorio
    Internacional de Prisiones
Acronyms: OIP
Languages: French; English; Spanish
Address: 16, avenue Berthelot
         B.P. 7083
         69301 Lyon cedex 07, France
Telephone Number: (33–4) 72–71–83–83
Fax Number: (33–4) 78–58–72–11
Email: 100536,153@compuserve.com
Web Page: http://www.oip.org

International Prison Watch (OIP), founded in 1990, keeps watch throughout the world on the custodial conditions of prisoners, and draws attention to any human rights violations. OIP publishes a yearly report reviewing conditions in prisons and treatment of prisoners worldwide. It also provides training to human rights advocates who want to undertake missions to prisons.

Name: L'Observatoire pour la protection des défenseurs des
    droits de l'homme
Other Name: The Observatory for the Protection of Human
    Rights Defenders; El Observatorio para la Proteccion de
    los Defensores de Derechos Humanos

Languages: English; French; Spanish
Address: c/o FIDH, 17
        Passages de droits de l'homme
        75011 Paris, France
        c/o OMCT, CP 119
        37–39 rue de Vermont
        CH 1211 Geneve, 20 CIC, Switzerland
Telephone Number: (33–1) 48–05–82–46;
   (41–22) 733–3140
Fax Number: (33–1) 40–39–22–42
Email: observatoire@iprolink.ch
Web Page: http://www.fidh.imaginet.fr, http://www.omct.org

The Observatory for the Protection of Human Rights Defenders, established as a joint project of OMCT and FIDH in 1997, responds to the grave violations and contributes to the protection of human rights defenders at the national and international levels. It works to alert the international community by sending out urgent appeals; assembles all the information concerning the situation of these activists (an emergency hot line is at their disposal 24 hours a day); organizes inquiry missions in countries where the activities of human rights activists are increasingly threatened, and any other activity relating to the protection of human rights defenders.

Name: Organisation mondiale contre la torture
Other Name: Organizacion Mundial Contra la Tortura;
    World Organization Against Torture; Weltorganisation
    Gegen die Folter
Acronyms: OMCT
Languages: French; English; Spanish
Address: C.P. 21, 8, ruc du Vicux-Billard
        CH-1211
        Geneva 8, Switzerland
Telephone Number: (41–22) 809–49–39
Fax Number: (41–22) 809–49–29
Email: omct@omct.org
Web Page: http://www.omct.org

The World Organization Against Torture (OMCT), founded in 1986, is a network of national organizations that fight to bring an end to torture and other serious human rights violations. Fighting for the rights of victims, OMCT provides its members with tools and services they need to carry out their work: to seek to prevent torture, confront torturers, bring them to justice, and provide rehabilitation to victims.

Name: Orville H. Schell, Jr. Center for International Human
    Rights
Language: English
Address: Yale Law School
        P.O. Box 208215
        New Haven, CT 06520–8215, USA
Telephone Number: (1–203) 432–7480

Fax Number: (1–203) 432–1040
Email: james.silk@yale.edu
Web Page: http://humanrights.law.yale.edu/

The Orville H. Schell, Jr. Center for International Human Rights, established at Yale Law School in 1989, is an interdisciplinary research organization that seeks to provide a broad conceptual framework for the day-to-day concerns of human rights advocates for both practitioners in the area of international human rights and scholars studying international human rights. The Center aims to integrate scholarship in a range of disciplines with the insights of human rights advocates from around the world to develop a comprehensive, realistic understanding of international human rights problems. The Schell Center's program has three components: scholarship, curriculum, and outreach. The Center encourages education related to international human rights at the undergraduate, graduate, and professional levels. It has a database of human rights documents.

Name: Peace Brigades International
Other Name: Brigades de paix internationale; Brigades
    Internacionales de Paz
Acronyms: PBI; BPI; BIP
Language: English, French; Spanish
Address: 5 Caledonia Road
        London N1 9DX, UK
Telephone Number: (44–171) 713–0392
Fax Number: (44–171) 837–2290
Email: pbiio@gn.apc.org
Web Page: http://www.igc.apc.org/pbi

Peace Brigades International (PBI), founded in 1981, works to research and implement nonviolent approaches to peacekeeping and human rights support. PBI provides protective international accompaniment for individuals and organizations who have been threatened by political violence or who are otherwise at risk. This enables local activists to work for social justice and human rights. In addition to protective accompaniment, PBI also trains people in nonviolence, conflict resolution, and human rights; fosters social and political reconciliation; documents conflicts and initiatives for peace and distributes this information worldwide.

Name: Penal Reform International
Other Name: National Association for the Care and
    Resettlement of Offenders
Acronyms: PRI
Languages: English; French
Address: Unit 114, The Chandlery
        50 Westminster Bridge Road
        London, SE1 7QY, UK
Telephone Number: (44–171) 721–7678
Fax Number: (44–171) 721–8785

Email: headofsecretariat@pri.org.uk
Web Page: http:/www.penalreform.org

Penal Reform International (PRI), founded in 1989, works on problems in penal systems. PRI strengthens the efforts of penal reformers by working together across national boundaries and having a presence in international forums. PRI promotes humane treatment of offenders according to international instruments and the elimination of racial, class, and ethnic discrimination in penal measures. It tries to reduce the use of prison throughout the world, and to replace prison whenever possible by constructive alternatives that are meaningful to victims and to abolish the death penalty.

Name: Parliamentary Human Rights Group
Acronyms: PHRG
Language: English
Address: House of Commons
              London SW1P OPW, UK
Telephone Number: (44–171) 219–6609; 274–4617
Fax Number: (44–171) 219–5943; 219–5943
Email: 104125.1657@compuserve.com

The Parliamentary Human Rights Group (PHRG) was founded in 1976 as an independent forum in the British Parliament concerned with the defense of international human rights. Members of the group represent all political parties, making it broadly representative. The objectives of PHRC are to increase awareness of human rights in Parliament as well as throughout the UK and abroad; communicate the group's concerns about human rights violations to governments, their representatives in the UK and visiting delegations; and to work for the implementation by all governments of the Universal Declaration of Human Rights, and of the UN covenants on civil, political, economic, social, and cultural rights.

Name: People's Decade of Human Rights Education
Acronyms: PDHRE-International
Language: English
Address: 526 West 111th St.
              Suite 4E
              New York, NY 10025, USA
Telephone Number: (1–212) 749–3156
Fax Number: (1–212) 666–6325
Email: pdhre@igc.apc.org
Web Page: http://www.pdhre.org/

People's Decade of Human Rights Education (PDHRE-International) was founded in 1988 to develop and advance pedagogies for human rights education relevant to people's daily lives in the context of their struggles for social and economic justice and democracy. PDHRE-International is dedicated to publishing and disseminating demand-driven human rights training manuals and teaching materials, and otherwise servicing grassroots and community groups engaged in a creative, contextualized process of human rights learning, reflection, and action. PDHRE-International views human rights as a value system capable of strengthening democratic communities and nations through its emphasis on accountability, reciprocity, and people's equal and informed participation in the decisions that affect their lives. PDHRE-International works directly and indirectly with its network, primarily women's and social justice organizations.

Name: People's Union for Civil Liberties
Acronyms: PUCL
Address: 81, Sahayoga Apartments
              Mayur Vihar I, Delhi 110 091, India
Telephone Number: (91–11) 225–0014
Fax Number: (91–11) 225–6931; 249–2342
Email: puclnat@yahoo.com
Web Page: http://www.pucl.org

The People's Union for Civil Liberties (PUCL), formed in October 1976, has branches throughout India and is dedicated to promoting civil liberties and the democratic way of life by peaceful means. PUCL monitors and reports on human rights violations throughout the country. It also constantly reviews penal laws and criminal procedures with a view to bringing them into harmony with humane and liberal principles, works for the withdrawal and repeal of all repressive laws, encourages freedom of thought and defense of the right of public dissent. PUCL works to ensure freedom of press and makes legal aid available to the poor, especially for the defense of civil liberties. It opposes discrimination on the ground of religion, race, caste, sex, or place of birth, and combats social evils that encroach on civil liberties, such as untouchability, and defends in particular the civil liberties of the society and of women and children.

Name: Philippine Alliance for Human Rights Advocates
Acronyms: PAHRA
Language: English
Address: Room 403, FMSG Building
              9 Balete Drive corner Third Street
              New Manila
              Quezon City 1112, Philippines
Telephone Number: (63–2) 271–7814
Fax Number: (63–2) 721–7814
Email: pahra@info.com.ph

The Philippine Alliance for Human Rights Advocates (PAHRA) brings together over 100 justice and peace groups, local human rights organizations, lawyers groups, families and victims of human rights violations, and documentation centers. Organized in 1986, it coordinates efforts to promote human rights in the country. PAHRA conducts campaigns for justice and indemnification for all victims of human rights violations, works for the institutionalization of human rights and democracy, and peace. It also educates people about their rights and their role in promoting human rights, and facilitates welfare and rehabilitation programs for victims of human rights violations.

Name: Physicians for Human Rights—USA
Acronyms: PHR
Languages: English, with capabilities in French; Spanish; Russian
Address: 100 Boylston St.
    Suite 702
    Boston, MA 02116, USA
Telephone Number: (1–617) 695–0041
Fax Number: (1–617) 695–0307
Email: phrusa@igc.apc.org
Web Page: www.phrusa.org

Physicians for Human Rights (PHR), founded in 1986, uses the knowledge and skills of the medical and forensic sciences to investigate and prevent violations of international human rights and humanitarian law. It works to stop torture, disappearances, and political killings by governments and opposition groups, as well as to improve health and sanitary conditions in prisons and detention centers. It also investigates the physical and psychological consequences of violations of humanitarian law in internal and international conflicts, and defends medical neutrality and the right of civilians and combatants to receive medical care during times of war. PHR works to protect health professionals who are victims of violations of human rights and to prevent medical complicity in torture and other abuses. PHR also conducts educational and training projects for health professionals, members of the judiciary, and human rights advocates on the application of medical and forensic skills in the investigation of violations of human rights.

Name: Privacy International
Acronyms: PI
Language: English
Address: c/o Simon Davies
    Computer Security Research Centre
    London School of Economics
    Houghton St.
    London WC2A 2AE, UK
Telephone Number: (44–81) 402–0737
Fax Number: (44–81) 313–3726
Email: pi@privacy.org davies@privacy.org
Web Page: http://www.privacy.org/pi

Privacy International (PI), founded in 1990, acts as a watchdog on surveillance by governments and corporations. PI conducts campaigns in Europe, Asia, and North America to counter abuses of privacy by way of information technology such as telephone tapping, ID card systems, video surveillance, data matching, police information systems, and medical records.

Name: Programa Radio Internacional Feminista
Other Name: Feminist International Radio Endeavor
Acronyms: RAIF; FIRE
Languages: Spanish; English
Address: P.O. Box 239–6100
    San Jose, Costa Rica
Telephone Number: (506) 249–1993
Fax Number: (506) 249–1993
Email: fuegocr@sol.racsa.co.cr
Web Page: www.fire.or.cr

The Feminist International Radio Endeavor (FIRE), founded in 1991, is a communications venue on shortwave where women's voices, in all their diversity, are heard by the international community, crossing barriers of nationality, culture, race, and geography. It is produced and transmitted by Radio for Peace International, a global community radio based at the University of Peace in Costa Rica.

Name: Rainforest Action Network
Acronyms: RAN
Language: English
Address: 221 Pine St.
    Ste. 500
    San Francisco, CA 94104, USA
Telephone Number: (1–415) 398–4404
Fax Number: (1–415) 398–2732
Email: rainforest@ran.org
Web Page: http://www.ran.org

The Rainforest Action Network (RAN), founded in 1985, works to protect tropical rain forests and the human rights of those living in and around those forests. RAN works with environmental and human rights groups in 60 countries, sharing information and coordinating the U.S. sector's role in worldwide campaigns to protect the rain forests and their inhabitants. It focuses on education, communication, conferences, and direct action in the United States and promotes the efforts of indigenous and environmental groups in tropical countries to achieve ecologically sustainable solutions within their own regions.

Name: Raoul Wallenberg Institute of Human Rights and Humanitarian Law
Language: English
Address: P.O. Box 1155
    S-221 05 Lund, Sweden
Telephone Number: (46–46) 222–1200 (Secretariat); 222–1230 (Library)
Fax Number: (46–46) 222–1222

The Raoul Wallenberg Institute of Human Rights and Humanitarian Law, founded in 1984, is an academic institution at the University of Lund, Sweden. It promotes research, training, and academic education in the fields of human rights and humanitarian law. It has a research library and initiates, develops, and supports other activities in these fields.

Name: Redress: Seeking Reparation for Torture Survivors
Language: English
Address: 6 Queen Square
          London WC1N 3AR, UK
Telephone Number: (44–20) 7278–9502
Fax Number: (44–20) 7278–9410
Email: redresstrust@gn.apc.org; redress@gn.apc.org
Web Page: http://www.redress.org

Redress: Seeking Reparation for Torture Survivors (Redress), founded in 1992, works to help torture survivors around the world use available legal remedies to obtain reparation and to campaign for effective remedies where they do not exist. It works for reparation (including compensation and rehabilitation) to help in healing and restoring the lives of those who have been tortured. It also works to combat the practice of torture and deter repressive regimes.

Name: Refugee Studies Centre
Acronyms: RSC
Language: English
Address: Queen Elizabeth House
          21 St. Giles
          Oxford OX1 3LA, UK
Telephone Number: (44–1865) 27–07–22
Fax Number: (44–1865) 27–07–21
Email: RSC@qeh.ox.ac.uk
Web Page: http://www.qeh.ox.ac.uk/rsp//http://
          www.rsl.ox.ac.uk/cgibin/rspnew.tcl

The Refugee Studies Centre (RSC) is part of the University of Oxford's International Development Centre. Founded in 1982, it carries out multidisciplinary research and teaching on the causes and consequences of forced migration; disseminates the results of that research to policy-makers and practitioners, as well as within the academic community; and tries to build understanding of the experience of forced migration from the point of view of the affected populations. The RSC regularly organizes and hosts conferences, workshops, and public lectures, in addition to holding its series of weekly public seminars. It maintains a documentation center dedicated to forced migration in the world.

Name: Rehabiliterings Center for Torturofre
Other Name: Rehabilitation and Research Centre for Torture Victims; International Rehabilitation Council for Torture Victims
Acronyms: RCT
Languages: Danish; English
Address: Borgergade 13
          P.O. Box 2107
          DK-1014 Copenhagen, Denmark

Telephone Number: (45) 33–76–06–00
Fax Number: (45) 33–76–05–10
Email: rct@rct.dk
Web Page: http://www.rct.dk

The Rehabilitation and Research Centre for Torture Victims (RCT), founded in 1982, runs a center for the rehabilitation of persons (and their families) who have been subjected to torture. It also instructs Danish and foreign health personnel in the examination and treatment of persons who have been subjected to torture, and engages in research on torture and on the nature and extent of its consequences for the purposes of treatment and eventual abolition. RCT also has an international documentation center for the purposes of disseminating facts about torture, studying the consequences of torture, and rehabilitating persons who have been subjected to torture.

Name: Rencontre africaine pour la défense des droits de
          l'homme
Other Name: African Meetingplace for the Defense of
          Human Rights
Acronyms: RADDHO
Language: French
Address: BP 15246
          Dakar-Fann, Senegal
Telephone Number: (221) 824–6056
Fax Number: (221) 824–6052
Email: raddho@telecomplus.sn

The African Meetingplace for the Defense of Human Rights (RADDHO), formed in 1990, works to promote and protect human rights in all of Africa by making the rule of law, democratic tolerance, and conditions for freedom of expression recognized in each country. RADDHO works to encourage the struggle for total emancipation of Africa and dignity of African persons, and toward peace and solidarity. It denounces states that violate human rights through statements published in the press and organizes conferences, roundtables, and workshops, as well as conducts field investigations.

Name: Reporters sans frontières
Other Name: Reporters Without Borders
Acronyms: RSF
Languages: French; English
Address: 5, rue Geoffroy-Marie
          75009 Paris, France
Telephone Number: (33–1) 44–83–84–84
Fax Number: (33–1) 45–23–11–51
Email: rsf@rsf.fr
Web Page: http://www.rsf.fr

Reporters sans frontières (RSF), established in 1985, works to defend press freedom and assists journalists who are threatened or imprisoned.

Name: Rights and Humanity
Language: English
Address: 2 St. Peters Street
          Ipswich IP1 1XB, UK
Telephone Number: (44–1473) 286–365
Fax Number: (44–1473) 286–720
Email: rights.humanity@pop3–poptel.org.uk

Rights and Humanity, the International Movement for the Promotion and Realization of Human Rights and Responsibilities, was established in 1986 simultaneously in Africa and Europe. It was formed in response to the appalling loss of life and human suffering caused by poverty and deprivation, discrimination, and social rejection. The African and European members have joined forces to establish the International Association of Rights and Humanity with three National Associations (in Nigeria, the Sudan, and the UK). It is committed to education in the field of human rights and the principles of humanity, so that all individuals and organs of society might be more aware of their responsibilities, both to members of their own societies and toward the global family. It works toward the establishment of fair economic relations, as well as the development of international protection law and the recognition of an effective humanitarian ethic.

Name: Service International pour les droits de l'homme
Other Name: International Service for Human Rights;
     Servicio Internacional para los Derechos Humanos
Acronyms: ISHR
Languages: French; English
Address: Case Postale 16
          1211 Geneva 20 CIC, Switzerland
Telephone Number: (41–22) 733–5123
Fax Number: (41–22) 733–0826

The International Service for Human Rights (ISHR), founded in 1984, is an international association serving human rights defenders by providing timely and accurate information, analysis, and relevant training, as well as legal, political, and practical advice and input on international human rights standards and procedures. ISHR also contributes to standard settings at the international level.

Name: Servicio Paz y Justicia en America Latina
Other Name: Service for Peace and Justice in Latin America
Acronyms: SERPAJ-AL
Languages: Spanish; Portuguese
Address: Carlos Ibarra 176 y 10 de Agosto
          Oficina 805
          Casilla Postal: 17–03–1567
          Quito-Ecuador
Telephone Number: (593–2) 57–15–21
Fax Number: (593–2) 57–16–36
Email: serpaj@ecuanex.net.ec
Web Page: http://www.nonviolence.org/serpaj/

Service for Peace and Justice in Latin America (SERPAJ-AL), founded in 1968, inspired by Christianity, works to promote the values of solidarity and nonviolence, and toward building a society based on the full realization of the rights of people and communities in the process of Latin American liberation. It has regional offices in Bolivia, Brazil, Chile, Costa Rica, Ecuador, Mexico, Nicaragua, Panama, Paraguay, and Uruguay.

Name: Servicio Paz y Justicia—Uruguay
Other Name: Service for Peace and Justice—Uruguay
Acronyms: SERPAJ-URUGUAY
Languages: Spanish; English
Address: Joaquin Requena 1642
          C.P. 11 200 Montevideo, Uruguay
Telephone Number: (598–2) 408–5301; 408–5701;
     408–4770
Fax Number: (598–2) 408–5701
Email: serpajuy@serpaj.org.uy, cedoc@serpaj.org.uy
Web Page: http://www.serpaj.org.uy

Service for Peace and Justice—Uruguay (SERPAJ-Uruguay), founded in 1968, was forced to stop work in 1980, and declared illegal in 1983. Since 1985, it has once again been able to work legally on issues of democracy and repression both in Uruguay and regionally, and produce documentation for use by the public, the courts, and/or parliament. SERPAJ-Uruguay trains teachers, supports victims of rights violations with legal, humanitarian, and social aid, and assists families of political prisoners and the disappeared. It also prepares reports for intergovernmental organizations, and works with other human rights groups in the country and region.

Name: Sisterhood Is Global Institute
Acronyms: SIGI
Language: English
Address: 1200 Atwater Avenue
          Suite 2
          Montreal
          Quebec H3Z 1X4, Canada
Telephone Number: (1–514) 846–9366
Fax Number: (1–514) 846–9066
Email: sigi@qc.aibn.com
Web Page: http://www.sigi.org

Sisterhood Is Global Institute (SIGI), founded in 1984, is dedicated to the support and promotion of women's rights at the local, national, regional, and global levels. With members in 70 countries, SIGI works toward empowering women and developing leadership through human rights education of basic rights guaranteed to women under international human rights conventions, and to increase public awareness and concern about human rights abuses committed against women. It also facilitates the direct participation of women from the Global South in international debates concerning their rights. SIGI also facilitates research and provides training models for women from the developing world in the areas of human rights education, communication, and leadership.

Name: SOS racisme internationale
Other Name: SOS Racism International
Acronyms: SOS
Language: French
Address: 64, rue Petites Ecuries
          Paris 75010, France
Telephone Number: (33–1) 5324–6767

SOS Racism International (SOS) works to fight racism in France and around the world. SOS also works to promote awareness in France of racism in other countries.

Name: South Asian Forum for Human Rights
Address: 3–23 Shree Durbar Tole
          Patan Dhoka
          Lalitpur, Nepal
Telephone Number: (977–1) 541–026
Fax Number: (977–1) 527–852
Email: south@safhr.wlink.com.np

The South Asia Forum for Human Rights (SAFHR) works to promote observance of and respect for international human rights in the region. SAFHR circulates information on the human rights situation in the region; appeals to all major human rights organizations, in times of crisis, to alert travelers and the world of impending human rights flashpoints; and implements a periodic training program for human rights activists on international instruments. SAFHR acts as a focal point for discussion of transborder human rights issues. SAFHR's long-term goal is to establish a South Asian Charter for Human Rights, which would be comparable in structure and purpose to the Charter of the OAS and the European Convention.

Name: South Asia Human Rights Documentation Centre
Acronyms: SAHRDC
Language: English
Address: B-6/6, Safdarjang Enclave Extension
          New Delhi 110029, India
Telephone Number: (91–11) 619–1120; 619–2717;
  619–2706
Fax Number: (91–11) 619–1120
Email: hrdc_online@hotmail.com
Web Page: http://www.hri.ca/partners/sahrdc/index.htm

The South Asia Human Rights Documentation Centre (SAHRDC) seeks to investigate, document, and disseminate information about human rights treaties and conventions, human rights education, refugees, media freedom, prison reforms, political imprisonment, torture, summary executions, disappearances, and other cruel, inhuman, or degrading treatment.

SAHRDC conducts a series of human rights training programs in the South Asian and East Asian region and offers placements as part of a formal internship program.

Name: Studie en Informatiecentrum Mensenrechten
Other Name: Netherlands Institute of Human Rights;
    Institut néerlandais des droits de l'homme; Instituto
    Holandes de Derechos Humanos
Acronyms: SIM
Languages: Dutch; English; French; Spanish
Address: Janskerkhof 3
          3512 BK Utrecht, Netherlands
Telephone Number: (31–30) 253–8033
Fax Number: (31–30) 253–7168
Email: sim@law.uu.nl
Web Page: http://www.law.uu.nl/english/sim

The Netherlands Institute of Human Rights (SIM), founded in 1981, researches and distributes information, and generally works to stimulate interest, with regard to the promotion and protection of human rights, both at the national and the international level. It is particularly interested in the question of the universality of human rights. SIM's research also looks at the foreign policy of the Netherlands and other countries with regard to human rights.

Name: Survival International
Acronyms: SI
Address: 310 Edgware Road
          London W2 1DY, United Kingdom
Telephone Number: (44–20) 72–42–1441
Fax Number: (44–20) 72–42–17–71
Email: info@survival-international.org
Web Page: http://www.survival-international.org

Survival International (SI), founded in 1969, supports tribal peoples' right to decide their own future and helps them protect their lives, lands, and human rights. SI works in close partnership with local indigenous organizations, conducts campaigns directed not only at governments, but at companies, banks, extremist missionaries, guerrilla armies, museums, and anyone else who violates tribal peoples' rights. It also provides educational material.

Name: Taskforce on the Churches and Corporate
    Responsibility
Acronyms: TCCR
Language: English
Address: 129 St. Clair Ave. West
          Toronto, Ontario M4V 1N5, Canada
Telephone Number: (1–416) 923–1758
Fax Number: (1–416) 927–7554
Email: tccr@web.apc.org
Web Page; htpp://www.web.net/~tccr

The Taskforce on the Churches and Corporate Responsibility (TCCR) was established by Canadian churches in 1975 to be the voice of the church with business corporations when they can or do impact human rights. It undertakes research and advocacy, and assists member organizations in promoting and implementing policies adopted by them on the social and environmental responsibility of Canadian-based corporations and financial institutions. TCCR publishes various materials, including articles and press clippings on issues related to its agenda, briefs and correspondence with governments, reports of company annual meetings, and occasional papers.

Name: Transition Monitoring Group
Acronyms: TMG
Language: English
Address: c/o CRP
             P.O. Box 4447
             Surulere
             Lagos, Nigeria
Telephone Number: (234–1) 584–3041; 584–8498
Fax Number: (234–1) 584–8571
Email: crplagos@crp.org.ng
Web Page: http://www.crp.org.ng

The Transition Monitoring Group (TMG), formed in 1998, is a coalition of human rights groups, NGOs, and civil society organizations who work to develop the integrity of the electoral process in Nigeria by monitoring and reporting on political programs.

Name: Turkiyc Insan Ilaklari Vakfi
Other Name: Human Rights Foundation of Turkey
Acronyms: TIHV; HRFT
Language: Turkish
Address: Menekse 2 Sokak 16/6
             06440 Kizilay
             Ankara, Turkey
Telephone Number: (90–312) 417–7180
Fax Number: (90–312) 425–4552
Email: tihv@tr-net.net.tr
Web Page: http://www.hrft.org.tr, http://www.tihv.org.tr

The Human Rights Foundation of Turkey (HRFT), was established in 1990 by 32 founding members of the Human Rights Association. HRFT bases its work on all international human rights accords whether signed by Turkey or not. HRFT issues publications and documentation on human rights and freedoms, and carries out scientific research and education. HRFT undertakes projects in a number of areas. It assists torture victims in getting treatment after having established a Treatment and Rehabilitation Centre for Torture Survivors and provides treatment for prisoners in ill health and for torture victims, as well as documenting prison conditions. HRFT also works to

protect those women subjected to violence or the threat of violence.

Name: Tutela Legal del Arzobispado de San Salvador
Other Name: Legal Aid Office of the Archbishopric of San
     Salvador
Language: Spanish
Address: Apartado 2253
             San Salvador, El Salvador
Telephone Number: (503) 225–2603

The Legal Aid Office of the Archbishopric of San Salvador (Tutela Legal), created in 1982, operates under the authority of the Justice and Peace Commission of the Archbishop of El Salvador. It documents human rights violations in El Salvador and provides legal assistance to the victims of such violations. Tutela Legal receives complaints of violations, records affidavits submitted by victims, and conducts on-site investigations of allegations, using both domestic and international law as a framework for impartial analysis. It also regularly visits persons detained by security forces, provides legal representation for victims of abuses, and coordinates the exhumation of deceased victims when unidentified bodies are discovered. Tutela reports on violations of both rebel and government forces in a strictly nonpartisan manner, and issues frequent detailed statistics of the violations, including politically motivated killings by the right (death squad and the military) and by the left (the FMLN). It also documents indirect killings, such as casualties resulting from land mines or other explosive devices.

Name: Union interafricaine des droits de l'homme
Other Name: Interafrican Union for Human Rights
Acronyms: UIDH
Languages: French; English
Address: 01 BP 1346, Ouagadougou 01
             Burkina Faso
Telephone Number: (226) 316–145
Fax Number: (226) 316–144
Email: uidh@fasonet.bf
Web Page: http://www.multimania.com/uidh

The Union interafricaine des droits de l'homme (UIDH) was created in 1992 to serve as a collective watchdog, at the African level, of the principles stated in the Universal Declaration of Human Rights and the African Charter of Human and Peoples' Rights. It does not replace but rather supplements and reinforces national human rights organizations. UIDH's activities include conducting field investigations in tension areas; promotion and information missions; organizing campaigns to promote the signing and ratification of international human rights instruments, and to educate people on the implementation of these international instruments; and establishing procedures for harmonizing domestic law with international human rights treaties.

Name: U.S. Committee for Refugees
Acronyms: USCR
Languages: English; Spanish; Cambodian
Address: 1717 Massachusetts Ave. N.W.
                 Suite 200
                 Washington, DC 20036, USA
Telephone Number: (1–202) 347–3507
Fax Number: (1–202) 347–3418
Email: uscr@irsa-uscr.org
Web Page: http://www.refugees.org

The U.S. Committee for Refugees (USCR) was established
in 1958 to protect the rights of refugees in the U.S. and
around the world. USCR works to draw attention to the plight
of refugees and internally displaced people, and translates
that attention into meaningful protection and assistance.
USCR engages in three types of activities. It responds to
emergency situations by going to the scene of a refugee
crisis, interviewing refugees and organizations involved, and
reporting its findings to public and private relief agencies
and human rights groups. Through media outreach, USCR's
information and analysis appear regularly in the national
and international media, drawing attention to the plight of
refugees. USCR also advocates on behalf of refugees to the
government.

Name: Unrepresented Nations and Peoples Organization
Acronyms: UNPO
Address: Postbox 85878
                 2508 CN, The Hague
                 The Netherlands
Telephone Number: (31–70) 360–3318
Fax Number: (31–70) 360–3346
Email: unpo@unpo.nl
Web Page: http://www.unpo.org

The Unrepresented Nations and Peoples Organization (UNPO),
founded in 1991, consists of over 50 members who represent
over 100 million persons. UNPO offers an international forum for those who are not represented in the world´s principal
international organizations, such as the United Nations. This
includes occupied nations, indigenous peoples, minorities, and
even oppressed majorities who currently struggle to regain
their lost countries, preserve their cultural identities, protect
their basic human and economic rights, and safeguard the natural environment.

Name: Urban Morgan Institute for Human Rights
Language: English
Address: College of Law
                 University of Cincinnati
                 Cincinnati OH 45221–0040, USA
Telephone Number: (1–513) 556–0068; 556–0093
Fax Number: (1–513) 556–2391

Email: nancy.ent@law.uc.edu
Web Page: http://www.law.uc.edu/morgan2/

The Urban Morgan Institute for Human Rights, founded in
1979, is affiliated with the University of Cincinnati College of
Law. It works to promote and protect human rights, particularly as they relate to the education of tomorrow's leaders.
The Institute also works to disseminate electronically information that will facilitate the review of human rights literature by human rights advocates and researchers around the
world in a timely way.

Name: Voix des sans voix pour les droits de l'homme
Other Name: Voice of the Voiceless for Human Rights
Acronyms: VSV
Languages: French; English
Address: BP 7248, Kinshasa I
                 Democratic Republic of Congo
Telephone Number: (243–88) 40–394; 50–832; 50–514
Fax Number: (243–88) 01–826 (243–12) 34–441
Email: vsv@ic.cd

The Voice of the Voiceless for Human Rights (VSV) operated
clandestinely for several years before its formal foundation in
1990. It undertakes fact-finding and reporting on human rights
abuses and collaborates with and even helps to finance other
human rights initiatives in Kinshasa. VSV also sponsors a theater troupe, produces a newsletter aimed at popular education
in human rights, and runs a program of assistance to victims
of torture.

Name: Women in Law and Development in Africa
Acronyms: WILDAF
Language: English
Address: P.O. Box 4622
                 Harare, Zimbabwe
Telephone Number: (263–4) 752–105; 751–189
Fax Number: (263–4) 781–886; 752–105
Email: wildaf@mango.zw
Web Page: http://www.hri.ca/partners/wildaf

Women in Law and Development in Africa (WILDAF),
founded in 1980, works to promote the effective use of legal
strategies by women in Africa for national, community, and
self-development. WILDAF provides assistance and training
in legal literacy, as well as lobbies and mobilizes groups
through networking.

Name: Women, Law and Development International
Acronyms: WLD
Languages: English; French; Spanish
Address: 1350 Connecticut Ave. NW
                 Suite 407
                 Washington, DC 20036–1701, USA

Telephone Number: (1–202) 463–7477
Fax Number: (1–202) 463–7480
Email: wld@wld.org/mschuler@wld.org
Web Page: http://www.wld.org

Women, Law and Development International (WLD), founded in 1997, promotes women's full and equal participation in nations around the world by advancing universal respect for human rights, expanding rights education and legal literacy among women, and challenging discriminatory socioeconomic barriers. Committed to capacity-building, advocacy, and expanding women's rights networks, WLD collaborates with thought-leaders, researchers, advocates, activists, and monitors throughout the world. WLD works with partners to identify legal, cultural, and economic impediments to women's enjoyment of human rights, to propose targeted approaches, to develop activist strategies, and to train women's groups to advocate before UN and governmental bodies for policies that recognize women's rights.

Name: Women Living Under Muslim Laws—International
    Solidarity Network
Other Name: Femmes sous lois musulmanes—Réseau
    internationale de solidarité
Acronyms: WLUML
Languages: French; English
Address: B.P. 20023
         34791 Grabels, Cedex
         Montpellier, France
Telephone Number: (requested that it not be printed)
Email: wluml@mnet.fr
Web Page: http://wluml.org

The Women Living Under Muslim Laws—International Solidarity Network (WLUML), founded in 1984, works to improve the status and lives of women living under Muslim law and to abolish unjust laws. It works to create links between women's groups in Muslim countries and communities and to share information.

Name: Women's Environment and Development
    Organization
Acronyms: WEDO
Language: English
Address: 355 Lexington Ave.
         3rd Floor
         New York, NY 10017–6603, USA
Telephone Number: (1–212) 973–0325
Fax Number: (1–212) 973–0335
Email: wedo@igc.apc.org
Web Page: http://www.wedo.org

The Women's Environment and Development Organization (WEDO), created in 1990, is a global organization working to increase women's visibility, roles, and leadership in public policy-making through peace, gender, human rights, environmental, and economic justice campaigns; through advocacy nationally, regionally, at the UN and in international financial institutions; and through local actions. WEDO works on a range of interconnected gender, environment, and development issues in a human rights framework. The organization, through its network of activists and experts, responds flexibly to the needs and interests of its worldwide constituency.

Name: Women's International League for Peace and
    Freedom
Other Name: Ligue internationale des femmes pour la paix
    et la liberté; Liga Internacional de Mujeres por la Paz y la
    Libertad; Internationale Frauenliga für Frieden und
    Freiheit
Acronyms: WILPF; LIFPL; LIMPAL; IFFF
Address: 1, rue de Varembé
         CP 28
         1211 Geneva 20, Switzerland
Telephone Number: (41–22) 733–6175
Fax Number: (41–22) 740–1063
Email: wilpf@iprolink.ch
Web Page: http://www.wilpf.int.ch

The Women's International League for Peace and Freedom (WILPF), founded in 1915, works through its national sections to bring together women who are opposed to war, violence, exploitation, and all forms of discrimination and oppression to establish peace based on economic and social justice for all, without distinction of sex, race, class, or creed. WILPF seeks to educate, inform, and mobilize women for action to achieve its goals. It organizes meetings, seminars, conferences, and campaigns to promote its goals. It sends missions to countries in conflict and reports to its members and friends and to the United Nations on their efforts to bring about peaceful settlements. WILPF also offers training to young women on disarmament, development, and human rights.

Name: World Council of Churches, Commission of the
    Churches on International Affairs
Acronyms: WCC—CCIA
Address: P.O. Box 2100
         1211 Geneva 2, Switzerland
Telephone Number: (41–22) 791–6111
Fax Number: (41–22) 791–0361
Email: info@wcc-coe.org
Web Page: http://www.wcc-coe.org

The World Council of Churches (WCC), founded in 1948, is an international Christian organization built upon the foundation of ecumenical collaboration. WCC's International Relations group works to inform and address public issues that have a claim on the Christian conscience by monitoring, analyzing, and providing information on global security, the reform of the UN and other international institutions, and the applicability of sanctions. It also provides a platform for information-sharing and joint advocacy on critical situations of human rights violations and conflicts, and on opportunities to support peacemaking initiatives. WCC conducts programs and training for its local members on human rights and religious freedom; impunity, truth and reconciliation; disarmament and arms control; peace and conflict resolution; global governance; and uprooted people—refugees, migrants, and internally displaced people.

Name: World Press Freedom Committee
Acronyms: WPFC
Language: English
Address: 11690–C Sunrise Valley Drive
                Reston, VA 20191, USA
Telephone Number: (1–703) 715–9811
Fax Number: (1–703) 620–6790
Email: freepress@wpfc.org; mgreen@wpfc.org
Web Page: http://wpfc.org

The World Press Freedom Committee (WPFC), founded in 1976, is an umbrella organization of print and broadcast professionals, labor and management, journalists, editors, publishers, and owners on six continents—united in the defense and promotion of press freedom. As well as providing legal assistance grants to journalists and news media prosecuted by governments, WPFC emphasizes monitoring and coordination, vigorous advocacy of free-press principles, and practical assistance programs.

Name: World University Service International
Other Name: Entraide universitaire mondiale; Servicio
      Universitario Mundial
Acronyms: WUS; EUM; WUS
Languages: English; Spanish; French
Address: WG-Plein 400
                1054 SH Amsterdam
                The Netherlands
Telephone Number: (31–20) 412–2266
Fax Number: (31–20) 412–2267
Email: wus-i@antenna.nl; admin@wis-i.antenna.nl
Web Page: http://www.antenna.nl/wus-i

World University Service (WUS), founded in 1920, focuses on education, development, and human rights. The Human Rights Program run by WUS-International promotes the rights to education, to academic freedom, and to university autonomy, and seeks to defend the human rights of members of the educational sector. WUS runs the Summer University on Human Rights and the Right to Education.

Name: Yayasan Lembaga Bantuan Hukum Indonesia
Other Name: Indonesian Legal Aid Foundation
Acronyms: YLBHI
Languages: Bahasa Indonesia; English
Address: Jalan Diponegoro No. 74
                Jakarta 10320, Indonesia
Telephone Number: (62–21) 314–5518; 390–4226;
      390–4227
Fax Number: (62–21) 330–140
Email: ylbhi@ylbhi.org
Web Page: http://www.ylbhi.org/

The Indonesian Legal Aid Foundation (YLBHI), founded in 1981, provides free legal aid to those who could otherwise not afford it. It raises consciousness and respect for the principle of the rule of law, human dignity, and human rights in general, and works to develop and modernize the law and monitors its implementation. YLBHI also undertakes public education on the concept and norms/values of the rule of law through courses, lectures, conferences, seminars, workshops, and through a variety of publications. It also makes suggestions, criticisms, and comments to authorities in the judicial, legislative, and executive branches of government and to society. YLBHI works with governments and institutions as well as NGOs in Indonesia and abroad and conducts research into social, political, economic, and cultural problems.

Name: Zimbabwe Human Rights Association
Acronyms: ZimRights
Language: English
Address: P.O. Box 3951
                Harare, Zimbabwe
Telephone Number: (263–4) 707–278; 705–898
Fax Number: (263–4) 707–277
Email: zimright@samara.co.zw

The Zimbabwe Human Rights Association (ZimRights) works to promote, educate, raise awareness, and defend human rights and dignity. ZimRights aims to foster among individuals and groups respect for dignity regardless of race, religion, sex, age, or social status. It promotes the practice of social, economic, political, and legal justice to bring about social harmony and peace. ZimRights conducts public education programs to inform people and create awareness about their rights. It also carries out investigations into alleged human rights abuses and encourages the Zimbabwean government to ratify international human rights instruments and to perform its duties under such instruments. ZimRights liaises and cooperates with other human rights organizations locally and internationally. It helps victims of human rights abuse to claim legal remedies.

Glossary

alien. An individual who is not a citizen of the country in which he or she resides.

amnesty. A pardon granted to an individual or group of individuals for crimes committed in the past. Beneficiaries of an amnesty cannot legally be prosecuted for past crimes.

Amnesty International. One of the most active international non-governmental organizations (NGOs) dedicated to fighting for human rights around the world.

anti-Semitism. A hatred or hostility directed against Jews.

apartheid. The system of government-sanctioned racial segregation in South Africa from 1948 to 1990, which guaranteed the dominance of the white minority over the country's black majority.

asylum. A status granted to an individual or individuals protecting them from being forced to return to their country of origin. Asylum is often granted to victims of human rights abuse.

bicameral. Having two legislative chambers. The United States has a bicameral legislature, divided between the House of Representatives and the Senate.

bill of rights. Summary of basic human rights and personal freedom guaranteed against violation by the government. In the United States the Bill of Rights refers to the first ten amendments to the Constitution.

bonded labor. Workers forced to labor because of debts incurred by themselves or family members. Bonded labor often is equivalent to slavery.

Cairo Declaration on Human Rights in Islam. Adopted in 1990, a statement on human rights by a collection of Islamic nations. In tone, it is more conservative than United Nations human rights documents.

capitalism. An economic system that favors allowing businesses and entrepreneurs to operate without interference.

capital punishment. The use of the death penalty to punish a crime.

CEDAW. *See* Convention on the Elimination of All Forms of Discrimination Against Women

centrally planned (or controlled) economy. An economy directly controlled by the government, usually characteristic of a communist government.

civil liberties. Rights protected by law. Civil liberties include the right to speak freely or the right to a fair trial.

civil service. Civilian government employees.

conscientious objection. A refusal to serve in the military for religious or ethical reasons.

constitution. The laws and principles that underlie a country's legal system, or the document containing those laws.

Convention on the Elimination of All Forms of Discrimination Against Women (CEDAW). Adopted by the United Nations in 1979, it obliges signatory nations to bring about equality of treatment between men and women.

coup (coup d'état). Violent overthrow of a government.

Cold War. The long period of hostility between the United States and the Soviet Union that developed in the aftermath of World War II. The Cold War ended with the fall of the Soviet Union in 1991.

Commonwealth. The name of an association of nations that were members of the British Empire. (The full name was the British Commonwealth of Nations.)

communism. A political and economic system based on the ideas of Karl Marx. In the twentieth century, communist countries were all one-party dictatorships.

declaration of independence. The official statement of a group severing ties with a former colonial or imperial power. The United States Declaration of Independence was signed on July 4, 1776 to signal American intentions to separate from Great Britain.

derogation. In international human rights law, the partial or complete deviation from a human rights commitment.

dictatorship. A government run by a person or group without consulting the wishes of the people. The political opposite of democracy.

disappearance. The sudden vanishing of a person because of kidnapping or murder. Often caused by oppressive governments and targeted against citizens who have resisted their governments.

Doctors Without Borders/Médicins Sans Frontières (MSF). An international non-governmental organization dedicated to providing medical aid to victims of natural disasters and wars. MSF received the Nobel Peace Prize in 1999.

domestic violence. Physical abuse of one family member by another. The most common forms are parents beating children and husbands beating wives.

EC. *See* European Community

ethnic cleansing. The use of violence or the threat of violence to force all people of one ethnicity out of a region.

EU. *See* European Union

European Community (EC). An association of European states. Called the European Union since 1994.

European Union (EU). The successor to the EC. The EU has fifteen members: Austria, Belgium, Denmark, Finland, France, Germany, Greece, Ireland, Italy, Luxembourg, Netherlands, Portugal, Spain, Sweden, and United Kingdom.

extradition. Forcible transfer of an individual from the control of one government, where he or she has sought refuge, to that of another, where he or she is accused of a crime.

extrajudicial. Actions taken by government officials (e.g., police, army troops) that do not have the sanction of law. Extrajudicial killings, for example, are essentially murders carried out by the police or army in the name of justice.

female genital mutilation (FGM). The ritual cutting of some part of the female genitalia, usually that of young girls, for religious or traditional reasons.

FGM. *See* female genital mutilation

formal and informal economy (or sector). The formal sector (or formal economy) is the official economy. The informal sector, or the black market economy, is hidden from government regulators and tax collectors.

freedom of assembly. The right to gather openly in marches or demonstrations.

freedom of the press. The right of newspapers, magazines, and other media outlets to publish freely, including, most importantly, the right to criticize the government.

freedom of religion. The right to practice any religious faith.

freedom of speech. The right to speak or write freely, without fear of government interference.

free-market economy. An economy that favors capitalism, free enterprise, and relatively little government interference.

GDP. *See* gross domestic product

Geneva Conventions. A series of international agreements, first adopted in Geneva, Switzerland, in 1864, that require the signatories (which include most of the world's nations) to respect the human rights of soldiers, prisoners, and civilians during war.

genocide. An attempt to murder all or a portion of a people or ethnic group.

GNP. *See* gross national product

gross domestic product (GDP). The total income resulting from a nation's economic activity. GDP is used to compare the relative economic strength of countries.

gross national product (GNP). The gross domestic product with the addition of investment income earned by residents and minus the investment income earned by foreigners in the domestic market.

habeas corpus. A writ issued to bring a person before a court. The right of habeas corpus prevents a person from being jailed without proper authority.

Hague Conferences. Two conferences held in the Hague, Netherlands, in 1899 and 1907 for the purpose of limiting the destructive consequences of war.

Holocaust. Nazi Germany's attempt to exterminate Jews during World War II. Six million out of Europe's nine million Jews were killed during the Holocaust.

Human Rights Watch. A prominent human rights non-governmental organization (NGO).

impunity. The ability of some human rights criminals to escape punishment for their crimes.

IMRCRC. *See* The International Movement of the Red Cross and Red Crescent

indigenous peoples. Peoples long native to an area. Often used in reference to traditional or tribal groups, which have been threatened by the arrival of foreign conquerors.

International Labor Organization. An international agency affiliated with the United Nations. Founded in 1919, it is dedicated to protecting the rights of workers around the world.

International Movement of the Red Cross and Red Crescent (IMRCRC). Founded in 1863, the Red Cross was dedicated to providing food and medical support for victims of war and natural catastrophes. It became the IMRCRC in order to include humanitarian organizations from the Muslim world. The symbol of the Red Cross is a red cross on a white background; the symbol of the Red Crescent is a red crescent on a white background.

intifada. Arabic for "shaking off." The name given to the period from 1987 to the early 1990s of unrest and turmoil among Palestinians opposed to Israel's occupation of the West Bank and the Gaza Strip.

League of Nations. International organization founded at the end of World War I in an attempt to avoid future wars. The League failed to prevent the outbreak of World War II but helped to lay the groundwork for the United Nations.

NATO. *See* North Atlantic Treaty Organization

NGO. *See* non-governmental organization

non-governmental organization (NGO). Organization, not associated with any one government, that supports activities across national boundaries in specific issue areas, such as healthcare or politcal rights. Amnesty International and the Red Cross are both NGOs.

North Atlantic Treaty Organization (NATO). NATO was created in 1949 as a security and military alliance dedicated to opposing the threat of Soviet power in Europe. Its nineteen members include Belgium, Canada, Czech Republic, Denmark, France, Germany, Greece, Hungary, Iceland, Italy, Luxembourg, Netherlands, Norway, Poland, Portugal, Spain, Turkey, United Kingdom, and United States.

Palestine Liberation Organization (PLO). The most prominent of the Palestinian resistance movements that are fighting to regain an independent homeland in Palestine.

PLO. *See* Palestine Liberation Organization

racism. The belief that the members of one racial or ethnic group are superior to another.

rapporteur. United Nations representative responsible for a particular issue.

Red Crescent. *See* International Movement of the Red Cross and Red Crescent

Red Cross. *See* International Movement of the Red Cross and Red Crescent

refugee. A person forced to flee his or her home because of political turmoil or persecution.

Roma ("Gypsies"). An ethnic group scattered throughout Europe. The Roma have a long history of facing discrimination.

sexual orientation. Describes the nature of a person's sexual attractions. Sexual orientations include heterosexuality (being attracted to the opposite sex), homosexuality (being attracted to the same sex), and bisexuality (being attracted to both sexes).

shari'a (also sharia). The legal code based on the Koran.

slavery. The practice of forcing people to work for no wages and treating them as a form of property.

solitary confinement. Imprisonment with little or no contact with other prisoners or guards. A harsh punishment causing great mental anguish.

subsistence agriculture. Agricultural practice in which farmers are growing just enough food to feed themselves and their families.

terrorism. The illegal use of violence against people in an effort to intimidate and influence society.

Tiananmen Square. A central square in Beijing, China. In spring 1989, Tiananmen Square was the site of pro-democracy human rights demonstrations that were brutally repressed by the Chinese government.

totalitarianism. A form of government that uses police and security forces to gain complete control over all aspects of its people's lives. Totalitarian governments are inherently hostile to most human rights. Stalin's Soviet Union and Hitler's Nazi Germany were both totalitarian states.

UN. *See* United Nations

UNESCO. *See* United Nations Educational, Scientific, and Cultural Organization

unicameral. Having only one legislative chamber. Israel, for example, has a unicameral legislature.

UNICEF. *See* United Nation's Children's Fund

United Nations (UN). The world organization of nations founded in 1945.

United Nations Educational, Scientific, and Cultural Organization (UNESCO). A United Nations organization dedicated to making the world aware of the importance of human rights and international justice and to end ignorance and prejudice.

United Nations High Commissioner for Refugees (UNHCR). The name refers to both the organization and the leader of the organization that serves to protect the interests of refugees around the world.

United Nations Universal Declaration of Human Rights (UDHR). Adopted by the United States in 1948, the UDHR is a statement of purpose on human rights by the nations of the world. Its articles outline the human rights that all people should be granted.

WHO. *See* World Health Organization

World Health Organization. A United Nations agency dedicated to improving the health of all people through education and medical assistance. The WHO works closely with UNICEF and UNESCO.

World Trade Organization (WTO). Major UN organization that oversees international trade agreements and treaties.

WTO. *See* World Trade Organization

xenophobia. A fear of or contempt for foreigners. Xenophobia and racism are closely related prejudices.

Bibliography

Abrahamson, Irving. *Against Silence: The Voice and Vision of Elie Wiesel.* New York: Holocaust Library, 1985.

Abrahamsson, Hans. *Mozambique, The Troubled Transition: From Socialist Construction to Free Market Capitalism.* Atlantic Highlands, NJ: Zed Books, 1995.

Abrams, Irwin. *The Words of Peace: Selections from the Speeches of the Nobel Prize Winners of the Twentieth Century.* New York: Newmarket Press, 2000.

Aciman, Andre. *Letters of Transit: Reflections on Exile and Memory.* New York: New Press, 1999.

Amnesty International. *Amnesty International Report 2000.* New York: Amnesty International Publications, 2000.

———. *Conscientious Objection to Military Service.* London: Amnesty International, 1991.

———. *Female Genital Mutilation: A Human Rights Information Pack.* London: Amnesty International, 1997.

———. *Out of the Margins: The Right to Conscientious Objection to Military Service in Europe.* London: Amnesty International, 1997.

Andreopoulos, George J., and Richard Pierre Claude. *Human Rights Education for the Twenty-first Century.* Philadelphia, PA: University of Pennsylvania Press, 1997.

Arendt, Hannah. *The Origins of Totalitarianism.* New York: Harcourt Brace, 1973.

Aristide, Jean-Bertrand. *Eyes of the Heart: Seeking a Path for the Poor in the Age of Globalization.* Monroe, ME: Common Courage Press, 2000.

Arms Project of Human Rights Watch and Physicians for Human Rights. *Land Mines: A Deadly Legacy.* New York: Human Rights Watch, 1993.

Asante, Clement E., ed. *Press Freedom and Development: A Research Guide and Selected Bibliography.* Westport, CT: Greenwood Press, 1997.

Aung San Suu Kyi. *Freedom from Fear.* London: Penguin Books, 1991.

Australian Privacy Charter Group. *The Australian Privacy Charter.* Sydney: University of New South Wales, 1994.

Baehr, P.R., and Leon Gordenker. *The United Nations in the 1990s.* New York: St. Martin's Press, 1992.

Bales, Kevin. *Disposable People: New Slavery in the Global Economy.* Berkeley, CA: University of California Press, 1999.

Ball, Desmond, and Jeffrey Richelson. *The Ties That Bind: Intelligence Cooperation Between the UKUSA Countries—The United Kingdom, the United States of America, Canada, Australia, and New Zealand.* Boston, MA: Allen & Unwin, 1985.

Ball, Howard. *Prosecuting War Crimes and Genocide: The Twentieth-Century Experience.* Lawrence, KS: University Press of Kansas, 1999.

Banisar, David, and Simon Davies. *Privacy and Human Rights 1999: An International Survey of Privacy Laws and Developments.* London: Electronic Privacy Information Center, 1999.

Barendt, Eric. *Freedom of Speech.* Oxford, UK: Clarendon Paperbacks, 1985.

Barnes, Jack. *The Changing Face of U.S. Politics: Working Class Politics and the Trade Unions.* New York: Pathfinder Press, 1994.

Barnett, Randy E. *The Structure of Liberty: Justice and the Rule of Law.* New York: Oxford University Press, 2000.

Bassiouni, M. Cherif. *Crimes Against Humanity in International Law.* Dordrecht, Netherlands: Martinus Nijhoff, 1998.

Baum, Dan. *Smoke and Mirrors: The War on Drugs and the Politics of Failure.* Boston, MA: Little, Brown, 1996.

Bayer, Ronald, and Gerald M. Oppenheimer. *AIDS Doctors: Voices from the Epidemic.* New York: Oxford University Press, 2000.

Beauchamp, Tom L., and Leroy Walters. *Contemporary Issues in Bioethics.* Belmont, CA: Wadsworth Publishing, 1999.

Beetham, David. *Democracy and Human Rights.* Malden, MA: Blackwell Publishers, 1999.

Bell, Daniel. *East Meets West: Human Rights and Democracy in East Asia.* Princeton, NJ: Princeton University Press, 2000.

Benedek, W., Ed. *Human Rights in Bosnia and Herzegovina After Dayton: From Theory to Practice.* Cambridge, MA: Kluwer Law International, 1999.

Bluglass, Robert, and Martin Roth. *Psychiatry, Human Rights, and the Law.* Cambridge, NY: Cambridge University Press, 1985.

Boland, Reed. *Promoting Reproductive Rights: A Global Mandate.* New York: Center for Reproductive Law and Policy, 1997.

Bosworth, Barry, and Gary Burtless, eds. *Aging Societies: The Global Dimension.* Washington, DC: Brookings Institution Press, 1998.

Brown, Robert McAfee. *Elie Wiesel: Messenger to All Humanity.* South Bend, IN: University of Notre Dame Press, 1984.

Buergenthal, T. *International Human Rights in a Nutshell.* St. Paul, MN: West Publishing, 1988.

Buergenthal, Thomas. "To Respect and to Ensure: State Obligations and Permissible Derogations." In *The International Bill of Rights: The Covenant on Civil and Political Rights,* ed. Louis Henkin. New York: Columbia University Press, 1981.

Bulmer, Martin. *Racism.* Oxford, UK: Oxford University Press, 2000.

Bunch, Charlotte. "Organizing For Women's Human Rights Globally." In *Ours By Right: Women's Rights as Human Rights,* ed. Joanna Kerr. London: Zed Press, 1993.

Burgat, Francois, and William Dowell. *The Islamic Movement in North Africa.* Austin, TX: Center for Middle Eastern Studies, 1993.

Burton-Rose, Daniel, Dan Pens, and Paul Wright. *The Celling of America: An Inside Look at the U.S. Prison Industry.* Monroe, ME: Common Courage Press, 1998.

Cameron, Maxwell A., Robert J. Lawson, and Brian W. Tomlin. *To Walk Without Fear: The Global Movement to Ban Landmines.* New York: Oxford University Press, 1999.

Campbell, Patricia J., and Kathleen Mahoney-Norris. *Democratization and the Protection of Human Rights: Challenges and Contradictions*. Westport, CT: Praeger, 1998.

Campbell, Tom, David Goldberg, Sheila McLean, and Tom Mullen, eds. *Human Rights: From Rhetoric To Reality*. New York: Basil Blackwell, 1986.

Carey, Alex. *Taking the Risk Out of Democracy: Propaganda in the U.S. and Australia*. Sydney, Australia: University of New South Wales Press, 1995.

Cassese, Antonio. *Inhuman States: Imprisonment, Detention and Torture in Europe Today*. Cambridge, MA: Polity Press, 1996.

Central Intelligence Agency. *The World Factbook 1999*. Washington, DC: Office of Public Affairs, 2000.

Chadha, Yogesh. *Gandhi: A Life*. New York: John Wiley & Sons, 1998.

Chang, Grace. *Disposable Domestics: Immigrant Women Workers in the Global Economy*. Cambridge, MA: South End Press, 2000.

Chirot, Daniel. *Modern Tyrants: The Power and Prevalence of Evil in Our Age*. New York: Free Press, 1994.

Clark, David J., David McCoy, Gerard Clark, and Gerard McCoy. *The Most Fundamental Legal Right: Habeas Corpus in the Commonwealth*. New York: Oxford University Press, 2000.

Clarke, Desmond M., and Charles Jones. *The Rights of Nations: Nations and Nationalism in a Changing World*. New York: St. Martin's Press, 1999.

Claude, Richard Pierre, and Burns H. Weston. *Human Rights in the World Community*. Philadelphia, PA: University of Pennsylvania Press, 1992.

Cocker, Mark. *Rivers of Blood, Rivers of Gold: Europe's Conflict with Tribal Peoples*. London: Jonathan Cape, 1998.

Coliver, Sandra, ed. *The Right to Know: Human Rights and Access to Reproductive Health Information*. Philadelphia, PA: University of Pennsylvania Press, 1995.

Committee to Protect Journalists. *Attacks on the Press in 1999: A Worldwide Survey by the Committee to Protect Journalists*. New York: Committee to Protect Journalists, 2000.

Conroy, John. *Unspeakable Acts, Ordinary People: The Dynamics of Torture*. New York: Knopf, 2000.

Constable, Nicole. *Maid to Order in Hong Kong: Stories of Filipina Workers*. Cornell, NY: Cornell University Press, 1997.

Cose, Ellis. *Color-Blind: Seeing Beyond Race in a Race-Obsessed World*. New York: HarperCollins, 1997.

Cotton, Samuel. *Silent Terror*. New York: Harlem River Press, 1998.

Cranston, Maurice. *What Are Human Rights?* London: Bodley Head, 1973.

Crenshaw, Martha, and John Pimlott, eds. *Encyclopedia of World Terrorism*. Armonk, NY: M.E. Sharpe, 1997.

Crosson-Tower, Cynthia. *Understanding Child Abuse and Neglect*. New York: Allyn & Bacon, 1998.

Crowe, David, and John Kolsti, eds. *The Gypsies of Eastern Europe*. Armonk, New York, and London: M.E. Sharpe, 1991.

Cuomo, Kerry Kennedy, et al. *Speak Truth to Power: Human Rights Defenders Who Are Changing Our World*. New York: Crown Publishers, 2000.

Curry, George E., and Cornel West. *The Affirmative Action Debate*. Reading, MA: Addison-Wesley, 1996.

Dalai Lama. *Ethics for the New Millennium*. New York: Riverhead Books, 1999.

Dalai Lama. *Freedom in Exile: The Autobiography of the Dalai Lama*. San Francisco, CA: Harper San Francisco, 1991.

Davies, Simon. *Big Brother: Britain's Web of Surveillance and the New Technological Order*. London: Pan, 1996.

Degener, Theresia, and Yolan Koster-Dreese. *Human Rights and Disabled Persons: Essays and Relevant Human Rights Instruments*. Boston, MA: Martinus Nijhoff, 1995.

Deloria, Jr., Vine, and Clifford M. Lytle. *American Indians, American Justice*. Austin, TX: University of Texas Press, 1997.

Derose, Laurie Fields, Ellen Messer, and Sara Millman. *Who's Hungry? and How Do We Know? Food Shortage, Poverty, and Deprivation*. New York: United Nations University Press, 1999.

Desai, Manisha. "From Vienna to Beijing: Women's Human Rights Activism and the Human Rights Community." In *Debating Human Rights: Critical Essays from United States and Asia*, ed. Peter Van Ness. London: Routledge. 1999.

Destexhe, Alain. *Rwanda and Genocide in the Twentieth Century*. New York: New York University Press, 1995.

Dinnerstein, Leonard. *Antisemitism in America*. New York: Oxford University Press, 1994.

Dinstein, Yoram. "The Right to Life, Physical Integrity, and Liberty." In *The International Bill of Rights: The Covenant on Civil and Political Rights*, ed. Louis Henkin. New York: Columbia University Press, 1981.

Duyvendak, Jan Willem. *The Global Emergence of Gay and Lesbian Politics: National Imprints of a Worldwide Movement*. Philadelphia, PA: Temple University Press, 1998.

Dyson, Michael Eric. *I May Not Get There with You: The True Martin Luther King, Jr.* New York: Free Press, 2000.

Edmonds, Beverly C., and William R. Fernekes. *Children's Rights: A Reference Handbook*. Santa Barbara, CA: ABC-CLIO, 1996.

Eldredge, Dirk Chase. *Ending the War on Drugs: A Solution for America*. Bridgehampton, NY: Bridge Works, 1998.

Evan, William M., and Stephen Hilgartner, eds. *The Arms Race and Nuclear War*. Englewood Cliffs, NJ: Prentice-Hall, 1987.

Fisler, Lori, and David J. Scheffer, eds. *Law and Force in the New International Order*. Boulder, CO: Westview Press, 1991.

Fitch, John Samuel. *The Armed Forces and Democracy in Latin America*. Baltimore, MD: Johns Hopkins University Press, 1998.

Flaherty, David. *Protecting Privacy in Surveillance Societies*. Charlotte, NC: University of North Carolina Press, 1989.

Forsberg, Randall, et al. *Nonproliferation Primer: Preventing the Spread of Nuclear, Chemical, and Biological Weapons*. Cambridge, MA: The MIT Press, 1995.

Forsythe, David P. *Human Rights and Peace: International and National Dimensions*. Lincoln, NE: University of Nebraska Press, 1993.

Fredrickson, George. *White Supremacy: A Comparative Study in American and South African History*. New York: Oxford University Press, 1981.

Friedman, Elisabeth. "Women's Human Rights: The Emergence of a Movement." In *Women's Rights, Human Rights: International Feminist Perspectives*, ed. Julie Peters and Andrea Wolper. New York: Routledge, 1995.

Gall, Carlotta, and Thomas de Waal. *Chechnya: Calamity in the Caucasus*. New York: New York University Press, 1998.

Galliher, John F. *Criminology: Human Rights, Criminal Law, and Crime*. New York: Prentice Hall, 1989.

Gandhi, Mohandas Karamchand. *An Autobiography: The Story of My Experiments with Truth*. Boston, MA: Beacon Press, 1993.

Garrow, David J. *Bearing the Cross: Martin Luther King, Jr. and* the *Southern Christian Leadership Conference*. New York: William Morrow & Company, 1999.

Gentile, Thomas. *March on Washington, August 28, 1963*. Washington, DC: New Day Publications, 1983.

Gibney, Mark. *Strangers or Friends*. Westport, CT: Greenwood Press, 1986.

Ginzburg, Eugenia. *Journey into the Whirlwind*. New York: Harcourt Brace, 1975.

Gora, Joel M. *The Right to Protest: The Basic ACLU Guide to Free Expression*. Carbondale, IL: Southern Illinois University Press, 1991.

Gourevitch, Philip. *We Wish to Inform You That Tomorrow We Will Be Killed with Our Families*. New York: Farrar, Straus, and Giroux, 1998.

Grewal, J.S. *The Sikhs of the Punjab (New Cambridge History of India)*. New York: Cambridge University Press, 1998.

Grunfeld, Tom. *The Making of Modern Tibet*. Armonk, NY: M.E. Sharpe, 1987.

Guest, Iain. *Behind the Disappearances: Argentina's Dirty War Against Human Rights and the United Nations*. Philadelphia, PA: University of Pennsylvania Press, 1990.

Guggenheim, Martin. *The Rights of Families: The Authoritative ACLU Guide to the Rights of Family Members Today*. Carbondale, IL: Southern Illinois University Press, 1996.

Hacker, Andrew. *Two Nations: Black and White, Separate, Hostile, Unequal*. New York: Ballantine Books, 1995.

Halperin, Morton H., and David J. Scheffer. *Self-determination in the New World Order*. Washington, DC: Carnegie Endowment for International Peace, 1992.

Harris, David, Michael O'Boyle, and Chris Warbrick. *Law of the European Convention on Human Rights*. London: Butterworths, 1995.

Hartmann, Betsy. *Reproductive Rights and Wrongs: The Global Politics of Population Control*. Boston, MA: South End Press, 1995.

Haspels, Nelien, and Michele Jankanish. *Action Against Child Labour*. Geneva: International Labour Office, 2000.

Hatcher, William S., and J. Douglas Martin. *The Bahai Faith*. San Francisco, CA: Harper & Row Publishers, 1985.

Havemann, Paul. *Indigenous Peoples' Rights in Australia, Canada, & New Zealand*. New York: Oxford University Press, 1999.

Henckaerts, Jean-Marie. *Mass Expulsion in Modern International Law and Practice*. The Hague: Kluwer Law International, 1995.

Henkin, Louis, ed. *The International Bill of Rights: The Covenant on Civil and Political Rights*. New York: Columbia University Press, 1981.

Hitchens, Christopher. *Cyprus*. London: Quartet Books, 1984.

Human Rights Watch. *World Report 2000*. New York: Human Rights Watch, 2000.

Human Rights Watch and the Natural Resources Defense Council. *Defending the Earth: Abuses of Human Rights and the Environment*. New York: Human Rights Watch, 1992.

Human Rights Watch Staff. *Shielded from Justice: Police Brutality and Accountability in the United States*. New York: Human Rights Watch, 1998.

Human Rights Watch. *"Germany for Germans": Xenophobia and Racist Violence in Germany*. New York: Human Rights Watch, 1995.

———. *Throwing Away the Key: Indefinite Political Detention in Syria*. New York: Human Rights Watch, 1992.

Humphrey, J.P. *Human Rights and the United Nations: A Great Adventure*. Dobbs Ferry, NY: Transnational Publishers, 1984.

Hurrell, Andrew, Ngaire Woods, and R. Albert Berry. *Inequality, Globalization, and World Politics*. New York: Oxford University Press, 1999.

Innes, Brian. *The History of Torture*. New York: St. Martin's Press, 1998.

Itzin, Catherine, ed. *Pornography: Women, Violence and Civil Liberties. A Radical New View*. London: Clarendon Press, 1993.

Izady, Mehrdad R. *The Kurds: A Concise Handbook*. New York: Crane Russak, 1992.

Jaimes, M. Annette, ed. *The State of Native America: Genocide, Colonization, and Resistance*. Boston, MA: South End Press, 1992.

Joyce, Peter. *The Rise and Fall of Apartheid: The Chronicle of a Divided Society as Told Through South Africa's Newspapers*. Capetown, South Africa: Struik Publishers, 1990.

Karmen, Andrew. *Crime Victims: An Introduction to Victimology*. Pacific Grove, CA: Brooks/Cole Publishing, 1990.

Keene, Ann T. *Peacemakers: Winners of the Nobel Peace Prize*. New York: Oxford University Press, 1998.

Kenrick, Donald, and Grattan Puxon. *The Destiny of Europe's Gypsies*. London: Heinemann-Chatto-Sussex, 1972.

Kershaw, Ian, and Moshe Lewin. *Stalinism and Nazism: Dictatorships in Comparison*. New York: Cambridge University Press, 1997.

Kleg, Milton. *Hate Prejudice and Racism*. New York: State University of New York Press, 1993.

Klinkner, Philip A. *The Unsteady March: The Rise and Decline of Racial Equality in America*. Chicago, IL: University of Chicago Press, 1999.

Kohn, Stephen M., and Howard Zinn. *American Political Prisoners*. New York: Praeger Publishers, 1994.

Kurlansky, Mark. *The Basque History of the World*. New York: Walker, 1999.

Kymlicka, Will. *The Rights of Minority Cultures*. New York: Oxford University Press, 1995.

———. *Multicultural Citizenship: A Liberal Theory of Minority Rights*. New York: Oxford University Press, 1995.

Lahav, Pnina, ed. *Press Law in Modern Democracies: A Comparative Study*. New York: Longman, 1985.

Laurance, Edward J. *The International Arms Trade*. New York: Lexington Books, 1992.

Lauren, Paul Gordon. *The Evolution of International Human Rights: Visions Seen*. Philadelphia, PA: University of Pennsylvania Press, 1998.

Lazare, Bernard. *Antisemitism: Its History and Causes*. Lincoln, NE: University of Nebraska Press, 1995.

Lemkin, Raphael. *Axis Rule in Occupied Europe*. Washington, DC: Carnegie Endowment for International Peace, 1944.

Loescher, Gilburt. *Refugees and the Asylum Dilemma in the West*. Philadelphia, PA: Pennsylvania State University Press, 1992.

Lohman, D. *Republic Of Belarus: Crushing Civil Society*. New York: Human Rights Watch, 1998.

Lowden, P. *Moral Opposition to Authoritarian Rule in Chile, 1973–90*. New York: St. Martin's Press 1996.

MacIntyre, Alasdair. *A Short History of Ethics*. Notre Dame, IN: University of Notre Dame Press, 1998.

Mandela, Nelson. *Long Walk to Freedom: The Autobiography of Nelson Mandela*. New York: Little, Brown, 1995.

Mann, Jonathan M., Sofia Gruskin, and Michael A. Grodin, eds. *Health and Human Rights*. London: Routledge, 1999.

Marshall, Paul. *Religious Freedom in the World: A Global Report on Freedom and Persecution*. Nashville, TN: Broadman & Holman Publishers, 2000.

Marx, Anthony W. *Making Race and Nation: A Comparison of South Africa, the United States, and Brazil.* New York: Cambridge University Press, 1998.

Maybury-Lewis, David. *Indigenous Peoples, Ethnic Groups, and the State.* Boston, MA: Allyn & Bacon, 1997.

Mayer, Ann Elizabeth. *Islam and Human Rights: Tradition and Politics.* Boulder, CO: Westview, 1998.

McDowall, David. *A Modern History of the Kurds.* New York: I.B. Tauris, 1996.

McWhinney, Edward. *The International Court of Justice and the Western Tradition of International Law.* Boston, MA: M. Nijhoff, 1987.

McWhirter, Darien A. *Freedom of Speech, Press, and Assembly.* Phoenix, AZ: Oryx Press, 1996.

Meisalis Susan. *Kurdistan: In the Shadow of History.* New York: Random House, 1997.

Meisler, Stalnley. *United Nations: The First Fifty Years.* New York: Atlantic Monthly Press, 1995.

Mendes, E.P., and Traeholt, A.M., eds. *Human Rights: Chinese and Canadian Perspectives.* Ottawa, Canada: Human Rights Research and Education Center, University of Ottawa, 1997.

Meredith, Martin. *Nelson Mandela: A Biography.* New York: St. Martin's Press, 1998.

Miller, Diane Helene. *Freedom to Differ: The Shaping of the Gay and Lesbian Struggle for Civil Rights.* New York: New York University Press, 1998.

Minority Rights Group International. *World Directory of Minorities.* London: Minority Rights Group International, 1997.

Minority Rights Group. *Co-existence in Some Plural European Societies.* London: Minority Rights Group, 1986.

Mittelman, James H. *The Globalization Syndrome: Transformation and Resistance.* Princeton, NJ: Princeton University Press, 2000.

Moore, John Bassett. *A Treatise on Extradition and Interstate Rendition.* Littleton, CO: Fred B. Rothman Company, 1997.

Moriarty, Laura J., and Robert A. Jerin. *Current Issues in Victimology Research.* Durham, NC: Carolina Academic Press, 1998.

Morris, Norval, and David J. Rothman. *The Oxford History of the Prison: The Practice of Punishment in Western Society.* New York: Oxford University Press, 1997.

Morsink, J. *The Universal Declaration of Human Rights: Origins, Drafting, and Intent.* Philadelphia, PA: University of Pennsylvania Press, 1999.

Moskos, Charles C., and John Whiteclay Chambers II, eds. *The New Conscientious Objection: From Sacred to Secular Resistance.* New York: Oxford University Press, 1993.

Mullan, Don, and John Scally. *Bloody Sunday: Massacre in Northern Ireland.* Boulder, CO: Roberts Rinehart Publishers, 1997.

Neier, Aryeh. *War Crimes: Brutality, Genocide, Terror, and the Struggle for Justice.* New York: Random House, 1998.

Newman, Graeme. *1999 Global Report on Crime and Justice.* New York: Oxford University Press, 1999.

Nizich, I. *Civil and Political Rights in Croatia.* New York: Human Rights Watch, 1995.

Noonan, John Thomas. *The Lustre of Our Country: The American Experience of Religious Freedom.* Berkeley, CA: University of California Press, 1998.

Oates, Stephen B. *Let the Trumpet Sound: The Life of Martin Luther King, Jr.* New York: HarperPerennial Library, 1994.

Parenti, Christian. *Lockdown America: Police and Prisons in the Age of Crisis.* New York: Verso Books, 1999.

Patrick, John J. *Constitutional Debates on Freedom of Religion: A Documentary History.* Westport, CT: Greenwood Publishing Group, 1999.

Pierre, Andrew J. *Cascade of Arms: Controlling Conventional Weapons Proliferation in the 1990s.* Washington DC: Brookings Institute Press, 1997.

Pierre, Andrew J. *The Global Politics of Arms Sales.* Princeton, NJ: Princeton University Press, 1982.

Pizzi, William T. *Trials Without Truth.* New York: New York University Press, 1999.

Plaut, Gunther. *Asylum.* New York: Praeger, 1995.

Pommersheim, Frank. *Braid of Feathers: American Indian Law and Contemporary Tribal Life.* Berkeley, CA: University of California Press, 1995.

Pryor, Douglas W. *Unspeakable Acts: Why Men Sexually Abuse Children.* New York: New York University Press, 1999.

Rahman, Anika, and Nahid Toubia, eds. *Female Genital Mutilation: A Guide to Worldwide Laws and Policies.* United Kingdom: Zed Books, forthcoming.

Ratner, Steven R., and Jason S. Abrams. *Accountability for Human Rights Atrocities in International Law: Beyond the Nuremberg Legacy.* New York: Oxford University Press, 1997.

Rehnquist, William H. *All the Laws but One: Civil Liberties in Wartime.* New York: Knopf, 1998.

Renner, Michael. *Small Arms, Big Impact: The Next Challenge of Disarmament.* Washington, DC: Worldwatch Institute, 1997.

Rhodes, Richard. *Why They Kill: The Discoveries of a Maverick Criminologist.* New York: Alfred A. Knopf, 1999.

Richards, David A. *Identity and the Case for Gay Rights: Race, Gender, Religion as Analogies.* Chicago, IL: University of Chicago Press, 1999.

Ridley, Aaron. *Beginning Bioethics: A Text with Integrated Readings.* New York: Bedford Books, 1998.

Rifkin, Jeremy. *The End of Work: The Decline of the Global Labor Force and the Dawn of the Post-Market Era.* New York: J.P. Tarcher, 1996.

Roht-Arriaza, Naomi. *Impunity and Human Rights in International Law and Practice.* New York: Oxford University Press, 1995.

Rosenfeld, Jona, and Bruno Tardieu. *Artisans of Democracy: How Families in Extreme Poverty, Ordinary Citizens and Social Institutions Become Allies to Overcome Social Exclusion.* Lanham, MD: University Press of America, 2000.

Rotberg, Robert I. *Truth v. Justice: The Morality of Truth Commissions.* Princeton, NJ: Princeton University Press, 2000.

Rothenberg, Daniel. *With These Hands: The Hidden World of Migrant Farmworkers Today.* New York: Harcourt Brace, 1998.

Rowbotham, Michael. *The Grip Of Death: A Study Of Modern Money, Debt Slavery, and Destructive Economics.* Charlbury, Oxfordshire, UK: Jon Carpenter, 1998.

Ruedy, John. *Modern Algeria: The Origins and Development of a Nation.* Bloomington, IN: Indiana University Press, 1992.

Sachar, Rajindar. *The Right to Adequate Housing.* New York: United Nations, 1996.

Said, Edward W. *Out of Place: A Memoir.* New York: Knopf, 1999.

Sampson, Anthony. *Mandela: The Authorized Biography.* New York: Knopf, 1999.

Sayce, Liz. *From Psychiatric Patient to Citizen: Overcoming Discrimination and Social Exclusion.* New York: St. Martin's Press, 2000.

Scharf, Michael P. *Balkan Justice: The Story Behind the First International War Crimes Trial Since Nuremberg.* Durham, NC: Carolina Academic Press, 1997.

Schirmer, Jennifer. *The Guatemalan Military Project: A Violence Called Democracy*. Philadelphia, PA: University of Pennsylvania Press, 1998.

Schrag, Philip. *A Well-Founded Fear: The Congressional Battle to Save Political Asylum in America*. New York: Routledge, 2000.

Shaw, Malcolm N. *International Law*. New York: Cambridge University Press, 1997.

Singer, Peter. *Practical Ethics*. New York: Cambridge University Press, 1993.

Solzhenitsyn, Aleksandr. *The Gulag Archipelago*. New York: Westview Press, 1997.

Spencer, Jonathan. *Sri Lanka: History and the Roots of Conflict*. New York: Routledge, 1990.

Spinner, Jeff. *The Boundaries of Citizenship: Race, Ethnicity, and Nationality in the Liberal State*. Baltimore, MD: Johns Hopkins University Press, 1994.

Squyres, Suzanne, Cornelia Blair, and Margaret A. Mitchell, eds. *Immigration and Illegal Aliens—Burden or Blessing?* Plano, TX: Information Plus, 1997.

Stauber, John, and Sheldon Rampton. *Toxic Sludge Is Good for You: Lies, Damn Lies and the Public Relations Industry*. Monroe, ME: Common Courage Press, 1995.

Steiner, Henry J., and Philip Alston, eds. *International Human Rights in Context: Law, Politics, Morals*. New York: Oxford University Press, 1996.

Stine, Gerald J. *AIDS Update 2000*. New York: Prentice Hall, 1999.

Tebbutt, Susan, ed. *Sinti and Roma: Gypsies in German Speaking Society and Literature*. New York and Oxford: Berghahn Books, 1998.

Tirman, John. *Spoils of War: The Human Cost of America's Arms Trade*. New York: Free Press, 1997.

Toubia, Nahid. *Female Genital Mutilation: A Call for Global Action*. New York: Rainbo, 1995.

Toubia, Nahid, and Susan Izett. *Female Genital Mutilation: An Overview*. Geneva: World Health Organization, 1998.

Tye, Larry. *The Father of Spin: Edward L. Bernays and the Birth of Public Relations*. New York: Crown Publishers, 1998.

United Nations. *Right to Adequate Food as a Human Right*. New York: United Nations Publications, 1989.

United Nations Department for Disarmament Affairs. *Nuclear Weapons: A Comprehensive Study*. New York: United Nations, 1991.

United Nations High Commissioner for Refugees. *The State of the World's Refugees 2000: 50 Years of Humanitarian Action*. New York: Oxford University Press, 2000.

U.S. Department of State. *Country Reports on Human Rights Practices for 1999*. Washington, DC: Bureau of Democracy, Human Rights, and Labor, 2000.

Van Ness, Peter, ed. *Debating Human Rights: Critical Essays from the United States and Asia*. London: Routledge, 1999.

Verney, Peter. *Slavery in Sudan*. London: Anti-Slavery International, 1997.

Vickers, Miranda. *The Albanians: A Modern History*. New York: J.B. Tauris, 1995.

Waldron, Jeremy. *The Right to Private Property*. Oxford, UK: Clarendon, 1988.

Wallace, Harvey. *Family Violence: Legal, Medical, and Social Perspectives*. Needham Heights, MA: Allyn & Bacon, 1998.

Waltz, Susan Eileen. *Human Rights and Reform: Changing the Face of North African Politics*. Berkeley, CA: University of California Press, 1995.

Wei Jingsheng. *The Courage to Stand Alone: Letters from Prison and Other Writings*. New York: Penguin, 1998.

Weiss, Thomas George. *Military-Civilian Interactions: Intervening in Humanitarian Crises*. Lanham, MD: Rowman & Littlefield, 1999.

Wenz, Peter. *Environmental Justice*. Albany, NY: The State University of New York Press, 1988.

Weschler, Lawrence. *A Miracle, a Universe: Settling Accounts with Torturers*. Chicago, IL: University of Chicago Press, 1998.

Westin, Alan F. *Privacy and Freedom*. New York: Atheneum, 1967.

Whitaker, Reg. *The End of Privacy: How Total Surveillance Is Becoming a Reality*. New York: New Press, 1999.

Wiesel, Elie. *All Rivers Run to the Sea: A Memoir*. New York: Alfred A. Knopf, 1995.

Winslow, Philip C. *Sowing the Dragon's Teeth: Land Mines and the Global Legacy of War*. Boston, MA: Beacon Press, 1997.

Wintemute, Robert. *Sexual Orientation and Human Rights: The United States Constitution, the European Convention and the Canadian Charter*. New York: Oxford University Press, 1997.

Wistrich, Robert S. *Antisemitism: The Longest Hatred*. London: Thames Methuen, 1991.

Wronka, Joseph. *Human Rights and Social Policy in the 21st Century*. Lanham, MD: University Press of America, 1998.

Yates, Michael. *Why Unions Matter*. New York: Monthly Review Press, 1998.

General Index

Name Index

Photo Credits Volume Three